THE GLOBAL FINANCIAL CRISIS

D1606698

Although banking and sovereign debt crises are not unusual, the crisis that has unfolded across the world since 2007 has been unique in both its scale and scope. It has also been unusual in being both triggered by and mainly affecting developed economies. Starting with the US subprime mortgage crisis and the recession in 2007–9, the problem soon erupted into financial crisis in Europe. A few of these countries came to the brink of bankruptcy and were rescued by the EU and the IMF on the condition they adopt austerity measures. The detrimental social effects of the crisis in both the US and Europe are still emerging.

Although there have been several studies published on the US crisis in particular, there has so far been an absence of an accessible comparative overview of both crises. This insightful text aims to fill this gap, offering a critical overview of causes, policy responses, effects, and future implications. Starting with the historical context and mutation of the crisis, the book explores the policies, regulations, and governance reforms that have been implemented to cope with the US subprime mortgage crises. A parallel analysis considers the causes of the European sovereign debt crisis and the responses of the European Union, examining why the EU is as yet unable to resolve the crisis. This book is supported with eResources that include essay questions and class discussion questions in order to assist students in their understanding.

This uniquely comprehensive and readable overview will be of interest and relevance to those studying financial crises, financial governance, international economics, and international political economy.

George K. Zestos is Jean Monnet Chair for European Integration Studies and Professor of Economics at Christopher Newport University, USA.

THE GLOBAL FINANCIAL CRISIS

From US subprime mortgages
to European sovereign debt

George K. Zestos

To JoJo
Best wishes
and good luck
In your studies
and research
on Malthus

George K Zestos

Routledge
Taylor & Francis Group

LONDON AND NEW YORK

First published 2016
by Routledge
2 Park Square, Milton Park, Abingdon, Oxon OX14 4RN

and by Routledge
711 Third Avenue, New York, NY 10017

Routledge is an imprint of the Taylor & Francis Group, an informa business

© 2016 George K. Zestos

British Library Cataloguing in Publication Data
A catalogue record for this book is available from the British Library

Library of Congress Cataloging in Publication Data
Zestos, George K.
The global financial crisis : from US subprime mortgages to European
sovereign debt / George K. Zestos.
pages cm
Includes bibliographical references and index. 1. Financial crises. I. Title.
HB3722.Z42 2015
330.9'0511–dc23
2015016222

ISBN: 978-1-138-80019-9 (hbk)
ISBN: 978-1-138-80021-2 (pbk)
ISBN: 978-1-315-75559-5 (ebk)

Typeset in Bembo
by Cenveo Publisher Services

To My Family
Eva, Kostis, and Alex

CONTENTS

FIGURES

TABLES

BOXES

PREFACE

Writing a book on the recent global financial crisis is a great challenge because the study covers a long time period, from the end of the Great Depression to the Eurocrisis which has not yet ended. The crisis affected the US and several countries in Europe.

To examine the causes of the US subprime mortgage crisis, it is important to consider the role of the government and its involvement in the housing industry. After the Great Depression, several public and quasi-public federal housing agencies were created to help increase home ownership in America. Financial innovation in the US increasingly became more important, which was indicated by the mounting pressure from investment banks and other financial institutions to repeal the strict banking legislation introduced after the Great Depression. Indeed, in 1999, the Glass-Steagall Act was repealed and since then, many opportunities to earn higher profits were created for the banks. Financial innovation, high risk-taking by banks, greed by bank executives, a very expansionary monetary policy, and strong interference by the US government aiming to increase home ownership all fermented the US subprime mortgage crisis.

The international financial system became more fragile and volatile starting in the early 1980s, because the US and UK became involved in a race-to-the-bottom financial deregulation war in order to attract financial capital. The US government put pressure on banks to extend more home loans to low-income individuals, minorities, and middle-class families, aiming to increase home ownership in the US. Several public and quasi-public housing institutions were created by the US government to pursue its objective of promoting home ownership. The most important of these institutions were Fannie Mae and Freddie Mac, which bought mortgages from banks, and thereafter securitized and sold them as mortgage backed securities (MBSs) to increase liquidity in the US housing market. Because some of the liberally extended mortgages were of low quality, the securities based on these mortgages were also of low quality. The US subprime mortgage crisis began when investment banks, Freddie Mac and Fannie Mae, securitized many of the subprime mortgages and sold them in the US and abroad.

The US subprime mortgage crisis initially entered Europe when US mortgage-related securities were sold to European investors who were searching for a higher rate of return and trusted the US banks. During this period, credit rating agencies (CRAs) and speculators revealed the weaker economies in the EU, and the latter found opportunities to earn huge profits through short selling the securities of these countries, thus driving the government bonds to junk status and the countries to bankruptcy. The victim countries were all members of the Economic and Monetary Union (EMU), which was introduced incomplete and incapable of defending itself and its member countries during the perfect financial storm which the Eurocrisis evolved to become.

The economically stronger countries' leaders did not do enough to prevent the crisis, thus there was an onslaught on the weaker groups of the population after the bailouts were extended. Millions of people were thrown into poverty, and many still have not recovered yet. The financially distressed EMU members were saved from bankruptcy through rescue packages (bailouts), jointly offered by the EU and IMF. The group of the bailout recipient countries includes Greece, Ireland, Portugal, Spain and Cyprus. Greece was affected more than any other EA country. It experienced a humanitarian crisis of unprecedented dimensions in the post-World War II Europe era causing immense poverty and misery to the weaker groups of its population. On June 30, 2015, the seemingly never-ending negotiations between the new government of Greece and international lenders led Greece to default on a €1.6 billion loan from the IMF. This event led the ECB to freeze liquidity to Greece which forced the closure of Greek banks. Such action allowed the Greek people to withdraw only small amounts of cash from ATMs resulting in perpetual queuing.

Sequence of chapters

To study the US subprime mortgage crisis, one must be familiar with the US banking and home finance system, and the regulatory regime that was established after the Great Depression. Thus Chapter 1 begins with a section describing the efforts of the US government to stabilize the crippled US economy from the Great Depression. The chapter introduces a few legislative acts, the most important being the Glass-Steagall Act that regulated both businesses and financial activities until 1999. The roles of several newly established US federal housing agencies in the US subprime mortgage crisis are critically analyzed.

In Chapter 2, possible factors that caused the US subprime mortgage crisis are examined. Such factors are many and diverse, and it is concluded that there was not one single cause of the crisis. Both government and private failures played a role, each in its own unique ways. The government's objective to increase home ownership is one such factor because it generated an increased volume of subprime mortgages that were securitized by the investment banks, Freddie Mac, and Fannie Mae that contributed to the creation and spread of toxic assets. Financial innovations flourished during this period as investment banks created novel and complex financial derivatives that the market could not correctly price.

The third chapter takes the reader to Europe and directly addresses its main issue, which is the excessive public debt. Several other important factors and macroeconomic variables are presented, and their roles in the crisis are discussed. One such important macroeconomic variable is the long-term interest rates on government bonds. The long-term interest rates capture the cost of borrowing to governments. With the onset of the crisis, all interest rates increased substantially, indicating a rise in default risk. In five countries, the long-term interest rates increased so much that it became prohibitively expensive for these governments to borrow in the markets. As a result, they had to be bailed out by the EU and IMF.

In Chapter 4, we discuss the reason the crisis has lasted such a long time in Europe. The creation of the EMU was based on strong political commitments among EU country leaders to unify Europe. This type of leadership has now been all but eclipsed. In addition, the crisis could not be contained because the economic foundations of the euro were faulty. The EMU took away the exchange rate and monetary policies, and to a great extent fiscal policy from member countries, rendering them incapable of defending themselves. The EU decided that the way out of the crisis would be through an internal devaluation, i.e. through austerity and reductions of prices and wages. In this way, the EU expect countries would become internationally competitive, and thus increase exports and induce economic growth.

Chapter 5 presents the US monetary and fiscal policies launched to cope with the Great Recession. Two presidents and the US Congress introduced three stimulus plans to cope with the crisis. The magnitude of the stimuli involved is unprecedented in US history. Similarly, the Federal Reserve (Fed), after it drove the federal funds rate down to zero bound, adopted two other monetary policies to help the US economy out of the recession. Thus the short term liquidity programs and quantitative easing (QE) were launched. The US recovered in 2009 and has successfully ended both the fiscal and monetary stimulus programs. This chapter provides a thorough analysis of how the US government effectively employed the two policies and all other available instruments to cope with the US subprime mortgage crisis.

The role of Germany in the European sovereign debt crisis is discussed in Chapter 6. Being the largest and strongest economy in the EU, it was expected to play a leading role during the recession. Germany did exactly the opposite. Instead of supporting growth policies, it adopted and promoted only austerity and neoliberal, supply-side policies as the means for the bailout recipient countries to exit the crisis. The chapter also discusses the policies adopted by Chancellor Gerhard Schröder and Angela Merkel that helped the German economy achieve growth; this was accomplished by introducing the Hartz IV reforms in Germany. However, austerity policies sank the periphery countries into a prolonged recession and misery. Most of the German leaders, along with their allies in Finland and the Netherlands, were not moved and showed very little, if any, flexibility. Germany, according to internal and mostly external critics in particular, is determined to make the rest of Europe follow its example. There exists evidence that during the last decade, the German leaders' attitude toward Europe has drastically changed. The country became more ethnocentric by more narrowly pursuing its own national interests. This will have a great impact on the future of European integration. Such attitudes surfaced in the middle of 2015, when the German Finance Minister, Wolfgang Schäuble, presented a plan in the Eurogroup meeting to throw Greece out of the EA. This initiative puts the entire European project at risk as French President, François Hollande, responded "There is no Grexit, but a Eurozone exit."

Chapter 7 examines the role of Greece in the European sovereign debt crisis. As Greece triggered the crisis with the fiscal revelations of its prime minister, George Papandreou, it became the epicenter of the crisis. The chapter goes into great depth analyzing factors that have played a role in causing the worst recession in the EA's history. The relationship of Greece with other EA countries, especially with Germany, and the humanitarian crisis that prevailed in the country is also presented. Greece is still at risk and is threatened with a Grexit, which continues to attract the world's attention and much fear of another global financial crisis. As the world focuses on Greece, many past economic and political problems of the country are carefully scrutinized, and some of them were suspected and found to be the causes of the rise in public debt that became unsustainable. Corruption and clientelism in the public sector top this list. These problems must be effectively addressed to assist both Greece and the EMU.

Chapter 8 analyzes the roles played by the credit rating agencies (CRAs) during the crisis. The CRAs were blamed for failing to warn investors of the poor quality of the securities that investors were buying, which were erroneously rated as high quality. CRAs were sued in the US, Australia, and Europe for being negligent in providing the ratings of corporate government bonds. In Europe, the CRAs overreacted and downgraded government bonds prematurely, causing several lawsuits to be filed against them. In a few countries, the CRAs have already been found guilty of misleading investors that bought low-quality securities. The chapter also presents the historical credit ratings of the five bailout countries, along with statistics about economic growth, public deficit and debt ratios. A few legislative measures were taken by the EU to improve the system of rating government securities and there exists evidence that more will be done in the future. In the US, legislatures began a campaign to undo the Dodd-Frank Act to give more freedom to banks to invest in risky securities in pursuit of higher profit. As a result, banks can invest in the same types of structured derivatives that were suspected to be a major cause of the US subprime mortgage crisis.

Personal anecdotes from the author related to the European economic crisis

A few years ago, before the euro was introduced, I attended a seminar at a major US university. The presenter was a German economist and his topic was monetary integration in Europe. The professor was much against the idea of a monetary union as he only saw the costs and not the benefits for Germany. He was so agitated, it was as if the forecast threat was coming to pass right in front of him, yet the euro had not even been introduced! Immediately, I realized that if the EMU was launched there would be problems and did not think it would be beneficial for other countries to share the same currency with Germany. In 2010, when the crisis entered Europe, I knew there would be millions of people like the presenter waiting to react to the issue and make the crisis worse instead of better. They would be eager to take an extreme position against countries which violated the rules of the EMU, since they were expecting them to do so even before the creation of the EMU. The attitude of many Germans during the Eurocrisis, particularly in Chancellor Merkel's party, the Christian Democratic Union (CDU), reminded me of the German presenter in that university seminar years before.

In June 2010, I participated in the annual meetings of the Global Finance conference at Poznan University of Economics in Poland. Besides my presentation, I was also interviewed by a Warsaw news channel. When I was asked whether I believed Poland should enter the EMU I responded that when the Polish government felt it was the right time, then they should join. I had developed tremendous respect for the Polish people as they were very friendly, polite, and very energetic. Such impressions convinced me that Poland was a country on the move and their hospitality impressed me. Poland and Sweden contributed to the European Stability Mechanism (ESM) bailout fund although they did not have to do this as they had not yet adopted the euro. However, when they do adopt the European common currency, I know Poland and Sweden will both be great stabilizing forces for the EMU.

One month later, I participated in a conference that took place in Frankfurt, Germany at the German Central Bank (Bundesbank). The conference was organized by the Athenian Policy Forum, an international group of economics and finance professors interested in European integration. In this conference, a hot discussion topic was the Greek public debt and the bailout that Greece had received not long before that, in May 2010. I vividly remember that at the conference it was suggested by a presenter that a possible solution to Greece's public debt problem could be a haircut on its public debt. I then remember well stating to the audience that such a solution would prolong the recession in Greece because no investors would be willing to return and invest in the country. A couple of years later, Chancellor Merkel had her way and a haircut was imposed on the holders of the Greek government bonds. The program came to be known as Private Sector Involvement (PSI) and is one of the main reasons the Greek economy sank deeper into the recession.

I also remember discussing this topic with one of the German professors, a very amicable and charismatic person, who was one of the organizers of the conference. I told him that France was helping Greece and suggested that Germany should do the same, to which he strongly agreed. Exactly two years after the Frankfurt Conference the Athenian Policy Forum held another conference in 2012 in Chalkidiki Peninsula, Greece.

I met again with my German friend and discussed the situation in Greece at a conference center overlooking the Aegean Sea. I immediately realized his perception of Greece had changed. He gave me the impression that he perceived Greece was suffering from some type of incurable disease. It took me several months to realize why his attitude toward Greece had changed so much. After reading several journal articles about how the German media had shaped German public opinion, I realized it had been very effective in creating a distorted picture of Greece. I was also informed that Greece had become a joke in the evening news on German television. The news media campaign was later branded as Greek bashing and is how the stereotype of the lazy Greeks developed. The German news media has committed a horrendous crime against a country which, for historical reasons, ought to use its name with extraordinary respect. This should be indisputable by any logical and fair person as, not long ago, it was Nazi Germany that was committing unthinkable atrocities around Europe, and in Greece with regard to its population. The German news media have provided a disservice to their country by unearthing old wounds that people have tried hard to forget. Their irresponsible journalistic attitude has poisoned the relationship between the peoples of these two countries for a long time and has punished the innocent and poor.

In February 2013, I participated in a conference at the University of Miami organized by the Miami-Florida European Union Center for Excellence. There I was introduced to a German professor who informed me that Germans and Greeks at the European Institute in Florence, Italy would not speak to each other. I realized then that things had gotten out of hand with regard to achieving the European project. He suggested we start a movement to set up a Greek-German reconciliation team, and to that I agreed responding "let us do it," but we have not as yet started down that path.

ACKNOWLEDGMENTS

I would like to express my gratitude to the Commissioning Editor of Economics, Emily Kindleysides, and the Editorial Assistant of Economics, Lisa Thomson, of Routledge UK for making the writing of this book a meaningful and rewarding project. I also thank Peter Williams for proficiently editing the manuscript. All were very supportive and very professional. I would also like to thank Christopher Newport University and the Faculty Senate for its continuous support and for awarding me a sabbatical to work on this project. Specifically, I would like to thank the University President Paul Trible, Provost David Dowdy, Dean Robert Colvin, and Economics Chairman Robert Winder for their support of this project. This book has also gained tremendously by contributions from the British press, such as the *Financial Times*, *The Economist*, and many applied research studies by UK universities.

I express my gratitude to my students in my International Economics and European Integration courses who gave me excellent feedback on the manuscript. I would also like to particularly thank several students who served as research assistants – they helped me by working long hours on this and other research projects. Chris Coffman, Katelyn Brown, Chad Cieslewicz, Spencer Busby, Richard Rosenfeld, and Annaliesa Selick-Butos all provided excellent research assistance. My sons, Alexander and Kostis Zestos, also read the manuscript and provided very helpful and insightful comments. I thank my wife, Eva, for her patience and continued moral support.

I am also grateful to the EU Commission for awarding me the honorary lifetime title of Jean Monnet Chair of European Integration and a generous grant that sponsored my teaching and research activities on European integration. I am thankful for and proud of the EU recognition and financial support. My great friend Roark Mulligan read the entire manuscript and edited each chapter, providing me constructive criticism. Professor Gemma Kotula is thanked accordingly for reading and editing the manuscript. I thank Aaron Smith and Michael Williamson, my research assistants, who for the last three years provided excellent research assistance that vastly improved the quality of this textbook. I can never thank them enough. Jason Benedict, a brilliant Christopher Newport University Student Research Fellow, assisted me in finalizing the book and I am grateful for his high-quality research.

ABBREVIATIONS

ABCP	Asset-Backed Commercial Paper
ABS	Asset-Backed Security
AfD	Alternative for Germany
AIG	American International Group
ANEL	Independent Greeks Party
ARM	Adjustable Rate Mortgage
ARRA	American Recovery and Reinvestment Act 2009
BEA	Bureau of Economic Analysis
BIS	Bank for International Settlements
BLS	Bureau of Labor Statistics
CA	Current Account
CAC	Collective Action Clause
CD	Certificate of Deposit
CDO	Collateralized Debt Obligations
CDS	Credit Default Swap
CDU	Christian Democratic Union
CEE	Central and Eastern Europe
CFTC	Commodities Futures Trading Commission
CPDO	Constant Proportion Cost Obligation
CPFF	Commercial Paper Funding Facility
CPI	Consumer Price Index
CPP	Capital Purchase Program
CRA	Credit Rating Agency
CSU	Christian Social Union
DM	Deutschmark
EA	Euro Area
EC	European Community

ECB	European Central Bank
ECOFIN	EU Economics and Financial Affairs Council
ECSC	European Coal and Steel Community
EEC	European Economic Community
EERP	European Economic Recovery Plan
EFSF	European Financial Stability Facility
EMFU	Economic, Monetary, and Fiscal Union
EMU	Economic and Monetary Union
EMS	European Monetary System
EP	European Parliament
ESCB	European System of Central Banks
ESM	European Stability Mechanism
ESMA	European Securities and Markets Authority
EU	European Union
FA	Financial Account
FDI	Foreign Direct Investment
FDIC	Federal Deposit Insurance Corporation
FHA	Federal Housing Association
FHFA	Federal Housing Finance Agency
FNMA	Federal National Mortgage Association
FOMC	Federal Open Market Committee
FSB	Finance Stability Board
GDP	Gross Domestic Product
GNMA	Government National Mortgage Association
GSEs	Government-Sponsored Enterprises
HOLC	Home Owners Loan Corporation
HUD	Department of Housing and Urban Development
IMF	International Monetary Fund
IRA	Irish Republican Army
KKE	Communist Party of Greece
LFPR	Labor Force Participation Rate
LLC	Limited Liability Company
LTRO	Long-Term Refinancing Operation
M5S	Five Star Movement
MBSs	Mortgage Backed Securities
MMIFF	Money Market Investor Funding Facility
MRO	Main Refinancing Operation
MTFS	Medium-Term Fiscal Strategy
MTO	Medium-Term Objective
NBER	National Bureau of Economic Research
ND	New Democracy Party
NGO	Non-Government Organization
NINJA	No Income, No Job or Assets
NPD	National Democratic Party

OCA	Optimum Currency Area
OECD	Organization for Economic Cooperation and Development
OMT	Outright Monetary Transaction
OTE	Hellenic Telecommunications Organization
PASOK	Pan-Hellenic Socialist Party
PSI	Private Sector Involvement
QE	Quantitative Easing
REER	Real Effective Exchange Rate
REIT	Real Estate Investment Trust
REPO	Repurchase Agreement Rate
RMBS	Residential Mortgage-Backed Securities
S&Ls	Savings and Loan Associations
S&P	Standard & Poor's
SD	Selective Default
SDR	Special Drawing Rights
SEC	Securities and Exchange Commission
SGP	Stability and Growth Pact
SIV	Structured Investment Vehicle
SME	Small and Medium-sized Enterprises
SMP	Securities Market Program
SPD	Socialist Democratic Party
SPV	Special Purpose Vehicle
Syriza	Coalition of the Radical lext
TAF	Term Auction Facility
TALF	Term Asset-Backed Securities Loan Facility
TARP	Troubled Assets Relief Program
TIP	Targeted Investment Program
UK	United Kingdom
UKIP	UK Independence Party
UMP	Union for a Popular Movement
US	United States of America
VAT	Value Added Tax
WTO	World Trade Organization
WWI	World War I
WWII	World War II

ABOUT THE AUTHOR

George K. Zestos is presently a Professor of Economics and Jean Monnet Chair of European Integration at Christopher Newport University in Virginia. Dr Zestos was born in the small town of Deleria, Thessaly, Greece, at the foot of Mount Olympus. He began his university studies at the Aristotelian University of Thessaloniki in Greece, where he studied economics and political science for two years. He continued his college education in the US at Saginaw Valley State University in Michigan where he received a BA degree in economics and business. He received his MA and PhD in economics from Michigan State University and Indiana University (Bloomington), respectively. Dr Zestos taught at DePauw University and Ball State University for six years before he started his academic career at Christopher Newport University. Professor Zestos teaches several courses including International Economics, Applied Econometrics, and European Integration.

His research interests are in international economics, particularly in European integration, a topic on which he wrote his PhD dissertation and a textbook, *European Monetary Integration: The Euro*. His research has appeared in a variety of journals, including: *Journal of Policy Modeling* (Belgium), *Journal of Economic Integration* (Korea), *Southern Economic Journal* (US), *Journal of International Economic Studies* (Japan), *Review of International Economics* (US), *Atlantic Economic Journal* (US), *Economia Internazionale* (Italy), *Journal of Business Society* (Cyprus), *International Journal of Banking and Finance* (Australia), and *Journal of Economic Asymmetries* (Canada). He involves several students in his research and collaborates with scholars from the US and other countries, such as China, Canada, and Greece. His hobbies include traveling, fishing, gardening, soccer, and reading.

1

FROM THE GREAT DEPRESSION TO THE GREAT RECESSION

Introduction: a brief overview of the US monetary and banking system

A plausible way to begin investigating the emergence and causes of the US subprime mortgage crisis is by starting with a brief synopsis of the evolution of the US monetary and banking system. Within this framework, the government's role in the housing industry following the Great Depression is discussed. Such an approach seems appropriate since the US subprime mortgage crisis emerged as a result of financial innovations and structural changes in the financial and regulatory system.

Prior to 1863, all US commercial banks were chartered and supervised by their respective State Banking Commissions. Because the US did not share an official national currency, each bank was allowed to issue its own currency. In such an environment, there was very little central supervision of the US banking system. Bank failures during this period were frequent as they were triggered by widespread fraud and lax or absent bank regulations. Under the National Bank Act of 1863, a federal system of national banks was chartered and supervised by the Office of the Comptroller of the Currency.[1]

The US presently maintains a dual banking system, thus preserving some freedom for each state's banking system. Such a banking regime suggests that Americans have not been inclined to opt for more centralization. This American preference was also demonstrated by the failure of Congress to renew the charter of the First Bank of the US in 1811, and by the veto of President Andrew Jackson to renew the charter of the Second National Bank of the US in 1832.[2]

US government legislative initiatives to stabilize the economy

The creation of the Fed

A series of bank panics that resulted in many bank failures and substantial losses among depositors convinced the US government and Congress to establish its central bank in 1913. The Federal Reserve Act of 1913 established the Federal Reserve System, commonly known as "the Fed." The initial objective of the Fed was to prevent bank panics, which so frequently occurred prior to its creation, and thus promote economic and monetary stability.[3] The Fed was able to achieve these objectives by applying monetary policy and by pursuing a dual mandate of price stability and economic growth. According to its charter, the Fed was established as one of the main regulators of all national banks, and more recently has evolved into the most important regulator of the US banking and financial institutions.[4]

Because Americans were overly concerned that Wall Street financiers and large corporations would seek to influence their central bank, the US Congress designed the Fed to be independent from the rest of the government, thus strengthening the US politico-economic system of checks and balances.[5] The independence of the Fed was surprisingly challenged about one hundred years after its creation by a few US legislators during the Congressional debates regarding the Fed's role in the US subprime mortgage crisis. These US legislators launched an unsuccessful campaign to curtail the Fed's authority through audits that were to be initiated by the US Congress.[6]

A brief history of the US government's role in market regulation

In the early 1930s after the Great Depression, the federal government adopted three important legislative acts to safeguard the stability of the economy from possible future economic and financial crises. For the next 65 years, the three acts dominated the entire US banking, financial, and legal environment. The Securities Act of 1933 was the first of the three acts that required all issuers of securities to disclose sufficient information to potential investors regarding their own financial status. In this way, the act promoted transparency, thus providing useful information to investors which contributed to the stability of the economy. The act also explicitly prohibited fraud in the sales of securities, and consequently it became known as the "Truth in Securities Act."

In addition, the Securities Act of 1933 required all public securities offers to be registered with the Securities and Exchange Commission (SEC). The SEC was established a year later by the Securities Exchange Act of 1934, the last of the three major acts of the 1930s. Since then, the SEC has become the main regulatory authority to oversee stock exchanges, credit rating agencies (CRAs), and private regulatory organizations involved in overlooking practices of auditing securities and accounting.[7]

The Glass-Steagall Act

The Glass-Steagall Act was the second major act of the 1930s, introduced in 1933. It is considered to be by far the most important piece of legislation that provided a legal oversight of the business and banking environment in the US. It is the hallmark of the New Deal banking regulations introduced by President Franklin Delano Roosevelt in response to the Great Depression. The Glass-Steagall Act prohibited commercial banks from underwriting or dealing in corporate securities, which were activities exclusively reserved for investment banks. Similarly, investment banks were prohibited from being involved in commercial banking activities. The intention of the act was to keep risky activities of trading securities away from commercial banks in order to safeguard both the banks and their depositors.

The Glass-Steagall Act has also created the Federal Deposit Insurance Corporation (FDIC) to guarantee each bank deposit account up to a certain maximum amount, thus strengthening financial and macroeconomic stability.[8] In order for banks to qualify for FDIC insurance, each bank must meet certain requirements set by the FDIC. Therefore the FDIC, along with the Fed, the SEC, and the Commodities Futures Trading Commission (CFTC), constitutes one of the four major financial regulatory institutions.

Governments have always demonstrated a strong concern for the stability and solvency of banks, as they differ from any other business firms. Banks are closely interlinked with businesses and the public, as they hold their deposits and extend loans to them. In this respect, a bank failure constitutes systemic risk to the entire economy because when a bank folds, it takes many others with it, triggering a domino effect. For this reason, governments take extraordinary measures to protect their banking systems. The Glass-Steagall Act lasted until 1999 when it was repealed and replaced by the Gramm-Leach-Bliley Act during the administration of President Bill Clinton.[9]

US public and quasi-public housing agencies

Government stabilization of the housing market

The Great Depression (1929–33) practically devastated every sector of the US economy and did not spare the housing market. During this period, home values dropped by approximately 50 percent; such a sharp decline in home prices triggered a wave of foreclosures. The number of home foreclosures during the Great Depression years reached 10 percent of all US homes, while the unemployment rate hit an all-time high close to 25 percent.[10] In response to the economic crisis, the US government, under President Franklin Delano Roosevelt, launched an unparalleled, massive spending program to pull the US economy out of the Great Depression. After the Great Depression, the role of the US government in the economic system was irrevocably changed. The President and

Congress launched a massive discretionary counter-cyclical fiscal policy aimed at stabilizing the economy.[11] According to a few studies, these economic policies reduced the frequency and duration of the recessions in the US after the establishment of the Fed.[12]

Since the Great Depression, the US government has been intervening in the economy to pursue its objective of protecting US families throughout and beyond the economic crisis. To achieve this objective, the government initially established two important federal housing agencies (institutions) that permanently marked the US housing market. These agencies were the Federal Housing Administration (FHA) and the Home Owners Loan Corporation (HOLC).[13]

The US government also established a few other federal housing institutions to promote home ownership in the US. The roles of these public or quasi-public agencies will be discussed in this chapter. These agencies have received much credit for increasing home ownership in the US and recently much criticism for enhancing systemic risk to the entire economy.

The Federal Housing Administration

The FHA is one of the two federal housing agencies created by the National Housing Act of 1934. It provides home insurance to certain groups of qualified homeowners who are required to pay a small fee incorporated in their monthly mortgage payment.[14] Such an arrangement motivates banks to provide loans to applicants who, without the FHA home insurance, could not qualify for a mortgage.[15] First, the FHA contributed to the increase in home ownership in the US by introducing the FHA extended insurance for mortgage contracts of 30 years. The long-term fixed-interest-rate contract allows mortgage borrowers to make smaller monthly installments which are preferable and affordable by the vast majority of homeowners. Second, in 1956, the FHA raised the maximum loan-to-home value ratio for all new homes to 95 percent from the initial 80 percent for its insured mortgages.[16] Both of these measures undertaken by the FHA boosted US home ownership as the government subsidized home insurance for more borrowers and for larger amounts of mortgages.

In its history of over 80 years, the FHA remained an independent public housing agency that did not receive recapitalization aid from Congress. Since 1934, the FHA has insured 34 million homes and 47,205 multi-family housing project mortgages.[17] However, after the subprime mortgage crisis, the FHA found itself under heavy financial distress because of the ever increasing number of foreclosures it had to prevent. As a result, the FHA required and received a $1.7 billion "bailout" from the US Treasury in 2013 in order to replenish its depleted capital reserves. Because the FHA issues insurance for homes up to a certain maximum price, it became possible for private home insurance firms to insure more expensive homes. Eventually, the share of privately insured mortgages exceeded the share of those mortgages insured by the FHA.

The Home Owners Loan Corporation

The Homeowners Loan Act of 1933, as a part of President Franklin Delano Roosevelt's New Deal legislation, established the Home Owners Loan Corporation (HOLC) in response to the 1929 crash. President Roosevelt declared the administration's national policy in a message addressed to the US Congress:

> This policy is that the broad interests of the nation require that special safe-guards should be thrown around home ownership as a guarantee of economic and social stability and that to protect home owners from inequitable enforced liquidation in time of general distress is proper concern of the government.[18]

The HOLC raised funds by issuing and selling securities that were guaranteed by the government to various investors for the purpose of buying, reinstating, and refinancing defaulted loans from financial institutions. The HOLC also converted variable interest rate loans, common during the Great Depression, to longer maturity and fixed rate mortgages.[19] It was customary during the Great Depression for most mortgage contracts to have a repayment period of three to five years for both the entire principal and interest payment. The HOLC extended the repayment period of mortgages to 15 years. Over 65 years later, during the subprime mortgage crisis of 2007–9, foreclosures again became a major problem in the US.

Several analysts who studied the subprime mortgage crisis suggested that an HOLC type of agency would have been very beneficial during the crisis as it would have protected many homeowners from losing their homes.[20] After the HOLC accomplished its objective, to protect homeowners from foreclosures, it was abolished in 1936. The HOLC was replaced in 1938 by the Federal National Mortgage Association (FNMA), which is popularly known as Fannie Mae. The FHA and the HOLC both contributed to the recovery of the housing sector from the Great Depression. The long-term contracts that were introduced in the mortgage market are the legacy of the FHA and the HOLC that will continue to benefit present and future generations of homeowners.

The Federal National Mortgage Association

Fannie Mae was established in 1938 as a government-owned federal housing agency, pursuing a dual purpose of promoting stability in the housing market and increasing home ownership. It initially pursued its objective by providing liquidity to the banking system through buying FHA-insured loans and mortgages guaranteed by the Veterans Administration. Fannie Mae was privatized in 1968 during Lyndon Johnson's presidency.[21]

Gradually Fannie Mae expanded its activities to purchase conventional mortgages and adjustable rate mortgages (ARM). In the early 1980s, for the first time it issued mortgage-backed securities (MBSs). Fannie Mae launched several new programs to expand purchases, which included mortgages from low- and middle-income families and minorities. However, Fannie Mae bought all of its mortgages from banks and lending institutions in the secondary market and never made loans directly to families. Most of the new programs were launched and undertaken to comply with directives from the US Congress and the Federal government.[22]

Fannie Mae was the third government housing agency introduced but it became the most important in terms of the number of mortgages that it has insured and financed to date. Fannie Mae is the largest buyer of mortgages in the world. It finances its purchases of mortgages by issuing MBSs that always carry an explicit or an implicit guarantee by the US government.[23] The mortgages Fannie Mae purchases serve as the underlying assets (collateral) of the MBSs it issues. In this way, Fannie Mae creates and offers opportunities for many US residents to become homeowners. In 1968, a new federal housing agency split from Fannie Mae, the Government National Mortgage Association (GNMA), also popularly known as Ginnie Mae.

Although Fannie Mae kept its name after the split, it was transformed into a privately owned housing agency pursuing the objectives of promoting home ownership for Americans and income for its shareholders, while it was regulated by the government. In the fall of 2008, because of unprecedented losses due to a large number of home foreclosures during the subprime mortgage crisis, Fannie Mae was nationalized by the government and placed under the conservatorship of the Federal Housing Finance Agency (FHFA). Fannie Mae finally began making profits again in 2012 after incurring six consecutive years of losses.

Government National Mortgage Association

In 1968, the US government introduced radical changes in the US housing market when it formed a fourth federal governmental housing agency that split from Fannie Mae. The Government National Mortgage Association (GNMA), or "Ginnie Mae" as it is commonly known, was established by the Fair Housing Act of 1968. Ginnie Mae is owned by the government and is part of the Department of Housing and Urban Development (HUD).[24] Ginnie Mae was created to issue and provide a full guarantee of all its MBSs. The underlying assets of the MBSs are all government-guaranteed mortgages. These government loans include FHA-insured mortgages, mortgages to farmers guaranteed by the Department of Agriculture, mortgages guaranteed by the Veterans Affairs to military personnel, and mortgages to a few other specific groups.

Ginnie Mae issued the first MBSs ever in 1970, before any other public or private institution. In this way, it raises capital in the global financial markets as it is able to sell its MBSs, which have the full guarantee of the US government. Such securities consequently are considered exceptionally safe. Ginnie Mae receives its income by charging fees to lending institutions which issue mortgages that are purchased and securitized by it.

The Federal Housing Loan Corporation

A fifth US governmental housing agency, established in 1970, is the Federal Home Loan Corporation (FHLC), which is popularly known as "Freddie Mac." It was created as a privately owned agency, regulated by the US government. Freddie Mac's primary objective was to finance mortgages originated by the savings and loan associations (S&Ls). Freddie Mac accomplishes this goal by issuing securities that are sold to investors and are backed by mortgages it holds as collateral. Fannie Mae and Freddie Mac are very similar and they are known as government-sponsored enterprises (GSEs). The two institutions pursue the same objective – to promote home ownership in the US – and as a result they compete against each other. The government created Freddie Mac to break up the monopoly of Fannie Mae. For this reason, the two federal housing agencies are often referred as the twin GSEs. According to their federal charters, the two GSEs are responsible for providing liquidity and stabilizing the MBSs secondary market. Freddie Mac and Fannie Mae were nationalized and placed under conservatorship in the fall of 2008 in the midst of the crisis. They are now administered by the Federal Housing Finance Agency (FHFA), which was created and authorized by the President and US Congress to determine on a future course for the two federal housing agencies.

Savings and loans associations

Prior to the 1980s, savings and loans associations (S&Ls) and mutual savings banks issued most US residential mortgages that they kept on their balance sheets and serviced until the loans were completely amortized.[25] S&Ls are similar to banks but for many years they have focused their lending mainly on mortgages. S&L bankers and homeowners (borrowers) usually lived for a long time in the same communities, thus their proximity helped them develop good social and business relations. Such an amicable environment based on good personal contacts between the home loan contracting parties created a stable system. The New Deal banking regulations, which restrained banks from being exposed to excessive risk, also contributed to the stability of the banking system.[26]

The structure of the US housing market began changing, however, in the late 1970s, starting with two major events. The first was the initial relaxation of Regulation Q during the years 1979–86, which was finally abolished at the end of this time period.[27] By enforcing Regulation Q, financial regulators imposed interest rate ceilings on savings and time deposit accounts with lending institutions. The second event that caused a major structural change of the US housing market was the rising inflation of the 1970s. High inflation led Fed chairman, Paul Volcker, to adopt a new approach to monetary policy in October 1979, focusing on controlling the growth of the money supply.[28] In October 1979, the Fed abandoned targeting the federal funds rate. This policy shift resulted in drastic increases in nominal interest rates and an abrupt reduction of inflation. These two new developments led the S&Ls to become uncompetitive in comparison to banks. The main problem was that S&Ls were no longer able to raise funds in the market by paying lower interest rates to depositors than they were receiving from their mortgages.[29]

Approximately 4,000 S&Ls became insolvent during this period. One-third of these were liquidated or bought by other financial institutions at a cost of approximately $150 billion to the US taxpayers.[30] By legislating the Depository Institutions Deregulation and Monetary Control Act of 1980, US Congress tried to resolve the crisis by allowing S&Ls and other depository institutions (thrifts) to operate like commercial banks. Specifically, the act allowed them to issue adjustable interest rate mortgages and have access to the novel structured financial derivatives already available to commercial banks. As a result, the percentage of adjustable mortgages issued by S&Ls increased from 5 percent in 1980 to 64 percent in 2006, which is a huge structural change in their loan portfolio. Nevertheless, S&Ls became less important in the total US housing market in terms of their share of issued mortgages. The percentage of S&L mortgages of total US mortgages decreased from 50 percent in 1980 to 8 percent in 2006.[31]

Major changes in the US home finance system

The New Deal banking regulations and home finance regime operated without major disruptions until the late 1960s. However, in the early 1970s, for many reasons, the Glass-Steagall Act of 1933, which incorporated most of the New Deal financial regulations, was seriously challenged. The source of the challenge primarily had its roots in the major structural changes that were taking place in the US political, economic, and financial system. The GSEs, by raising funds in the global money markets, were able to increase liquidity for the US housing sector. In doing so, they relied exclusively on the mortgage securitization model to help US families achieve the "American Dream" of becoming homeowners.

Several authors attribute the government's involvement in the housing industry to be a cause of the subprime mortgage crisis. Barth *et al.* (2012) claim that few countries, without the massive governmental programs, attained as high rates of home ownership as the US. This claim is supported by Figure 1.1 where the home ownership of the US and Canada is compared. From the early 1980s, the home ownership rates of the two countries increased at similar rates. The US home ownership rate was higher than the Canadian rate until 2005. Just two years prior to the outset of the subprime mortgage crisis (2007–9), the home ownership rate of the two neighboring countries became equal. From 2006, the two rates diverged. Although the Canadian home ownership rate kept rising and reached 70 percent in 2012, the US home ownership rate has been declining since 2004. Canada accomplished such an increase in its home ownership without establishing similar housing agencies to those in the US. This reduction in home ownership can be almost exclusively attributed to the subprime mortgage crisis. The decline in US home ownership in 2012 by 4 percentage points since its peak in 2004 is a major setback inflicted by the subprime mortgage crisis on the American people. Such a negative effect is in

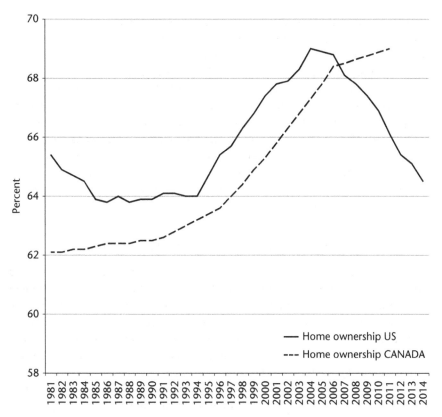

FIGURE 1.1 US and Canadian home ownership rate

addition to the rising unemployment rate which has almost doubled during the subprime mortgage crisis.[32]

It will never be known how US home ownership would have developed without the extensive government presence in the housing market, which is still very strong to this day.[33] However, it is a common understanding that millions of low- and middle-income American families would not have been able to buy their homes without the government's active presence and subsidization of home purchases. Thus government involvement in the housing market contributed to the democratization of credit and increased home ownership in the US. This is something that was reversed during the years of the subprime mortgage crisis. The US government could have prevented this if it had directed all of its efforts into directly providing aid to homeowners and thus indirectly helping the financial institutions.

Initially, the US government explicitly guaranteed the MBSs issued by the GSEs. Such a guarantee strongly motivated investors to purchase their securities. The trust of investors in the MBSs continued even after Fannie Mae was privatized in 1968, because there was an implicit guarantee that the federal government would intervene and bailout the GSEs if they ever became insolvent.[34] For many years, Fannie and Freddie issued securities backed only by high-quality performing home mortgages; consequently, their MBSs received AAA ratings.

Lower quality mortgages, such as subprime and Alt-A, were initially purchased and securitized by investment banks.[35] MBSs issued by GSEs were then sold to various investors in the US and abroad. Salomon Brothers issued the first private MBSs for the Bank of America in 1977. The decision by investment banks to securitize subprime and Alt-A mortgages is considered to be a major factor behind the subprime mortgage crisis. Defenders of the investment banks claim that securitization of subprime mortgages promoted credit democratization in the US and thus increased home ownership.

The US government's influence on the housing market

During and after the end of the Great Depression, all US administrations and Congress were committed to increasing home ownership. The US government pursued such a policy by establishing several federal housing agencies exclusively authorized to achieve this objective. The US Congress passed the Community Reinvestment Act in 1977, which required banks to extend mortgages to low- and middle-income families that could not have been obtained in the market without assistance from the government.

Several years later in 1995, the Department of Housing and Urban Development (HUD) directed the GSEs to expand their home loan portfolios by buying more mortgages issued to low- and moderate-income families. This decision, although directed to the GSEs, encouraged banks to issue a larger number of subprime and Alt-A type of mortgages. This policy aimed to close the gap in home ownership among social groups of different races and income levels. Consequently, the GSEs became heavily exposed to risk to the extent that they came close to the brink of bankruptcy.

The federal government, initially, bailed out the two GSEs at a total cost of approximately $187.5 billion. The two GSEs, however, paid out dividends of $65.2 billion, which were kept by the government and reduced the cost to $123.5 billion.[36] In September 2008, the government nationalized both GSEs, as it applied macro-prudential policy to avoid systemic risk and cope with the "too big to fail" problem.[37]

On 30 July 2008, President George W. Bush signed into law the Housing and Economic Recovery Act of 2008. Under this act, the two GSEs came under the conservatorship of the Federal Housing Finance Agency (FHFA). The FHFA was delegated the authority to oversee the two GSEs and the twelve federal home loan banks. In addition, the act gave authority to the FHFA to consolidate several housing regulatory agencies along with their staff under the FHFA umbrella. The objective of the FHFA is to provide stability in the housing market by supporting the financing of homes at reasonable prices that families can afford. It is the responsibility of the

FHFA to search for a solution for the future of the two GSEs and thus improve the US housing and financial markets while protecting the taxpayers.

The restructuring of the two federal housing giants was to take place under the direction of the federal government and the US Congress. The Dodd-Frank Act, also known as the Financial Regulatory Reform Act, was adopted by the US in July 2010. One of the major criticisms of this act was that it had not specified a course of action for the future of Freddie Mac and Fannie Mae. This might have happened because US legislators and President Obama expected the FHFA to permanently resolve the future of the two GSEs, as it was delegated the authority by the Housing and Economic Recovery Act of 2008. Indeed, the FHFA has been planning for some time now to transfer activities of the two GSEs to the private sector and thus resolve the "too big to fail" problem that the two home finance giants pose to the US economy. (For a more detailed plan designed by the FHFA to privatize the two GSEs see Box 1.1.)

BOX 1.1 A plan for the two GSEs and a dilemma for the US Congress

In February 2012, a plan was announced by the acting director of the FHFA at that time, Edward DeMarco, to wind down the two GSEs and transfer their activities to the private sector. About a year later, on 5 March 2013, Mr Demarco released more information regarding the plan which was backed by President Barack Obama's administration and the Republicans in Congress. According to the plan, a new public utility housed outside of Freddie Mac and Fannie Mae was going to be formed and will be responsible for creating a securitization platform for the entire US secondary mortgage market.

According to this plan, all securitizations of the US home mortgage industry will employ the same platform. The processing of the payments from all issuers of MBSs to investors (buyers) of MBSs and following through all of the payments will take place in the same system. The plan will standardize the securitization process as it is designed to be an improvement in comparison to the unregulated securitization system that previously existed – and still exists – that is considered one of the factors that fermented the subprime mortgage crisis. Looking ahead, the FHFA and Mr Demarco had to find a way to wind down Fannie Mae and Freddie Mac by following directions from Congress and the Obama administration. The biggest problem ahead faced by the FHFA and Mr Demarco was that they were not quite certain how to securitize the entire secondary US mortgage market without the participation of the two GSEs. Fannie Mae and Freddie Mac securitized about half of the total US secondary mortgage market amounting to about $5 trillion of a total $10 trillion industry.

It is, nonetheless, embarrassing for the FHFA and the Obama administration because, as the plan for dismantling the two federal housing agencies is in the process of being designed, both GSEs generated record high net incomes in 2012, 2013, and 2014. Fannie Mae made $17.2, $83.96, and $14.2 billion whereas Freddie Mac generated $11, $48.7, and $7.7 billion in income respectively. Also, both GSEs have been paying dividends to the Treasury. Table 1.1 shows the annual dividend payments of the two GSEs to the government.

TABLE 1.1 Fannie Mae and Freddie Mac dividends to government ($bn)

Year	Fannie Mae	Freddie Mac
2012	11.60	7.20
2013	82.50	47.60
2014	20.60	19.62
Total	114.70	74.42

Because private securitization after the crisis dried up, the role of the two GSEs in home finance became more important. As the two GSEs began making profits, the government received the entire amount. By April 2015, the government received $228 billion from the two GSEs, which is roughly $40 billion more than the government originally invested (Light, 2015). Fannie's securitizations alone amounted to 48 percent of all the new MBSs for 2012. As many politicians are determined to "scale down" the government involvement in the home finance industry, the news of the record high income of the two GSEs caused a great dilemma. This becomes more complicated and interesting as politicians aim to make the home finance industry more efficient. Considering the budget disputes and the perpetual bickering between Republicans and Democrats to reduce public deficits and debt, it is difficult for anyone to imagine that politicians will easily decide to reduce public revenues by privatizing the two GSEs.

Bank resistance to regulation

The Glass-Steagall Act of 1933 for many years had prohibited commercial banks from issuing or trading securities for their own account. This activity, which was considered very risky, was performed exclusively by investment banks.[38] Some countries, however, that have not adopted the distinction between investment banks and commercial banks have not experienced a major financial crisis.[39] Much pressure, however, was mounting through the years because banks were seeking freedom to trade in non-traditional and more risky investments. The Fed permitted an exception to this Glass-Steagall regulation in 1987 when for the first time it authorized a subsidiary of Citibank in London to create a Special Purpose Vehicle (SPV).[40] The creation of SPVs allowed banks to get around the Glass-Steagall Act which prohibited them from dealing and underwriting securities such as stocks and bonds. As the banks gained freedom to invest through their SPVs, financial uncertainty, instability, and fragility also entered the US financial system. The Gramm-Leach-Bliley Act of 1999 repealed the Glass-Steagall Act and provided the freedom for banks to begin investing in risky activities.

The Dodd-Frank Act that became effective in July 2010 aimed to restrict banks from trading in securities on their own account. US legislators considered it imprudent to expose taxpayers to risk by allowing banks to take unnecessary risk and, thus, jeopardizing the banks' solvency and their customers' deposits which are insured by the FDIC. The Dodd-Frank Act requires banks to spin off their trading desk operations of derivatives and other proprietary trades. A last minute compromise, nevertheless, after immense pressure from banks, was reached to allow banks to keep 3 percent of their total trading desk operations.[41] This regulation, which is now part of the Dodd-Frank Act, is known as the Volcker Rule, bearing the name of a former chairman of the Fed who was a strong proponent in the debates of prohibiting banks from trading in securities with depositors' money.

The US housing bubble

Figure 1.2 shows the home price indices for 20 individual US cities and two composite home price indices for the entire US economy. Karl Case and Robert Shiller were the first economists to construct and publicize US housing price indices; as a result, these indices were named after them. Figure 1.2(b) shows the home price indices for 20 major US cities. Most of the individual home price city indices follow the same pattern as the two composite home price indices. The home price city indices began rising sharply after the early 2000s and reached a peak in 2006, after which they began declining rather abruptly. Consequently, most housing indices for the single cities and the two composites behaved as leading economic indicators since they turned up before the real economy went into a recession. Initially, they indicated strong evidence of the formation of a bubble in the US housing market during 2000–6, which triggered the expansion prior to the crisis. Finally, the balloon burst in 2006 when the home price indices began declining, and this brought the subprime mortgage recession in 2007–9.

Figure 1.2(a) depicts two composite home price indices for 10 and 20 major US cities, which are denoted by composite-10, CSXR-SA, and composite-20, SPC20R-SA, respectively. By examining the two home composite price indices, it is also evident that US home prices remained rather stable until the late 1990s. Since then, the two US home price indices drastically increased until they reached a peak in February 2006. For the next year until February 2007, the home composite price indices declined slightly. Starting in February 2007, both indices began to drop sharply and in March 2009 they leveled off to reach close to the same value as in 2003. Since January of 2013, almost all housing indices began to increase indicating that possibly another housing bubble is forming.

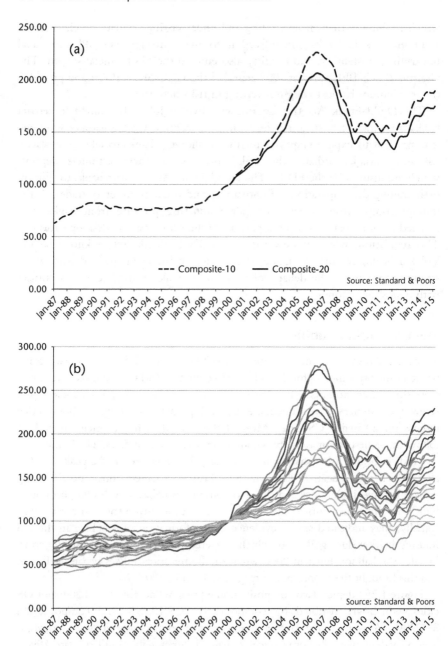

FIGURE 1.2   (a) Case-Schiller two composite home price index; (b) Case-Schiller 20 US city home price indices

Examination of the two composite home price indices clearly indicates how and when the subprime mortgage crisis evolved. The US home price indices began rising in the early 2000s, when the housing boom started as a result of the excessive monetary and fiscal policies and foreign financial capital inflows that kept US interest rates low. Such economic policies were launched to cope with the 2001 dot-com recession, the corporate scandals crisis, and the negative climate created by the September 11, 2001 terrorist attacks in the US. As the home price indices turned down in February 2006, they affected the real economy. Families started losing their homes and workers began losing their jobs. After a year's lag, unemployment in 2007 began increasing and real GDP was in decline until 2009, the last year of the recession.

US unemployment rate and GDP growth

The US unemployment rate and the real GDP growth are shown in Figures 1.3(a) and 1.3(b). The horizontal axis of the two graphs are aligned so one can clearly observe both the dot-com and subprime mortgage crisis recessions, as indicated by the shaded columns. The beginning and ending dates of the recessions are those exactly determined by the Business Cycle Dating Committee of the National Bureau of Economic Research (NBER).[42] The inverse relation of the real GDP growth and unemployment for the dot-com and the subprime mortgage crises are very clearly depicted in Figures 1.3(a) and 1.3(b).

In Figure 1.4, the US unemployment rate and the real GDP growth are shown for the period 1916 to 2014. The most important recessions and the Great Depression are depicted by the respective shaded columns. The duration of each recession in terms of number of months is placed on the top of each shaded column. The US experienced its longest recession during the period 1929–33, therefore this recession has been named the Great Depression. It lasted 43 months and it is associated with the highest US unemployment rate ever recorded for which macroeconomic data are available for the country.[43]

The two recessions, caused by the oil crises, lasted for 16 months each, but the second oil crisis resulted in a higher unemployment rate than the first. The recession caused by the dot-com crisis lasted a short period of less than a year. The expansionary US fiscal and monetary policies to cope with the dot-com crisis helped the US economy quickly recover from this recession. Such policies, however, planted the seeds for a new, longer, and more catastrophic recession, the subprime mortgage crisis, that lasted 18 months. Because the duration of this contraction is only second to the Great Depression, the subprime mortgage crisis has been named the Great Recession. The effects of the Great Recession are far from over as the crisis has spread abroad. Particularly in Europe, countries have been experiencing stagnation that seriously threatens several economies and the very foundation of the Economic and Monetary Union (EMU) and the euro.

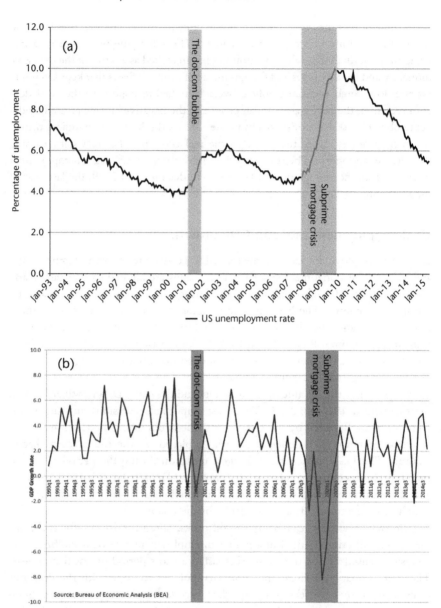

FIGURE 1.3 (a) US unemployment rate; (b) US real GDP growth rate

Concluding comments

The US government has a long tradition of being a major participant in the financing and insuring of homes in America. During and after the Great Depression, the US government established several public and quasi-public institutions to assist families which otherwise would have been unable to purchase their homes. Starting with

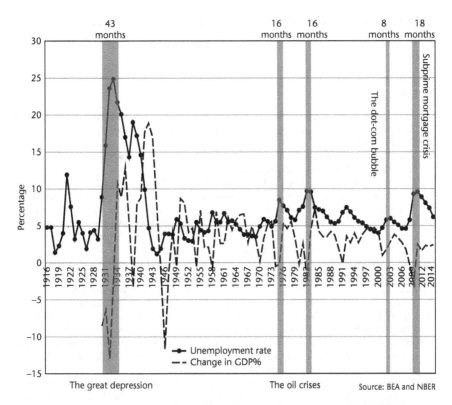

FIGURE 1.4 US recessions as indicated by the unemployment rate (1916–2014)

the FHA and the HOLC, the US government provided homeowners with insurance and bought foreclosed mortgages to save their homes. A few years later, it created Fannie Mae and Freddie Mac which purchased mortgages in the secondary market, thus helping finance homes for many qualified borrowers. The two housing agencies indirectly financed homes by buying mortgages from banks and raising capital via securitization by selling MBSs in the global financial markets while they used the mortgages as collateral.

The two GSEs along with several investment banks also purchased many mortgages that were of poor quality, namely subprime and Alt-A. Consequently, a great share of the MBSs were of low quality. When investors realized that a large share of MBSs was based on low-quality mortgages, the subprime mortgage crisis began. Both GSEs and a few investment banks, along with several other financial institutions, were devastated by the crisis. The two GSEs, however, were saved as the US government nationalized them. This decision prevented systemic risk that would have more severely spread the crisis to the entire country. A plan drawn by the FHFA aimed to eventually privatize Fannie Mae and Freddie Mac. Since 2012, however, the two GSEs have generated substantial profits. Such news would have been welcome for the President and Congress, provided they were not planning to privatize them. Privatization of the two GSEs would have resulted in a loss of public revenue in the midst of a period of partisan confrontation regarding fiscal contraction.

Notes

1 The Office of the Comptroller of the Currency is part of the Department of the US Treasury. This regulatory banking institution still exists to this day.
2 Mishkin (2013).
3 The US, prior to the establishment of the Fed, experienced bank panics in 1797, 1819, 1839, 1857, 1873, 1893, and 1907. See Shiller (2008).
4 The Federal Reserve Act of 1913 gave the US its permanent central bank.
5 An independent Fed, for example, can resist pressure from the incumbent government to apply easy monetary policy by reducing interest rates in order to boost economic growth prior to an election year. A non-accommodating monetary policy in this case can better serve the country because it promotes price stability, a prerequisite for long-term economic growth and development.
6 Such a recent legislative initiative was triggered by the Fed's unwillingness to reveal the names and the respective amounts of bailout recipient institutions during the subprime mortgage crisis. Finally the "audit the Fed" bill did not pass to become US law.
7 The Securities Act of 1933 exists to this day, but it was amended in 2009.
8 The Federal Deposit Insurance Corporation (FDIC) insured every bank account up to $100,000 before the subprime mortgage crisis, provided the accounts were held with different banks. As a result of the subprime mortgage crisis, the FDIC increased the insurance on every bank account, starting in July 2010, to $250,000. See www.fdic.gov/news/news/press/2010/pr10161.html for more information.
9 Another important law that aimed to achieve financial stability was introduced much later: the Bank Holding Company Act of 1956. This act prohibits bank holding companies from acquiring non-banking businesses and vice versa. To this day, bank holding companies cannot acquire or merge with non-banking companies. This act aimed to reduce the concentration of power as a result of the merging of financial and non-financial institutions.
10 The US subprime mortgage crisis caused 14 percent of all mortgages to be either delinquent or in foreclosure. See Wachter and Smith (2011).
11 The European Union is not following the US's example of adopting a centralized discretionary counter-cyclical fiscal policy to fight its own crisis. The US government's influence on the economic system prior to the Great Depression was limited. This was in line with the views of the classical economists who believed that a free-market laissez-faire system will be efficient, self-correcting, and will always move the economy to full employment equilibrium.
12 An exception is the Great Depression (1929–33) that occurred after the establishment of the Fed. Figure 1.4 in this chapter depicts the number and duration of the most important US recessions after the establishment of the Fed.
13 See Green and Wachter (2005) for more information.
14 Qualified homeowners are those who obtained government guaranteed mortgages.
15 The FHA is part of the US Department of Housing and Urban Development (HUD).
16 For example, if a borrower's home was worth $200,000, under the 80 percent maximum loan-to-home value ratio, the borrower would qualify for a $160,000 insured mortgage by the FHA. Under the increased 95 percent loan-to-home value ratio, the borrower would qualify for a $190,000 insured mortgage.
17 See "US Department of Housing and Urban Development," at: portal.hud.gov/hudportal/HUD.
18 See A. Hillier (n.d.) "Redlining in Philadelphia," at: www.nis.cml.upenn.edu/redlining/HOLC_intro.html.

19 Approximately one million mortgages were purchased and reinstated by the HOLC. Variable interest rate mortgages are very risky because interest rates always increase when the interest rates in the economy rise. This often makes it difficult, if not impossible, for borrowers to afford to pay their monthly loan payments, thus they often end up losing their homes. See Green and Wachter (2005).

20 This was the initial intent of the Troubled Asset Relief Program (TARP), introduced by the Bush administration, until the Secretary of the Treasury, Henry Paulson, realized that rescuing homes from foreclosures would have taken trillions instead of billions of dollars. As a result, the TARP plan was redirected to rescue financial and other institutions instead of helping families to save their homes.

21 The US government, at that time, decided to reduce the burden on the US budget, which was heavily stressed by the Vietnam War that the US was fighting during this time. Thus it privatized Fannie Mae but the agency remained under government supervision.

22 See "History of Fannie Mae," at: www.alliemae.org/historyoffanniemae.html.

23 Fannie Mae still issues bonds for the same purpose.

24 See "Inside Ginnie Mae," at: www.ginniemae.gov/inside_gnma/company_overview/Pages/our_history.aspx.

25 A balance sheet is the financial picture of a business firm. It shows on one side the assets of the firm and on the other the sources of the assets. These are the liabilities and the capital of the owners of the firm which is called net worth or owner's equity. Keeping the loans on the balance sheet simply means that the bank does not sell the loans, but it keeps them until they are fully amortized, i.e. until the loans are paid off.

26 See Wray (2007).

27 Regulation Q was first introduced on 1 November 1933 to protect banks from failing due to fierce competition.

28 To achieve this new policy objective, the Fed controlled either total reserves or unborrowed reserves.

29 This problem arose because the S&Ls mortgage interest rates were low as most of their mortgage contracts were signed during a period when the interest rates in the economy were also low.

30 See Barth et al. (2012) for a more detailed analysis.

31 See Barth et al. (2008).

32 Reduction of home ownership is mainly the result of the increased number of foreclosures during the subprime mortgage crisis.

33 In 2013, nine out of ten homes in the US were either financed or insured by the government (see Pickard, 2013).

34 This indeed happened in September of 2008 when the federal government nationalized both Freddie Mac and Fannie Mae·

35 The risk of Alt-A mortgages is higher than the risk of the prime mortgages, but lower than the risk of the subprime mortgages. However, almost all analysts group Alt-A with subprime mortgages rather than with prime mortgages.

36 See Timiraos (2013).

37 The "too big to fail" problem is one of the major problems governments must address to prevent financial instability and contagion. During financial crises, governments face a dilemma between allowing an institution to fail or bailing it out. Both options can be detrimental to the economy. If a big institution fails, it will affect many other institutions and the entire economy. Similarly, bailing out a big institution can be costly to taxpayers, but it will not affect other institutions through a domino effect.

38 Investment banks, according to the Glass-Steagall Act, were not allowed to offer deposit accounts (Banking Act of 1933, H.R. 5661, 73rd Cong. (1933) (enacted)).

39 Ibid., 30.

40 SPVs are also called structured investment vehicles (SIVs). They are investment funds created and owned by banks to allow them to get around the Glass-Steagall Act and

invest in profitable but very risky assets held outside the balance sheet of the banks. In this way, banks can protect their balance sheet assets in case the SPV goes bankrupt.
41 Trading desk operations are a bank's most profitable activity. It is therefore obvious why banks were much opposed to giving them up.
42 "US Business Cycle Expansions and Contractions," at: www.nber.org/cycles.html.
43 There were several other recessions but two of the most severe were caused by the two oil crises. The first started in the fourth quarter of 1973 and ended in the first quarter of 1975. The second oil crisis was from the third quarter of 1981 to the fourth quarter of 1982.

References

Barth, J. R., Caprio, G., and Levine, R. (2012) *Guardians of Finance*. Cambridge, MA: MIT Press.
Barth, J. R., Li, T., Lu, W., Phumiwasana, T., and Yago, G. (2008) *Capital Access Index 2007 – Best Markets for Business Access to Capital*. Santa Monica, CA: Milken Institute.
Green, R. K. and Wachter, S. M. (2005) "The American mortgage in historical and international context," *Journal of Economic Perspectives*, 19 (4): 93–114.
Hillier, A. (n.d.) "Home Owners' Loan Corporation," at: www.nis.cml.upenn.edu/redlining/HOLC_intro.html.
"HUD/U.S." (n.d.) HUD/US Housing and Urban Development [online].
Light, J. (2015) "Treasury Department: Fannie, Freddie bailout wasn't a loan," *Wall Street Journal*, April 21.
Mishkin, F. S. (2013) *The Economics of Money, Banking, and Financial Markets*. Boston: Addison-Wesley.
"Our History" (n.d.) Ginnie Mae [online].
Pickard, J. (2013) "Property of the state: housing policy," *Financial Times*, 19 April.
Shiller, R. (2008) *The Subprime Solution*. Princeton, NJ and Oxford: Princeton University Press.
Timiraos, N. (2013) "Fannie's windfall blurs debate over its fate," *Wall Street Journal*, 3 April.
"US Business Cycle Expansions and Contractions" (n.d.) National Bureau of Economic Research [online].
Wachter, S. and Smith, M. (2011) *The American Mortgage System: Crisis and Reform*. Philadelphia, PA: University of Pennsylvania Press.
Wray, L. R. (2007) *Lessons from the Subprime Meltdown*, Working Paper No. 522. Annandale-on-Hudson, NY: Levy Economics Institute of Bard College.

2

CAUSES OF THE US SUBPRIME MORTGAGE CRISIS

Introduction

Several years have passed since the end of the recession caused by the subprime mortgage crisis in the US. The causes of the crisis are still subject to debate, and it seems they will always be disputed, especially among proponents of opposing politico-economic ideologies. The main disagreement between these opposing ideological groups is in regard to the degree of government intervention in the economy and, more specifically, the housing market. Most researchers, nonetheless, are convinced that both government and market failures played a major role in the formation of the US subprime mortgage crisis and a large majority of analysts agree that many factors were responsible. What follows in this chapter is a brief analysis of the most important factors that fermented the crisis. All of these factors are discussed and critically analyzed, though they are not presented in order of significance.

The dot-com and the corporate scandals crises of 2000–3

The dot-com and corporate scandals crises that occurred at the turn of the twenty-first century were preceded by the longest economic expansion in modern US history, the decade of the 1990s. This expansion brought the unemployment rate down to 4 percent, the inflation rate to about 2 percent, and generated federal government surpluses for the years 1998–2001.[1] Several authors support the view that the US subprime mortgage crisis has its roots in the expansionary US monetary and fiscal policies, adopted to cope with the dot-com and corporate scandals crises, and the negative climate that followed the terrorists attacks of September 11, 2001. The Fed, after a sequence of incremental cuts, drove the federal funds rate, its main monetary policy instrument, from 6.5 percent down to 1 percent, a 42-year record low.

The US federal government reduced taxes and increased expenditures during this period to prevent a further deepening of the anticipated recession. The expansionary monetary and fiscal policies of this time were effective as low interest rates and increased government spending triggered a boom. Output, income, consumption, and prices all increased during this period. Monetary policy was exceptionally effective because it boosted consumption of automobiles as auto companies were able to increase car sales by offering zero percent interest rate loans to finance purchases of new vehicles.

The Fed was successful in reducing long-term interest rates; therefore, monetary policy was very effective as families purchased new homes, refinanced existing homes, and even borrowed more on existing mortgages. Furthermore, households spent excessive amounts of money on other items, such as home renovations, boats, vacations, and other purchases. Increasing home prices encouraged many families to go on an extended spending spree.[2] In addition to rising home prices, stock prices also increased. As a result of booming markets, asset prices increased and a wealth effect was generated among consumers, which helped pull the US out of the recession.[3]

The expansionary monetary and fiscal policies that created euphoria among consumers and helped the US out of the crisis also became a major cause of the upcoming subprime mortgage crisis. The extraordinary increase in consumer spending that generated the boom in the housing and stock markets also created bubbles in these markets due to the rising and unsustainable consumer debt. In addition, the countercyclical expansionary policies adopted by the US to overcome the dot-com and corporate scandals crises also contributed to the creation of bubbles in the housing and stock markets prior to the subprime mortgage crisis. If there was a lesson to be learnt from the dot-com and corporate scandals experience, it was that policymakers ought to be extremely careful regarding the magnitude of the injected stimuli adopted by the government to implement countercyclical policies to combat the recession. Policymakers overreacted, and as they put out an old fire, a new one had begun. It is now certain that the countercyclical policies that engineered the recovery also planted the seeds for a newer and much bigger crisis.

Several high-level executives and other professionals such as accountants, auditors, and bankers, were found guilty of fraudulent behavior having devastating effects on their companies and the entire economy. It is also interesting to note that during the last two US crises, the corporate scandals and the subprime mortgage crisis, there was plenty of evidence of unethical behavior among high-level business executives. During both crises, the vast majority of the victims were among the lower- and middle-income classes of society. The corporate scandals crisis resulted in the loss of the pensions of many hourly workers, whereas the 2007–9 subprime mortgage crisis resulted in millions of foreclosures of homes owned by the lower- and middle-income class families and minorities.

Trade and financial flows

Trade liberalization and financial deregulation

Many analysts are convinced that the US subprime mortgage crisis had its roots in the rapid increase of trade liberalization and financial deregulation policies starting in the early 1980s under the administrations of President Ronald Reagan and British Prime Minister Margaret Thatcher. Both US and UK administrations promoted trade liberalization and financial deregulation. In such a laissez-faire environment, financial regulators provided minimal oversight of financial institutions. The Gramm-Leach-Bliley Act of 1999, also known as the Financial Services Modernization Act, replaced the Glass-Steagall Act which legalized many financial activities that were formerly prohibited.

Financial and banking deregulation allowed the introduction of several structured financial products that, according to their proponents, created new investment opportunities that helped increase liquidity and credit in the banking system to finance mortgages. These new financial products were created to increase profits; however, they were very risky. Former Fed president, Alan Greenspan, is on record stating: "This was done by allocating risk to those investors who were willing and able to accept."[4] Nonetheless, it is not certain that such increased efficiency in the allocation of financial capital attracted only investors that were well aware of the risk involved in these new investment opportunities.[5] Financial innovation has often masked risk, especially when several of the multi-level securitizations produced financial derivatives that were so complex and opaque that they were mispriced by markets.

International trade imbalances

Another factor that often is presented as a possible cause of the US subprime mortgage crisis is large and increasing international trade imbalances, particularly the US's chronic and increasing trade deficit. Starting in the early 1980s, when trade liberalization policies were adopted by the US and many other countries, the US began generating massive trade deficits in relation to the rest of the world. Figure 2.1 shows the US Current Account (CA) and Financial Account (FA). The CA consists mainly of the goods and services balance, i.e. exports minus imports, and a few other components.[6] The FA captures the financial flows most often taking place to accommodate the CA. For the US, the FA is almost the mirror image of the CA and it shows how the US CA deficit is financed (see Figure 2.1).

From 1991, the US experienced a sequence of CA deficits that reached unprecedented magnitudes in terms of both absolute levels and as a percentage of gross domestic product (GDP). The increasing US CA deficits attracted much attention and raised serious concerns among policymakers and academics; consequently it became a major issue of dispute in the US and abroad. Many economists were then

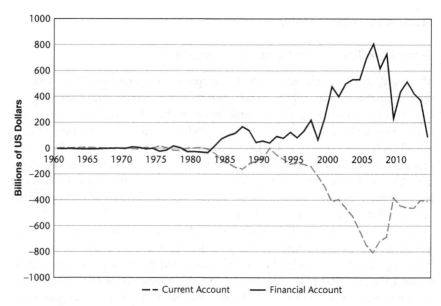

FIGURE 2.1 US balance of payments accounts
Source: Bureau of Economic Analysis.

convinced that the US trade deficit was unsustainable and could have triggered a major world economic crisis.

In 1991, a rollercoaster of US trade imbalances began. By 2006, the US trade deficit explosion reached its maximum at approximately $800 billion, just above 6 percent of GDP. This magnitude constitutes the greatest trade imbalance that has ever occurred in any country in the world.[7]

Such trade imbalances occurred just before the onset of the US subprime mortgage crisis in 2007. It is interesting to note that the US CA deficit explosion from 1991–2006 lasted a period of 16 years, an interval during which two of the most severe post-World War II crises began or occurred, the Asian crisis in 1997–8 and the US subprime mortgage crisis in 2007–9. The US CA deficit began shrinking only when the subprime mortgage crisis was well rooted and US consumers and businesses substantially cut spending. During this time, the only source of growth was the US government. Indeed, the US government applied the most expansionary fiscal and monetary policies in its history to protect the US economy from another Great Depression.

Since the beginning of 2010, the US has been officially out of the subprime mortgage crisis. During the crisis, the US did not experience capital outflows, as usually happens with countries that are hit by major financial problems. The flow of financial capital during the crisis in the US had been moving in the wrong direction. According to international trade theory, under normal conditions, capital is flowing from the capital-abundant countries like the US to the capital-scarce countries, i.e. countries in the developing world. However, during the US subprime mortgage crisis, capital flows were moving in the opposite direction. The uninterrupted capital inflow to the

US during the crisis provides a convincing reason that US trade imbalances did not cause the crisis. The explanation of this anomaly is based on the fact that the US is a unique country: it has the largest economy in the world, and its currency still serves as the world's most important, but unofficial, reserve currency.

Trade of derivative financial instruments

In 2006, the US CA imbalance had reached its peak, as shown in Figure 2.1.[8] This was the year prior to the eruption of the US subprime mortgage crisis. It could, therefore, be inferred that the CA imbalance caused the crisis, or this could be a good example of the post-hoc fallacy. The CA, however, "is dwarfed" in comparison to total capital flows in the world.[9] The above claim can be supported by the following information: in 2012, the world's GDP was approximately $70 trillion; however, the total annual volume of traded derivative financial instruments amounted to $740 trillion.[10] The largest share, an amount of about $640 trillion, was traded over-the-counter. This means that there exist no public records of these trade transactions because they simply are not recorded in any official exchange.[11]

Despite the evidence of the relatively small amounts of the trade flows as compared to the total financial flows, the IMF, the EU, and the G20 nevertheless all launched programs aiming to reduce or "unwind" large global and regional trade imbalances. Obstfeld claims monitoring CA global imbalances is important for stabilization purposes.[12] However, because the CA global imbalances are so small in comparison to the total financial flows, it is the financial flows that constitute the greater potential risk to the global economy. This risk is more serious considering the fact that a great amount of these financial transactions are opaque and the traded assets are extremely risky. To avoid another major crisis, it is imperative that data are gathered and become accessible in order to provide information regarding the direction, magnitudes, and trades of all financial flows. Such information must be shared and used by both national and international policy circles to increase understanding of all major financial flows. This information can be useful in assisting with the adoption of common or coordinated policies and enabling countries to take the necessary precautionary measures to reduce financial fragility and uncertainty in the US and the global financial system.

A major factor in the US subprime mortgage crisis and the European sovereign debt crisis was the introduction of several novel structured financial products, popularly known as derivatives. The most common derivatives are mortgage backed securities (MBSs), collateralized debt obligations (CDOs), and credit default swaps (CDSs) that are mainly traded by hedge funds and other financial companies and by the trading desks of investment banks. It is evident from Figure 2.2 that the share of OTC derivatives has been increasing exponentially. Beginning in 2007, the first year of the US subprime mortgage crisis, the growth of the OTC derivatives nevertheless leveled off, but slowly increased again starting in 2010. As a result, many analysts are very suspicious of these transactions.

Defenders of OTC derivatives claim that since these securities are tailored for two parties, they are useful financial instruments and serve the purpose of hedging

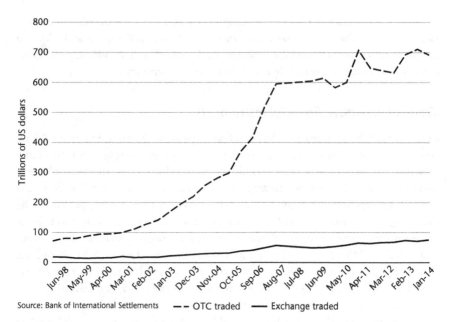

Source: Bank of International Settlements   - - OTC traded   — Exchange traded

FIGURE 2.2 Derivative financial instruments traded over the counter and on organized exchanges

specific needs by transferring market credit risk between counterparties. It is interesting to note that, after the end of the subprime mortgage crisis in 2009, the total supply of OTC derivatives increased by approximately $100 trillion, whereas the exchange traded derivatives leveled off to an amount of about $70 trillion.

Regulatory reforms on the trading of financial derivatives gave hope that by October 2, 2013, opaque derivatives would start trading in electronic exchanges. However, it was later known that it would be delayed as US regulators demanded control of all platforms that trade with US counterparties.[13]

Did government failure cause the crisis?

The US government, according to its critics, is mainly responsible for the development of the US housing bubble. However, the bubble could not have lasted forever, and as a result, a drastic drop in home prices in 2007 signaled the burst. The government's objective was to offer opportunities to many underprivileged citizens in the middle- and lower-income levels as well as to minority groups to fulfill "the American Dream."[14] Fannie Mae and Freddie Mac are two such important US federal housing institutions. They both raise capital in the private markets by issuing MBSs to enhance liquidity for the home lending institutions. They accomplish this by buying and insuring residential mortgages from banks and other lending institutions such as savings and loan associations (S&Ls), mutual savings banks, credit unions, and a few others.

For many years, Fannie Mae and Freddie Mac purchased only high-quality prime mortgages. For this reason, Fannie and Freddie's MBSs received AAA ratings from the credit rating agencies (CRAs). The federal government, as far back as 1977, adopted a policy requiring banks to increase lending to families of lower- and moderate-income level.[15] Under such circumstances, although many mortgage applicants lacked the necessary credit quality, their applications for home loans were approved. Consequently, a large number of nonperforming mortgages, which became known as subprime and Alt-A, are a major cause of the US subprime mortgage crisis. This happened because the subprime and Alt-A mortgages consti-tuted a substantial share of the underlying assets (collateral) of the novel structured synthetic financial products.

Government regulatory institutions did not deter this explosion of financial derivatives – as a matter of fact they often encouraged it. A fair evaluation of the government is that in its noble efforts to increase home ownership in the US it contributed to the creation of the bubble by directing banks and other financial institutions to increase lending to lower-income classes and minority groups. Whereas many analysts agree that the overall role of the government was positive in raising home ownership in the US, they also believe that the government increased the fragility and instability of the financial system prior to and during the crisis. Consequently, the government negatively contributed to the formation of the subprime mortgage crisis, despite the fact that its objective was to increase home ownership through the democratization of credit for home financing.

Innovation in US housing finance

Financial innovation and perverse incentives

A great number of analysts attribute the causes of the US subprime mortgage crisis to major structural changes in the US financial system that had begun even before the repeal of the Glass-Steagall Act in 1999. The Glass-Steagall Act had provided a legal oversight and a regulatory umbrella for the US financial and banking sector during the period 1933–99. Under this strict regulatory environment, commercial banks and other depository institutions were prohibited from investing in risky investments that could enhance systemic risk and endanger the stability of the financial system. The removal of such restrictions allowed financial institutions to undertake excessive risk, as they heavily invested in the novel structured financial products, also known as financial derivatives.

Financial innovation and structural changes in the US banking system have played a crucial role in the development of the crisis. The new originate-to-distribute model of financing homes created incentives for banks to sell their mortgages as soon as they were signed. Banks under this model earned their profit mainly from the fees they received from each loan granted. This model flourished during and prior to the crisis within a laissez-faire unregulated financial regime, which was very much favored among the key US financial regulators.

Many loan applicants borrowed larger amounts than they could afford. Bankers were often more than eager to approve almost all loan applications and sometimes in larger amounts than requested by unqualified applicants. This attitude can be explained because the banks had "no skin in the game." This was an expression often used describing the practice of banks not keeping their loans on their balance sheets, which was a common phenomenon during this period. For this reason, bankers easily approved a plethora of loans, as the quality of the borrower's credit and the ability to repay the mortgages were not a restraining factor and thus of no significance to them. When the crisis erupted, borrowers who did not qualify for the loans or who borrowed more than they could afford found themselves in a difficult position. The only way for them to keep their homes was through refinancing. As long as home prices kept increasing refinancing was feasible, but when home prices began decreasing, refinancing was no longer a viable option to them.

Since many low-quality credit borrowers paid very small down payments or because some borrowers had a second mortgage on top of the first, many of their homes were "underwater".[16] This expression means that the borrowers had accumulated a negative equity, i.e. they borrowed more than the home was worth. Under such difficult situations, borrowers were sometimes forced to turn in their home keys to their banks. This was a socially undesirable phenomenon and an admission of a failed national policy that diverted from the government's initial objective of increasing home ownership. Consequently, both lenders and borrowers demonstrated plenty of irresponsibility that was tolerated and often encouraged by the financial regulatory institutions. Under this scenario, borrowers, lenders, and government finance regulators were all responsible in encouraging the adoption and use of the originate-to-distribute model, which triggered the eruption of the crisis.[17]

Proliferation of structured finance products

A few years prior to the spread of the subprime mortgage crisis, financial innovation thrived. Exponential growth of structured financial products such as MBSs, CDSs, and CDOs were prevalent in the financial markets. The CDO was a popular synthetic product, which combined different assets of varying risk that were bundled together and often ranked into three major tranches (categories). The highest tranche generated the vast majority of the securities that have a first priority on all incoming cash from the underlying assets in terms of both principal and interest payments. Such securities receive the highest rating, i.e. AAA, and pay the lowest interest rate because they are considered to be the safest investment.

The second-level tranche, known as the mezzanine, generates the second largest share of securities, which are based on riskier underlying assets and, therefore, pay a higher interest rate to compensate investors for the risk. The mezzanine tranche distributes income to securities owners only if there are sufficient funds available after paying the owners of the securities of the first tranche. Lastly, the third tranche, which is subordinated by the first two, is designed to generate the smallest share of securities. These securities are extremely risky because they receive the last priority in paying interest and principal to the investors. This of course happens if and only if sufficient earned income is generated by the underlying assets to pay all investors.

The intention of investment banks in creating synthetic assets was to produce a larger number of AAA securities than the total AAA-ranked available underlying assets. In this way they were intended to increase liquidity in the banking system while spreading the risk among many investors. The imagination and creativity of financial engineers in their effort to achieve this objective had no limit in creating new CDOs by combining existing CDOs, re-bundling, and slicing them again. By doing so, they introduced new financial products of securities that became known as CDO^2, having plain CDOs as their underlying assets. Financial engineers went even further when they formed a third level of securities by combining and repackaging tranches of underlying CDO^2 and re-slicing them to create an even higher order of securities, called CDO^3. One could easily characterize these novel financial products as devices to deceive.[18] The ultimate objective of the investment bankers was always maximization of sales (total revenue) or short-term profit.

Investment banks flooded the US and the world markets with these types of equivocal securities, thus creating an environment of intense financial uncertainty. Investors, however, eventually became skeptical about the quality of these novel securities, as they were suspected of being based on non-performing mortgages and, therefore, were perceived to be almost worthless. As a result, they soon became known as toxic securities or assets. The creation of this massive asset toxicity played a central role in the formation of the subprime mortgage crisis.[19]

Financial engineers either intentionally or unintentionally contributed to the creation of a market environment that lacked the necessary foundation of a transparent legal system. It was impossible for markets to determine the prices of such opaque financial derivatives because buyers – and even suppliers – of such products had only a vague notion of their intrinsic value. It was therefore impossible for markets to assign a price to an asset without knowing what exactly this asset was. One might imagine these products as packages that are completely wrapped and could not be opened by the buyer before they were purchased. It is certain that these products with such undisclosed features would not be popular among consumers. Some financial derivatives were so opaque that investors had hardly any knowledge of the products they were buying.

Missing ethics

During the crisis, notorious predatory lending behavior was widespread in the real estate and home finance professions. This is evident by the new types of mortgage contracts that were popular during this time. A good example of this is the adjustable rate mortgage (ARM) contracts that started with very low interest rates for the first two or three years. These rates, however, quickly spiked afterwards, following the market interest rates as they were set according to a benchmark rate that periodically increased.[20] These were the notorious teaser rates.

Similarly, balloon contracts were widespread prior to and during the crisis. These contracts required borrowers to repay the entire amount of the loan and interest after about 5–7 years from the time the loan was signed.[21] In addition, the liberal and dubious lending practices of this period are well portrayed by the no income, no job or assets (NINJA) mortgage contracts. NINJA is an acronym that reminds one of the popular Japanese video game characters among youngsters, the Teenage Mutant Ninja Turtles, which fascinated America's youth in the 1990s.

Unprecedented aggressive and unethical lending practices by bankers, realtors, real estate developers, mortgage brokers, title companies, investment bankers, lawyers, and others involved in the housing market contributed to the formation of a frenzied environment that led to the spreading of the crisis. All such individuals and particularly the top bank executives earned extraordinarily high remunerations consisting of fixed salaries and huge bonuses that could not have been supported under conditions of a normal economic environment. During this period, the home finance industry gave the impression that it operated under the false premise that the boom would never end. Based on such incorrect perceived fundamentals, the participants in the supply side of the market pursued a single objective of short-term sales, i.e. total revenue maximization.

The explanation for this type of socially irresponsible behavior, considering the fact that the bonuses were mainly determined by the banks' level of revenues, should be obvious. Large increases in sales were associated with big increases in executive bonuses. People up in the top hierarchy of the financial institutions, nonetheless, knew very well that the party would not last forever, but the attitude was "as long as the music is playing, you've got to get up and dance."[22]

The US mortgage party resembles a fish feeding frenzy of all kinds of predators – tuna, white bass, dolphins, and sharks – on a school of sardines which is strategically and repeatedly attacked while on its voyage along the coasts of South Africa. These sardines migrate from the colder waters of the Cape and move up along the east coast of South Africa to the warmer waters of KwaZulu-Natal. Of course, the sardines are defenseless, especially when they dare to venture into deeper waters. Their only "weapon" is the immense numbers in the school, each fish expecting another will be the victim in each attack. The feeding frenzy only ends when the school of sardines arrives, totally demolished, at its destination. The sardines in this analogy are the homeowners, many of whom had lost their homes to foreclosures.[23]

The mortgage frenzy of course ended as soon as home prices began declining, and a bust followed the boom. Just before the crisis began, lending by banks almost completely ceased as a result of the overwhelming number of mortgage defaults. Bank credit practically froze in the US, due to distrust and lack of confidence. There is no doubt that unethical behavior was an important factor that fermented the crisis. Some people that played a central role in the formation of the subprime mortgage crisis exhibited perverse and predatory behavior. Among these people were many bankers that for a long time were held in high esteem in their society.

Much blame rightly is placed on investment bankers and financial engineers that created the opaque toxic securities. Several novels were written with the main theme being the subprime mortgage crisis. These novels eloquently describe the greedy, arrogant, and aggressive behavior of high-level executives in several major US financial institutions.[24] Their behavior was a great disappointment, but not a surprise, as these people were simply responding to selfish and perverse incentives. Such attitudes among the high-level executives had been nourished since the early 1980s by the US financial and political system which was undergoing a major structural transformation by adopting trade liberalization and financial deregulation.

Minsky time

Hyman Minsky (1919–96), an American heterodox economist, did not live long enough to witness how popular his theory became.[25] Minsky argued that the US and other capitalist economies were not self-regulating and as stable as classical economists such as Smith and Walras purported. Minsky extended the Keynesian approach, assuming the economy does not always settle in full employment equilibrium. Minsky's main theory is the "Financial Instability Hypothesis." According to this theory, there exist endogenous destabilizing factors within the economy. Stability itself generates factors that give way to fragility and lead to instability of the economic system. Banks and other financial institutions play a very important role in Minsky's theory. Banks, in their effort to maximize profit, seek financial innovation which leads to prosperity, expansion, and stability in the economy.[26]

A few economists influenced by the writings of Hyman Minsky claim that the subprime mortgage crisis was an expected event given the inherently unstable US financial system that generated excessive fluctuations in economic activity. Expansion was triggered by an easy monetary policy, financial innovation, and credit expansion, which led to increases in income, consumption, home prices, and a high leverage in households and banks. Once the economy reached a peak, a contraction followed. This was triggered by declining home prices, lower income, higher unemployment, reduced consumption, an increased number of foreclosures, and deleveraging of households and banks.[27] Minsky claimed that securitization allows banks to extend credit and loans without any limits, as bank credit and loans are disassociated from the bank's own capital.[28] This means that securitization is a source of fragility for the financial system as the explosion in credit leads to unsustainable household debt.

Asymmetric information, moral hazard, and adverse selection

If information is not equally shared by all economic agents in a contract, then certain behavior of those parties possessing more information, by pursuing their self-interest, can be damaging to the other parties, and could possibly become a systemic risk to the entire economy. This problem is known as moral hazard and is caused by the presence of the asymmetric information described above.

Policymakers can reduce the probability of the occurrence of the next economic and financial crisis if they identify and successfully address areas in the economy where problems of moral hazard are developing. A few episodes of moral hazard problems that played a crucial role in the formation of the US subprime mortgage crisis will be presented and critically analyzed in this section. Adverse selection – another problem that arises in the presence of asymmetric information – is also discussed.

Principal-agent conflict: managers/executives vs. shareholders

One example of moral hazard is the principal-agent problem that boomed prior to and during the subprime mortgage crisis. A conflict of interest existed between the executives (managers) and the shareholders (owners) of a financial institution.[29]

Executives contractually are the fiduciaries of the shareholders of financial institutions.[30] Consequently, executives have the legal obligation to pursue and serve the interests of the financial institutions that are identical with the interests of the shareholders. This, however, did not often happen during the crisis. It is obvious that managers have more knowledge than the shareholders regarding the financial situation of the institutions as they are full-time employees and caretakers of the business on a day-to-day basis.

In contrast to the executives, shareholders have much less information about the banks. The limited information held by the shareholders comes from the financial reports, such as the income statements and annual balance sheets that executives often help prepare and approve.

Shareholders also gain information about their firm at shareholder meetings, which are infrequent. The conflict between the two groups received much attention from the popular news media during and after the US subprime mortgage crisis.

Whereas shareholders were interested in the long-run growth and profitability of their banks, executives were concerned with maximizing short-term sales or profits. The reason for the different objectives of the two groups is rather simple: it pertains to the way executives are paid. Executive remuneration in general was based on both salaries and bonuses. The annual salary was usually fixed, but the bonus varied with the sales or profits of the financial institution. For this reason, financial institutions, following the guidance and interests of the executives, heavily invested in very profitable but risky assets. A few years before the crisis, banks invested in such risky securities at unprecedented levels. Therefore bank executives were frequently and liberally awarded extraordinarily large bonuses. It became common knowledge during those times that one good year's bonus was more than sufficient to support an early retirement, even for the most extravagant of executive spenders.

Investment in risky assets, however, led to the downfall of several financial institutions that triggered the subprime mortgage crisis, which rapidly spread to the real economy and abroad.[31] Former Fed chairman Alan Greenspan once said that he ". . . could not believe how bankers led their own banks to bankruptcy." The executives' perverse incentive to pursue short-term revenue or profit maximization seems to explain what has happened. A way to address and possibly resolve this issue is to adopt a new policy regarding how executives are compensated.

As news spread about the exceptionally large executive salaries, there was a public outcry about the unbelievably large bonuses many US executives received. The public was particularly outraged with the investment bankers, especially when the news media publicized the fact that some of them had driven their firms to bankruptcy and several institutions were bailed out by the US federal government. Many years have passed since the peak of the subprime mortgage crisis in the fall of 2008, yet the US Congress has not yet addressed this problem as of June 2015.[32] The EU, however, introduced on January 1, 2014, bonus caps on the executive bonuses of bankers. Bonuses were allowed to increase to twice the level of the fixed salary but in order for the increase to take place, a super-majority shareholder vote of 66 percent is necessary. There is opposition to salary caps in some EU countries as some analysts argue that, because of this regulation, extremely qualified and talented executives will leave the EU.

The originate-to-distribute model

A moral hazard problem of the principal-agent type has also developed as a result of the originate-to-distribute model that induced mortgage brokers and banks to sell their mortgages as soon as they signed them. Since the income of the banks and mortgage brokers (the home loan originators) increased with the value and numbers of home loans issued, banks had an incentive to approve as many mortgages as possible. To reach this objective, banks relaxed the credit quality standards of the loan applicants. As banks and mortgage brokers' strategic interests were against the interests of buyers of mortgages, i.e. investment banks and GSEs, a moral hazard problem was created. This is indicated by the plethora of subprime mortgage and Alt-A mortgages that were issued during this period.

One way to fix this problem is to require banks to keep a certain percentage of their mortgages on their balance sheets instead of selling all of them. Under this policy, banks and other lending institutions are required to maintain "skin in the game," as the popular expression so eloquently describes the problem. Such a solution necessitates banks to bear responsibility of their decisions, and by doing so, they reduce the amount of worthless mortgages they generate and thus reduce systemic risk to the entire economy. These low-quality mortgages were the underlying assets of the toxic securities that are considered to be a main cause of the subprime mortgage crisis.

Explicit guarantees by the FDIC to the bank depositors that their money is safe caused another moral hazard problem to develop. As a result of these guarantees, depositors did not have a strong incentive to keep a close watch that lending institutions were prudent in how they were investing their money. The principal-agent and moral hazard problem that cultivated the perverse incentive and the inappropriate and unethical transfers of funds from shareholders and depositors to executives continues to constitute a major issue even after the failure or near failure of a few investment banks.

The principal-agent and moral hazard problems were issues even after some of these institutions were bailed out. A few executives dared to pocket a portion of the bailout money as bonuses despite the fact that the aim of the bailouts was to restore financial and economic stability by inducing banks to resume lending to consumers and businesses. When such news leaked, the public became even more outraged. Considering such information, it is surprising the US government did not prosecute all illegal actions and unethical behavior and try to confiscate the loot much earlier.

Mortgage securitization and the "too big to fail" problem

Securitization is another example that led to the creation of the moral hazard problem under conditions of asymmetric information that gradually spread prior to the subprime mortgage crisis. It is certain that investment banks had a better knowledge about the quality of the securities they structured and were selling than the investors who were buying them. However, the investment banks did not always reveal such information to the investors.[33]

The unprecedented growth of the GSEs securitizations was encouraged by the explicit or implicit guarantees of their securities by the US government. Such guarantees were created by the existence of the "too big to fail" problem. The government was expected to intervene and bail out institutions at risk in order to avoid financial contagion and thus protect the economy. For example, even when Fannie Mae and Freddie Mac were both privately owned, their investors strongly believed that the US government would always be backing up their securities. The default option for the two GSEs was never perceived as a possibility because their collapse would be a great threat to the entire economy. When the two GSEs did come very close to collapsing in the fall of 2008, the US government intervened and saved them, proving that the investors' expectations were correct. Therefore it can be inferred that the two GSEs were "too big to fail" for the US economy.

The US government, nonetheless, did not bailout all the private financial institutions which were near collapse based on the "too big to fail" argument. Remarkably, Lehman Brothers, an investment bank with $600 billion in assets and 25,000 employees, was not rescued by the government. It is still not known why Lehman Brothers was excluded from receiving a bailout, although it was widely expected that its collapse would shake-up the markets and trigger a crisis, as has indeed occurred. Many analysts suspect that the government wanted to send a strong signal to all possible future bailout candidate recipients that the rescue of financially distressed firms is not guaranteed and should not always be expected. By doing so, the government wanted to avoid a queuing line of hopeful bailout recipients. However, it can be argued that if Lehman Brothers was bailed out, the crisis could have been prevented from spreading to the rest of the economy in the US and abroad.[34]

Adverse selection

Another situation that occurred under conditions of asymmetric information during the subprime mortgage crisis is the problem of adverse selection. This problem can arise when a certain number of mortgage applicants devote a lot of time and effort to succeed in obtaining a home loan. As a result of their efforts, these applicants succeeded in having their loans approved. However, some of these successful applicants were dishonest and did not intend to abide by the mortgage contract.

Many other applicants, however, who did not put forth much effort and preparation for the approval of their home loans, did not succeed in having their mortgages approved. This is how the problem of adverse selection was developed. Thus bad creditors were able to buy a house, whereas several good creditors who would have honored the agreement and paid off the mortgages were not able to do so. However, because banks reduced the credit requirements during the crisis, and even extended credit to many unqualified applicants, the adverse selection problem could not have been such a major factor contributing to the increase in the number of defaulted mortgages and foreclosures. Therefore, as an extension, adverse selection was not a major cause of the subprime mortgage crisis.

Credit rating agencies

For many years, credit rating agencies (CRAs) provided their services to firms by rating corporate bonds. When securitization became popular, however, the composition of CRAs' services to customers changed drastically. By 2007, half of the revenue of the CRAs was earned by rating securitizations. These new services were not the same as rating bonds. The main difference was the complexity and opacity of securitizations. This, nonetheless, did not deter the CRAs from expanding in the new business, by employing the same method for rating securitizations as the one used in rating corporate bonds. Consequently, the CRAs' performance in rating the novel structured financial products was far from perfect.

CRAs failed to reveal problems as they often rewarded AAA ratings to firms only a week before they defaulted. Consequently, it can be stated that CRAs proved to be incapable of sending early warnings to prevent the crisis, although they were designed and paid to do so. For example, during the dot-com crisis, CRAs had failed to downgrade Enron's corporate bonds below investment grade to junk until four days before the company filed for bankruptcy on December 2, 2001.

CRAs were criticized for their inability to provide early warnings of the US subprime mortgage crisis. Similarly, CRAs have grossly failed to accurately rate the debt of several financial and non-financial institutions in the US prior to the crisis. Furthermore, firms requesting the rating of their securities paid the CRAs, as the "issuer pays" model was employed to compensate CRAs.[35] Such a payment system for CRAs constitutes an outright conflict of interest.[36] Thus a new model of how CRAs evaluate securities should be sought in order to avoid the conflict of interest problem. A better system of rating securities could have warned investors much earlier of the problems regarding financial institutions at risk.

Credit default swaps

A big problem also arose with the credit default swaps (CDSs), derivatives that are traded in the over-the-counter market that amounted to trillions of dollars prior to the crisis. The idea of the CDSs is rather simple as it is similar to an insurance policy. By buying CDSs, an investor for a certain fee is guaranteed to always receive the original price of the security regardless of the present market price of the security. Because CDSs are negotiable and traded, some investors buy CDSs for securities that they do not even own or have borrowed. In other words, the purchase of the CDSs in such a situation is pure speculation. The parallel in home insurance is if one were to purchase fire insurance for a randomly selected home without knowing the owner and not being interested in the protection of the home. These CDSs are known as naked CDSs, and were prohibited from May 19, 2010 until March 31, 2011 in Germany.[37] CDSs have been used in ways that are often suspected of being highly destabilizing. Several analysts, including government leaders, pointed out that CDSs contributed to the formation of the crisis because they allowed speculators to take a short position on both private and public securities when they believed that the market prices of such securities were overpriced and could not be defended.

Massive short-selling of such securities enabled speculators to bring down their prices. Once the security prices declined substantially, the purchasers of CDSs profited as they receive the difference between the original price and the reduced market price of the security from the issuers (sellers) of the CDSs. The supporters of CDSs, however, claim that these derivatives allow firms and countries to insure their securities for a small fee. In this way, CDSs help markets make quick adjustments by correcting weaknesses that in the absence of CDSs would have taken a longer time to be corrected. As CDSs are negotiable over-the-counter traded derivatives, they are very opaque. CDSs are usually issued by banks and a few other financial institutions.

The American International Group (AIG) was bailed out by the US government with an extraordinarily large amount of over $180 billion. AIG issued massive amounts of CDSs prior to the crisis. In 1996, the Fed allowed banks which purchased CDSs to lower their own contributed capital. Such a decision turned out to have detrimental effects on the economy because it induced banks to invest in risky assets that masked their low quality. As long as the banks had purchased CDSs, the reduction of the banks' own capital was approved by the Fed. For example, the risky securities that a bank purchased, i.e. the CDOs or the MBSs, were rated according to the rating of the institution which issued the CDSs (the counterparty). Therefore the Fed's decision to allow banks to use CDSs in order to reduce their own bank-contributed capital requirements is considered by a few analysts as one of the major causes of the subprime mortgage crisis.[38]

Hedge funds

Hedge funds are another institutional financial innovation that is suspected to have played a major negative role in the creation and duration of both the US subprime mortgage and the European sovereign debt crises. Many hedge funds are aggressively managed portfolios of very large investments created for the sole purpose of seeking high profits in the US and abroad. Hedge funds are not registered in any official exchange market, thus their transactions are not transparent. Because hedge funds move undisclosed amounts of financial capital in various investments, both domestically and abroad, for a variety of strategic purposes, they have been suspected of being destabilizing and are considered by some analysts to be one of the causes of the financial crisis. The response to this criticism by their supporters is that hedge funds, in pursuit of profit, simply increase liquidity by shifting financial capital to where it is needed and valued the most.

Shadow banking

It has been pointed out that shadow banking was another major cause of the subprime mortgage crisis. The term "shadow banking" was used for the first time by Paul McCully in 2007, coinciding with the onset of the crisis.[39] The vast majority of activities of shadow banking are opaque. Consequently, nobody knows the specifics of these activities and, particularly, the amount of trades. Because shadow bankers are "lightly regulated" and perform the same functions as banks, they became very popular among investors who wished to avoid the heavy regulation of commercial banks.[40]

Although public data on shadow banking is rather scarce one study found that assets in shadow banking grew from $3 trillion in 1980 to $40 trillion in 2010.[41] By the end of November 2012 shadow banks held $67 trillion. This is a relatively large amount considering that the world GDP in 2012 was approximately $70 trillion.[42] With such an extraordinary volume of financial transactions, the concern is that shadow banking constitutes systemic risk to the entire economy. Shadow banking includes money mutual funds, structural investment vehicles (SIVs), hedge funds, finance companies, investment banks, mortgage brokers, and the two GSEs before they were nationalized in September 2008.

Shadow banking also includes several financial instruments, such as asset backed commercial paper, CDOs, repurchase agreements (repos), and asset-backed securities (ABS). Because most of the securitizations were carried out by shadow banks, the latter were at the top of the suspect list of causes of the crisis. Shadow banks have neither the access to liquidity from the Fed, nor the guarantees of the FDIC. As a result, they are highly risky.

Concluding comments

The excessively expansive monetary and fiscal policies employed by the US to cope with the dot-com and corporate scandals crises are partially responsible for the creation of the boom in the housing market. When home prices began declining, the expansion abruptly ended and was followed by a recession.

The repeal of the Glass-Steagall Act in 1999 by the government led to fundamental structural changes in the US financial regime and particularly in the home finance industry. The heavily regulated financial regime was replaced with a laissez-faire system of financial freedom. Within this system, banks and other financial institutions, in order to increase profits, aggressively adopted numerous financial innovations. Novel financial products were introduced and spread quickly throughout the US and abroad; MBSs, CDOs, CDSs, and ABSs constitute a small sample of these financial derivatives. Some of these financial derivatives were so complex that the markets were unable to price them correctly, thus creating uncertainty and instability.

In addition, the federal government, in its effort to democratize credit and help low- and middle-income families, directed banks to extend credit to the aforementioned groups of families and minorities. Many home-buyers in these groups were approved mortgages although they did not always meet the required credit standards to obtain home loans on their own in the market. Investment banks also issued MBSs to finance mortgages. Because many of the low-quality mortgages served as the collateral assets to many of the structural financial derivatives, the latter were also of low quality and thus became known as toxic. CRAs were unable to reveal this, and as a result, there was no early signal to warn of the crisis which could quickly spread in the US.

Many analysts pointed out several other factors as important causes of the sub-prime mortgage crisis. Minsky's theory supports the view that the US financial system is inherently unstable and generated the financial crisis. Micro decisions under asymmetric information played a role in the creation of the crisis. The principal-agent problem that allowed the perverse incentives of managers and chief executives to pursue maximization of short-term profits or sales also contributed to the crisis.

Lastly shadow banking, which includes both financial products and activities that are not supervised by the Fed and thus have neither access to its liquidity nor the protection of their deposits by the FDIC, thrived during the crisis. Thus shadow banking is a primary cause of the fragility of the financial system. As bank regulations increased after the crisis, shadow banking began replacing customary banking operations and thus is becoming a greater threat to the financial system.

It can be safely stated that many factors played a crucial role in the creation of the US housing bubble, which burst as home prices eventually collapsed and the crisis spread throughout the US economy and beyond. Securitization of subprime mortgages, however, is at the center of the crisis. Thus it can be concluded that the crisis will remain known in history by its true name, which is not a misnomer – the subprime mortgage crisis.

Notes

1 This was a remarkable achievement for an advanced economy like the US. It was accomplished with the cooperation of President Clinton, a Democrat with a Republican-dominated Congress.
2 See Zestos *et al.* (2011) for more on the effects of the US monetary-fiscal policy mix in the US economy during this period.
3 A wealth effect is a condition under which consumers gain confidence that they are wealthier and, thus, boost consumption. However, in this case, their increased wealth was unsustainable and began to evaporate as home prices started declining in February 2006.
4 This was an expression used by the Federal Reserve Chairman Alan Greenspan in a congressional hearing before the Committee on Banking, Housing, and Urban Affairs of the US Senate, July 16, 2003 (see www.banking.senate.gov).

5 Whether this claim is correct is still highly debatable. Many investors strongly disagreed that they were informed of the concealed risks in their investments. Investment banks are still in litigation by the Federal Housing Finance Agency (FHFA) and the US Department of Justice. However, there is no final ruling yet to create precedent for all similar cases. There are several settlements according to which, investment banks paid billions of dollars to US Department of Justice and other financial regulatory institutions.

6 The CA, in addition to the trade balance, also includes the income balance, i.e. income earned abroad by US labor and capital minus income earned by foreign labor and capital in the US. Another item of the CA is unilateral transfers; this component of the CA is relatively small.

7 See Cooper (2008) for more details on this issue.

8 See Obstfeld (2012).

9 Ibid., p. 8.

10 The source of the data is the Bank for International Settlements (BIS).

11 Whether the US trade deficits initially triggered the crisis is doubtful because when the CA started increasing in the early 2000s, the US unemployment rate was declining until the onset of the crisis in 2007.

12 Ibid., p. 9.

13 See Braithwaite and Mackenzie (2013).

14 To achieve this goal the US government created a few public and quasi-public institutions to pursue its objective.

15 See the Community Reinvestment Act of 1977 and the 1995 decision of the HUD directing banks to purchase mortgages of low- and moderate-income families discussed in the previous chapter.

16 Second mortgages or even third mortgages were popular during this time as bankers were more than eager to approve them.

17 See Kregel (2008) and Barth *et al.* (2012) for a thorough and critical analysis of the originate-to-distribute model.

18 See Donnelly and Embrechts (2009), and also see Acharya (2009) for more information on structured finance products.

19 See Wray (2007).

20 Such a benchmark was usually the London Interbank Offered Rate (Libor).

21 The only hope for the borrowers with balloon contracts to be able to keep their home was through refinancing, which could only happen when home prices increased. However, who can guarantee that the price of an asset always increases?

22 This expression is attributed to Charles O. Prince (2007), a former CEO of Citigroup (Nakamoto and Wighton, 2007).

23 Attacks of predator fish such as rock bass on schools of small fish are also often seen along the coast of the Atlantic Ocean in Virginia and other states. Sardine voyages like the one in South Africa take place in other parts of the world with no better luck for the sardines.

24 See, for example, Sorkin (2012).

25 A new school of thought was founded by adherents to his theories. Several economists, most of them associated with the Levy Economic Institute housed at Bard College in Annandale-at-Hudson, New York, pursue research on the same line of thinking that Minsky introduced about three decades ago.

26 See Minsky (1992).

27 See Wray (2007) and Kregel (2008).

28 See Minsky (2008).

29 The principal-agent problem, of course, does not occur only with financial firms, but also with all business firms whenever there exists a separation between ownership and management. It occurs also in so many other cases when a legal representative (the agent) is delegated the authority to act on behalf of and represent another party (the principal).

30 Since banks are the most common depository financial institutions, in this text we often refer to all financial depository institutions for convenience as banks.

31 See Acharya (2009) and Krugman (2009).

32 Reduction of excessive salaries and bonuses that are not supported by the executives' productivity is plausible and necessary. In addition, any action to limit the gap in the compensation between ordinary workers and executives is desirable, especially considering the fact that this gap in the US is by far larger than in any other country in the world.

33 This is an issue that is still highly debated, as banks do not admit claims that they misled investors by hiding the fact that their securities were based on subprime mortgages. Although Citigroup, for example, agreed to settle class-action lawsuits by paying in 2012 and 2013 amounts of $590 and $730 million respectively, still denies the allegations and insist they agreed to the settlement only to reduce uncertainty (*Financial Times*, March 18, 2013). JP Morgan Chase paid $13 billion while the Bank of America settled out of the court and paid $16.65 billion in fines, the largest penalty paid of all investment banks (see: seattletimes.com/html/editorials/ 2022364255_jpmorganchasesettlement30xml.html).

34 Similarly, many analysts believed that if Greece had initially been offered a bailout on favorable terms, i.e. lower interest rates and a longer repayment period, it would have quickly stabilized its economy and the European crisis would have never spread via contagion.

35 This arrangement is still employed today as the issuers of the securities are paying the CRAs.

36 The parallel in education is when students pay the professors' salary. One can only imagine the types of grades these students would be receiving.

37 See Walker and Shah (2010).

38 See Barth *et al.* (2012).

39 See Whitney (2012).

40 Pozsar *et al.* (2012).

41 Ibid., p. 39.

42 Financial Stability Board, Report, ibid., p. 39.

References

Acharya, V. (2009) *Restoring Financial Stability: How to Repair a Failed System*. Hoboken, NJ: John Wiley & Sons.

Barth, J. R. (2008) "A short history of the sub-prime mortgage market meltdown," *GH Bank Housing Journal*, 2–8.

Barth, J. R., Caprio, G., and Levine, R. (2012) *Guardians of Finance: Making Regulators Work for Us*, 1st edn. Cambridge, MA: MIT Press.

Braithwaite, T. and Mackenzie, M. (2013) "US rules endanger derivatives reforms," *Financial Times*, September 27.

Cooper, R. N. (2008) "Global imbalances: globalization, demography, and sustainability," *Journal of Economic Perspectives*, 22 (3): 93–112.

Donnelly, C. and Embrechts, P. (2010) "The devil is in the tails: actuarial mathematics and the subprime mortgage crisis," *ASTIN Bulletin*, 40 (1): 1–33.

Kregel, J. (2008) *Minsky's Cushions of Safety: Systemic Risk and the Crisis in the U.S. Subprime Mortgage Market*. Annandale-at-Hudson, NY: Levy Economics Institute of Bard College.

Krugman, P. R. (2009) "The road to global economic recovery, 2009", *Revista de Economía del Caribe*, 4: 1–18. Retrieved from: rcientificas.uninorte.edu.co/index.php/economia/article/viewFile/562/303.

Minsky, H. P. (1992) *The Financial Instability Hypothesis*, Working Paper No. 74. Annandale-at-Hudson, NY: Levy Economics Institute of Bard College.

Minsky, H. P. (2008) *Stabilizing an Unstable Economy*, 1st edn. New York: McGraw-Hill.

Nakamoto, M. and Wighton, D. (2007) "Citigroup chief stays bullish on buy-outs," *Financial Times*, July 9.

Obstfeld, M. (2012) "Does the current account still matter?" *American Economic Review*, 102 (3): 1–23.

Pozsar, Z. *et al.* (2012) *Shadow Banking*, Staff Report. Federal Reserve Bank of New York.

Sorkin, A. R. (2012) *Too Big to Fail*. New York: Viking.

Walker, M. and Shah, N. (2010) "Germany to ban some naked short-selling," *Wall Street Journal*, May 19.

Whitney, M. (2012) "How Wall Street 'privatized' money creation: shadow banking," *CounterPunch*, November 28. Retrieved from: www.counterpunch.org/2012/11/28/shadow-banking/.

Wray, L. R. (2007) *Lessons from the Subprime Meltdown*. Annandale-at-Hudson, NY: Levy Economics Institute of Bard College.

Zestos, G. K., Geary, A. N., and Cooksey, K. S. (2011) "US monetary-fiscal policy mix evidence from a quartovariate VECM," *International Journal of Banking and Finance*, 8 (2): Article 3.

3

THE CRISIS SPREADS TO EUROPE

Introduction

The US subprime mortgage crisis of 2007–9 had devastating effects on the US economy. It constitutes the second most significant US recession, next only to the Great Depression of 1929–33. A great number of Americans lost their homes and millions became unemployed. To cope with the crisis, the US applied extraordinary expansionary monetary and fiscal policies which were effective in preventing a further catastrophe. The US financial crisis, however, had spread to other parts of the world, particularly to Europe. The crisis is still seriously threatening the European Union (EU), particularly the Euro Area (EA), and the single European currency, the euro.[1] The EA countries that were affected the most by the crisis are those in Southern Europe: Greece, Portugal, Italy, Spain, Cyprus, and Ireland.[2]

In contrast to Southern EA members, most Northern EA countries were not significantly affected, as they proved capable of quickly recovering from the crisis. Starting in the first quarter of 2013, nevertheless, all EA members, with the exception of Austria, experienced negative growth. In the second quarter of 2013, however, the EA unexpectedly generated a 1.2 percent annualized rate of growth and in 2014 every EA periphery country with the exception of Cyprus attained a positive real economic growth. Nonetheless, several analysts and EU officials pointed out that this should not be interpreted as a definite turning point as several EA countries were still experiencing extraordinarily high unemployment. Such weak economic performance raises concerns of a further spreading of the crisis in Europe and the rest of the world. As the US subprime mortgage crisis impacted the two EA groups differently, it constitutes the first asymmetric shock experienced by the Economic and Monetary Union (EMU).

Greece, Ireland, and Portugal were the first EA victims of the European financial crisis that was triggered by the US subprime mortgage crisis.[3] The crisis was first revealed in Europe by the interbank lending freeze in the summer of 2007. This led to a sharp increase in long-term government bond rates. The very high interest rates deterred the three countries from borrowing in the market. Consequently, Greece, Ireland, and Portugal, in chronological order, were rescued, with massive and unprecedented bailout packages that were jointly provided by the EU and the International Monetary Fund (IMF). In order to receive the bailouts, the rescued countries had to comply with the austerity programs imposed by the IMF. The common requirement of these programs was the IMF's notorious and controversial conditionality that accompanies all such rescue packages.

Fiscal discipline and austerity

The EU, mainly under the influence of the governments of Germany, the Netherlands, and Finland, initiated legislation to promote fiscal discipline to all EU members as a way to cope with the crisis. As a result, in January 2012, 25 out of the then 27 EU member countries signed the Fiscal Compact Treaty.[4] The intention of Germany and its Northern allies was to reach an agreement that would require and enforce fiscal discipline on all EU member countries. The Fiscal Compact Treaty required that EU member countries adhere to stricter fiscal stability rules that were to be implemented by the EU Commission. Consequently, the taxpayers of Germany and its Northern allies would be protected from the burden of guaranteeing additional bailouts to other financially distressed EA countries. Despite the initial expectations to resolve the crisis, economic conditions in the periphery EA countries that adopted the draconian fiscal austerity programs have rapidly deteriorated as the crisis spread further to other European countries.

As the recession was prolonged in the countries of the periphery, the effectiveness of the IMF/EU approach in resolving the crisis by simply pursuing austerity and programs of structural reform has been seriously challenged. Several economists and millions of people in the Southern EA countries, Cyprus and Ireland (the periphery), and other countries have repeatedly expressed strong opposition to the austerity programs that led these countries into a prolonged recession and to the deterioration of the standard of living of their people.

Surprisingly, in October of 2012, the IMF revealed grave reservations regarding the effectiveness of the macro-economic austerity programs. A new IMF study found that the imposed austerity measures had stronger recessionary effects than originally expected.[5] The managing director of the IMF, Christine Lagarde, in an effort to avoid further deepening of the recession, recommended that countries must be allowed more time to reduce their public deficits.[6] Ms Lagarde's views were vehemently opposed by Wolfgang Schäuble, the German finance minister, one of the strongest advocates for fiscal austerity, and also by the German Chancellor, Angela Merkel. Austerity and fiscal consolidation are topics that European leaders have been fiercely debating since the crisis began.

As soon as he was elected president of France on May 6, 2012, François Hollande visited Chancellor Merkel in Berlin. During this visit, President Hollande strongly recommended growth policies and the introduction of eurobonds in addition to austerity measures as a means to pull financially distressed EA countries out of the crisis. Such policies, according to President Hollande, were going to induce economic growth and reduce the ratio of public debt to GDP of the heavily indebted countries. Surprisingly, since his visit to Berlin, President Hollande has toned down his initial approach to the European crisis. He quickly adopted a more conciliatory and less controversial approach towards Germany. The shift in his position could possibly be explained by the weakening of the French economy and its inability to meet the fiscal requirements of the Stability and Growth Pact (SGP), which requires a public deficit of less than 3 percent. Another reason for President Hollande's shift in attitude could be a financial scandal that afflicted his administration.[7] The quick and unexpected shift in President Hollande's approach to the crisis reduced hopes for a drastic policy change on how to resolve the crisis. In the second quarter of 2013, however, France unexpectedly returned to positive economic growth.

Several other politicians and economists before President Hollande have also recommended the issuance of eurobonds as a solution to the European sovereign debt crisis. As far back as 2010, Italian minister of the economy and finance Giulio Tremonti, and the prime minister, treasury minister, as well as the former president of the EU Economics and Financial Affairs Council (ECOFIN), Jean-Claude Juncker of Luxembourg, jointly called for the introduction of eurobonds as a means to end the crisis.[8] The philosophy of jointly issuing eurobonds is logical and convincing to many people. If the EU and the EA jointly guarantee the eurobonds, then these securities will be a very safe investment because the taxpayers of these countries will jointly be backing these bonds. As a result, the eurobonds could be used to assist all financially distressed EA members to raise funds at very low interest rates and thus resolve the European sovereign debt crisis.

It is not difficult for the EA or the EU authorities, which would be responsible for the funding through the issuance of eurobonds, to keep records using an internal accounting system. In this way they will assure that the country receiving the funds would be solely responsible for the interest payments and the redemption of the eurobonds. Such an arrangement would be attractive because the issuance of eurobonds would not be a burden to all the other EA countries. This arrangement would resolve the moral hazard problem. Such a scenario would also be appealing to investors, since they would know that the entire EU would be responsible for guaranteeing the eurobonds that they buy.

The European sovereign debt crisis developed because the periphery EA countries could no longer borrow at the market interest rates to refinance their public debt. Furthermore, eurobonds could be used to finance major European infrastructure projects, which promote more European integration and growth in the entire EU. For these projects, the entire group of EA countries would be responsible for paying the interest rates and principal of these eurobonds.

Despite the support that the eurobond proposal received from the Southern EA countries, the EU Commission, and many economists, the French President's proposal found strong opposition from the German Chancellor, Angela Merkel.

The German government is opposed to the joint issuance of eurobonds by the EA countries because such debt mutualization through issuing jointly guaranteed eurobonds would increase the cost of borrowing to Germany. It would consequently increase the burden on the German taxpayers if one or more of the countries defaulted on their public debt. In addition, during 2013, national elections were held in Germany, therefore anything that potentially raised taxes on German voters would have made the re-election of Chancellor Merkel more difficult.

After the victory of Chancellor Merkel in the national elections in September 2013, the chancellor reaffirmed the voters that her European policy would not change. Since her Christian Democratic Union (CDU) party did not receive the required 42 percent of the popular vote to form its own independent government, Chancellor Merkel sought the participation of another party to form a coalition government. As a result, only pressure from the participating party in the coalition could have put some pressure on Chancellor Merkel to change her position on austerity programs for the Southern EU countries and Ireland. The Socialist Democratic Party (SPD) became the major partner in the coalition in addition to the Christian Social Union of Bavaria. The SPD announced that a condition of its participation in a coalition government would be a change in Germany's policy towards those countries in receipt of a bailout with regard to the austerity programs. The SPD, however, did not deliver on this promise.

As a result of the European sovereign debt crisis, Germany was able to borrow at exceptionally low interest rates, because it attracted foreign capital inflows since it is considered a safe-haven country. This has been a major cause of the European crisis, since financial capital has been flowing into the country that needed it the least, i.e. Germany. Some critics, as a result, claim that Germany achieved domestic growth partially at the expense of its EA partner countries, which starved themselves of liquidity. Such a benefit alone was sufficient for Germany to maintain policies that prolonged the crisis.

The austerity programs prolonged the crisis

The austerity programs and fiscal consolidations adopted were aimed at reversing the effects of the expansionary fiscal and monetary policies which were strongly recommended in 2009 by the major world country leaders of the G20, the OECD, and the IMF to prevent the subprime mortgage crisis from spreading to the rest of the world.[9] Following these policy recommendations, contractionary policies were applied by many countries after the US subprime mortgage crisis. The draconian austerity measures imposed on the EA periphery countries that received the bailouts, however, prolonged the recession and increased unemployment instead of expediting the path to recovery of these countries. These austerity programs, therefore, have created much tension among Northern and Southern EA members.

The unemployment rates in Greece and Spain exceeded 25 percent in 2013. Such extraordinarily high unemployment rates, under normal circumstances, would have raised a red flag for the mobilization of the EU and the member countries' resources to fight the recession. The US launched a massive government spending program during the Great Depression when its unemployment rate came close to 25 percent of its labor force. The German and IMF approach to the European crisis which was also imposed on EU member countries was to pursue recovery through austerity and internal devaluation, i.e. through the reduction of real wages and prices. The austerity programs imposed brought a reduction in the standards of living of these countries for the purpose of improving their international competitiveness.[10]

Many young people in the recession-afflicted countries have been emigrating and seeking employment abroad. Greece, for example, in 2015 has been undergoing its seventh year of recession. On May 6, 2012 economic stagnation and instability led to despair as angry voters in Greece, for the first time since the 1960s, failed to send a clear message regarding which political party would form the next government. Greek voters particularly punished the two major political parties, the New Democracy Party and mostly the Pan-Hellenic Socialist Party (PASOK), which negotiated and signed the two Greek bailout programs with the EU and the IMF.

Similarly, in 2013, Italy also experienced political instability, as no political party emerged as a clear winner in the national election of February 24–25, 2013. Thus Italy could not form a government for several weeks after the election. A party that received a substantial share of the votes was an anti-establishment, anti-EU protest party, the Five Star Movement (M5S), headed by the comedian and blogger, Pepe Grillo. Finally, the Democratic and the Republican parties formed a coalition government, headed by Enrico Letta, which stabilized the political situation in Italy for a short period.

On June 17, 2012, a second election was held in Greece, which also did not produce a single winning political party to form a government alone. However, three political parties emerged to form a coalition government and temporarily stabilize the political conditions in the country. The formation of the new government in Greece was perceived as a great relief to many people. This was indicated by a sharp decrease in the Greek long-term interest rates. Political stability in both Greece and Italy at that time was expected to be short-lived as any unexpected event that increased friction between the coalition parties in the two countries could trigger political instability. Greece and Italy, as a result of the instability and strong interference by EU country leaders and officials, had their elected prime ministers removed from office.

Much is at stake for the future of the EU, as there still exists a strong general disapproval of the fiscal austerity programs in many European countries. This is indicated by the fact that, so far, several EA government leaders who supported the austerity programs in their countries have lost the national elections and were removed from office. However, economic conditions, starting in 2014, changed as periphery countries generated current account surpluses and positive economic growth. As a result, citizens of periphery EA countries began to look more favorably at their elected leaders and the EU austerity programs.

The first major signal of the crisis in Europe: rising interest rates

Starting in 2009, Europe was in the midst of its worst crisis since World War II. The EA was definitely confronted with the most severe financial crisis since the euro was introduced in January 1999. The EU was also undergoing an identity crisis, as it has become evident that the European countries, the people, and the political parties within those same countries were divided. The dilemma was, and still is, whether EU countries would continue to strongly pursue the European project promoting further integration or revert to more ethnocentric policies by even considering a possible exit from the EU/EMU. The financial crisis entered Europe via international economic and financial integration and contagion; it first affected those countries of which the financial institutions had heavily invested in US and domestic mortgage-related securities. EU countries that ran chronic government deficits, either prior to or during the crisis, and accumulated excessive and unsustainable public debt were the countries affected the most. For this reason, the crisis became known as the European sovereign debt crisis.[11]

The first indicator that revealed the crisis had arrived in Europe was the freezing of the interbank lending market which led to the increase in the long-term bond interest rates of the most heavily indebted countries: Greece, Portugal, Ireland, and, to a lesser degree, Spain and Italy. Starting at the end of 2008, the ten-year government bond interest rate spreads of these countries, in relation to the German government bonds, began rising rapidly. As a result, the first three EA countries mentioned above were cut off from borrowing from the markets. Similarly, the prices of CDSs, which are contracts to insure the sovereign debt (bonds) of these countries, also began swiftly increasing. The EA interest rate spread increase coincided with the most turbulent period of the US subprime mortgage crisis, a time when several US financial institutions, a few systemically important firms, and the two major quasi-public housing agencies were under serious financial stress.

The Eurocrisis was triggered in October 2009 when the Prime Minister of the newly elected government of Greece, George Papandreou, accused the preceding government of fabricating and misrepresenting the national statistics on the Greek public deficit in its report to the EU Commission. After such shocking revelations were made, the three major world CRAs repeatedly downgraded the Greek sovereign bonds. Since then the Greek economy has entered a prolonged recession that has brought the country to the verge of bankruptcy.[12] Greece was the first country to be rescued on May 10, 2010 with an exceptionally large and unprecedented bailout package of €110 billion jointly provided by the EU countries and the IMF. Ireland and Portugal were also bailed out with the very large joint EU/IMF rescue packages of €85 and €78 billion, on November 28, 2010 and on May 16, 2011, respectively.

Figure 3.1 clearly shows that during the 2000–8 period, the interest rate spreads, measured with the ten-year government bond yields spread, of Greece, Italy, Spain, Portugal, and Ireland in relation to the equivalent German bond yield declined so much that they came close to zero. This means that all of the EA member countries'

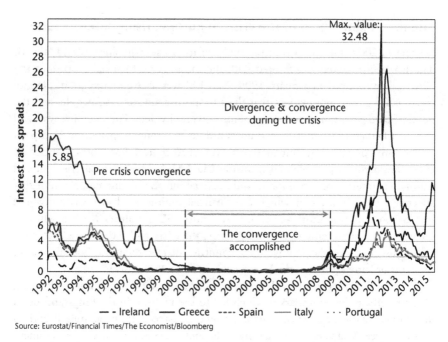

FIGURE 3.1 Southern European countries' interest rate spreads vs. German bonds

interest rates converged to the German ten-year government bond interest rate. This amazing success was an outcome based on the campaign of all candidate EMU members to reduce inflation, interest rates, public deficits, and debt. Successful government campaigns were launched to comply with the 1992 Maastricht Treaty, which required all candidate EMU countries to meet the Maastricht convergence criteria prior to joining the EMU.[13] As a result EMU candidate countries applied contractionary monetary and fiscal policies to qualify for EMU membership.

The convergence of long-term interest rates is also attributed to the conviction of the markets that European integration is an ongoing process and that the euro is the permanent and irrevocable currency of the EMU member countries. Such a market perception drove the risk premia of the EA countries' long-term interest rates down to zero.[14] The markets' initial assumption about the euro's stability turned out to be incorrect despite the repeated declarations and promises by the European leaders to resolve the crisis and save the euro. The irrevocability of the euro was shaken when a few EU country leaders did not perceive and accept EA national economic problems as common European problems. Similarly, some EA country leaders led voters to form expectations that an exit from the EMU was a viable option if it became too costly for their country to remain an EMU member. As a result, the euro is still challenged and its future is uncertain.

In Figure 3.2, the long-term interest rate spreads of the two EA country groups are depicted in relation to the German government bond interest rate. The interest rate spreads of the four Southern EA countries and Ireland are shown in Figure 3.2(b).

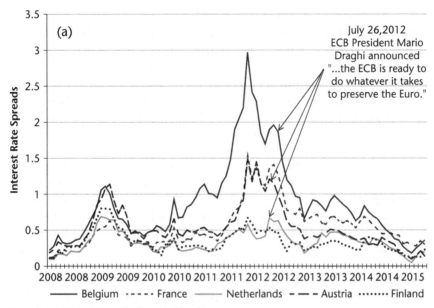

Source: Eurostat/Financial Times/The Economist/Bloomberg

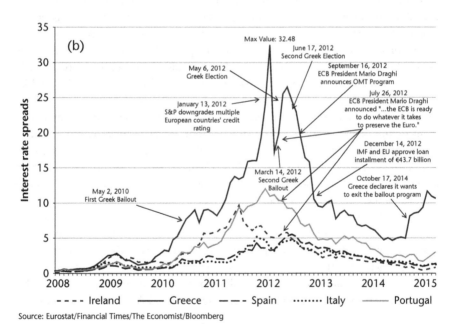

Source: Eurostat/Financial Times/The Economist/Bloomberg

FIGURE 3.2   (a) Northern European countries' ten-year interest rate spreads vs. the equivalent German bond rate; (b) Southern European countries' ten-year interest rate spreads vs. the equivalent German bond rate

In Figure 3.2(a), the interest rate spreads of five Northern EA countries, Belgium, France, the Netherlands, Austria, and Finland, are portrayed in relation to the long-term interest rate of Germany.[15] A comparison of the interest rate spreads of the two EA groups of countries indicates that a substantial difference exists between them. Whereas the Northern EA countries' maximum interest rate spread range is approximately three percentage points, the Southern EA countries' interest rate spread range exceeds 30 percent. It can be observed in Figures 3.1 and 3.2 that the interest rate spreads substantially increased in the periphery countries, but minimally increased for the Northern EA group of countries.

Figure 3.2 shows that the Greek interest rate spread increased the most during the crisis; this is undoubtedly the result of the leaks regarding the falsification of the government deficits. Long-term interest rates also substantially increased in Ireland and Portugal. Consequently, for the three countries it became prohibitively expensive to borrow from the market, therefore it was necessary for them to receive bailouts which were jointly offered by the EU and the IMF. It is almost certain that interest rates in Greece would not have skyrocketed if the fabricated Greek government deficit leaks had not become front page news. With the same reasoning, the European sovereign debt crisis that was triggered by the Greek fiscal revelations could have also been avoided altogether.

It is intriguing to observe the interest rate spreads of the Southern EA countries. It is also very revealing to notice how the turning points and fluctuations of the Greek interest rate spread reveal the unfolding Greek financial saga since November 2009, when the world was informed about the public fiscal profligacy by the new Greek Prime Minister. Events including the two bailouts to Greece, the two Greek elections, and the release of a major loan installment on March 14, 2012 by the EU to Greece, which was publicized as required to save the country from a disorderly default can be observed in a single line plot in Figure 3.2. A premature announcement by the New Democracy/PASOK Coalition government to exit the bailout programs on October 17, 2014 is indicated by the steep increase in the Greek long-term interest rates. Lastly, the reignited Greek public debt crisis, after the election of new government headed by Syriza in January 2015, is depicted with a sharp increase in the Greek interest rate.

In both Figures 3.2(a) and 3.2(b), a few distinct turning points of the interest rate line graphs exist that are associated with critical events and developments that were anxiously and carefully followed as they evolved during the crisis. The first Greek bailout, on May 2, 2010, despite the initial expectations, did not impress the markets. Investors quickly sensed that the €110 billion bailout was insufficient to reverse the deteriorating fiscal situation in Greece. Consequently, all EA interest rates continued to rise.

Another critical event is associated with the agreement on the second bailout to Greece that took place on March 14, 2012; this is indicated by a sharp decline in all interest rate spreads. The second Greek bailout agreement was received with a great relief by those interested in the survival of the EMU and the euro. The perception was that failure in the negotiations among the Greek government representatives, the EU, the IMF, and the Greek private bondholders (investors) may have led Greece into financial chaos. A collapse in the negotiations among the bargaining parties was anticipated to have grave repercussions on the EA economies and could have triggered a major global crisis.

The first Greek national election on May 6, 2012 resulted in a further increase in the Greek interest rate spreads. The outcome of this election was perceived as a great disappointment, since the Greek voters failed to elect a political party with a majority in parliament and able to form a government. The expectation was that a newly elected Greek government would have supported the second bailout agreement since the two major Greek political parties had already complied with the Troika request and signed an agreement to continue with the structural reforms and the austerity program.[16] The perception was that the second bailout to Greece, although extremely harsh, would have prevented the worst scenario of disorderly default, i.e. bankruptcy of the country.

Greece held a second election on June 17, 2012. The outcome of this election was critical for the future course of Greece, as it was to determine whether the country would remain in the EA. The election results could also have affected the very survival of the euro. The election of June 17, 2012 again produced no clear winner. However, a three-party coalition government was formed that stabilized the political situation in Greece, which then gained credibility among the EU member states. On June 25, 2013, the smallest of the three Greek parties that formed the coalition withdrew its support for the government over a disagreement concerning massive layoffs in the public sector. From that point the coalition government consisted of two parties, New Democracy and Pasok, which governed with a thin majority of only four seats in the parliament.

Another significant event, shown in Figure 3.2(b), was an important decision made by the President of the European Central Bank (ECB), Mario Draghi, on July 26, 2012. The ECB president stated in a speech given in London that the ECB will do "whatever it takes" to preserve the euro, as is shown in Figure 3.2(a). This event is indicated by a sharp decline in all interest rate spreads of the EA members. President Draghi's announcement was the most encouraging message since the crisis began which triggered a substantial decline in interest rates in all EA countries.

On September 6, 2012, the ECB President followed through with his promise and announced at a press conference in Frankfurt the Outright Monetary Transactions (OMT) program. He stated that the ECB, under certain conditions, would buy unlimited amounts of short-term government bonds in the secondary market to help those countries at risk experiencing high long-term interest rates, as shown in Figure 3.2(b).[17] The OMT program of the ECB was adamantly opposed by the President of the Central Bank of Germany (the Bundesbank), Jens Weidmann, who considered it to be a serious violation of the "No Bailout Clause" of the Maastricht Treaty which established the EMU. The aforementioned clause was enshrined in the EU/EMU treaties that established the EMU, upon the insistence and persuasion of Germany. The German Chancellor, Angela Merkel, rather hesitantly and with about a month's delay, indicated to the news media that she did not disagree with the proposed plan of Mario Draghi. The OMT program has already proved to be very successful as it calmed down the markets without the ECB having to buy a single national bond. Mr Weidmann opposed the OMT program not only in the ECB Governing Council of which he is a member, but also at the Federal Constitution Court of Germany where, as a representative of the Bundesbank, he tried to stop the new ECB program, claiming it violated the EMU/EU treaties. (For more details on this lawsuit, see Box 3.1.)

BOX 3.1   The Federal Constitutional Court of Germany (Bundesverfassungsgericht)

Jens Weidmann, the president of the Bundesbank, who had cast the only dissenting vote in the ECB Governing Council against Mario Draghi's OMT program, continued his efforts to permanently block the program. President Draghi's OMT program of purchases of short-term national government securities by the ECB was intended to reduce the market interest rates of the financially distressed countries and thus prevent bankruptcy of these EMU members.

On June 11 and 12, 2013, Mr Weidmann represented the German Bundesbank as a plaintiff in a hearing at the Federal Constitutional Court of Germany located in the city of Karlsruhe. The ECB was represented by its German member of the ECB executive board, Jörg Asmussen, another German. Mr Weidmann claimed that the ECB's OMT program is in violation of the EU treaty because it exceeded its narrowly defined delegated authority on monetary policy. Bundesbank President Weidmann suggested the ECB buying national government securities is very close to mixing monetary with fiscal policy. Saving financially distressed countries, Mr Weidmann claimed, is the responsibility of governments and elected politicians and not the job of the ECB, which was given a single mandate to exclusively pursue price stability.

The German Constitutional Court, however, does not have jurisdiction over the ECB. The court delayed its decision to 2014, until after the German national elections, on whether the ECB's OMT program violated German law. The court decided that the OMT did not violate German law and that the European Court of Justice should have the final say on this decision.

The German Constitutional Court had also delayed announcing its decision when it was requested to rule whether the European Stability Mechanism (ESM) and the Fiscal Compact Treaty had violated German law by shifting fiscal authority from the German parliament (Bundestag) to Brussels. This hearing was brought by 37,000 citizens, a Bavarian politician, a few academics, and the left-wing political party Die Linke. At that hearing in July 2012, the colorful constitutional court of eight scarlet robed judges did not find that the ESM or the Fiscal Compact Treaty had violated the German law. The court, however, took a lot of time to announce its decision and this could have been fatal for the survival of the financially distressed countries, as speculators could have launched a sequence of speculative attacks on their government bonds.

A similar approach to the German Constitutional Court was adopted by Chancellor Merkel who had several times commented that it will take years to correct the economic problems in Europe and save the euro. In both cases brought to the court, the plaintiffs had the right to question decisions of democratically elected German representatives and institutions. These rights were gained back in 1933 when a lawfully elected party had terminated the German parliament and the democratic regime of the Weimar Republic replacing them with tyranny. The political and judicial system in Germany delays the decision-making process in the EA. This places EA members at increased risk and also makes the EMU and the euro vulnerable. It is not, however, certain whether the majority of Germans are overly concerned about the well-being of the citizens of other EMU members.

Public debt at the center of the Eurocrisis

The accumulated excessive public debt of a few EA countries is a core issue in the current crisis. As a matter of fact, the name of the crisis, "the European sovereign debt crisis," reveals the importance of public debt. After 2008, as shown in Figure 3.3, the debt to GDP ratio of the periphery countries increased to an unsustainable level. The debt to GDP ratio of all the Southern European countries and Ireland has exceeded the 60 percent of the Maastricht maximum reference value since 2010. The best performer regarding the public debt of the five periphery countries was Spain. Figure 3.3(b) shows that for the Northern EA countries, the increase in the public debt to GDP ratio during the crisis was relatively small in comparison to that of the Southern EA members. The asymmetric effects of the financial crisis on the long-term interest rates and on the public debt of these two distinct EA groups sets this crisis apart from any other past crises in Europe.

If we observe Figure 3.3(a), the debt to GDP ratio of two EA countries, Greece and Italy, was close to 100 percent for the entire 17-year sample period. Portugal and Ireland have also experienced increasing debt to GDP ratios starting in 2005. If we examine Figure 3.3(b), which shows the debt to GDP ratio of the Northern EA countries, it is evident that all these countries, with the exception of Belgium, maintained a public debt to GDP ratio below or slightly above the Maastricht reference value of 60 percent, but not above 100 percent.

It is interesting to note that Italy, Greece, and Belgium became members of the EMU and adopted the euro although they exceeded the maximum allowed Maastricht debt to GDP ratio value of 60 percent. EU country leaders compromised over public debt and launched the EMU in 1999, although not all candidate countries met this criterion.[18] Economists had predicted that it was going to be very difficult for countries to drastically reduce the public debt to GDP ratio within a short period of a few years.

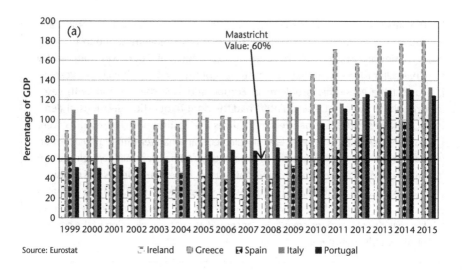

Source: Eurostat   ⌐ Ireland   ▣ Greece   ▨ Spain   ▦ Italy   ■ Portugal

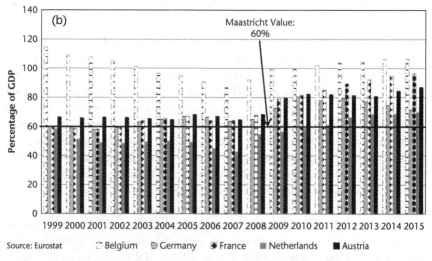

Source: Eurostat   ⌐ Belgium   ▣ Germany   ◉ France   ▦ Netherlands   ■ Austria

FIGURE 3.3 (a) Southern EA gross public debt as a percentage of GDP; (b) Northern EA gross public debt as a percentage of GDP

Consequently, it is not a surprise that more than 15 years after the launch of the EMU, the same three countries, Greece, Italy, and Belgium, are still struggling with an excessive public debt to GDP ratio. The decision to launch the EMU as a result could not be supported according to agreed selected fiscal criteria by the EU members. However, the European leaders made the historical decision to launch the euro according to their strong political will and commitment to unify Europe. The implicit assumption was that all the EU governments would adopt all necessary policies and take the appropriate measures to integrate Europe. If the integration process had been completed, EA countries would have been more resilient to asymmetric shocks. The integration process, however, was slow, and the US subprime mortgage crisis found the EMU countries unprepared to deal with the external shocks.

Ireland and Spain increased their private debt by heavily borrowing from abroad; most of these capital inflows were channeled to the booming real-estate sectors of the two countries. Ireland quickly transformed almost all of its private debt into public debt when the Irish government decided to guarantee the country's bank deposits. Such a decision was based on the fact that the three major Irish commercial banks had accumulated a large number of non-performing (bad) property loans. In a spontaneous decision to protect the entire banking system and the bank depositors, the Irish government offered a blanket guarantee of its banks for an amount equal to 2.5 times its total GDP.

Like Ireland, Spain experienced problems within its banking system that put the entire Spanish economy at risk. Because of the large size of the Spanish economy, a possible collapse of its banking system poses a major concern that the crisis will quickly spread to neighboring countries. If such an event occurs, it could be catastrophic because it would be extremely difficult for the EU/IMF to provide a sufficient bailout package to rescue Spain and prevent the crisis from spreading abroad. On December 4, 2012, nevertheless, Spain negotiated with the Troika to receive a bailout of €100 billion to recapitalize its banks, which sustained major losses by lending heavily to its booming construction and real-estate industry. Greater concerns were raised about Italy, which has an even larger economy than Spain. The sustainability of the Italian and Spanish debt is therefore an issue of extraordinary importance tantamount to the survival of the EMU.

Can highly indebted countries maintain low interest rates?

The European sovereign debt crisis convinced many people that heavily indebted countries will eventually experience high interest rates which would cause financial distress. In Figure 3.4, the ten-year government bond yield spreads of the US, Japan, and the UK are depicted vis-à-vis the corresponding ten-year government German bond interest rates. According to Figure 3.4(a), the ten-year government bond interest rate spreads of the US, Japan, and the UK are below 1 percent. The Japanese ten-year government bond spread was consistently negative, meaning that this interest rate was always lower than the German bond interest rate.

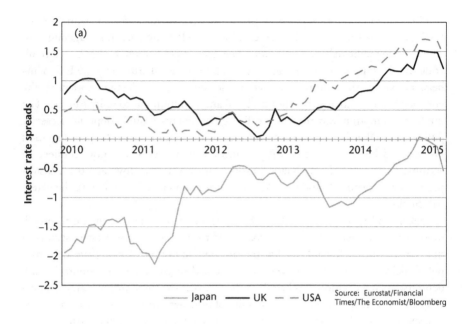

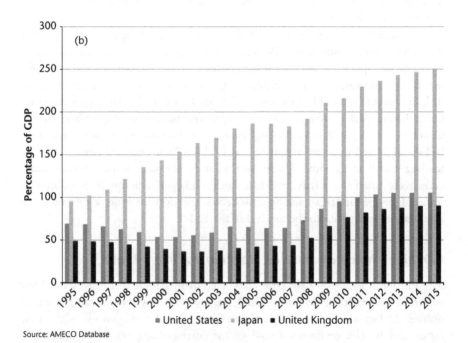

FIGURE 3.4 (a) USA, UK, and Japanese ten-year interest rate spread vs. the equivalent German bond rate; (b) USA, UK, and Japanese public debt to GDP ratio

In Figure 3.4(b), the debt to GDP ratios for the US, Japan and the UK are also depicted. According to Figure 3.4, the three countries have accumulated a very high debt to GDP ratio. As a matter of fact, Japan accumulated the highest debt to GDP ratio of all the developed countries, standing at 250.8 percent by June 2015. High public indebtedness, however, did not necessarily result in high interest rates. Similarly, in the US, a very expansionary fiscal policy designed to cope with the subprime mortgage crisis increased the public debt to GDP ratio above 100 percent, but the US still enjoys a relatively low interest rate and a steady growth rate after the end of the rather short-lived recession caused by the subprime mortgage crisis. In 2013, the US began reducing its public deficit as the US Treasury was paid back substantial amounts of the fiscal stimuli that it granted to assist various US private and quasi-public institutions in its efforts to stabilize the economy.

In the summer of 2012, bipartisan political disputes in the US Congress prevented Republicans and Democrats from reaching an agreement on the US fiscal deficit problem. This indecision triggered the Sequester in March 2013.[19] This was an automatic, across-the-board increase in taxes and a reduction in government expenditures. Such economic developments helped the US restore fiscal stability. In these three countries that had accumulated a very high public debt to GDP ratio, the long-term interest rates remained low. The US, Japan, and the UK are by no means threatened by default, as they are three of the largest and most dynamic economies in the world.

Fiscal academic disputes

Carmen Reinhart and Kenneth Rogoff (2010), two Harvard University economists, established an empirical relationship between economic growth and government debt. According to these two authors, economic growth and public debt to GDP ratio are negatively related after the public debt to GDP ratio exceeds a critical value of 90 percent. The two authors derived their empirical findings from a sample that included a large number of countries. These empirical results served as an intellectual academic endorsement of the austerity programs imposed by the IMF on the over-indebted bailout recipient countries that were advised to reduce government expenditures and raise taxes.[20]

More recently, Professors Reinhart and Rogoff's empirical results were challenged by a student, Thomas Herndon, and two professors, Michael Ash and Robert Pollin, from the University of Massachusetts at Amherst. The three authors, employing the same data, reported that they could not replicate the results of the negative relation of economic growth and public debt to GDP ratio when this ratio exceeds the 90 percent critical value.[21] Therefore the three authors expressed skepticism over the validity of the Reinhart-Rogoff results. The findings of the three authors were much publicized and presented as a strong counter-thesis to the imposed austerity programs.

TABLE 3.1 EA government deficits and debts

As a percentage of GDP	2009	2010	2011	2012	2013	2014
Government expenditures	51.2	51.0	49.0	49.5	49.4	50.5
Government revenues	44.9	44.8	45.3	46.2	46.5	47.6
Government deficit	−6.4	−6.2	−4.2	−3.7	−2.9	−2.9
Government debt	80.0	85.4	87.3	90.6	90.9	96.4

Source: Eurostat/IMF.

EA fiscal statistics

In Table 3.1, government expenditures, revenues, deficit, and debt are reported as a percentage of the EA GDP during the period of 2009–14. According to this table, government expenditures have declined slightly while government revenues have been increasing. As a result, the public deficit to GDP ratio of the EA countries for the 2009–14 period decreased by 3.5 percent, whereas the public debt to GDP ratio increased by 16.4 percent. Such results are not a surprise, as applied contractionary fiscal policy, measured by a reduction in the public deficit of the EA countries, also reduced GDP. This finding is something to be expected under normal macroeconomic conditions. It is possible, however, but very rare for highly indebted countries to apply contractionary fiscal policy (fiscal consolidation) and, as a result, increase national income while the country simultaneously reduces its government deficits and public debt.[22]

Who did it in Greece?

With the eyes of the entire world focused on the public indebtedness of Greece it make sense to examine how this €335 billion mountain of public debt was created. Which political party was responsible for this sharp increase in the Greek public debt? Figure 3.5 portrays the Greek public debt to GDP ratio on the vertical axis from 1975 to 2015. The debt to GDP ratio is denoted by shaded or non-shaded bars depending on which political party was in government that year and therefore is mainly responsible for the public debt changes.

During the 40 years shown in Figure 3.5, the Pan-Hellenic Socialist Party (PASOK) (shaded) ruled Greece alone for 20 years whereas the New Democracy party (non-shaded), a right-center party, ruled Greece alone for 15 years. As shown in Figure 3.5, both parties increased the Greek debt to GDP ratio. The two major Greek political parties are therefore both responsible for the reckless fiscal management of the economy and the increase in the debt to GDP ratio. Both political parties were accused of playing a major role in increasing government expenditures, which led to a bloated public sector. A larger public sector resulted in more jobs for their constituency. Politicians, year after year, were in the habit of exchanging favors for votes. Consequently, such a clientelistic

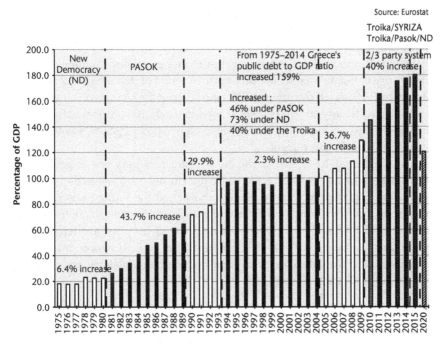

FIGURE 3.5 Greek debt as a percentage of GDP

type of relationship was developed among politicians and voters, as both voters and politicians received short-term benefits. Such interdependency, however, led to the financial devastation of the country in the long run because the increasing public debt to GDP ratio became unsustainable and the problem surfaced during the crisis when interest rates increased and Greece could not service its public debt.

Since 2010, however, Greece has been under IMF/EU supervision and the imposed conditionality; as a result, the IMF and EU bear a major share of the responsibility for the Greek public debt explosion during the years 2010–15. This period is depicted by the dotted bars in Figure 3.5. The last column, shown by a striped bar, denotes the Greek debt to GDP ratio forecasted by the IMF/EU at the second bailout agreement to be 120 percent in 2020. As the Greek governments followed the austerity programs imposed by the Troika, the Greeks lost governance of their country. The agreed austerity programs sank Greece into a prolonged recession with little hope of return to growth. The very harsh initial terms of the two Greek bailout programs played a major role in the high indebtedness of Greece. The first bailout was particularly detrimental, as it was purposefully designed to be harsh on Greece in order to discourage other countries from seeking bailouts, thus aiming to minimize the moral hazard problem.[23]

In Figure 3.5, it is evident that both Greek parties experienced mixed periods of stable and unstable fiscal performance. The New Democracy party left the public debt to GDP ratio practically unchanged during its first term in government, but drastically increased it during its second two terms. New Democracy increased the total public debt to GDP ratio by 73 percent during its three terms. PASOK tripled the public debt to GDP ratio during its first term, but stabilized it during its three consecutive terms in government that lasted for a period of eleven years (1994–2004). However, PASOK left the debt to GDP ratio at about the same level as it was when it was elected to government in 1994 at approximately 100 percent, indeed a very high level. The total increase in public debt to GDP ratio by PASOK was 46 percent over its 20 years in government.

The sub-period 2005–9 when the New Democracy party was in government the fiscal performance of Greece was worse than in any other sub-period prior and in relation to any other country. During this period the Prime Minister, Kostas Karamanlis, only two years in to his second term in government, announced a snap election in 2009 hoping to increase the members of his party to strengthen the government in order to be able to better handle the crisis. However, many critics commented that he looked for an easy exit from his responsibilities, as the country was already in financial trouble.

Public debt composition and private saving in the EA

The question arises, what factors other than the public deficit and debt to GDP ratios play a crucial role in influencing a country's economic and fiscal condition, particularly the interest rate a country has to pay to refinance its public debt? The composition of a country's public debt is one such crucial factor. It makes a difference whether the public debt is owned domestically or by foreigners. If a substantial share of total debt is owned by foreign investors, then a country is in a disadvantageous position for three reasons: first, because the country makes annual interest payments abroad to its foreign bond owners; and second because the government does not receive taxes on the interest payments made to foreign lenders.[24] The third and most important factor for the country to rely on the domestic financing of its public debt is that the negotiations with domestic creditors would be easier and more favorable. This point of view is supported by considering the harsh treatment of all bailout recipient countries by the Troika.

By observing the government bond yield spreads and the public debt to GDP ratio of the periphery countries, it is clear that for Greece, Ireland, and Portugal, high government bond yield spreads are associated with high public debt to GDP ratios. Italy, however, constitutes an exception because although it has accumulated a large public debt to GDP ratio of over 100 percent, its ten-year government bond yield spread was relatively low in comparison to that of Greece, Ireland, and Portugal. This discrepancy can be explained by comparing the shares of the total general government debt in these countries that is owned by foreigners. As it turns out, Italy is the country with the lowest percentage of foreign debt to GDP ratio among the four countries.[25]

For many years, Italy has also maintained a relatively high private saving rate; thus the country did not have to rely heavily on borrowing from abroad, as can be seen in Figure 3.6. Spain maintained a private saving rate even higher than Italy's after 2008. The high saving rate helped Spain maintain lower long-term interest

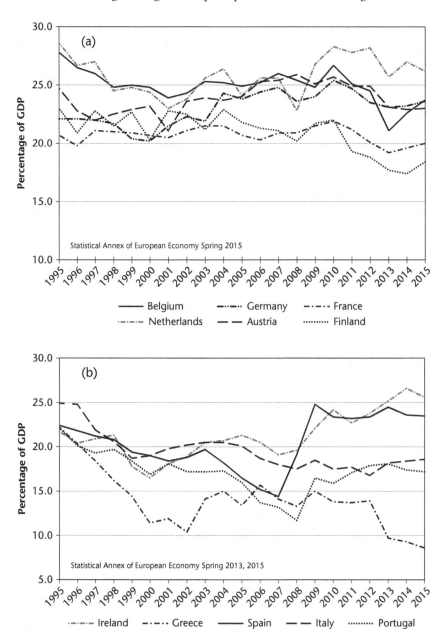

FIGURE 3.6 (a) Gross private savings Southern EA countries; (b) Gross private savings Northern EA countries

rates than Greece, Ireland, and Portugal as well. However, Spain's banks borrowed heavily from abroad at the outset of the Eurocrisis to finance its booming real estate and construction sector.

It can be seen in Figure 3.6(a) that since the mid-1990s, Greece generated the lowest private saving rate. Such an exceptionally low saving rate for Greece is associated with high public and trade deficits and a high public debt to GDP ratio which resulted in the highest long-term interest rate spread in the EU. If we look at Figure 3.6(b), it is evident that France has the lowest private saving rate among the Northern EA group. Consequently, it is not a coincidence that France began experiencing fiscal problems and pays relatively higher interest rates in relation to most other Northern EA countries. The exception is Belgium, which accumulated the highest public debt to GDP ratio among the Northern EA group. From this analysis, it can be inferred that if an economy is large and has a relatively high private saving rate, then it will rely less on foreign capital inflows and will be more resilient to external shocks. It was demonstrated that foreign capital flows are very volatile and sensitive to the information leaks and CRA downgrades that brought at least six EA countries to the brink of bankruptcy.

International competitiveness

International competitiveness was also a factor that played a role in how countries were affected during the European sovereign debt crisis. Countries that are internationally competitive are capable of generating large trade and CA surpluses; consequently, over the years, these countries generate a high and positive international investment position.[26] Countries that accumulate chronic CA deficits will eventually experience a net international indebtedness position. It is difficult nonetheless to find direct indicators that measure a country's international competitiveness.

It is possible, nevertheless, to evaluate a country's international competitiveness indirectly by comparing the country's historical CA balances and net international investment (indebtedness) positions. A comparison of the historical statistics of the two EA groups of countries in reference to these two variables indicates that substantial differences exist between the two groups. Figure 3.7(a) shows the CA of all Southern EA countries and Ireland. Each one of these countries from 2000 to 2012 has generated relatively large CA deficits. It is also evident from Figure 3.7(a) that Greece, Portugal, and Spain experienced the largest CA deficits. In Figure 3.7(b) it can be seen that the Northern EA countries have consistently generated CA surpluses. These findings suggest that the Northern EA countries remained internationally competitive during the crisis.[27]

Historical statistics regarding the international investment position of Northern and Southern EA countries are portrayed in Figure 3.8. As shown, the Northern EA countries over the 1999–2013 period generated a net international investment

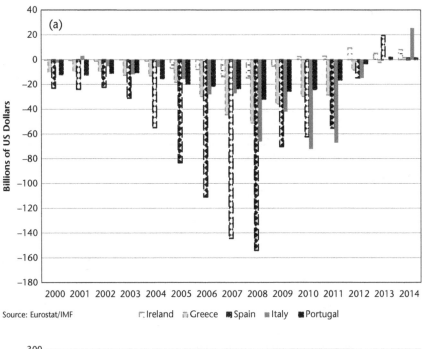

Source: Eurostat/IMF   Ireland Greece Spain Italy Portugal

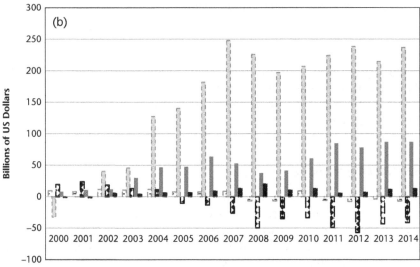

Source: Eurostat/IMF   Belgium Germany France Netherlands Austria

FIGURE 3.7 (a) Southern EA countries' Current Accounts; (b) Northern EA countries' Current Accounts

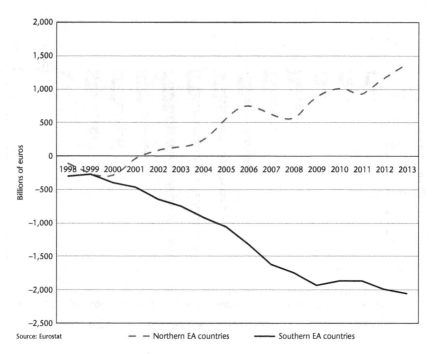

FIGURE 3.8 Net international investment position

position that resembles almost a mirror image of the Southern EA countries' international indebtedness, which amounted to over 2 trillion euros at the end of 2013. As the European sovereign debt crisis began to slowly subside, both international investment and indebtedness gradually started declining, but after 2011 these figures began to increase again.

Rebalancing in the EA

Large trade imbalances were thought to be a cause of the European crisis; as a result, many economists support the view that an exit from the crisis will take place through trade rebalancing. Figure 3.9 clearly shows that rebalancing in the EA has been taking place. However, a reduction in trade imbalances was attained through an automatic mechanism, which was a byproduct of the crisis that caused a substantial decrease in the national incomes of the Southern EA countries and Ireland and thus a reduction in their trade deficits. Figure 3.9 shows that the five Southern EA countries' cumulative trade deficits have been declining since 2008 and by 2013 they generated a surplus in relation to the rest of the world. The five Northern EA countries have generated a rising cumulative trade surplus since 1995, which has reached a level of almost $290 billion in 2014.

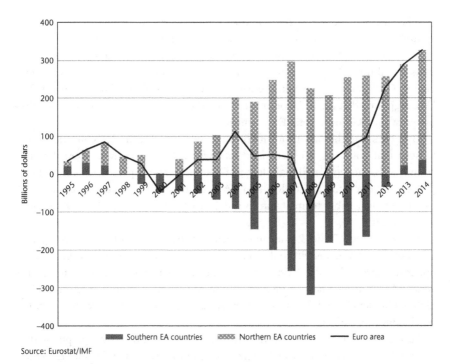

Source: Eurostat/IMF

FIGURE 3.9 Rebalancing in the EA

Concluding comments

The US subprime mortgage crisis quickly began spreading to Europe during the fall of 2008, a time when the crisis was at its peak in the US, just after the collapse of the Lehman Brothers. The most affected EA countries included those that were over-indebted and those which experienced a decline in their international competitiveness. Over-indebted countries witnessed the continuous degrading of their sovereign debt by the three major CRAs. The presence of the crisis in Europe was initially felt by a crunch in the interbank liquidity that triggered the rise in the long-term interest rate spreads of those countries which ran large and chronic government deficits and, consequently, had accumulated excessive and unsustainable public debt.

The EU and IMF decided to rescue these financially distressed EA countries by jointly offering bailouts to those EA countries that were unable to refinance their public debt in the market. Greece, Ireland, Portugal, Spain, and Cyprus all received bailouts. The EU and the IMF approved the bailouts on the condition that bailout recipient countries would adopt austerity programs. These programs were designed to help the countries attain fiscal stability and economic growth. Despite the original expectations, bailout recipient countries experienced prolonged recessions, record rates of unemployment, political instability, and a humanitarian crisis of unprecedented dimensions.

The austerity programs were opposed by many citizens of the bailout recipient countries. Millions of people became outraged and expressed their anger through riots and strikes. The validity of the austerity programs was challenged after several years of failure to help countries return to growth in order to reduce their public debt to GDP ratio. As a result, the bailout programs prolonged the recession. The IMF suggested that the EU Commission ease the rules on deficit reduction requirements of the SGP on several EA countries.

By examining the historical data on the saving rates of the EA countries, it can be seen that countries that generated relatively lower saving rates were the same countries that accumulated high debt to GDP ratios and experienced extraordinarily high interest rates. Most Northern EA countries attained high saving rates and, as a result, were able to maintain low debt to GDP ratios and borrow at lower interest rates.

From Figures 3.7 and 3.8, it can be seen that the Southern EA countries generated both large CA deficits and international indebtedness positions. Exactly the opposite happened in the Northern EA countries. It is interesting to note that the same EA countries that experienced prolonged fiscal instability, as measured by high public deficits and debt to GDP ratios, also experienced high net international indebtedness positions.

Several economists claim that the crisis was caused not only by high public debt but also by large trade imbalances. These economists recommended that EA countries must reduce their trade imbalances. Figure 3.9 shows that trade imbalances were reduced substantially by 2012. In 2013 and 2014 the periphery countries generated a trade surplus. However, this reduction of the imbalances was a byproduct of the crisis as the recession reduced the countries' national incomes and their ability to import.

Notes

1 The EA is the group of EU countries that adopted the euro as their common currency. They are often referred to as the Eurozone or – rarely – as Euroland. As of July 2015, these EA includes 19 countries: Austria, Belgium, Cyprus, Estonia, Finland, France, Germany, Greece, Ireland, Italy, Latvia, Lithuania, Luxembourg, Malta, the Netherlands, Portugal, Slovakia, Slovenia, and Spain.

2 Although Ireland is a Northern European country, it is included with the South because its economy was affected in a similar way to the Southern European economies. The four Southern EA countries, along with Cyprus (a Mediterranean republic), and Ireland are referred to as the EA periphery countries in this and other chapters of the book since they are located around the central EA countries. Cyprus was the last country affected by the European crisis, thus some of the early developments of the crisis are not related to Cyprus.

3 Stating that the European crisis was triggered by the US subprime mortgage crisis does not necessarily mean that the US caused the crisis in these countries. If these countries had not developed weaknesses or "preconditions," the crisis would never have spread in them. With the same reasoning, it can be argued that the US is the origin of the crisis and must accept much responsibility for the recent fragility and instability of the international financial system. There are, however, EU countries that developed their own housing bubble without having been exposed much to the US toxic assets.

4 The UK and the Czech Republic decided to opt out and not sign the Fiscal Compact Treaty.

5 Olivier Blanchard, the IMF's chief economist, admitted in an article he wrote for the *World Economic Outlook: 2012*, that fiscal multipliers are larger than they were perceived to be. Thus fiscal consolidation efforts by increasing taxes and reducing government expenditures caused more destructive effects on the economies where they were applied than initially expected. As a result, countries pursuing austerity programs such as Greece, Portugal, Spain, and Ireland experienced a sharp decline in GDP and therefore an increase in their public debt to GDP ratio instead of a decrease. In particular, the IMF study found that fiscal multipliers were in the range of 0.7–1.7 instead of 0.6 as they were believed to be prior to this study.

6 Such a view about austerity was expressed by IMF Chief Lagarde in a news release at the annual joint conference of the IMF and World Bank in Tokyo on October 13, 2012.

7 Both of these factors, along with his non-confrontational personality, could be the reason why President Hollande no longer offers a promise for a radical change to the EMU governance that could lead to a solution to the crisis. The news media commented that he chose not to be the leader of a second division league by uniting and leading the periphery EA countries. The switch of President Hollande's position disappointed many people, especially in his own Socialist Party. This however, changed after the May 2015 Brussels Summit when he and Italy's Prime Minister Mateo Renzi supported Greece's membership in the EMU.

8 See Tremonti and Juncker (2010).

9 The G20 consists of the 20 most important economies in the world from which representatives have been meeting to find common policies in order to address global economic problems. The OECD (Organization of Economic Corporation and Development) is a group of 34 developed member countries, also known as the Club of Paris. The purpose of the OECD is to provide a forum for member countries to seek common policies that will improve the economic and social well-being of people around the world.

10 The IMF and German approach to the European crisis is reminiscent of the classical economic theory that supports the view that free markets and minimal government interference can quickly restore full employment. One could imagine how long the US Great Depression and the Great Recession would have lasted if the US had followed the failed German/IMF approach to the European crisis.

11 When a country accumulates unsustainable debt it has limited options to cope with the over-indebtedness. The worst of these options is disorderly default (bankruptcy), but the most common alternative involves restructuring the debt. This requires an agreement with its creditors who will volunteer for any of the following: a partial write-off ("haircut") of the public debt, a reduced interest rate, or an extension of the repayment period of the sovereign debt. Most often, the restructuring agreement includes all previously mentioned options.

12 The world's three most important CRAs are Moody's, Standard & Poor (S&P), and Fitch.

13 For the Maastricht Convergence Criteria, see Zestos (2006: chapter 3).

14 A risk premium is measured by the difference in the interest rate that a country or a corporation has to pay above a risk-free interest rate to sell its securities. Examples of risk-free securities usually accepted by investors are the US Treasury bill and the German government bond.

15 The German bond is considered to be one of the safest securities, as Germany has achieved price stability for a long period. For this reason, the ten-year German government bond yield is the benchmark rate.

16 The Troika refers to the EU Commission, the European Central Bank (ECB), and the IMF. These are the institutions that approved the bailouts and imposed the lending conditions on Greece and the other countries. The new Greek government no longer refers to the IMF, ECB, and the European Commission as the Troika, but instead as "the institutions" since the Troika is associated with the austerity imposed on and the pain caused to the Greek people.

17 When the ECB buys national government bonds, the demand for bonds increases which leads to lower interest rates, as there exists a negative relation between the price of bonds and interest rates.

18 See Zestos (2006: chapter 6).

19 Blake (2013).

20 This has been, and still is, Germany and its Northern allies' approach to the EA crisis, which so far has failed to resolve the crisis and is heavily criticized by many economists, world leaders and millions of people in the impoverished countries.

21 See Herndon *et al.* (2013).

22 See, for example, Levy (2001) who provided evidence from the US Omnibus Reconciliation Act of 1993, when President Bill Clinton, with the cooperation of a Republican-dominated Congress, was able to generate a sequence of four years of government surpluses and an increase in economic growth by means of government expenditure reductions and tax increases on high-income earners.

23 Greece's only alternative to the bailouts, according to Greek government representatives negotiating with the Troika, would have been disorderly default. There were, of course, other much better alternatives, but Germany and its Northern allies wanted to make the bailout program to Greece as painful as possible in order to send a strong message to possible bailout candidate countries. In this way, Germany and its allies, namely Finland and the Netherlands, tried to resolve the moral hazard problem by discouraging countries from easily resorting to seeking bailouts.

24 See Cabral (2010).

25 Ibid.

26 The international investment position consists of the accumulation of a country's net assets abroad minus the accumulated net foreign assets at home.

27 A possible exception is France, which, although grouped with the Northern EA countries, since 2005 has generated small but increasing CA deficits. For this reason, a case can be made that France could be included in the Southern group, although its economy was more resilient than the other Southern countries. On April 10, 2013, the EA Commission, however, gave warnings to France to restore fiscal stability and international competiveness, but it also gave France, along with a few other EA countries, two extra years to meet the public deficit requirement according to the provisions of the SGP.

References

Blake, A. (2013) "When does the Sequester start?" *Washington Post*, March 1.

Blanchard, O. (2012) *World Economic Outlook: October 2012.* Washington, DC: IMF.

Cabral, R. (2010) "The PIGS' external debt problem", *VoxEU.org*, May 8.

Herndon, T., Ash, M., and Pollin, R. (2013) *Does High Public Debt Consistently Stifle Economic Growth? A Critique of Reinhart and Rogoff.* Political Economy Research Institute, University of Massachusetts at Amherst, April 15.

Levy, M. D. (2001) "Don't mix monetary and fiscal policy: why return to an old, flawed framework?" *Cato Journal*, 21 (2): 277–83.

Reinhart, C. M. and Rogoff, K. S. (2010) "Growth in a time of debt," *National Bureau of Economic Research Digest.*

Treaty on European Union (Maastricht text), July 29, 1992, O.J. C 191/1 [hereafter Maastricht TEU].

Tremonti, G. and Juncker, J. C. (2010) "E-Bonds would end the crisis," *Financial Times*, December 5.

Zestos, G. (2006) *European Monetary Integration: The Euro.* Mason, OH: Thompson Southwestern.

4

WHY THE EUROPEAN SOVEREIGN DEBT CRISIS HAS LASTED SO LONG

Introduction

This chapter examines the reasons why the European sovereign debt crisis has not yet been resolved. Since the Economic and Monetary Union (EMU) and the euro are at the center of the crisis, the focus of this analysis will be on European economic and monetary integration. During the most recent recession, the GDP of the Euro Area (EA) declined for six consecutive quarters and the unemployment rate reached 12.1 percent, the highest ever on record for the EA.[1] Only during the second quarter of 2013 did the EA GDP increase by 1.2 percent, driven mainly by Germany and, surprisingly, France and Portugal. Both the EU and the EA experienced anemic GDP growth during 2014. Nonetheless, all of the periphery EA countries except Cyprus generated a positive growth in 2014.

One major reason that the crisis has deepened and endured so long is because the EMU was introduced as an incomplete structure, lacking the necessary tools to fight asymmetric shocks that afflicted some of its members and not others. According to some economists who have contributed to the theory of monetary integration, the member countries that formed the EMU in 1999 did not constitute an Optimum Currency Area (OCA).[2] The decision upon which countries qualified for EMU membership was based on five Maastricht convergence criteria. The Maastricht Treaty, also known as the Treaty on European Union, required all EMU candidate countries to meet five convergence criteria prior to joining the EMU. Maxima reference values were set for four of the criteria: inflation, long-term interest rate, public deficit and debt. Candidate EMU countries had to comply with the Maastricht criteria limits in order to qualify for EMU membership. For the fifth convergence criterion, the exchange rate, the Maastricht Treaty set a band of upper and lower limits of ± 2.25 percent, within which the exchange rates of candidate EMU countries could fluctuate.

The Maastricht convergence criteria, however, were not pertinent to real economic convergence. Measures or proxies of real economic convergence pertain to the level of economic development of countries; this is often measured with convergence in the real per capita income or GDP.[3] Due mainly to different levels of economic development and reasons related to the idiosyncratic nature of the various economies, business cycles among the EMU countries were not synchronized in the EA. In such a diverse group of economies of asynchronous business cycles, it became impossible for the European Central Bank (ECB) to successfully apply a common monetary policy. The most distinctive factor dividing the EA countries appears to be geographical, as the main differences lie between Northern and Southern groups.[4] Whereas the Northern EA countries were economically advanced, the Southern EA countries, initially, were lagging in terms of economic development. Several studies have shown that the periphery EA countries have been catching up with the Northern ones over the last five decades.[5] Such convergence was occurring until the crisis began spreading in Europe.[6]

The EU adopted several programs designed to cope with the crisis and fight the recession. In this chapter, the most important of these programs are critically analyzed and explanations are provided as to why none of these turned out to be sufficient to resolve the crisis. The ECB also launched a few monetary programs to safeguard the EA economies and particularly those countries that were most affected by the crisis. Such ECB programs are presented and analyzed in this chapter. The EU Commission, the ECB, and the IMF, referred to as the Troika, designed and granted bailout packages to assist the financially distressed EA economies.[7] All countries that received bailouts were required to accept and adhere to the terms of the bailout programs. The austerity programs were expected to restore fiscal stability in the EA countries and thus help them return to economic growth. Despite the original expectations, the austerity programs are now considered to be a major reason for the prolonging of the crisis.

A few major EU country leaders have consistently demonstrated a lack of determination to do what is necessary to resolve the crisis, protect the EMU, and maintain the euro as their permanent currency. This lack of determination among the EU country leaders to safeguard the EMU is discussed in this chapter and the chapters to follow as efforts are made to explain the reasons for their missing commitment to finding a permanent solution. Speculators quickly sensed the lack of commitment of the EU leaders to keep the EMU intact, thus repeatedly bet against the sovereign bonds of the EA periphery countries. Similarly, credit rating agencies (CRAs) revealed the weakness of the financially distressed economies by downgrading the government bonds of a few of these countries to junk status. Were the CRAs simple messengers of the bleak economic conditions or did they play a negative role in triggering an economic malaise in these EA countries, along with speculators?

EU country leaders and EU institutions, primarily the Commission, were continuously engaged in searching for programs and policies that would resolve the crisis. It is now evident that a solution to the crisis requires more integration and unity among member countries.[8] This was pointed out by many Europeans and non-Europeans who are interested in seeing a permanent solution and an exit from the crisis. A series of mistakes, gaffes, and half-baked proposed programs by European country leaders and the IMF have kept Europe away from its path to recovery. The most important proposed programs, rules and regulations, policies, and governing reforms are also discussed and critically analyzed in this chapter.

The EMU: an incomplete structure

One main reason that the recession in the EA countries has not subsided is because the EMU was introduced as an incomplete structure in January 1999. It took away both monetary and exchange rate policies and, most recently, their fiscal policies from countries after the signing of the Fiscal Compact Treaty. Nevertheless, the EMU gave nothing back to the member countries in return, leaving them defense-less against possible future economic recessions caused by asymmetric shocks. The "one-size-fits-all" interest rate monetary policy of the ECB proved to be incorrect to protect all of the EMU member countries' economies. During the recession caused by the crisis, an expansionary monetary policy would have been appropriate for the periphery EA countries to maintain low interest rates. Such a monetary policy would have boosted economic activity through increases in consumption and investment.[9] In contrast, for the Northern EA countries that experienced eco-nomic growth for most of the years of the crisis, a contractionary monetary policy of much higher interest rates would have been more appropriate. High interest rates would dampen economic activity and thus suppress inflation.[10]

The ECB was established in 1998 to apply monetary policy in the EMU and was assigned a single mandate to pursue price stability, i.e. to keep the inflation rate close to but below its target rate. This target inflation rate was set close to but below 2 percent. The ECB has no mandate on economic growth, which is at least an equally, if not more, important objective.[11] For this reason, the ECB's single man-date of the ECB is inferior to the US Federal Reserve's (Fed) dual mandate of pursuing both price stability and economic growth. Thus the Fed, the US Congress, and the President successfully applied monetary and fiscal policies that helped the US quickly recover from the subprime mortgage crisis. The US pulled rather quickly out of the recession and managed to keep inflation low despite its massive increase in the monetary base through exceptionally aggressive monetary policy. US economic growth, although relatively low, remained positive after the crisis. Such economic growth occurred even in the presence of a tight fiscal policy imposed by the Sequester in March 2012.[12]

Economic conditions were expected to deteriorate, nonetheless, in the US because in addition to contractionary fiscal policy, a tight monetary policy was also adopted. Chairman of the Fed, Ben Bernanke, announced that the Fed was ready to discontinue its quantitative easing policy at the end of 2013. Bernanke's announce-ment of phasing out the monthly purchases of securities, by reducing purchases by $10 billion each consecutive month, started in January 2014 and triggered an increase in interest rates. The announcement caused a major inflow of financial capital from several emerging economies suggesting that a global recession may be imminent. The possibility of a US recession increased after the US partisan fiscal disputes led to the shutting down of many federal government services on October 1, 2013 for 16 days. However, the US overcame its partisan disagreements and the two political parties came to an agreement on October 17, 2013. As a result, the US raised the public debt ceiling to allow the government to operate again. The US generated positive GDP growth in 2014 of 2.4 percent. In addition the US Congress passed a budget for 2015, the first in several years.

By adopting a single European common currency, EA countries lost their exchange rate policy. Prior to the adoption of the Euro, if EA countries were afflicted by a recession, they could devalue their national currencies or adopt policies leading to depreciation of their currency. In this way, countries could induce economic growth through improvement in the trade balance by increasing their exports and reducing imports. After joining the EMU, the foreign exchange rate policy is jointly applied by the ECB and the Economics and Finance Ministers Council (ECOFIN). The ECB and the ECOFIN always seek to find a middle-of-the-road solution aiming to serve all countries, but sometimes end up not serving any very well.

The Maastricht Treaty required all candidate EMU member countries to attain both price and fiscal stability before joining the EMU. Indeed, all candidate countries, by the end of the 1990s, prior to the launching of the EMU, attained price stability. However, not all countries were able to achieve fiscal stability. Belgium, Greece, and Italy joined the EMU although they exceeded the maximum allowed public debt to GDP ratio of 60 percent. The launching of the EMU was therefore based on the strong political will and determination of EU country leaders to unify Europe. As a result, they violated the self-imposed fiscal rules.

Economists who studied the required characteristics of candidate member countries to form an OCA expected the EMU to be at risk upon its exposure to the first asymmetric shock.[13] Not only did the candidate EMU member countries not constitute an OCA, but the EMU was ill-designed, as it lacked the necessary tools to cope with a recession caused by an asymmetric shock. This deficiency was first realized during the fall of 2008 when the US subprime mortgage crisis entered Europe and began affecting a few EA countries more than others. It was then revealed that the strong political will and commitment of the present EU country leaders to keep the EA countries unified and safeguard the EMU was indeed missing. It therefore depends on the political will and determination of the European country leaders to quickly relaunch the EMU correctly in a second round is, consequently, the present problem. Country leaders must reverse their stand and convince their constituencies regarding the importance of the protection of the EMU. This would unlock the gate to a path to the solution of the crisis. However, if such commitment is missing, EU leaders need to be pragmatic that countries would have to return to 1999, or to 1957, status and unwind the massive project of European integration, which would be exceptionally difficult if not impossible.

Early EU response to the European sovereign debt crisis

The Central and Eastern European (CEE) countries were the first to be affected at the outset of the European crisis. These countries suffered as a result of the international liquidity freeze following the Lehman Brothers bankruptcy in the fall of 2008. EU country leaders chose to assist the CEE countries immediately, through increases in the IMF member country contributions. Such an arrangement enabled the IMF to double its resources. The IMF implemented these bailout programs as it had done in the past for so many other countries. The CEE countries suffered from the accumulated large current account (CA) deficits and excessive private borrowing of their banks from abroad in foreign currency. As a result, their banks faced a currency mismatch problem, although their public finances were in excellent condition.[14] The first countries to receive aid from the IMF were Latvia, Ukraine, and Hungary.

The EU leaders, however, decided to help all other EA countries that required assistance through joint EU/IMF bailouts. Several critics, including high EU officials and EU country leaders disagreed with the idea of the IMF assisting European countries on the grounds that Europe is a rich continent and should be able to help itself without IMF assistance.[15] In addition, the same critics insisted that the EU has sufficient resources and expertise, which, if carefully and promptly employed, would have been able to quickly resolve the crisis on their own.

Another factor that deepened and prolonged the crisis is the fact that candidate bailout recipient countries postponed admitting that they were in need of a bailout for as long as possible.[16] Such resistance from these country leaders certainly worsened the situation as speculators exploited the weaknesses of countries' economies and profited through short selling at the expense of entire nations by betting against their government securities. For some time, many analysts have been convinced that Spain, for example, should have already received a full bailout; however, Spain's government was against the standard EU/IMF bailouts. The Spanish resistance to a bailout is attributed to the fact that the country wished to keep its sovereignty intact and avoid the extreme hardship of an austerity program and the humiliation which accompanies the bailouts. In addition, because Spain is the fourth largest EA economy, the required bailout would have been so large that it is unthinkable that the EU country leaders, considering the political constraints they face at home, would have been willing or able to have it approved by their national parliaments.

As the crisis began spreading in Europe, the EU Council approved and adopted the European Economic Recovery Plan (EERP) in 2008, a joint stimulus program between the EU countries and the EU Commission for a total of €200 billion. The plan promoted growth in the green economy and boosted demand by helping the most vulnerable people during the crisis.[17] This program, however, was very small in comparison to the two US fiscal stimuli plans that amounted to approximately $1.5 trillion to cope with the subprime mortgage crisis under Presidents Bush and Obama.

During the fall of 2008, the EU member countries adopted another, much larger program to fight the recession, which provided €3.5 trillion of aid to financial institutions. This funding was provided by the EU member states. These programs supported four different functions: bank deposit guarantees, bank recapitalizations, liquidity support, and treatment of impaired assets. State guarantees, however, constituted the largest component, comprising of €2.9 trillion. This was the program that permitted Ireland to guarantee all its bank deposits.[18]

The way out of the crisis

Once the crisis spread to Europe, the EU accepted the IMF method of bailing out countries on the condition that they abide with the imposed austerity programs. This approach was mainly supported by Germany, which persuaded EA members to accept that it was the best way to resolve the crisis. Germany, more than any other country, insisted on the participation of the IMF in the negotiations and implementation of the bailout programs. This decision of the German government was based on the fact that the IMF had many years of experience with the design and implementation of bailout programs. In addition, it would have been much easier for the IMF to impose the austerity programs that included privatization of state assets, pension cuts, and labor reforms that were painful for the vast majority of the populations of these countries. In this way, the IMF could bear most of the blame for the hardships sustained by the people. The austerity programs imposed on the periphery countries, however, have failed to restore fiscal stability and economic growth for a long time.

Restoring fiscal stability, i.e. reducing public deficits and public debts, was going to be achieved through drastic decreases in government spending and increases in taxes. Declines in prices and sharp reductions in both private and public wages were also imposed on all bailout recipient countries. Such an approach, known as internal devaluation, aims to improve the international competitiveness of countries and prepare for their return to economic growth through improvement in their CA and international investment position. This is exactly how Germany gained a competitive edge, when in 2003 labor reforms were launched by the Social Democratic Party (SPD), headed by Chancellor Gerhard Schröder.

For various reasons, the German success story should not be expected to be repeated in all of the countries that adopted the EU/IMF programs, especially when each of them shared the same trading partners. The austerity programs applied during the crisis are an application of contractionary fiscal policy during a recession. This policy recommendation is contrary to the mainstream macroeconomic countercyclical fiscal policy aiming to restore macroeconomic stability that recommends government deficits during recessions and surpluses during expansions. It is possible, however, that policies pursuing government deficit reductions through fiscal consolidation can sometimes be successful in increasing GDP and even reversing government deficits to surpluses.[19] This, nevertheless, is considered the exception rather than the rule and it rarely occurs.

Real effective exchange rates and real unit labor costs of ten EA countries

In order to analyze the recent developments regarding the international competitiveness of EA countries, we examine two economic indicators: the real effective exchange rates (REER) and the real unit labor costs for the ten EA countries. These economic indicators are helpful in evaluating countries' international competitiveness. Figure 4.1 depicts the REER and the real unit labor cost of ten EA countries.[20] The REER is one of the best indicators for international competitiveness because it captures the true price to foreign buyers (importers) of a country's products and services. In these graphs, some encouraging developments can be revealed. For example, Ireland's REER began drastically declining in 2008, and in 2014 was one of the lowest along with the Greek and Portuguese. Germany's REER has been declining since 1995, and it was the lowest of all for the period 2005–11. As for the rest of the EA countries' REERs, most have declined since 2008. Exceptions are the REERs of Belgium, Finland, and Italy. A country's recovery from the recession through a gradual reduction in the REER is a rather slow process and will only lead to recovery if the REER of the country declines faster than the REERs of its trading partners.

A major factor affecting the REER is the real per unit labor cost; this was sharply reduced by the austerity and the labor reforms imposed by the Troika. The real per unit labor costs of the ten EA countries are presented as indices for the period 1995–2015 below the REER time plots in Figure 4.1. It is evident from this figure that the real per unit labor costs of all ten EA countries began declining at the onset of the crisis. The Greek and Portuguese real per unit labor cost indicates a drastic reduction in the labor remuneration and are the lowest among the ten EA members. As for the unit labor costs of the rest of the EA countries, they have been mildly declining. The exception is the Irish real per unit labor cost which drastically declined up to 2012.

The evidence provided from the REERs and real per unit labor costs of the ten EA countries raises hope for the problem of trade imbalances in the EA that are clearly indicated by the CA and international investment position of the two EA groups shown in Figures 3.7 and 3.8. Such developments in the REER and the unit labor cost indicate that an eventual exit from the crisis is possible. However, the austerity measures adopted by the governments in their effort to achieve international competitiveness often reduced real wages for urban workers below subsistence levels. This led to social unrest, crime, homelessness, and poverty. In this respect a true humanitarian crisis spread from Lisbon to Athens.

Furthermore, a drastic reduction in wages and salaries decreased the aggregate demand in these economies, causing a further reduction in GDP and prices. This is something that was observed in the periphery EA countries that experienced recession, disinflation, and even deflation. Intra-EA rebalancing generally requires CA deficit countries' real wages to decrease and CA surplus countries' real wages to increase. More generally, rebalancing required an internal devaluation for the periphery and an internal revaluation for Northern EA members. This, however,

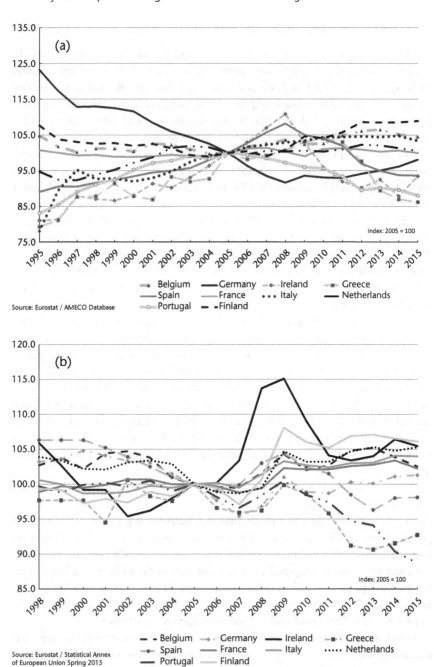

FIGURE 4.1 (a) Real effective exchange rate for Eurozone countries; (b) Real unit labor costs for Eurozone countries

was happening rather slowly, as Northern countries did not revalue fast enough to trigger growth in periphery EA countries.

There is no evidence for the redirection of trade within EA countries. For example, in 2011 Germany generated 70 percent of its trade surplus with non-EU countries. About 23 percent of Germany's trade surplus was with the EU, but non-EA, countries and only 7 percent with EA member countries. This information implies disintegration within the EA.[21] Redirection in German exports has possibly occurred due to the recessions that reduced national incomes in the EA periphery countries, which consequently reduced imports from Germany. In response, Germany expanded exports to non-EU countries to make up for the intra-EA trade slack. Such evidence suggests that the EMU is experiencing disintegration.

The euro: an overvalued currency

Another reason that may have delayed the EA recovery was its overvalued currency. The euro was first introduced in January 1999 as a floating currency in relation to the US dollar and a few major world floating currencies. In Figure 4.2, the dollar per euro exchange rate is presented. The initial exchange rate vis-à-vis the dollar was $1.179. In its first ten months, the euro depreciated against the dollar until October 26, 2000, when it reached its minimum of $0.8252. Since then, it mildly oscillated for almost two years until March 2002. Thereafter, it began a rollercoaster of rapid appreciation against the

FIGURE 4.2 US dollars per euro exchange rate

US dollar until July 15, 2008, when it reached its maximum of about $1.60. After that, it oscillated again for roughly six years around the rate of $1.35 per euro. Since then, the euro has depreciated drastically to reach approximately $1.12 per euro in June 2015.

Two major factors may have played a role in the 2014–15 depreciation of the euro. First is the continuous missing of the target inflation rate of 2 percent by the ECB that gave rise to the fear of possible deflation. Such fears caused the ECB to announce a new monetary policy, quantitative easing (QE), which was introduced March 2015. The other reason for the euro's depreciation is the reemergence of the Eurocrisis, which is centered around an agreement between Greece and the Troika (Institutions) to resolve the Greek public debt problem.

Several studies have shown that the euro was overvalued in relation to the US dollar as well as a few other major world currencies when it was first introduced in 1999. Afterwards, it remained overvalued during 2008 to 2014. Economists suggested long ago that a weak euro would improve the trade balance for the entire EA, especially the over-indebted periphery countries. One way to achieve this objective was for the ECB to apply a more expansionary monetary policy by reducing its key policy interest rate employed for the main refinancing operations, the Repurchase Agreement (REPO) rate. This decision was made by the ECB on May 2, 2013, when it reduced the REPO rate by 25 basis points (0.25 of 1 percent) and again in November 2013 by another 25 basis points. Beginning in January 2008, the REPO rate was always higher than the corresponding US monetary policy key interest rate, the federal funds rate. Figure 4.3 shows the REPO rate and the federal

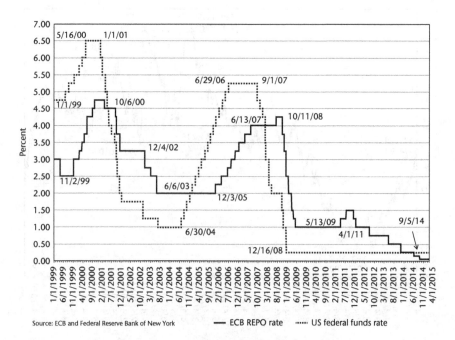

Source: ECB and Federal Reserve Bank of New York

FIGURE 4.3 ECB REPO rate vs. US federal funds rate

funds rate, the two monetary policy instruments of the ECB and the Fed, respectively, since January 1999 when the EMU was established.

A few empirical studies have found that the most important variable affecting the euro-dollar exchange rate was the long-term interest rate.[22] On September 10, 2014, the ECB reduced its REPO rate to an all-time low of 0.05 of 1 percent. Furthermore, because inflation, in the beginning of 2015, was not an issue in the EA, the ECB decided to apply a more expansionary monetary policy by employing an unorthodox monetary policy. Thus, in March, 2015, the ECB launched QE to increase liquidity in the EA.[23]This was a plausible decision considering the fact that the central banks of the US, Japan, and the UK had all adopted quantitative easing to revamp their economies long before the ECB.

Several EA countries experienced improvement in their trade balances due to the depreciation of the euro starting at the onset of the US subprime mortgage crisis. These unexpected benefits arose as investors were seeking a safe haven in the world's most important currency, the dollar. Investors behaved in this way despite the fact that the subprime mortgage crisis developed in the US. The ECB and the ECOFIN are capable of deliberately engineering further depreciation of the euro. Such a policy could improve all EA member countries' trade balances and would induce economic growth. As far back as 2010, a recommendation was made that the euro-dollar exchange rate shall be driven to parity, implying a substantial depreciation of the euro.[24]

ECB monetary policy to cope with the crisis

Introduction

The reduction, on November 13, 2013, of the REPO rate to 0.25 of 1 percent was a move in the correct direction. This should have happened much earlier considering that the US key monetary policy interest rate, the federal funds rate, since January 2009 stood in the range of 0–0.25 percent. In addition to the US Fed, the Bank of England and the Bank of Japan have all employed QE to pursue a more expansionary monetary policy. It was, therefore, plausible for the ECB to also adopt QE as it was not feasible to exert pressure onto the other three major central banks to refrain from applying QE.[25]

There are limits, however, to how much the ECB could accomplish through a reduction of the REPO rate. For example, Jörg Asmussen, the German member of the ECB executive board, expressed skepticism that the reduction of the REPO in May 2013, by 25 basis points, would have much impact on the Southern European businesses that experienced high borrowing costs.[26] The ECB, in early May 2013, announced that it would undertake additional measures to boost the EA economy. Such measures were going to particularly help the Southern European banks, which would have been able to borrow unlimited amounts from the ECB until at least the middle of 2014.[27] If banks could borrow at a low cost from the ECB, they would have been able to extend loans to small and medium-sized enterprises (SME) in Southern Europe. This would have restored the competitive position of the Southern businesses in relation to their Northern counterparts. President Mario Draghi announced that the ECB intends to correct the interest rate disparity by restoring credit conditions so interest rates are no higher for the Southern SMEs than they are in the Northern SMEs.

The ECB was established one year prior to the launch of the euro in 1998 to conduct monetary policy in the EMU. The German government then insisted and prevailed that the ECB would be located in Frankfurt, only a few miles away from the German central bank, the Bundesbank. Due to the German influence, the ECB was designed almost as a replica of the Bundesbank. Such an arrangement probably convinced the Germans to give up their beloved deutschmark (DM) for an untested currency, the euro. The national central banks of the EA countries together with the ECB constitute the Eurosystem, which is responsible for the conduct of monetary policy in the EMU. The national central banks, nonetheless, have no power of their own so they can be thought of as branches of the ECB. The EA national central banks, nonetheless, own the ECB's capital.

The Eurosystem applies monetary policy by employing open market operations as it buys and sells securities to and from the financial institutions that are also known as counterparties. In this way, it provides liquidity for one week via its main refinancing operations (MROs). The ECB sets its key policy interest rate, the REPO, for the repurchase agreements for these securities. The Euro-system also provides additional long-term liquidity with maturity of 1, 3, 6, 12, and 36 months through its long-term refinancing operations (LTROs). The national central banks carry out all necessary financial transactions as they are familiar with their own national financial markets. The national central banks, which own the ECB capital, are not necessarily always concerned with stability in the EMU as they perceive their capital share as their nation's investment instead of as the means for the ECB to apply monetary policy.[28]

In September 2008, the ECB launched an expansionary monetary policy through a sequence of reductions in the REPO rate that continued into 2014.[29] During this period, however, the REPO rate always exceeded the US federal funds rate until November 2013, when the ECB decreased its REPO to 0.25 of 1 percent; the two interest rates then coincided. This indicates that the Fed applied a more aggressive, expansionary monetary policy than the ECB, even during the period that the US was not in the recession. As the recession deepened in the EA, the ECB began an unorthodox policy of providing unlimited massive credit to financial institutions while it lowered the quality rating of securities that it was accepting as collateral. Figure 4.3 portrays the REPO rate and the federal funds rate starting in January 1999 when the euro was introduced.

The Securities Markets Programme

On May 12, 2010, the ECB began purchasing sovereign and private bonds in the secondary market. The purpose of this policy was to prop up the sovereign debt market of the highly indebted EA countries such as Greece, Ireland, Portugal, and possibly Italy and Spain. The demand for government securities (national debt) of these countries during the crisis had practically vanished, and became almost non-existent during the crisis. The new policy was criticized by two prominent German monetary officials, Alex Weber and Jürgen Stark, the two members of the ECB's Governing Council during that period. Such purchases of the highly indebted countries' government securities were criticized and portrayed as a first endeavor by the ECB to monetize national debt in the EA, which is explicitly prohibited by the EMU founding treaties.[30]

The ECB purchases of government bonds from highly indebted EA countries were expected to have favorable effects on the interest rates of these countries and eventually allow them to gain access to markets so they would have been able to borrow at a lower cost. A downside of this policy, according to the ECB critics, was a higher expected inflation rate. It was feared that such a monetary policy could also plant the seeds of another upcoming financial crisis. With the "Securities Markets Programme," as this policy became known, the ECB announced that it was purchasing national government bonds aiming to correct market irregularities and that it had no plans or intention to exercise quantitative easing similar to that adopted by the UK, the US, and Japan. The ECB was purchasing these securities in the secondary market under the condition that these interventions would be sterilized, i.e. the ECB would reduce the money supply by an amount equal to that of the purchased securities by intervening and using other methods. Therefore the ECB sterilization would leave the money supply unchanged. The ECB's transactions, however, regarding purchases of national bonds were opaque and thus the accurate amounts and the issuing countries of these securities were not known.

A comparison between the EA and the US in reference to the application of monetary policy is appropriate, as the two economies are almost of equal magnitude. In response to the subprime mortgage crisis of 2007–9, the Fed increased its monetary base by $3.2 trillion through purchases of various private and public securities.[31] The Fed accomplished this by employing the unorthodox monetary policy of quantitative easing through buying all kinds of private and public securities. In comparing the purchases of government securities by the ECB to the Fed's purchases, the amount of ECB government securities purchased is small, estimated to be €212 billion as of June 4, 2012. The ECB, as part of the Securities Markets Programme, purchased government bonds from Greece, Ireland, Portugal, Italy, and Spain.[32] Strong criticism of this policy, however, is almost certain to have influenced the central bank to slow down and even abandon such purchases in the future.

The hesitancy of the EU country leaders to take the necessary measures to resolve the crisis has put pressure on the ECB to intervene, thus taking the risk of becoming a "bad bank" by inflating the EA economy. Among many critics of the EU leaders was the former ECB president Jean-Claude Trichet, who made it well known that it was the responsibility of the EU leaders to resolve the crisis. Although the EU country leaders had the means to restore economic stability, they were lacking the will or the determination to do so. This frustrated Trichet, who repeatedly expressed his anger publicly against EU country leaders for not doing enough to resolve the crisis.[33] Such indetermination of the EU country leaders possibly stems from the fact that they were not convinced that their voters would support such programs to save the EA countries and the euro, or because they had hardly prepared their countries' electorate for this type of scenario.

Long-term refinancing operations

On November 1, 2011, Mario Draghi was appointed president of the ECB. President Draghi, as an MIT-trained economist with extensive experience in monetary policy as president of the Central Bank of Italy, raised great hopes for a fast recovery from the financial crisis. The news media, prior to President Draghi's appointment, were proclaiming that the ECB with President Draghi would provide the firepower of a "big bazooka" to save the euro.

The new ECB president, however, did not deliver a quick solution as some had expected by employing the unused firepower of the ECB to reverse the crisis. However, on his first day on the job, on November 1, 2011, the ECB reduced the key monetary instrument, the REPO rate, by 25 basis points (0.25 percent). This was perceived as a signal that new initiatives from the ECB should be expected. Indeed, in December 2011, the ECB Governing Council decided to extend liquidity to financial institutions through its long-term refinancing operations (LTROs) in a 36-month maturity program. As a result, on December 22, 2011, approximately €489 billion were allotted to the EA financial institutions through the LTROs. Similarly, on March 1, 2012, the ECB allotted about €529 billion also through LTROs. Thus both allotments amounted to over one trillion (€1.018), offered at the low interest rate of 1 percent. Consequently, in a period of a little over three months, the ECB increased liquidity which came as a temporary relief, particularly to the financially distressed countries. The program was considered successful because it provided the necessary liquidity to the banks at a very low cost. The program, nonetheless, did not provide much impetus to the real economy because the banks remained hesitant to lend to businesses and to consumers.

Outright monetary transactions

ECB President Draghi announced on July 26, 2012 that he would do "whatever it takes to preserve the Euro."[34] The new "Outright Monetary Transactions" (OMT) program presented by President Draghi would empower the ECB to buy unlimited amounts of short-term government bonds of 1–3 years maturity. These securities were to be purchased by the ECB provided that the countries abide by strict conditionality involving the participation of the IMF as well as the two EU funds: the European Financial Stability Facility (EFSF) and the European Stability Mechanism (ESM). The program was to be terminated if a country did not comply with the new conditionality. The OMT program received support from 22 out of the 23 ECB

Governing Council members, with the exception of the President of the Bundesbank, Jens Weidmann.[35]

The announcement of the program by President Draghi had positive effects on investors, as stock prices around the world began rising and Spanish and Italian government bond interest rates began declining. The OMT program of President Draghi was a step in the right direction, provided it was going to be supported by EU country leaders. Nevertheless, if a country that was willing to sell its bonds to the ECB did not comply with strict requirements, the program could not be employed. As of June 2015, the ECB has not bought any country's government bonds. However, EMU members such as Spain and Italy have already indirectly gained from the OMT program as their interest rates declined. This came about only as a result of the announcement of the program which helped form favorable expectations among investors. As it turns out the President of the ECB along with the Governing Council saved the euro, or at least prevented another intensification of the Eurocrisis with a simple announcement regarding the OMT program. The ECB received much criticism, although the program should not constitute a violation of the treaties because OMT requires full sterilization.[36] Therefore OMT could not be considered a program that creates inflation by printing money to bail out countries.

Two European rescue funds

The European Financial Stability Facility

The EU created two rescue funds to stand as firewalls and prevent the financial crisis from spreading. The first fund, the European Financial Stability Facility (EFSF), was created as a special purpose vehicle (SPV) chartered in the city of Luxembourg.[37] The EFSF was established as a rescue fund for the period 2010–13. Similar to the SPV investment funds created by banks to protect their assets, the EFSF fund protects EA countries by not holding them responsible to bondholders beyond the maximum amount of capital held by the EFSF. The EFSF received no capital contributions from the EA countries. The total amount of the EFSF capital was €440 billion, all of which was borrowed in the market through the issuance of bonds. It has been used to lend money to Portugal and Ireland. The EFSF was complemented with other programs to preserve financial stability in the EU.

Thus the EFSF was joined with another €60 billion from the European Financial Stabilization Mechanism (EFSM). The funding of the EFSM was borrowed by the EU Commission through the issuance of bonds that are guaranteed by the EU budget. On June 24, 2011, the EA member states decided to increase the guarantee commitment to the EFSF to €780 billion. This set the lending capacity of the EFSF to €440 billion; the remainder of the amount is kept in a reserve account so the EFSF receives the highest credit ratings by the CRAs. During the same time, the IMF created another fund for €250 billion for the same purpose of safeguarding financial stability in Europe. The three funds together therefore amounted to €750 billion.[38]

The European Stability Mechanism

On June 24, 2011, the European Council established a permanent crisis resolution mechanism, named the European Stability Mechanism (ESM). The ESM is similar to the EFSF, as it raises funding for the purpose of rescuing countries at risk during this and other future financial crises. The ESM has a total subscribed capital of €700 billion, €80 billion of which was paid by the EA members, phased in starting July 12, 2012. The lending capacity of the ESM is €500 billion. The ESM has already issued bonds that are backed by the EA members and two EU countries, Sweden and Poland, which, although not EMU members, have still volunteered to contribute to the fund. The EU Heads of Governments and States agreed that the amount still left with the EFSF was to join with the ESM; thus the two funds have created a joint firewall to protect the EA countries from the present and future crises.

The permanent ESM fund provides bailouts to applicant EA countries that abide by the IMF conditionality and may or may not include private sector involvement (PSI) programs. A PSI program is an agreement between a debtor country and its private bond owners who volunteer to accept a loss in their bond holdings, popularly known as a haircut. The ESM also includes standardized Collective Action Clauses (CACs).[39] The decision on whether or not each new rescue program, provided by the ESM to distressed economies, will include a PSI program will be made on a case-by-case basis. This means that a country that cannot pay its public debt and requires official assistance by the EU/IMF is likely to be required by the Troika to request the bond owners of its public debt to take a loss, i.e. accept a haircut.

The PSI program that was imposed only on Greece was an agreement between the Greek government and the private owners of Greek bonds to restructure the Greek public debt. Restructuring public debt in Greece involved the replacement of existing bonds with longer maturity bonds having lower interest rates, and a reduction (haircut) in the total Greek privately held nominal debt by 52.5 percent. The PSI is a voluntary program and will not work if a substantial group of bondholders decides to hold out and not participate. In such a case, it is possible that a credit event can occur that amounts to a disorderly default of the country.[40]

Bailout programs

Greece, Ireland, and Portugal were the first three countries to be affected the most by the crisis. All three EA members, as a result, were offered bailouts, but all three refused to accept them for a long time, as they were hoping to totally avoid them. Most analysts strongly supported the view that these three EA countries would have been better off if they had accepted the bailouts much earlier. The EU's insistence that the three countries had to accept the bailouts was based on the fact that once a financially distressed country accepts a bailout it protects itself from bankruptcy and relieves the ECB from having to provide additional liquidity to the country's banks. In this way, the ECB does not risk its reputation of being the guardian of price stability in the EMU.

TABLE 4.1 Bailout terms for Greece, Portugal, and Ireland (euros)[a]

Bailout	Greece: first bailout	Greece: second bailout	Ireland	Portugal
Amount	€110 bn	€130 bn	€85 bn	€78 bn
Interest	5.2%	Variable	5.8%	5.7%
Lenders and amounts	EU countries: €80 bn IMF: €30 bn	EFSF: €102 bn IMF: €28 bn	Ireland: €17.5 bn ESM: €22.5 bn EFSF: €22.5 bn IMF: €22.5 bn	ESM: €26 bn EFSF: €26 bn IMF: €26 bn
Maturity	3 years	IMF: 10 years EU: varies	7.5 years Renegotiated extension (4/12/13) 7 years	7.5 years Renegotiated extension (4/12/13) 7 years
Date funds available	May 19, 2010	2012–14	November 28, 2010	May 16, 2011

a EFSF contributed €17.7 bn for Ireland. The rest were bilateral loans: €3.8 bn from the UK, €0.4 bn from Denmark and €0.6 bn from Sweden.

Table 4.1 presents the amounts of the bailouts and the terms of the loans in chronological order that the bailouts were received, along with the sources of financing and interest rates. The first country to receive a bailout was Greece. The approved loan, after a long period of negotiations, was for the unprecedentedly large amount of €110 billion for a three-year repayment period at an interest rate of 5.2 percent. The bailout loan was offered to Greece jointly by the EU member states and the IMF. The bailouts to Ireland and Portugal were offered jointly by the EFSF, ESM, and the IMF. Greece, for example, was supposed receive €80 billion from the European Union member states and €30 billion from the IMF.[41]

Along with the IMF bailouts came the usual conditionality that the IMF imposes on bailout recipient countries; conditionality refers to the austerity programs that each bailout recipient country has to adopt to restore macroeconomic stability by reducing its public debt to GDP ratio. One would tend to think that the two Southern EA countries and Ireland, after they received such large bailouts, should be rapidly moving on their way to recovery. The reality, however, is that the periphery countries' economies did not quickly overcome the crisis and the recession and, as a result, have not reduced their excessive public debt.

For Greece, the situation deteriorated so much that EU officials and country leaders agreed that a second rescue bailout package was necessary to prevent Greece falling into a disorderly default. The irony is that many European leaders and analysts knew all along that the Greek bailout package, with the terms imposed on Greece, could not be anything more than temporary relief thus the program had to be renegotiated if Greek debt was to become sustainable.[42] Ireland was scheduled to be the first country to move out of the bailout program before the end of 2013. Ireland's ten-year government bond interest rate decreased to approximately 3.5 percent by

January 2014. Furthermore, Ireland has built its cash reserves to over €20 billion since it started borrowing from the international money markets in 2012. Thus Ireland successfully pulled out of the bailout program without an auxiliary credit line at the end of 2013. Greece had a more difficult time coping with the IMF conditionality than any other country.

In October 2011 at the Brussels Summit the European Council decided that Greece would receive a second rescue package of €130 billion. This new program would involve the participation of the private bond owners in the restructuring of the Greek public debt. This meant that bondholders of the Greek debt had to receive a haircut. By combining the two bailouts, the European Council approved a total of €172 billion for Greece. This amount is the result of €130 billion from the second bailout and the amount of the already dispersed funds from the first bailout. Journalists often incorrectly report that the Greek total bailout is €240 billion, i.e. the sum of the first and second bailouts. The PSI program that was part of the second bailout was strongly supported by the EU and the IMF, which convinced the vast majority of the Greek bondholders to participate in the program.[43] The small share of bondholders who did not sign the PSI agreement triggered a credit event, i.e. bankruptcy of the country, for a very short time. The Greek government, however, paid most of these bondholders. A declaration of a credit event triggers payments to holders of the Credit Default Swaps (CDSs). Indeed this happened and holders of Greek CDSs made large profits as they cashed in their CDSs after the Greek default. Alas, the Greek fiscal drama is not over yet as Christine Lagarde, the IMF Chief, warned that Greece will need an additional bailout to stabilize its debt. After much bickering and disagreements, it seems that most EU leaders and officials were convinced that Greece will require an additional bailout in 2015, although the new Greek government insists it does not want another such bailout.[44]

Spain is the fourth country to receive a bailout (see Table 4.2) to rescue its banks that had lent excessively during its property (real estate) boom period. Spain was approved for a relatively small amount of €100 billion to recapitalize the banking sector. In addition Spain avoided receiving a fully-fledged bailout accompanied by

TABLE 4.2 Bailout programs for Spain and Cyprus

Bailout	Spain	Cyprus
Amount	€100 bn	€10 bn
Interest	Variable	2.5%
Lenders and amounts	EU Commission	EU Commission
	ESM	ECB
	IMF	IMF
Maturity	15 years	10 years
Already used funds	€41 bn	€9 bn
Date funds available	December 11, 2012	May 2013

the IMF conditionality and the stigma that goes with the IMF austerity programs. Spain, which has received only €41 billion from the €100 billion that was approved, has exited the bailout program. The exit was agreed by the EA finance ministers in November 2013.

The last country to receive a bailout was the Republic of Cyprus (see Table 4.2), which received €10 billion after its two major banks became insolvent. Cyprus was forced to impose a tax (haircut) on large depositors on accounts over €100,000. This was a very different rescue package to the bailouts received by the previous three EA countries. The Cyprus case created a heated debate because it introduced a precedent and caused much uncertainty among all bank depositors in many countries around the world about the security of their bank deposits. Such a negative climate about bank deposit safety was created because the Cyprus bailout program received the official approval of the EU, the IMF, and ECB following the strong insistence of the German Christian Democratic Party (CDU) which wanted to convince voters and small political parties that the German government was imposing tough conditions on the bailout recipient countries. Strong opposition to these unprecedented conditions by the government of Cyprus was of no avail. A few Northern EU country leaders were initially against bailing out the Cypriot banks because there was a great suspicion that large amounts of deposits were of a questionable nature, such was the case for the suspected money laundering by Russian oligarchs.

Lack of commitment from the EA country leaders

The EU has experienced many crises in the past, but EU leaders have always worked out solutions that served the common objective, which was European unity and harmonious development.[45] This crisis, however, is different because for the first time markets have repeatedly tested the determination and commitment of the European country leaders to safeguard the EU and EMU. Speculators during the Eurocrisis quickly sensed that EU leaders were not totally committed to do what it takes to defend the common European currency and the EMU. Every program they adopted to resolve the crisis was insufficient to restore the leaders' lost credibility and reestablish stability in the EU and the EA.

Trade imbalances caused high indebtedness in the Southern EU countries and Ireland,[46] which resulted in high interest rates, but the crisis could still have been prevented. The crisis would have been avoided if the EU leaders had demonstrated that they were committed to preserving the EMU. It is unlikely that the crisis would have occurred if all countries had complied with the Stability and Growth Pact (SGP) and refrained from borrowing during expansionary periods. The roots of the crisis, therefore, are mainly found in the lack of fiscal discipline prior to the crisis and a lack of commitment among the EU country leaders and their constituency to pursue the vision of the founding fathers of the EU. More European integration is now necessary for an exit from the crisis; however, EU country leaders will have the last word on this decision. Because of the crisis, the EU is increasingly becoming less popular, and many EU citizens and politicians demanding less European integration. If such views prevail, the EMU will implode.

Several countries have violated the EMU fiscal rules prior to the European sovereign debt crisis; nonetheless, when small countries violated the SGP, they were instructed by the EU Commission to comply with the Maastricht fiscal criteria. Contrary to this, when large countries such as Germany, France, and Italy broke the fiscal rules, they convinced the other EA members and the Commission to relax the SGP fiscal requirements. A very important reason that the crisis is not resolved yet is the fact that EA countries did not quickly adopt the necessary policies and required governance reforms that would have convinced markets that the euro was their permanent currency. The Northern EA countries and particularly Germany blocked or postponed practically every proposed program that they perceived would create inflation, raise the interest rate for Germany, or result in a burden to its taxpayers. All of this happened despite the fact that Germany received more benefits than any other country in the EU, since Germany has been the largest exporting country and its growth is heavily dependent on exports to EU countries.

The two rescue funds, the EFSF and ESM, were established to create a firewall to prevent financial crises from spreading. However, both funds were given limited uses to prevent the crisis. The requirement of the PSI program on Greece deepened the recession and is responsible for the contagion to the other EA countries. Rational investors have been unwilling to return to a country that had officially accepted a haircut, regardless of whether the haircut had received the approval and the encouragement of the EU and the IMF. This decision sank Greece into a deep and long recession which quickly spread to other EA countries.

Germany convinced 25 out of the 27 EU countries[47] to agree on a fiscal compact that would assure countries pursue fiscal discipline and maintain a structured balanced budget. Countries that violate the fiscal treaty would be penalized by the EU Commission and the Court of Justice.[48] The IMF/EU bailout programs, by imposing austerity, caused recession in and humiliation of the people of the recipient countries. Despite the large amounts of the bailout programs, the terms of the bailouts were very harsh and recessionary to the extent that public debt became unsustainable, as it violated a simple rule of thumb for public debt sustainability. Such a rule states that when the implicit interest rate on the debt is higher than the rate of growth of an economy, the public debt is unsustainable.[49] Furthermore, if the EU member countries' leaders had demonstrated more solidarity at the onset of the crisis, then they would have kept a lid on the pot and the crisis would have never exploded. Thus billions, if not trillions, of euros would have been saved, as the crisis that has caused misery for millions of people would have been avoided.

Policy recommendations and governance reforms

The European sovereign debt crisis has already had devastating effects on the periphery EA countries. Since the summer of 2012, the European crisis lost some of its intensity, as the risk of the EMU breakup subsided. The recession, however, is far from over and is spreading to several European countries. Many fear that the European crisis could turn into a major world recession.[50] The way out of the crisis has been proven difficult by relying on strict austerity programs by suppressing the compensation and pensions of a country's employees and at the expense of the employees of their trading partner countries. A better way for Europe to overcome the crisis is if it stands united.

This can be attained through further integration and less self-centered nationalistic policies. To achieve this objective would be difficult because a climate of distrust has developed during the crisis. More European integration is a meaningful and plausible solution, as the benefits would be extended to all countries and not only to those that are in financial distress.[51] With the ongoing international economic and financial integration, no country can afford to be an island or a fortress. More integration and solidarity will lead to stability and growth which would benefit all EMU member countries.

It is important that the new EMU governance reforms and the new EMU rules address and resolve the problem of moral hazard. European integration cannot be achieved at the expense of the taxpayers of a few countries because such an arrangement is both unfair and unsustainable.[52] This means that financially distressed countries cannot expect permanent transfers of funds from the taxpayers of other countries. However, until now, Northern EA countries were not spending large amounts helping financially distressed countries, despite the fact that many citizens of these countries incorrectly believe otherwise. As was seen in this chapter, the vast majority of the funding for bailout purposes was borrowed in the capital markets and was guaranteed by all EA countries. If the EMU stabilizes, the bailout recipient countries would recover and become able to repay their debts.

There are, however, ways for countries to help each other without developing a dependency culture. This means that the new governance reforms and financial rules and regulations must address and resolve the moral hazard problem. Within the reformed EMU, it should not be possible for member countries to pursue narrowly defined national interests. Above all, European countries and citizens must set the common good as their highest priority. Such a common good is the strengthening of European unity. To attain further European integration, adoption of efficient and fair policies and regulatory reforms are required to achieve balanced economic growth and harmonization in the standards of living of all the European peoples, regardless of which country they live in. These objectives were set in the founding treaties of the EU.[53]

The question arises of how the Europeans can achieve such an ideal and noble objective. One may begin by recognizing the accomplishments of more than 60 years of integration. Europe was rapidly transformed from a vastly devastated area of fearful people who distrusted each other to a civilized and culturally rich continent of democratic and peaceful countries, thanks to the founding treaties that unified most of Europe. More gratitude belongs to the founding fathers of the EU who dared to dream for a peaceful and prosperous European continent. These Europeans dedicated their lives to achieving the dream of European unification. They created a Europe that includes under the same umbrella yesterday's mortal enemies. Such great visionaries, nowadays, have obviously been eclipsed, but their idealism and vision are more necessary now than ever to help complete the grand European project. Therefore country leaders and EU officials must draw from the vision of the founding fathers to continue on their path to restore trust and unity among the European peoples and countries; this vision is what is presently missing. The vision is missing in Germany, which ought to have a surplus of it considering the great generosity of the Allies at the end of World War II and their decision in 1989 to allow its reunification.

What can be done to achieve these goals? The ideal approach for the completion of the EMU is for the EU countries, which are not yet members, to eventually join.[54] Furthermore, European countries which are not members of the EU must also join the Union before they become members of the EMU.[55] Neither of these two recommendations can be achieved successfully, unless the EMU is first relaunched and finalized as a complete structure capable of withstanding all kinds of storms. To accomplish this, EA countries must first break the vicious cycle of over-indebted governments and their financially unsound and failing banks. Over-indebted governments and their ailing banks are so interdependent that the sovereign debt crisis is also a banking crisis. As a consequence, the EMU members must establish a complete banking union. Indeed, the EA country leaders have already begun negotiating the launch of the banking union to complement the EMU; nevertheless, the launching of the banking union has been slow.

According to most analysts, a complete banking union should include three major components:

1. A single European bank supervisor to introduce and enforce common banking regulations, first on the major European banks and eventually on all banks.
2. A European bank resolution authority to be responsible for liquidating failing banks and to determine who will pay to restore financial stability by recapital-izing the ailing banks that would be kept in operation. This is a major issue that has divided the EU policymakers and has left the EU's reputation damaged. This happened because of the way the EU handled the Cyprus crisis through imposing a haircut on large bank depositors as a condition to approve the €10 billion bailout. A new system must be sought and accepted and must be both efficient and equitable to all parties concerned.
3. A European insurance deposit agency to prevent bank panics and failures and promote banking stability. The deposit insurance corporation will require a joint European fund that will guarantee all bank depositors up to a certain maximum amount. The US, for example, introduced the FDIC immediately after the Great Depression with the Glass-Steagall Act of 1933.

All three proposed components of the banking union can be under the umbrella of the ECB, as it appears to be the most appropriate institution to undertake these new functions. The ECB, furthermore, has to be delegated authority to apply a fully independent monetary policy. Thus the ECB must be allowed to buy member countries' sovereign bonds to assist financially distressed countries. Mutualization of the public debt is also necessary. The EU and the EMU countries must jointly guarantee all new public debt that will become a safe investment. Jointly issued eurobonds will make it possible for EA countries to raise as much capital as is necessary at very low rates. Low interest rates will relieve countries that were excluded from the markets and lead them out of the crisis. A permanent solution of the present and future European sovereign debt crises would be found only when the EMU is transformed into a complete fiscal and banking union. This implies that the ECB has to be granted full independence to freely design and exercise monetary policy in the EA and to eventually become the single supervisor of all EMU countries' banks.

Equally important to the independence of the ECB is the establishment of the fiscal union governed by its own fiscal EU authority. The fiscal authority can be established within the EU Commission. Such a fiscal union will introduce fundamental and radical structural changes to allow the EMU countries to embark on a new era of fiscal stability and economic growth. The fiscal authority must be delegated independence to apply discretionary fiscal policy in the EMU. Such a major shift will also solve once and forever the moral hazard problem. The fiscal union would not, however, be bound by rigid fiscal rules such as balancing the annual budgets or the SGP requirements on public debt and public deficits. The existing Fiscal Compact Treaty will have to be radically amended or completely relaunched to emphasize in addition to fiscal responsibility also flexibility and adoption of discretionary fiscal policy. The new EU Commission with enhanced powers as the main European fiscal authority must cooperate with the ECB and the EMU member governments to promote economic growth, high employment, and monetary and fiscal stability.

Furthermore, The EU Commission as the supreme European fiscal authority must be delegated the powers to request both increases in revenue and spending to enhance its fiscal power. Such changes must be approved by the European and national parliaments. Fiscal policies are now mainly conducted by the national governments, which have been proven unable to coordinate policies and protect the EMU. The proposed structural changes would have to be democratically supported by the EMU member countries' voters and expressed through their representatives if they are given a chance to succeed. This implies that many people in the new high-level positions of the new fiscal authority and the ECB must be directly elected by the European people. In this way, the new institutions and the individuals filling the positions will establish credibility and legitimacy.

The European Parliament would have to be bestowed with vested authority to exercise oversight and control of the new institutions and also to monitor their actions. In this way, a stronger system of checks and balances would be created that will promote a fair and equitable system among European people and EU member states. Authority in the new Economic, Monetary, and Fiscal Union (EMFU) will be based on democratic principles, as the national parliaments and European

Parliament would both elect its members and oversee its operations. Eventually, if such proposed changes do take place, they must become part of the founding treaties, which may require a long time to be agreed upon and signed. Nonetheless, in the short-run, close cooperation among the EU and EA countries and the EU authorities can reverse the trend towards stability much earlier, before existing treaties are revised or new treaties are signed.

Concluding comments

The European sovereign debt crisis caused the most severe recession ever experienced by the EMU countries. It lasted several years and had devastating and lasting effects on several countries, particularly the Southern EA member countries, Ireland and Cyprus.

A question naturally arises as to why the European crisis endured for such a long time. To answer this question, one must focus on the history and the decision-making process of the EU and the EMU. The EMU was established as an incomplete structure when eleven EU countries in 1999 adopted the single European currency, the euro, and gave up their monetary and exchange rate policies. More recently, with the adoption of the fiscal compact treaty, the EU countries have also surrendered their fiscal policies. The common monetary policy applied by the ECB during the crisis in the presence of an asymmetric shock proved incapable of helping all EMU countries. The founding treaties of the EMU have prohibited the ECB from buying the sovereign bonds of financially distressed countries therefore the ECB cannot help those EA countries at risk. In addition, the EU, according to the Treaty of Lisbon, has a very small budget of about one percent of the EU GDP; consequently, the EU cannot apply an effective discretionary fiscal policy to help financially distressed EU/EA countries.

During the crisis, the EU decided instead to assist highly indebted countries with bailout programs jointly offered with the IMF. Thus far, five EA countries have been rescued with EU/IMF packages. Bailout recipient countries had to agree to abide within the imposed austerity conditions of the programs in order to qualify for the bailouts. The austerity programs were designed to restore financial stability to the bailout recipient countries. However, the bailouts have failed to achieve their objectives in a reasonable time, and as a result the recession has been prolonged in several EA member countries for over several years.

To finance the bailout programs, the EU established two funds: the EFSF and the ESM. The two funds borrowed most of their capital from the market by issuing bonds. Both funds were authorized limited use of their resources to help countries at risk. There exists some evidence provided by the REERs and the real unit labor costs that the EA countries' international competitiveness is improving; this is an encouraging signal especially for the bailout recipient countries. Indeed four of the five bailout countries generated a positive real rate of growth in 2014.

The European sovereign debt crisis has not been resolved yet because EU country leaders failed to convince the markets that they are determined to safeguard the EMU and keep the euro as their irrevocable currency. Markets sense this and remain unconvinced that each of the plans presented by the EU leaders could be a solution to the European sovereign debt crisis.

A permanent solution to the crisis requires major structural changes that will calm the markets and the CRAs, which kept downgrading the sovereign bonds of the periphery EMU member countries during the crisis. The ECB has to be granted full independence to apply discretionary monetary policy, free from the scrutiny, the watchful eye, and the interference of the national governments. Furthermore, the ECB must be authorized to buy EMU members' sovereign bonds and become the main regulatory authority of the major banks in the EA countries. In order for the EU and the EMU to successfully fight future crises, the EMU and eventually the EU must be transformed into a fully-fledged banking and fiscal union.

It is evident that the EMU and the EU, in order to be successful in providing harmonious economic development and peace, must follow the US example and create the United States of Europe. The alternative would be to return to the nineteenth-century concept of the nation state. It is certain that the vast majority of Europeans would reject such a regression.

Notes

1 Steen (2013).
2 As a result, common macroeconomic policies would not be appropriate to restore stability in the EMU countries.
3 Real economic convergence is often measured by the cross-sectional standard deviation of the countries' real per capita GDP or by the rate of convergence, denoted in the economic literature by beta (β), which is based on the neoclassical growth model. See, for example, Barro and Sala-Martin (1991).
4 As the EA is a large subset of EU countries, in many ways the EU and EA are similar. Therefore, on certain occasions, they can be used interchangeably without the need to differentiate between the two.
5 Periphery here refers to Southern EA countries and Ireland. Ireland was a laggard country in terms of economic growth for many years. It grew rapidly once it joined the EU in 1973. Thus Ireland ended up having the second highest real per capita GDP in the EU prior to the crisis, next only to Luxembourg. The crisis, however, affected Ireland so much that it became necessary to receive a bailout. For this reason, Ireland, along with Cyprus which also received a bailout, is also grouped with the Southern EA countries.
6 See Zestos and Yin (2009) and Yin et al. (2003) among several other empirical studies that found evidence of the real convergence in terms of real per capita GDP of the EU countries.
7 "Troika" is Russian for a carriage drawn by a team of three horses abreast. From January, 2015, the new Greek government is refusing to refer to the IMF, ECB, and the EU Commission as the Troika. This is because the name is associated with the imposed austerity and the misery inflicted on Greece. Now the three are referred to as the "Institutions"; however, the change of name has not altered anything.
8 This assumes that the EU and the EA countries are committed to keeping and expanding what they have accomplished in a period of over sixty years of European integration. A few EU leaders, however, have been campaigning for less European integration and the return of some of the decision-making back to the national capitals and away from Brussels. David Cameron, the Prime Minister of the UK, is one such leader.
9 Of course, after the recession spreads to almost all of the EA countries, a single monetary policy would be appropriate.

10 The problem appeared during the crisis when a few EA countries experienced low inflation and almost unprecedentedly high rates of unemployment. In contrast, Northern EA countries attained positive economic growth and very low unemployment rates, and therefore inflation for these countries was a concern.

11 It is irrational for a country to maintain low prices for goods and services, if most consumers cannot afford to buy what they need. With the same reasoning, a central bank must not create very high inflation in its effort to generate economic growth because high inflation is known to have detrimental effects on the economy.

12 A Sequester refers to the automatic increases in taxes and reduction in government expenditures that became effective in the US after the failure of the Democrats and Republicans, in the summer of 2012, to find a mutually agreeable solution to the US fiscal problem.

13 For elaborate analysis of the economics of an OCA, see Mundell (1961) and McKinnon (1963).

14 This is mainly related to the fact that the CEE countries inherited no public debt from their former communist era.

15 The IMF's resources admittedly were needed much more to assist other less fortunate continents and countries such as South Sudan in Africa for example, which has been fighting for its freedom for a period of over twenty years and had just recently gained its independence.

16 These countries' leaders were hoping to slide through the storm without admitting the wreckage of their ship, and, thus, avoid the stigma of the IMF conditionality and the painful austerity programs imposed by the Troika.

17 Growth in the green economy is an expression used to describe economic projects that are environmentally friendly.

18 See Eijffinger (2010).

19 See Levy (2001).

20 In Figure 4.1, the same sample of EA countries was employed as in Chapter 3.

21 See Darvas (2012). Such redirection of trade is not opposed by economists if the redirection is determined according to the principle of comparative advantage. It could also be the result of a change in strategic German trade policy. In either case, such a trade redirection may have implications on the future of the EMU and the EU.

22 See Apergis *et al.* (2012).

23 Inflation in the EA countries in November 2013 stood at 0.7 of 1 percent, which was below the ECB's maximum target rate of 2 percent. As of May 31, 2015, the inflation rate in the EA is still low at 0.3 of 1 percent, much below the target rate.

24 Callero and Giavazzi (2010).

25 It was possible for the ECB not to resort to quantitative easing if the Federal Reserve followed through with its announced intention to end quantitative easing in the US by the end 2014 and if the other two major central banks followed suit as well (Harding and Politi, 2013).

26 Hannon and Blackstone (2013).

27 Blackstone (2013).

28 This was clearly indicated in June 2013 when the national central banks refused to rollover the Greek bonds that they owned, although their governments had agreed to do so in the second bailout agreement with Greece. Their position caused the reaction of the IMF that threatened to suspend payments to Greece by July 2013, because the national banks' decision, according to the IMF, would have rendered the Greek public debt again unsustainable. See Spiegel (2013a).

29 There was an interruption in the decline of the REPO in 2011 at a time when the inflation rate began rising above the ECB target rate of 2 percent. The ECB then increased the REPO rate by 50 basis points (0.5 of 1 percent).

30 See Gerlach (2009). This means that the ECB was creating money to finance countries' public debt. The problem was that this program would increase inflation.

31 Such an increase in the monetary base did not result in a great increase in the money supply because lending had practically frozen during the US subprime mortgage crisis due to the general distrust and drastic reduction to the money multiplier (see Von Hagen, 2009).

32 See *RTE News* (2012).

33 Allen (2011).

34 Birnbaum and Plumer (2012).

35 Peel (2012).

36 Sterilization is defined as the reduction in money supply by the central bank (ECB) via any method by an equal amount of its government securities purchases that leaves the money supply unchanged.

37 An SPV was a device first introduced to allow banks to place part of their assets in very profitable but risky investment funds outside the bank thus leaving unexposed to risk the rest of the bank's assets.

38 See www.efsf.europa.eu/attachments/faq_en.pdf .

39 If issued government bonds include CACs, then once a country comes to an agreement with a substantial majority of its bondholders (usually 90 percent or above) it is mandatory for the rest of the minor bondholders to also accept a haircut.

40 See more on the PSI in Zestos and Williamson (2012).

41 However, since Slovakia did not participate in the program, and Ireland and Portugal received bailouts themselves, the original amount of €80 billion was reduced by €2.7 billion.

42 Markets revealed that the first bailout was insufficient to restore stability because the Greek long-term interest rates, although they had declined, initially still remained high and did not return to a normal range.

43 See more on the PSI program imposed on Greece in Zestos and Rizova (2012a).

44 EU leaders also refused to discuss the possibility of a new haircut during that time as well.

45 See Treaty of Rome (1957), Article 2.

46 See Zestos and Smith (2013).

47 The UK and the Czech Republic initially decided to opt out of signing this treaty, but the Czech Republic joined later. Croatia was not a member of the EU when the Fiscal Compact Treaty was signed in March 2012.

48 Under the Fiscal Compact Treaty, the EU countries lost their fiscal policy, particularly their discretionary policy, which was replaced by rigid rules. The loss of fiscal policy in the EA countries comes as an addition to the loss of monetary and exchange rate policies after the adoption of the euro.

49 The implicit interest rate is equal to the total interest payments of a country's public debt divided by the total public debt.

50 For example, the news media in the US often wrote about the "double dip" recession, the possibility that the recession would return to the US from Europe.

51 This is the case because the existing situation in the EU/EMU is not sustainable and the EMU would break up if new structural changes are not introduced.

52 This will happen because the taxpayers, or voters, will no longer wish to be a part of the EMU or because they will run out of resources to continue supporting financially distressed countries.

53 See Treaty of Rome (1957), Article 2.

54 The last two members of the EMU that adopted the euro are Latvia (2014) and Lithuania (2015).

55 Cohen (2013).

References

Allen, P. (2011) "The EU leaders didn't listen on debt: Trichet," *CNBC*, October 31.

Apergis, N., Zestos, G., and Shaltayev, D. (2012) "Do market fundamentals determine the dollar euro exchange rate?" *Journal of Policy Modeling*, 34 (1): 1–15.

Barro, R. J. and Sala-Martin, X. (1991) "Convergence across states and regions," *Brookings Papers on Economic Activity, 22* (1): 107–82.

Barro, R. J. and Sala-Martin, X. (1992) "Convergence," *Journal of Political Economy*, 100 (2): 223–51.

Birnbaum, M. and Plumer, B. (2012) "Central Bank chief vows to fight for euro," *Washington Post*, July 26.

Blackstone, B. (2013) "Europe's bank eases as downturn spreads," *Wall Street Journal*, May 3.

Callero, R. and Giavazzi, F. (2010) "Long live the euro at parity with the dollar," *Financial Times*, July 11.

Cohen, N. (2013) "Croatia: the EU's newest member," *Financial Times*, July 1.

Darvas, Z. (2012) "Intra-euro rebalancing is inevitable but insufficient," *Bruegel*, 31 August.

Eijffinger, S. C. W. (2010) "Spread of the crisis – impact on public finances," European Parliament. See: www.europarl.europa.eu/thinktank/en/document.html?reference=IPOL-JOIN_NT%282010%29429990.

European Council (2012) *ESM Treaty*. Retrieved from: http://www.european-council. europa.eu/media/582311/05-tesm2.en12.pdf (accessed March 2012).

Gerlach, S. (2009) "Defining and measuring systemic risk," European Parliament, Brussels.

Hannon, P. and Blackstone, B. (2013) "Europe woes bolster case for rate cut," *Wall Street Journal*, May 1.

Harding, R. and Politi, J. (2013) "Bernanke sees 2014 end for QE3," *Financial Times*, June 19.

Levy, M. D. (2001) "Don't mix monetary and fiscal policy: why return to an old, flawed framework?" *Cato Journal*, 21 (2): 2773.

McKinnon, R. (1963) "Optimum currency areas," *American Economic Review*, 53: 207–22.

McKinnon, R. (2004) "Optimum currency areas and key currencies: Mundell I vs Mundell II," *Journal of Common Market Studies*, 42 (2): 689–715.

McKinnon, R. (2005) "Trapped by the international dollar standard," *Journal of Policy Modeling*, 27: 477–85.

Mundell, R. (1961) "A theory on optimum currency areas," *American Economic Review*, 51: 657–65.

Patrick, A. (2012) "The EU leaders didn't listen on debt: Trichet," *CNBC*, October 31.

Peel, Q. (2012) "Merkel's man becomes the Becket of the Bundesbank," *Financial Times*, August 3.

RTE News (2012) "ECB holds back on bond purchases for 11th week," May 28. See www.rte. ie/news/business/2012/0528/322716-ecb-holds-back-on-bond-purchases-for-11th-week/.

Spiegel, P. (2013a) "Eurozone faces pressure over Greek aid after IMF warning," *Financial Times*, June 21.

Spiegel, P. (2013b) "Latvia to become Eurozone's 18th member," *Financial Times*, July 9.

Steen, M. (2013) "Eurozone sets bleak record of longest term recession," *Financial Times*, May 16.

Von Hagen, J. (2009) *The Monetary Mechanics of the Crisis*. Brugek Policy Contribution, Brussels, August.

Yin, L., Zestos, G. K., and Michelis, L. (2003) "Economic convergence in the European Union," *Journal of Economic Integration*, 18, March.

Zestos, G. K. and Rizova, T. P. (2012a) "A plan to rescue Europe from its economic crisis," *Ekathimerini*, January 11.

Zestos, G. K. and Rizova, T. P. (2012b) "US subprime mortgage crisis and the European sovereign debt: why the European sovereign debt crisis has not been resolved yet," *The State of the Union(s): The Eurozone Crisis, Comparative Regional Integration, and the EU Model*. Miami, FL: Thomson-Shore, pp. 69–83.

Zestos, G. K. and Smith, A. (2013) *Causal Links Between Northern-Southern Eurozone Trade Imbalances and Over-indebtedness of Southern Eurozone Countries*. Presented at the World Finance Conference, Cyprus 2013.

Zestos, G. K. and Williamson, M. (2012) "German rigidity: an obstacle to the resolution of the European crisis," *Journal of Regional and Socio-Economic Issues*, 2 (3).

Zestos, G. K. and Yin, L. (2009) "Global economic convergence," *International Journal of Economic Research*, 6: 175–203.

5

US FISCAL AND MONETARY POLICY TO COPE WITH THE GREAT RECESSION

Introduction

On Wednesday, December 18, 2013, both the Federal Reserve and the US Congress announced historical decisions that seemed to be perfectly synchronized. The chairman of the Fed, Ben Bernanke, in his press conference announced that the Fed was going to slow down its third round of quantitative easing (QE3) that began in September 2012 by purchasing $85 billion of government and mortgage-backed securities (MBS) each month.[1] The QE3 program had been launched by the Federal Open Market Committee (FOMC) on December 2012 with the purchase of $45 billion of long-term government securities and $40 billion of MBSs each month. This decision to reduce QE3 was expected and received well by the markets. The Fed's partial reversal on the QE policy became possible after the announcement of the positive news on the economy published earlier in 2013, regarding the reduction of the unemployment rate to 7 percent and the real GDP growth which increased to 4.1 percent during the third quarter of 2013.[2] At about the same time as the Fed's press release, the US Senate announced its approval of a federal budget, after operating for four years without one.[3] Such a decision came as a great relief to all those concerned about the health of the US economy, particularly the vast majority of Americans who despised the artificially created political and fiscal crisis during the 2012–13 period.

The year 2013 had been a time of uncertainty caused by political and fiscal confrontation as a result of bipartisan brinkmanship that frustrated many American people. The Fed began to taper its QE3 program in January 2014 by $10 billion MBSs and government securities each month. As a result, the Fed ended its QE3 program by making its final large purchase of $15 billion in October 2014. The two announcements at the end of 2013 were expected to put an end to the artificially created crisis.[4]

The inability of the Democrats and Republicans to reach an agreement and adopt a long-term fiscal plan that would have reduced public debt led the two US political parties to accept an automatically triggered alternative fiscal mechanism to achieve fiscal stability. Thus in March 2013, a fiscal program known as sequestration imposed automatic federal tax increases and government expenditure reductions. The sequestration program followed a previous fiscal threat, which became known as the "fiscal cliff." The fiscal cliff was set to take place on December 31, 2012, when several taxes were due to expire and government expenditures were to be reduced. The fiscal cliff, a term created by the news media, was to be triggered if the two political parties did not reach an agreement prior to the end of 2012. After last-minute negotiations, the US partially escaped "falling off" the fiscal cliff. The simultaneous announcements of the Fed and the US Senate were, consequently, expected to be the beginning of a new period in the US economy that would reverse the effects of the aggressive expansionary monetary and fiscal policies launched to fight the Great Recession caused by the subprime mortgage crisis.

Fiscal policy

The US fiscal authorities, i.e. the President and the Congress, launched three fiscal stimulus plans to fight the Great Recession.

The Economic Stimulus Act of 2008 (Bush's tax rebates)

On February 13, 2008, President George W. Bush signed the Economic Stimulus Act of 2008. This stimulus plan provided tax rebates to taxpayers who earned an income of up to $75,000 for single individuals and $150,000 for couples. The US Treasury Department mailed the tax rebate checks to 130 million Americans. The program also provided funding to disabled Americans and senior citizens, and offered generous tax breaks for investments. Each tax rebate amounted to up to $600 for individuals and up to $1,200 for couples. In addition, families earning less than $3,000 per year and not paying any taxes also received $300 in rebates. The US legislators expected that the larger share of the rebates would be spent and thus help the economy pull out of the recession. As a matter of fact, President Bush called the Economic Stimulus Act of 2008 a "booster shot" for the American economy.[5] The Bush administration was very optimistic that the tax rebate stimulus program would either help prevent the US from falling into a deep recession or would shorten the recession. Several economists, nonetheless, had serious doubts that a total of $152 billion in tax rebates were sufficient to prevent the crisis from further deepening and spreading in the US economy and abroad.

A tax rebate in general has a direct effect on increasing the taxpayer's disposable personal income and, consequently, indirectly on consumption. However, for tax rebates to have the most expansionary effects on the economy, taxpayers must allocate a substantial part of the rebates to consumption. If taxpayers saved a significant share of the rebates then the fiscal stimulus would not be able to generate a substantial increase in national income. The larger the percentage saved out of the total rebates, the weaker the fiscal program would be in boosting the economy.

After the fall of 2008, with the spreading of the crisis, it became apparent that the US government had underestimated the severity of the recession. This explains why the US administration launched such a small fiscal stimulus program that was only able to scratch the surface of the problem.

Figure 5.1 shows the performance of the US economy during the subprime mortgage crisis in terms of both real GDP in Figure 5.1(a) and also in terms of the unemployment rate in Figure 5.1(b). The recession is indicated by a sharp decline in the real GDP expressed in real 2009 US dollars. Figure 5.1(b) shows that the US unemployment rate began increasing after 2007 and reached a peak in 2010.[6] A persistent decline in real GDP and a rise in unemployment induced the US government and the Fed to react decisively. Both fiscal and monetary US authorities adopted extraordinarily expansionary policies to cope with the rapidly evolving crisis. In Figure 5.1(b), it is clearly shown that the subprime mortgage crisis caused a substantial increase in the unemployment rate by approximately five percentage points, implying millions of Americans lost their jobs. More detailed statistics on US employment are presented in the appendix of this chapter in Figures A5.1(a) and (b) and A5.2(a) and (b).

The Emergency Economic Stabilization Act of 2008 (Bush's fiscal stimulus program)

Economic and financial conditions in the US rapidly deteriorated by the end of 2006. The American Mortgage Association reported a high increase in home foreclosures and delinquencies starting in the fourth quarter of 2006. Consequently, many mortgage lenders began defaulting during and after this period. For example, the second largest US mortgage company, New Century Financial, filed for Chapter 11 bankruptcy protection on April 2, 2007. New Century Financial, however, was not a bank but a real estate investment trust (REIT). More than half of the subprime mortgage companies were set up as REITs. These companies financed their mortgages through the issuing of commercial paper as they did not hold deposits or have the protection of the FDIC. New Century Financial specialized in subprime mortgages and became a highly leveraged company. With a little over $2 billion in equity, New Century Financial accumulated more than $25 billion in assets (mortgages). The explosive growth and rapid decline of New Century Financial portrays a reasonably accurate view of how the subprime mortgage crisis had fermented.[7]

As the US housing bubble burst and home prices began tumbling, interest rates started rising, consequently borrowers became unable to refinance their mortgages. During this period, many mortgage companies experienced massive losses. As a result, their securities, which were mostly backed by subprime and Alt-A mortgages, became almost worthless.

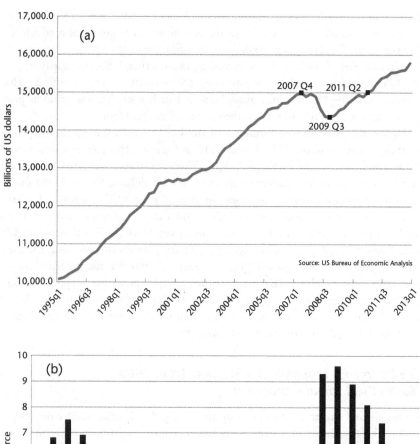

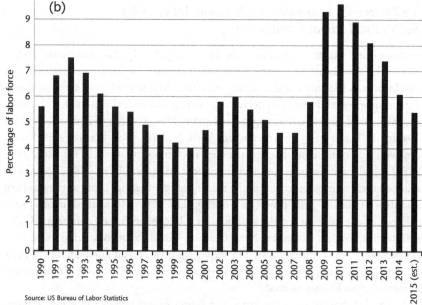

FIGURE 5.1 (a) US real GDP in 2009 dollars; (b) US unemployment rate

Countrywide Financial Corporation was another company that experienced downgrades of its securities. The three major US-based credit rating agencies (CRAs) became very active during this period, downgrading hundreds of issues of securities and thus accelerating the crisis.

As economic conditions continued to deteriorate, the US government decided to launch a second stimulus plan to boost the US economy by fighting the looming recession. Upon the request of the US Treasury and the President, the US Congress approved the Emergency Economic Stabilization Act of 2008 that was signed into law on October 3, 2008 by President George W. Bush.

Initially, the Treasury and the President launched the Troubled Assets Relief Program (TARP) aiming to remove the toxic assets from the balance sheets of the financial institutions. However, when the administration realized that it would have taken trillions instead of billions of dollars to remove all toxic assets, the administration abandoned the initial program. The Treasury subsequently launched a few other programs, such as the Capital Purchase Program (CPP), which instead injected direct investments into institutions by buying their pre-ferred and common stock, depending on the institution. Another program that the Treasury launched was the Targeted Investment Program (TIP). With this program the Treasury invested $20 billion in the Bank of America and another $20 billion in Citigroup. These two banks were considered critical to the func-tioning of the entire US financial system; consequently, their failure had to be prevented. Furthermore the Treasury extended very liberal funding to various other institutions under different programs.[8] All institutions, however, were con-tractually obligated to repay a priori an agreed rate of return on the government's investment. This is one of the reasons that many bailout recipient institutions repaid the government quickly.

Initially, Congress, according to the TARP, approved the purchase of $250 billion of troubled assets. The US Treasury in addition could also buy another $100 billion, and even another $350 billion of troubled assets upon the initiation of the President and the approval of the Congress, provided such government bailout was deemed necessary.

Table 5.1 lists the most important bailout recipient institutions in terms of the amounts involved that were allocated, received, and repaid to the government. The recipient institutions were bank holding companies, investment banks, two auto companies, an automobile finance corporation, and an insurance company. The TARP program distributed funding to a total of 934 recipients.[9] Only $457 billion of the original $700 billion that was initially allotted to TARP was approved to be dispensed to the diverse and numerous institutions. The vast shares of the TARP funds, however, were quickly repaid to the government.

It is interesting to note that the institution which received the largest bailout is not a financial institution per se, but an insurance company, the American International Group (AIG). However, AIG was such an important firm that it was considered to be a systemic risk to the global economy. AIG had issued a massive number of credit default swaps (CDSs) that insured the securities of many institutions

TABLE 5.1 Troubled Asset Relief Program (TARP) bailouts to US institutions
(all amounts in $ bn)

Name	Type	Amount allocated	Amount received	Amount returned
AIG	Insurance company	67.84	67.84	67.84
General Motors	Auto company	51.30	51.30	38.99
Bank of America	Bank	45.00	45.00	45.00
Citigroup	Bank	50.00	45.00	45.00
JPMorgan Chase	Bank	25.00	25.00	25.00
Wells Fargo	Bank	25.00	25.00	25.00
Goldman Sachs	Investment firm	10.00	10.00	10.00
GMAC (Ally Financial)	Private bank holding company	16.29	16.29	8.17
Chrysler	Auto company	12.37	12.37	9.44
Morgan Stanley	Bank	10.00	10.00	10.00
Totals		312.8	307.80	284.44
All other companies		143.76	114.13	83.40
Total TARP		456.56	421.93	367.84

Source: All figures gathered from Daily TARP Updates from the US Treasury and author's calculations.
See: www.treasury.gov/initiatives/financial-stability/reports/pages/default.aspx

and governments.[10] As a result, the US government regulators considered AIG to be a "too big to fail" institution, i.e. an institution which, were it to fail, would cause contagion to the rest of the economy. Two of the ten institutions listed in Table 5.1 are automotive companies, the Chrysler Group and General Motors. The US government made a strategic decision to assist the two automotive companies as it considered them of national importance and it did not want the US auto industry to collapse as a victim of the crisis.

The TARP was criticized by many analysts because it protected financial institutions which took unnecessary risk without having to pay the consequences. A few bailout recipient institutions even wasted bailout money, paying large bonuses to their executives. When such news was publicized, the American public became outraged.

Another criticism of the Emergency Economic Act of 2008 was that it contributed to the merging of financial institutions, creating larger banks that would be subject to systemic risk. There exists evidence suggesting such a tendency since failing investment banks were taken over by bigger holding companies. Under such restructuring and reorganization, financial instability can increase and may lead to another Minsky moment.[11] Since very large banks are considered "too big to fail" institutions, the fiscal stimulus program did little to solve this problem. The two financial institutions that failed, however, were investment banks with neither access to demand deposits and the Fed's supervision, nor the Federal Deposit Insurance Corporation's (FDIC) protection as the bank holding companies by which they were absorbed did.[12]

The American Recovery and Reinvestment Act of 2009 (Obama's fiscal stimulus plan)

Despite the two fiscal programs launched by the US government and the Fed's expansionary monetary policy, the US economy entered into a recession by the end of 2007. In the fall of 2008, the recession deepened further. It was estimated by the government then that the US economy had already lost approximately 3.6 million jobs over the past 13 months. The government was convinced that the US economy was heading towards a two-digit unemployment rate if no corrective action were to take place. To prevent the further deterioration of the economy, the US Congress quickly passed the American Recovery and Reinvestment Act of 2009 (ARRA). President Obama signed the bill into law on February 17, 2009.[13] The Act provided a fiscal stimulus amounting to $787 billion to boost the US economy and prevent the spreading of the subprime mortgage crisis to other sectors of the US economy and abroad.

The new fiscal stimulus was designed to inject funding and provide tax relief for the next 11 years (2009–19). The intention of the US legislators and the President was to stimulate every sector of the economy and assist many working people and families, particularly the middle income class. President Obama characterized the ARRA as the most "sweeping stimulus bill" in US history. The actual amount of the stimulus program could reach $840 billion.[14] The Obama fiscal stimulus plan provided both tax reductions and funding of over $80 billion to each of the following programs: healthcare, education, and social welfare. Substantial funding was provided to alternative energy – the aim was to double the renewable energy capacity of the country during the first three years of the program.

Massive funding was also allocated to states to support several educational programs ranging from early childhood to advanced university studies and research. The objective of the ARRA was to restore state-provided services disrupted by reduced state budgets as a result of the recession.[15] The ARRA document is exceptionally long, over 400 pages, as it combines the detailed work of several committees and subcommittees. The act is divided into three major parts: 1. Tax Incentives; 2. Contracts and Grants; and 3. Entitlements. A rather brief description of the three components of the ARRA follows.

Tax benefits or revenue provisions are the largest of the three components amounting to $290.7 billion.[16] Tax benefits include both individual and business tax credits relevant to a variety of economic activities. The next two parts of the ARRA pertain to spending. The first of the two components is total contracts and grants. This component amounts to $257.8 billion and includes only discretionary spending. Such discretionary spending was expected to have a positive impact on the economy and increase employment by about 3.5 million jobs. Other subcomponents of discretionary spending are funding for education, transportation, infrastructure, energy and environment, and research and development. Lastly, the third component of ARRA is entitlements or mandatory spending which amounts to $254.6 billion. Entitlements include spending on Medicaid/Medicare, unemployment insurance programs, energy, and a few other items.[17]

Table 5.2 provides a complete list of all the subcomponents of the three categories of the ARRA. It is interesting to note that the Obama fiscal plan affected almost every sector and activity in the US economy as it was purposefully designed to reinvigorate the economy battered by the recession.

The projected streams of expenditures and tax reduction revenues are shown in Table A5.1 in the appendix to his chapter. As depicted in this table, the vast amounts of spending and tax revenue changes took place within the first five years (2009–13) after the launching of the fiscal stimulus program.

TABLE 5.2 American Reinvestment and Recovery Act

Program	Amount paid ($bn)
Tax Incentives (Revenue Reduction)	
Individual Tax Credits	131.8
Making Work Pay	104.4
Incentives for Businesses	32.6
Energy Incentives	10.9
Manufacturing and Economic Recovery	7.3
COBRA (Assistance with Continuation of Health Coverage)	3.7
Total	**290.7**
Contracts and Grants (Discretionary Spending)	
Education	93.8
Transportation	39.1
Infrastructure	33.7
Energy/Environment	30.1
Research & Development	15.9
Housing	14.0
Health	12.1
Other Programs	6.2
Public Safety	5.7
Family	5.0
Job Training/Unemployment	4.8
Total for Contracts and Grants	**257.8**
Entitlements (Mandatory Spending)	
Medicaid/Medicare	104.3
Unemployment Insurance	61.3
Family Services	55.3
Energy	21.4
Economic Recovery	13.8
Housing	5.6
Agriculture	1.0
Total for Entitlements:	**254.6**
Total as of November 2013	***803.1***

Source: www.recovery.gov/arra/Pages/default.aspx

The largest public deficits and debts in the world

Figure 5.2 below portrays the US government's fiscal response to the Great Recession. The left-hand axis of Figure 5.2 depicts the US public deficit to GDP ratio and indicates that it increased drastically after 2007, the first year of the recession, from approximately 1 percent to over 10 percent in 2009, the last year of the recession. This is an extraordinarily larger increase in relation to the small US deficits generated after 2001, none of which exceeded 3.5 percent. The high deficits during the crisis constitute a significant increase especially in comparison to the federal surpluses generated during 1998–2001 by President Clinton's administration.

The right-hand axis of Figure 5.2 also indicates the government surplus/deficit in terms of current dollars. This figure shows that the public deficit increased substantially during the crisis, reaching the extraordinary amount of $1.4 trillion in 2009. However, since that time, the US federal deficit has been steadily declining. Such drastic deficit reductions according to some analysts provide some evidence that the US partisan fiscal battles during 2012 and 2013 were unnecessary and artificially created by politicians as the US had already began moving towards a stable fiscal position after the crisis. It is possible, however, that the public deficit reduction would not have occurred without the partisan confrontation.

Annual fiscal deficits are financed through the issuance of government bonds. The newly issued bonds are added to outstanding government securities that comprise a country's public debt, but government surpluses enable countries to retire (reduce) their public debt.

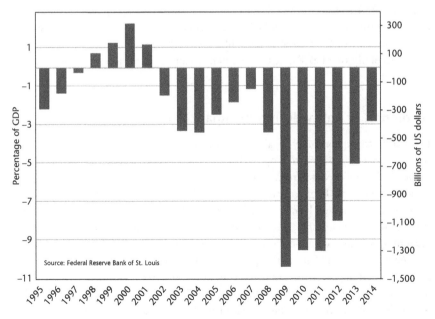

FIGURE 5.2 Federal government public surplus/deficit

It is clearly shown in Figure 5.3 that both nominal US GDP and public debt have been increasing since the early 1950s. Nominal GDP was, nonetheless, higher than public debt almost throughout the entire period. Up to 2001, GDP was growing faster than the public debt. During the period 2001–7 both nominal GDP and public debt grew at approximately equal rates. Starting in 2007, the first year of the crisis, the US public debt grew at a higher rate than GDP. This was a consequence of the exceptionally expansionary fiscal policy launched to cope with the crisis. In 2012, public debt and GDP became equal.[18] Since 2012, US public debt exceeded GDP; large increases in public debt can be detrimental to a country as investors become more hesitant to purchase government securities of highly indebted countries. Investors are induced to purchase securities of indebted countries if they are compensated through a higher rate of return on their investment. This translates to higher interest rates on the government bonds they purchase, because they include a default risk premium. Credit rating agencies (CRAs) usually send early warnings by downgrading government securities or placing a country's debt under a negative outlook. Even the US lost its AAA rating in 2011 for the first time in the country's history.[19]

Figure 5.3(b) depicts the US public debt to GDP ratio. This ratio is a better metric of indebtedness than the nominal public debt because it is a relative measure free of inflation. It also takes into consideration the size of the economy as large countries can afford to have larger absolute amounts of public debt. The debt to GDP ratio, after a continuous decline for three and a half decades after WW II, began increasing in the early 1980s. With a minor exception during the period 1998–2001, during the Clinton Administration, when the US generated surpluses in the government account and the public debt declined, the public debt has followed an upward trend, and in 2012 it exceeded 100 percent. Such an increase in the public debt to GDP ratio is most likely what triggered the Republican Party, and particularly the Tea Party, to vehemently campaign for a reduction of the US public debt.

US monetary policy during the financial crisis

In addition to expansionary fiscal policy, the US also applied unprecedented expansionary monetary policy to cope with the Great Recession. The Fed gradually reduced the target federal funds rate, its main monetary policy instrument. After the collapse of Lehman Brothers on October 29, 2008, the federal funds rate was lowered to unprecedented levels, down to the 0–0.25 percent range. After driving the federal funds rate close to "zero-bound," the Fed lost its most important monetary instrument because it cannot reduce it further below this level. On October 2008, the Fed launched a new monetary policy, the short-term liquidity programs through short-term lending to firms and markets in order to restore confidence in the economy. These programs lasted until February 10, 2014.

On December 28, 2008, the Fed also launched an unorthodox monetary policy, widely known as quantitative easing (QE). This provided liquidity to the economy by

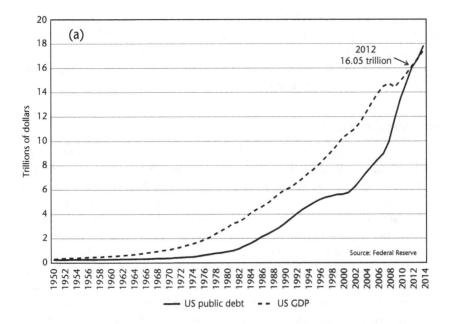

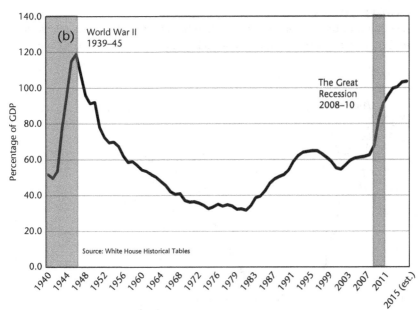

FIGURE 5.3 (a) US GDP and public debt in current dollars; (b) US public debt to GDP ratio

increasing the size of the Fed's balance sheet and total reserves of the banking system. The Fed carried out the QE policy by buying agency debt and MBSs from the government-sponsored enterprises (GSEs) and by purchasing Treasury securities.[20] Consequently, by April 2014, the Fed increased excess reserves in the banking system by an unprecedented $2.7 trillion (see Figure 5.5).

The federal funds rate

Figure 5.4 shows the target federal funds rate, the most important monetary policy variable (instrument) of the Fed till the most recent US financial crisis. This is a short-term overnight rate at which commercial member banks of the Fed borrow federal funds from each other to meet the reserve requirement. The Fed, by setting the federal funds rate, aims to affect all other short- and long-term interest rates. US monetary policy can be traced throughout the years by following the line graph of the target federal funds rate – this is depicted as a step function of discrete incremental changes. Supply and demand of federal funds by the Federal Reserve member banks determine the effective or market federal funds rate. However, when necessary, the Fed intervenes in the federal funds market through buying and selling government securities to maintain the effective, or market, rate close to the announced target rate.

In addition to the federal funds rate, two other interest rates are also depicted in Figure 5.4, the ten-year government bond yield, which is considered to be one of the

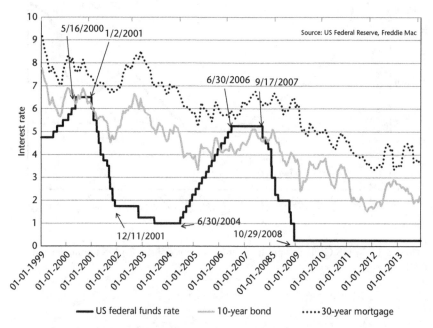

FIGURE 5.4   Three US interest rates

most important US long-term interest rates, and the 30-year mortgage rate. The
30-year mortgage rate is set according to the ten-year government bond yield and is
by far the most important interest rate for the housing market as it allows home buyers
to borrow for an extended period of 30 years at affordable terms. It is clearly shown
in Figure 5.4 that the Fed pursued an exceptionally expansionary monetary policy
during the last two recessions 2001–3 and 2007–9. Indeed, after September 2007 the
Fed applied the most expansionary policy ever to cope with the Great Recession.

Figure 5.4 clearly indicates that the Fed was effective in influencing the two long-
term interest rates. However, the change in the two rates is lagging the federal funds
rate and the movement of the three rates is not a close fit. In periods of expansionary
monetary policy the long-term interest rates, although declining, are always higher
than the federal funds rate. The difference between the two interest rates and the
federal funds rate depends on their term to maturity thus the 30-year bond rate is
always the higher of the two rates. Both rates kept decreasing for several years after
2007 and only started increasing in 2013. The two long-term interest rates always
follow a similar pattern, keeping about a two percent spread between each other.

Many economists believe that the 2001–3 recession was caused by three major
events: the dot-com crisis, the US corporate scandals of this period, and the terrorist
attacks on the US on September 11, 2001. To cope with this crisis, the Fed rapidly
and incrementally reduced the federal funds rate down to one percent, a 42-year
record low. The impact on the excess reserves in the banking system during this
period was rather insignificant. This is shown in Figure 5.5 by the exceptionally

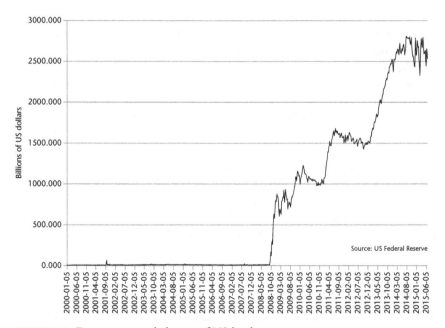

FIGURE 5.5 Excess reserves balances of US banks

small and temporary increase in excess reserves. Such a small increase in excess reserves does not support the generally accepted claim that the US subprime mortgage crisis had its roots in the expansionary monetary policy launched to fight the recession, created after the burst of asset bubbles.[21]

In July 2004 the Fed launched a prolonged contractionary monetary policy to suppress prices in the economy that began rising after the end of the dot-com recession. At increments of 0.25 of 1 percent (25 basis points), the FOMC kept increasing the federal funds rate until June 2006 when it reached 5.25 percent. The Fed kept the federal funds rate at 5.25 percent until September 17, 2007 (see Figure 5.4). When signals of the forthcoming subprime mortgage crisis began making news, this led to the burst of the housing bubble that drastically reduced home prices. Then the Fed embarked on its most expansionary monetary policy since its creation in 1913. With drastic and frequent decrements of 25, 50, 75, and even 125 basis points, the Fed drove the federal funds target rate down to the range of 0–0.25 percent and has kept this rate for a period of several years.[22]

For all practical purposes the zero-bound federal funds rate implies that the Fed is no longer able to employ its traditional, "orthodox," approach to conducting monetary policy. The Fed adopted two new major monetary programs to cope with the US subprime mortgage crisis: short-term liquidity programs and quantitative easing. These two programs are analyzed in the next two sections of this chapter.

Short-term liquidity programs

The Fed exercised its delegated authority as a lender of last resort and launched several short-term lending programs to provide liquidity to financial institutions, firms, markets, and foreign central banks. By extending massive amounts of short-term liquidity, the Fed was aiming to restore and safeguard the smooth functioning of the financial and banking system. Such Fed policy assumes that the problem was liquidity. However, some Fed critics believe that the problem – at least for some of the bailout recipient institutions – was insolvency and not liquidity. Under these programs, the Fed provided liquidity to several institutions that totaled almost astronomical and unprecedented amounts. By the end of 2008, the extended liquidity reached 1.6 trillion dollars.[23] Such a massive inflow of liquidity, however, did not trigger inflation because the liquidity was offered for a short period and was quickly returned to the Fed by the institutions that borrowed the money when they no longer needed it.[24] Five short-term liquidity programs are described and analyzed below and their magnitudes between January 2007 and April 2014 are shown in Figure 5.6.

Other assets

The major components of "Other assets" include the accrued interest of all Fed loans issued by the Fed under the short-term liquidity programs and the Fed's

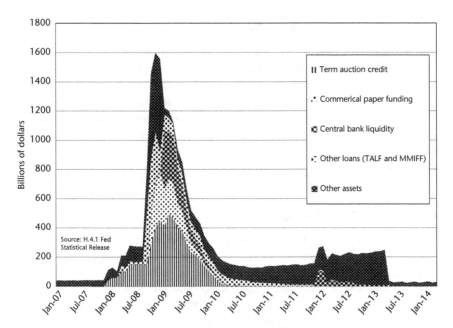

FIGURE 5.6 Short–term lending to financial firms and markets

accounts receivables. As loans were repaid and the short-term liquidity programs were phased out, the other assets drastically dropped at the beginning of 2013. After January 2014, other assets reached very low levels, close to $10 billion. This latter program is the only one that still exists till 2014, although it is very small, as shown in Figure 5.6.

Other loans

Other loans consist of two main components, the Term Asset-Backed Securities Loan Facility (TALF) and the Money Market Investor Funding Facility (MMIFF).

Term Asset-Backed Securities Loan Facility

The Fed, on November 25, 2008, announced the creation of the Term Asset-Backed Securities Loan Facility (TALF). Through the TALF program the Federal Reserve Bank of New York extended collateralized loans up to five years to eligible institutions that held asset backed securities. Such loans were expected to help increase loans to consumers and businesses that had practically stalled since the crisis began. The New York Fed was authorized to lend up to $200 billion for such loans.

The Money Market Investor Funding Facility

The MMIFF was created by the Fed to provide liquidity to money market investors. The New York Fed provided the liquidity to money market investors through five special purpose vehicles (SPVs). The SPVs were buying commercial paper and certificates of deposits (CDs) with a short maturity of 7–90 days from eligible investors. The SPVs borrowed funds from the MMIFF in order to finance the purchases of commercial paper and CDs. Lastly the SPVs sold asset-backed commercial paper (ABCP) and thus were able to pay back their (MMIFF) loans to the New York Fed. The Fed authorized the lending of $540 billion via the five SPVs.

Foreign central bank swap lines

To ease pressure on short-term dollar-funding overseas that emerged during the crisis starting in 2007, the Fed created temporary liquidity swap arrangements with 14 foreign central banks. The Fed took this initiative to protect the US economy from possible knock-on effects from a dollar shortage overseas. As a result, the FOMC approved, on December 12, 2007, dollar liquidity swap arrangements. In May 2010, the Fed authorized dollar liquidity swap lines to another five foreign central banks. Due to the continuous international financial stress in short-term dollar funding these reciprocal currency arrangement authorizations were extended several times up to February 1, 2014. Beyond July 2013, nevertheless, no additional dollar loans were extended to foreign central banks.

The Fed legally, according to FOMC procedures and policies, had extended the credits to these foreign central banks. With the same swap lines, the foreign central banks agreed also to lend their currencies to the Fed. Furthermore, the foreign central banks were liable to repay their loans to the Fed regardless of whether their counterparties failed to honor their agreements and pay back the loans. The short-term liquidity swap lines successfully restored short-term liquidity dollar funding overseas. For the Fed, however, it was never necessary to use the foreign central bank swap lines.

Commercial paper funding (lending to business)

From the onset of the crisis, many firms found it very difficult to borrow from the markets by issuing commercial paper. Traditional investors in commercial paper, such as money mutual funds, either lacked the funding to invest or became skeptical and reluctant to purchase commercial paper. As a result, the interest rates on commercial paper increased as the outstanding amount of commercial paper decreased substantially. Since commercial paper constituted a major source of short-term finance for many corporations, the Fed decided to boost the commercial paper market. To achieve its objective, the Fed established the Commercial Paper Funding Facility (CPFF) as a limited liability company (LLC). The New York Federal Reserve Bank provided short-term liquidity (three-month loans) to the CPFF LLC for the purchase of both secured asset-backed and unsecured commercial paper from qualified firms. The program operated successfully from October 27, 2008 when the CPFF LLC began purchasing commercial paper till February 1, 2010. All the commercial paper purchases made by the CPFF LLC have been fully repaid to the Fed.

Term Auction Facility (bailing out banks)

Because bank funding drastically declined from the onset of the crisis, the Fed created the Term Auction Facility (TAF) in December 2007 to provide liquidity to financially stressed institutions. Through this program, the Fed auctioned 28- and 84-day collateralized loans to financially sound banks. The TAF was announced in December 2007 and was terminated on March 8, 2010, when it offered its last auction of such loans. Several US banks and a few European US branches borrowed money under the TAF program. Figure 5.7(a) shows the five US banks that borrowed the largest amounts from the Fed. Similarly, Figure 5.7(b) shows the five European bank branches that borrowed the largest amounts under the TAF program. The graph shows the amounts each bank borrowed at any point in time during the period the TAF program was effective.

Four US banks that received bailouts from the Fed, JP Morgan, Bank of America, Citigroup, and Morgan Stanley, had also received loans from the US Treasury TARP program. These are major US and world financial institutions that were considered "too big to fail"; thus both the Treasury and the Fed extended loans to them to protect the US economy from a further spreading and deepening of the crisis. These banks along with a few other investment banks turned out to be at the center of the crisis and received heavy criticism when their role in the creation of the crisis was revealed. The public was outraged when it became informed that the major US financial institutions were responsible for the creation of the toxic financial derivatives. The public became even more outraged that the banks used some of the bailout money to award bonuses to executives instead of extending loans to consumers and businesses to revitalize the economy.

After strong pressure from Congress, several major US and foreign banks were investigated by a task force created by President Barack Obama in 2012. Several lawsuits against the foreign and domestic banks were filed before 2012 by the Federal Housing Finance Agency, the Commodities Futures Trading Commission (CFTC), the Securities Exchange Commission (SEC), and the Department of Justice. In 2013, a few of these banks paid over $51 billion in fines. Some analysts have doubts that such punishments meted out on the banks will change the attitude or behavior of the bankers if the bank executives are not prosecuted as well.

The Fed, besides providing liquidity to domestic institutions, extended loans to several European banks that maintained a strong presence in the US. Failure of any of these European banks was also perceived as a systemic risk to the entire US economy. It is interesting to note that three US banks, Morgan Stanley, Citigroup, and Bank of America, borrowed more than $200 billion each. Figure 5.7 indicates the exact debt owed to the Fed by the US and European banks at any point in time during the

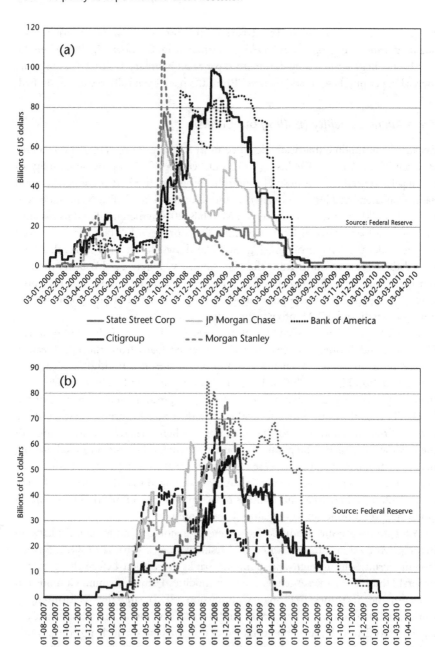

FIGURE 5.7   (a) Debt owed to Fed by US banks; (b) Debt owed to Fed by European banks

period 2008–10. The largest bailouts were received during the most critical years of the crisis from September 2008 to September 2009. It is interesting to note that both US and European banks paid off the entire bailout amounts prior to February 2010. As a result of the short duration of the bailouts, it is evident that this program never caused a serious inflationary threat. Figures A5.1(a) and (b) in the appendix list the maximum cumulative debt to the Fed of the most important domestic and European banks.

Quantitative easing

After the Fed drove the federal funds rate down to zero-bound territory and adopted the short-term liquidity programs, it also launched a new monetary policy. It purchased a variety of public and private securities, such as Treasury bonds, GSE debt, and MBSs. Such securities were issued by the Treasury, the government-sponsored enterprises (GSEs), and the investment banks. In doing so the Fed increased the reserves in the US banking system to unprecedented levels, which is tantamount to printing money. Such policy had the potential to create inflation, as it could have increased the amount of money in circulation.[25] This approach to the monetary policy is known as quantitative easing (QE) because it focuses on the quantity of money in the economy.[26] Purchases of securities by the Fed turned out to help ease tight credit conditions because banks and other financial institutions practically froze credit due to the lack of trust. QE, nonetheless, during the recession never posed a threat to trigger inflation in the US. Although QE resulted in an increase in reserves to unprecedented levels, the freezing of lending in the economy kept the money supply from expanding. The money multiplier was exceptionally low during the crisis.[27]

The Fed launches three QE programs

Quantitative easing 1 (QE1)

As a response to the financial contagion following the September 2008 collapse of Lehman Brothers, the Fed announced in November 2008 purchases of $100 billion GSEs debt and $500 billion MBSs issued by the GSEs.[28] A second announcement by the Fed on March 2009 stated that the Fed would purchase $100 billion of Fannie Mae and Freddie Mac debt along with $750 billion of MBSs. In addition the Fed announced its intention to purchase during the next six months another $300 billion of long-term Treasury securities. The Fed ended up buying $1.25 trillion of MBSs, $300 billion of government securities, and $175 billion of agency debt instead of the $200 billion it originally planned. Economists were convinced that the massive purchase of MBSs by the Fed restored confidence in the markets and the mortgage rates declined substantially to approximately 5 percent.

A few economists claimed that QE1 failed since the ten-year, long-term Treasury yield rose after the end of QE on March 31, 2010. Such criticism, nonetheless, is not accurate because QE1 led to the massive purchases of MBSs worth $1.25 trillion, not treasuries, since the Fed purchased only $300 billion of the latter.[29] The FOMC had stated that QE1 aimed to reduce the cost of borrowing to assist general financial conditions. In this respect QE1 was successful as the mortgage rate for the period QE1 was employed declined by approximately 1 percent.

Quantitative easing 2 (QE2)

A sluggish economic recovery and low inflation rate below one percent induced the Fed on November 3, 2011, to announce a second round of QE. This round became known as QE2. The Fed announced its plan to purchase $600 billion of long-term Treasury securities.[30] The Fed's main objective was to reduce long-term interest rates via massive purchases of government securities. Reduction of interest rates could induce increases in consumption and investment that would boost economic growth. Interest rates began decreasing immediately with the first signal by the Fed that it was going to launch QE2 on August 10, 2010. However, when the announcement was made on November 3, 2011, interest rates returned to the pre-announcement levels. As a result, QE2 was effective neither in reducing long-term interest rates nor in reversing the course of the US economy towards a higher rate of economic growth; however, it deterred further deterioration of the economic environment.

Complementing QE

Prevailing economic uncertainty and fears of inflation returning in the US led the Fed to adopt a policy that aimed to alter the composition of its balance sheet. The objective of the Fed was to reduce the long-term interest rates. This idea is very simple: the Fed sold short-term government securities and used the proceeds to purchase long-term government securities. One such program became known as "Operation Twist" as the Fed intended to twist the yield curve by purchasing $400 billion of long-term government securities on September 21, 2011. The Fed announced the continuation of "Operation Twist" on June 20, 2012. Because labor market conditions did not improve, increasing long-term interest rates triggered the launching of a third round of QE.

Quantitative easing 3 (QE3)

Federal Reserve Chairman Ben Bernanke announced on August 31, 2012, at his annual Jackson Hole speech, that worrisome labor conditions in the US required the Fed to undertake new monetary policy to stabilize the economy. Thus the Fed announced on September 13, 2012, that it had decided to embark on a third round of quantitative easing that became known as QE3. The new monetary program was an open-ended round that started with monthly purchases of $40 billion of MBSs from GSEs. QE3 was reinforced when the FOMC decided to increase purchases of securities to $85 billion a month by adding another $45 billion of long-term government securities. As a result, the US monetary base began increasing by $85 billion each month.

Because the US economy had sufficiently stabilized in 2013, the Fed decided to begin tapering its QE policy and eventually return to normal economic policy. As a result the Fed announced on December 18, 2013, a gradual scale-back of government securities from $85 billion to $75 billion a month. Furthermore the Fed announced a new policy known as future guidance to create certainty about expected Fed policy. The Fed announced that it would keep the federal funds rate to zero-bound until 2015, unless the unemployment rate dropped below 6.5 percent.[31]

Similarly on January 29, 2014, the Fed announced that it would continue its QE tapering policy by cutting purchases of securities from $75 to $65 billion. Lastly, on March 19, 2014, the Fed made its third announcement of tapering to reduce purchases of securities from $65 to $55 billion per month starting in April 2014. Figure 5.8 presents a timeline of the adoption and implementation of the QE policy by the Fed for each of the three programs and the adopted exit strategy that

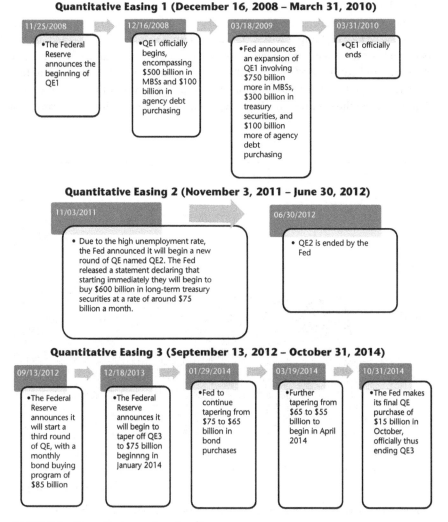

FIGURE 5.8 Quantitative easing timeline

extended to April 2014. During the second meeting of the FOMC on April 30 2014, under the new chair Janet Yellen, the Fed reduced QE3 bond purchases by another $10 billion to $45 billion a month.

The bigger picture

Figure 5.9 clearly shows the Fed's operations during the Great Recession. Both the short-term liquidity programs and the QE policy are shown in this figure. Five short-term liquidity programs and the amounts dispensed for each program throughout their duration are also shown in Figure 5.9. As purchases of government securities started declining by the middle of 2008, funding for lending to financial firms, markets, and foreign banks were increasing. Such expenditures constitute the short-term liquidity programs.

Since QE was launched in December of 2008, purchases by the Fed have been increasing. The Fed bought MBSs, US long-term Treasury securities, and agency debt, and as can be seen from Figure 5.9, the sum of the assets in the Fed's balance sheet has reached almost $4 trillion dollars. The job of the Fed thereafter was to find an exit strategy to bring its balance sheet to normalcy towards the pre-crisis level. This was done through the tapering of QE which coincided with the departure of

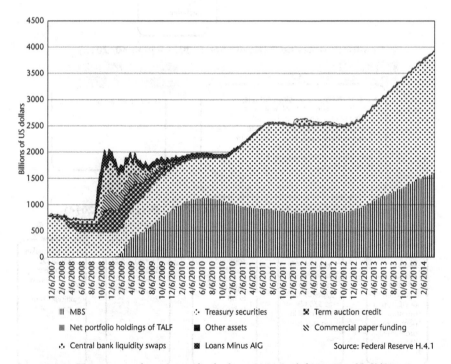

FIGURE 5.9 Treasury- and mortgage-backed securities and short term liquidity programs

Chairman Bernanke and the appointment of the new Chairman of the Fed Janet Yelen.

Evaluation of fiscal and monetary policies

Disentangling policy effects

It is very difficult, if not impossible, to isolate the effects of fiscal and monetary policies because such effects occur simultaneously and therefore are practically inseparable. As a result it is also almost impossible to separately evaluate the effectiveness of fiscal and monetary policy during and after the end of the Great Recession. Three major fiscal programs were adopted to fight the crisis. The three programs were introduced in addition to the fiscal built-in stabilizers that kicked in with the onset of the recession and strengthened with the deepening and the spreading of the crisis. Consequently, the effects of the fiscal programs, which constitute the discretionary part of fiscal policy and the non-discretionary policy effects that are generated by the built-in stabilizers, are only jointly observed.

Automatic built-in stabilizers were enacted to help stabilize the economic system by smoothing out the business cycles (economic fluctuations). Consequently, built-in stabilizers, once enacted, automatically become effective when necessary without any governmental interventions. Built-in stabilizers are free of the time lag problems, unlike discretionary fiscal policy.[32] Built-in automatic stabilizers generate new injections of spending during recessions and reductions in spending during expansions.[33] Similarly, because of the overlapping of the monetary policy programs, it is impossible to separate the effects of the zero-bound federal fund policy from the short-term liquidity programs and QE.

Although it is difficult to disentangle the effects of the fiscal and monetary policies and the impact of each specific monetary and fiscal program on the economy, it is plausible for one to form a fairly good view about the overall effectiveness of these programs by observing the performance of the economy during this period. US fiscal authorities launched during the crisis stimulus programs of unprecedented magnitudes.[34] The US government and the Fed adopted such massive programs because they anticipated the subprime mortgage crisis would lead to an exceptionally severe recession. For this reason the government and the Fed responded with policies designed for abnormal times reminiscent of the Great Depression.

As the recession turned out to be a rather short-lived one, the Fed and the fiscal authorities attributed the recovery to their massive and successful intervention. Many people were indeed surprised at the unexpected recovery of the economy, especially after taking into consideration the frequent negative economic news with which they were bombarded during this period. Several critics of the government and the Fed opposed these policies as being excessive and subsequently responsible for planting the seeds of a new and possibly more destructive crisis. It will never, however, be known whether the US economy would have rebounded so quickly without the application of the extraordinary expansive monetary and fiscal policies.

This is the case because it is impossible to create the state in which the US economy would have been without the massive fiscal and monetary stimuli.

Findings from other studies on the effectiveness of fiscal policy

Economic studies that evaluated the effectiveness of fiscal policy on real GDP and employment often reported a small boosting of GDP and employment mainly for two theoretical reasons: (1) the Ricardo equivalence and (2) the crowding out effect. The Ricardo equivalence refers to the possibility that forward-looking consumers and businesses tend to reduce spending and increase saving in order to be able to pay for expected future tax increases. Increases in savings and reductions in spending offset the government expenditures and thus can leave the aggregate (total spending in the economy) reduced or unchanged. Crowding out arises when the government finances its spending by borrowing from the market thus competing with the private sector for funding. As a result increased government spending causes an increase in interest rates which displaces (crowds out) private investment and consumption.

John F. Cogan *et al.* (2009) challenged the results reported in this chapter that the ARRA of February 2009 was expected, according to the government report, to raise output by 3.6 percent and generate or protect three and a half million jobs.[35] These authors performed simulations based on two neo-Keynesian type models that allow for some market rigidity and forward-looking expectations for consumers and businesses. They found that the Obama fiscal stimulus had a very small impact on GDP. However, the authors assumed in the model simulations that the interest rates would start to increase after 2011. This of course did not happen, as the Fed kept the federal funds rate close to the zero-bound range. Specifically, the Fed announced the rate would remain in the zero range till 2015.

John Taylor (2010, 2014) has been very critical of the Fed and the government approach to fight the Great Recession. He argues that as discretionary policies, both fiscal and monetary, replaced "rules-based policies," they increased economic instability and prolonged the recovery. Taylor consequently recommends that the US policy must "get back on track," i.e. the US should re-adopt rules-based policies that have worked well for almost two decades prior to the Great Recession.

Some general observations

Fiscal policy during the crisis was not very effective in drastically increasing GDP for several reasons. For example, the two major fiscal stimuli programs under Bush and Obama resulted in a relatively small increase in income because the fiscal multipliers were small. Under the Bush fiscal stimulus, the Fed was authorized to spend $700 billion by lending to institutions that were in financial distress. Several bailout recipient institutions used the bailouts to reduce the large amounts of preexisting debts. In order for GDP to substantially increase, it required the institutions that received the bailouts to have directly purchased goods and services, and hired workers.

Very little of this type of expenditure took place and as a result of which the fiscal multipliers turned out to be very low.

The Obama plan supported many programs. The most important of all turned out to be tax reductions. Several authors claim that tax reduction programs are the most efficient and effective way to raise GDP. Such authors even suggest that the tax multipliers, based on several studies, turned out to be higher than the government multipliers.[36] The Bush and Obama fiscal plans were not an exception to these reported empirical results.

Government spending, under the ARRA, was subject to heavy bureaucracy, which delayed quick spending that was the initial intention of the Federal government to boost GDP. Worse than this was the fact that most funding received by states was used to reduce existing debt or to reduce new borrowing. Such allocation of the fiscal stimulus resulted in small increases in GDP as the program generated a very small increase in indirect spending. It is therefore concluded that although the programs were useful in promoting financial stability by providing liquidity and overcoming financial distress, they did very little to increase US GDP and particularly employment. The crisis had its most devastating effect on employment particularly among young workers and minorities. None of the programs targeted a direct reduction of unemployment; it is sometimes possible for GDP to increase through programs that boost aggregate demand and still have little or no effect in reducing unemployment.[37] Such a phenomenon became known as a jobless recovery.

In Figure 5.10(b), the number of unemployed workers in the US is shown starting in 2000. It can be clearly seen from this chart that the Great Recession had a major negative impact in the labor market as over 8.6 million workers lost their jobs in the 31-month period of March 2007 to October 2009. Once the number of unemployed workers reached a peak on October 1, 2009, a very slow decline began thereafter. More than six years later, in 2015, the number of unemployed is still about 2 million above the 6.7 million that were unemployed in March 2007 at the beginning of the recession. Such a prolonged delay in employment recovery can be easily characterized as hysteresis, although a mild one in comparison to the prolonged EA crisis.

In Figure 5.10(a), the number of US employed workers is depicted. In January 2008, the number of US employed workers reached an all-time peak of approximately 138.3 million. By February 2010, employment dropped by 8.7 million, as a result of the Great Recession. Since then the number of employed workers began continuously increasing and employment reached the pre-crisis peak of 138.3 million in April 2014.[38]

A5.2(a) and (b) in the appendix to this chapter indicate that the US economy has been significantly affected by the Great Recession. In Figure A5.2(b), the labor force participation rate (LFPR), shown on the left-hand axis, has been declining since July 2008. A decline in LFPR after the crisis implies that the labor force in the US is increasing at a lower rate than the US population. On the right-hand side, the US unemployment rate is shown. This had been increasing during the crisis, and steadily declined after October 2009. The decline in the labor force is suspected to have been caused during the crisis by many discouraged workers exiting the

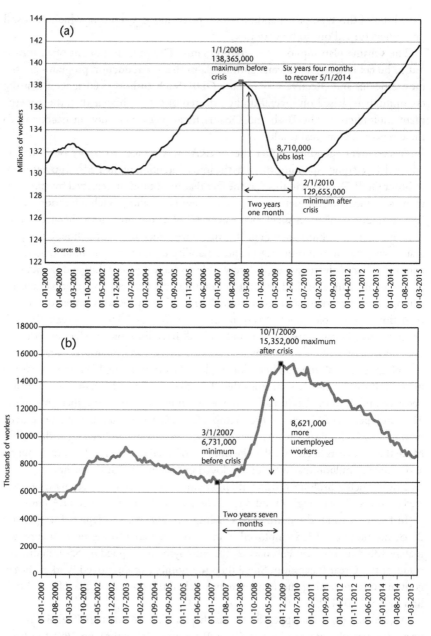

FIGURE 5.10   (a) Total number of US workers employed; (b) US unemployed workers

labor force. The impact of the crisis on the labor market is also shown by the effect it had on the number of discouraged workers. According to Figure A5.2(a) in the appendix, there was a major increase of discouraged workers starting in August 2007, the beginning of the crisis. The number of discouraged workers increased until it reached its peak in December 2010. Thereafter, they began to decline, but have not yet, as of 2014, reached their minimum pre-crisis level. These statistics provide further evidence that hysteresis is occurring in the US.[39]

Another negative impact of the recession is indicated by Figure A5.3 in the appendix, where real average weekly earnings of manufacturing workers are shown. There was a drop in the average real weekly wages of about $17 from $729.80 in July 2008 to $712.51 in March 2009. Since then, average weekly real wages for manufacturing workers have been increasing. This is a positive signal that the economy has been improving.

Concluding comments

The US monetary and fiscal authorities launched unparalleled expansive policies to cope with the Great Recession. After the US Fed drove its main monetary policy variable, the federal funds rate, down to zero-bound territory it launched two major monetary programs. It first adopted the short-term liquidity programs for the main purpose of providing liquidity to financially distressed institutions, markets, and foreign central banks. Five short-term liquidity programs were adopted by the Fed, which increased temporarily the Fed's balance sheet and excess reserves. Since the loans were quickly repaid by the Fed these programs were not a risk to trigger inflation. The second major monetary program launched by the Fed was QE, i.e. purchases of long-term Treasury securities, agency debt and MBSs. As long as these securities were held by the Fed the QE program had a potential to increase inflation. For this reason the Fed began to taper QE, removing the monetary stimulus through the sale of its purchased securities. In addition to expansionary monetary policy conducted by the Fed, the US President and Congress passed three fiscal bills to cope with the US subprime mortgage crisis.

The three fiscal stimuli programs were designed to provide the impetus together with the expansionary monetary policy to pull the US economy out of the long anticipated deep recession that was feared to be of a magnitude tantamount to that of the Great Depression. The two policies indeed prevented the feared devastation of the economy, and the US pulled out of the recession by the end of 2009. However, many economists and other analysts are very critical about the effectiveness of the fiscal and monetary policy. The quick reaction of the government to suppress the crisis from spreading resulted in a waste of resources and has possibly planted the seeds of a new crisis. As of June 2015 the US economy has not yet fully recovered according to some indicators such as the labor force participation rate, the number of discouraged workers. However, from a closer examination of the US economy, according to more popular indicators such as the unemployment rate and GDP growth, the US has recovered remarkably well.

Appendix

TABLE A5.1 Projected budgetary impact of the ARRA 2009 through the fiscal year 2019

(Amounts in $bn)	2009	2010	2011	2012	2013	2009–13	2014	2015	2016	2017	2018	2019	2009–19
Discretionary spending													
Estimated budget authority	288.7	7.1	4.6	3.6	2.5	306.5	1.1	1.1	1.1	1.1	0.5	0.0	311.2
Estimated outlays	34.8	110.7	76.3	38.1	22.9	282.8	12.8	7.0	3.1	1.6	0.8	0.1	308.3
Mandatory spending													
Estimated budget authority	90.3	107.6	49.0	7.6	7.3	261.8	15.1	4.7	−4.7	−4.1	−1.9	−1.4	269.5
Estimated outlays	85.3	108.6	49.9	8.1	7.4	259.3	15.1	4.7	−4.7	−4.1	−1.9	−1.4	267.0
Revenues													
Estimated revenues	−64.8	−180.1	−8.2	10.0	2.7	−240.4	5.5	7.1	5.8	5.1	5.0	0.1	−211.8

Sources: Congressional Budget Office and own calculations; Recovery and Reinvestment Act of 2009; *American Recovery and Reinvestment Act of 2009 (P.L. 111–15): Summary and Legislative History*, Congressional Research Service.

(a)

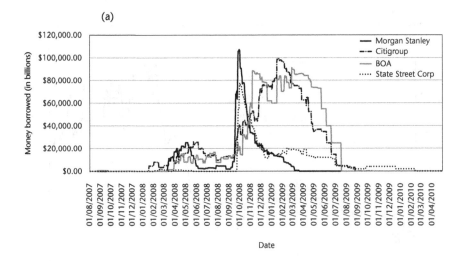

(b)

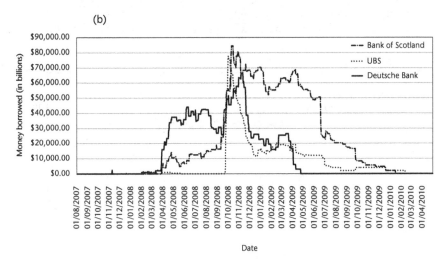

FIGURE A5.1 (a) Cumulative debt owed to Fed by US banks; (b) Cumulative debt owed to Fed by European banks

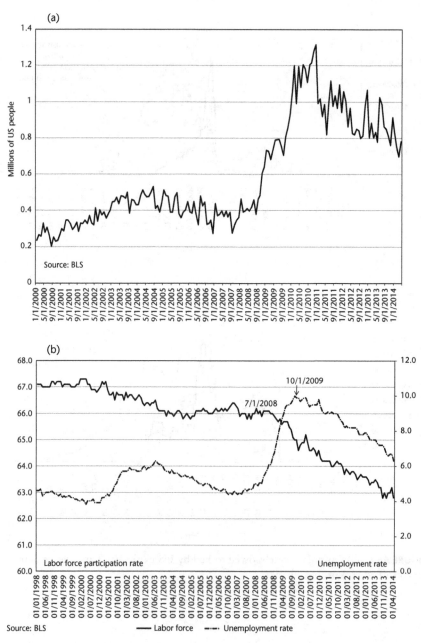

FIGURE A5.2   (a) Discouraged workers in the US; (b) Labor force participation and unemployment rate

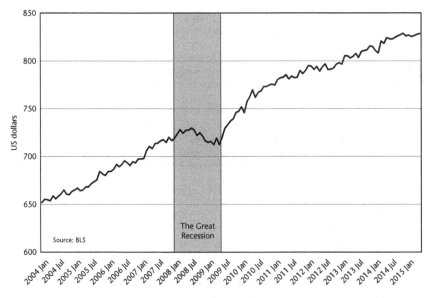

FIGURE A5.3 Average weekly earnings of production

Notes

1 See Federal Reserve Board of Governors FOMC Press Release, December 18, 2013 (www.federalreserve.gov/newsevents/press/monetary/20131218a.htm).
2 This was the third upward revision of the annual real GDP growth for 2013 from the 3.6 that was calculated in the second estimate (Bureau of Economic Analysis News Release, December 20, 2013).
3 See Weisman (2013).
4 There was a small possibility for the fiscal crisis to reemerge after February 2014, as the US public debt was approaching its limit if Congress failed to approve an increase in the US Federal debt ceiling. This probability has been reduced as the Tea Party was substantially weakened, and Congress lifted the ceiling of the public debt for the next two fiscal years.
5 N. Irwin (2008) "Fast-moving economy challenged architects of stimulus," *Washington Post*, February 18.
6 The employment rate increased in 2010 despite the fact that the US was officially out of the recession at the end of 2009.
7 Barry Nelson (2009) "A ride and demise of new century financial," *Investopedia*, February 22.
8 Often the same institutions received aid from different bailout programs.
9 The name of the TARP program was officially kept, although it was a completely different program aiming to assist financially distressed institutions instead of buying toxic securities.
10 A credit default swap is insurance of securities against a non-payment by a third party.
11 See Kregel (2008).
12 Therefore the criticism may be challenged as the most important bank holding companies came out winners after the crisis, even stronger, and indeed bigger, albeit with the help and approval of the government.
13 Brass *et al.* (2009).
14 This amount would be in line with the 2012 federal budget.

15 Note that all US states except Vermont have a legal requirement to always balance their budgets, thus they cannot employ deficit spending to boost their economies.

16 Originally, the tax benefits were not the largest component of ARRA. As a matter of fact, the tax benefits originally provided the smallest amount of the three components.

17 http://www.recovery.gov/arra/Pages/default.aspx

18 This is seen in Figure 5.3 by the intersection of the two line graphs in 2012.

19 See Detrixhe (2011).

20 Agency debt refers to bonds issued by GSEs to raise capital for their own purpose.

21 The bubble, however, began forming during the dot-com crisis and burst prior to the onset of the US subprime mortgage crisis. Low or no excess reserves simply means that lending institutions had extended many loans and could not extend additional ones.

22 Federal funds were most often traded during this period at 10 to 15 basis points. See Blinder (2010).

23 Federal Reserve Statistical Release (H.4.1 Factors Affecting Reserve Balances), April 2014.

24 See Bullard (2010).

25 See Blinder (2010).

26 The traditional monetary policy focuses on the interest rate which is the price of money.

27 See Von Hagen (2009).

28 GSEs, here, include Fannie Mae, Freddie Mac, Ginnie, Mae and the 12 Federal Home Loan Banks. It is, however, customary that the news media and others use the term GSEs to refer only to the two former US quasi-public housing giants Fannie Mae and Freddie Mac which were nationalized in September 2008.

29 See the QE timeline in Figure 5.8 of this chapter.

30 In addition to $600 billion the Fed also planned to purchase another $250–300 billion of Treasury securities from the proceeds of the MBSs. The latter, however is not considered QE as it was the replacement of one asset by another and not an injection of new money.

31 This policy has already run into problems because unemployment rates dropped below 6.5 percent (April 2014) and on May 5, 2014 the unemployment rate dropped to 6.3 percent. As of June 2015, the Fed has still not delivered on this announcement as it has not raised the federal funds rate above 0–0.25 of 1 percent even though the unemployment rate was at 5.5 percent.

32 It usually takes some time to recognize that the economy needs a fiscal stimulus (recognition time lag). It also takes time from the recognition of the need for a fiscal stimulus to the implementation (action time lag). Lastly, once the fiscal stimulus bill is implemented it takes time to observe the expected effect on the economy (effect time lag).

33 The personal income tax system, the unemployment compensation and the US welfare programs are the three major built-in stabilizers in the US economy.

34 The only exception was spending during the Great Depression 1929–33.

35 Such optimistic results were reported in a paper by Christina Romer and Jarod Bernstein. Note: Christina Romer served as the head of the Council of Economic Advisors in the Obama Administration (2009–10).

36 See Mankiew (2007).

37 See Tcherneva (2001).

38 Bureau of Labor Statistics, June 2015.

39 Hysterisis means that after the end of the crisis the unemployment rate did not return to the pre-crisis level.

References

Blinder, A. S. (2010) "Quantitative easing: entrance and exit strategies," *Federal Reserve Bank of St. Louis Review*, 92 (6): 465–79.

Brass, C. T., Vincent, C. H., Jackson, P. J., Lake, J. E., Spar, K., and Keith, R. (2009) "American Recovery and Reinvestment Act of 2009 (P.L. 111-5): Summary and Legislative History", Congressional Research Service, April 20.

Bullard, J. (2010) "Three lessons for monetary policy from the panic of 2008," *Federal Reserve Bank of St. Louis Review*, 92 (3): 155–63.

Cogan, J. F., Cwik, T., and Taylor, J. B. (2009) *New Keynesian Versus Old Keynesian Government Spending Multipliers*. National Bureau of Economic Research, Working Paper No. 14782.

Detrixhe, J. (2011) "U.S. loses AAA rating at S&P on concern debt cuts deficient," *Bloomberg Business*, August 6.

Federal Reserve Board of Governors (2013) Press Release. Federal Reserve Board of Governors. December 18. See: www.federalreserve.gov/newsevents/press/monetary/20131218a.htm.

Kregel, J. (2008) *Will the Paulson Bailout Produce the Basis for Another Minsky Moment?* Levy Economics Institute, January.

Mankiew, G. N. (2010) "Questions about fiscal policy implications from the financial crisis of 2008–2009," *Federal Reserve Bank of St. Louis Review*, 92 (3): 177–83.

Neely, C. J. (n.d.) *How Persistent are Monetary Policy Effects at the Zero Lower Bound?* Working Paper. See http://research.stlouisfed.org/wp/2014/2014-004.pdf.

Romer, C. and Bernstein, J. (2009) "The job impact of the American recovery and reinvestment plan," January 8. www.illinoisworknet.com.

Schroeder, R. (2008) "Bush signs economic stimulus package," *MarketWatch*, February 13.

Taylor, J. B. (2010) "Getting back on track: macroeconomic policy lessons from the financial crisis," *Federal Reserve Bank of St. Louis Review*, 92 (3): 165–76.

Taylor, J. B. (2014) "The role of policy in the great recession and the weak recovery," *American Economic Review: Papers & Proceedings*, 105 (5): 61–6.

Tcherneva, P. R. (2011) *Fiscal Policy Effectiveness: Lessons from the Great Recession*, Levy Economics Institute, Working Paper No. 649.

Von Hagen, J. (2009) *The Monetary Mechanics of the Crisis*, Brugek Policy Contribution, August.

Weisman, J. (2013) "Senate passes $3.7 trillion budget, setting up contentious negotiations," *New York Times*, March 23.

6

THE ROLE OF GERMANY IN
THE FINANCIAL CRISIS

A graphical presentation of German trade and growth

Despite the Allies' influence in governing Germany after World War II (1945–55), the German people played a crucial role in the formation of the economic and political system of their country. They accomplished this by successfully developing the model of the social market economy. For Germany, this was a rather unique system, relying on free markets, strong cooperation of employers with workers, and an important role for the government to promote social inclusion to reduce income inequality. This economic system also became known as the Rhineland model of capitalism.[1]

The German people were exceptionally successful in rebuilding their economy in a relatively short period of time.[2] Figure 6.1 depicts the real GDP growth of Germany for the period 1951–2013. During the first decade, 1951–60, Germany grew at a spectacular rate of 8.3 percent. Economists still debate the sources of economic growth in Germany during this period. Because of the phenomenal rise in real GDP, economists justifiably named this the miracle growth period (*Wirtschaftswunder*). During the next five decades, Germany generated a positive rate of growth, but much lower than in the first decade. Despite this moderate rate of growth, after the 2008–9 recession, Germany's economy performed relatively better than most other European economies; thus Germany is still considered the engine of the Euro Area (EA) economy.

During this last sub-period, 2010–13, the European sovereign debt crisis spread, and Germany, along with a few other Northern European countries, was criticized for having contributed to the increase in the public debt of the periphery EA members, and was subsequently considered partially responsible for the recession.[3] Although Germany experienced its worst post-World War II recession in 2009, its economy has since recovered and attained positive but declining real rates of economic growth.

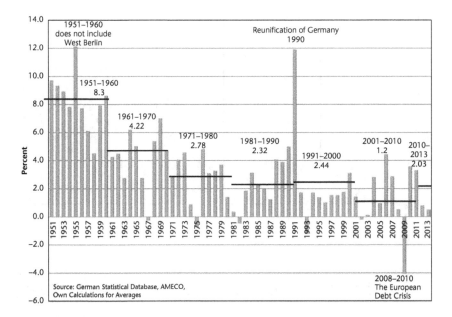

FIGURE 6.1 Growth of German GDP 1951–2013

Many economists attribute the miraculous rate of growth of Germany to sound market-oriented economic policies adopted by the German governments.[4] On the other hand, Rudi Dornbusch, the late MIT economist, suggested that this growth could not be exclusively attributed to the German free market approach because a few other countries, such as Japan and France, that also attained high growth rates did not embrace the German liberal market approach.[5] During the period 1950–2014, the economic growth of Germany was strongly associated with the boom in the German export sector. The policy adopted by Germany after World War II was rather mercantilistic as the value of exports (X) always exceeded the value of imports (M), generating a sequence of trade balance surpluses.

Figure 6.2 depicts the German trade balance as a percentage of GDP for the period 1950–2013. It is evident from this figure that Germany did not generate a single trade deficit after 1951. The figure clearly indicates that, prior to 1990, Germany's trade surpluses can be grouped into three main sub-periods each lasting for over a decade.[6] The last sub-period of trade expansion (1990–2014) lasted about twice as long as each of the previous three trade sub-periods.

During the last part of this sub-period (1990–2014), the European sovereign debt crisis spread across the EA periphery countries. Germany, along with a few Northern EU countries, was criticized because many analysts believed their trade imbalances were destabilizing the EA economy. The German government responded to this criticism by stating that the trade deficit countries were responsible for such imbalances.

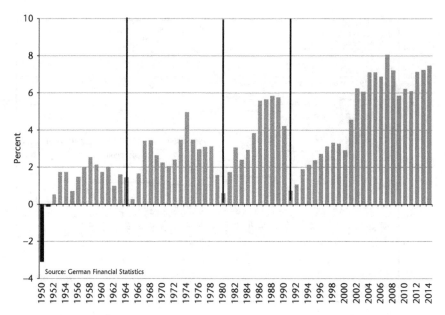

FIGURE 6.2 German trade balance (X – M) as a percentage of GDP 1950–2014

Many economists agree that Germany's economic growth can be explained by the export-led growth model. In October 2014, for example, Germany generated a larger Current Account (CA) surplus than any other country in the world. In 2014, Germany's CA surplus was $289.6 billion, amounting to 7.1 percent of its GDP. The country with the second largest CA was China: China generated a CA surplus of $213 billion, which is over half of Germany's CA and is only 2.1 percent of its GDP.[7] In the early 2010s, Chinese surpluses, particularly with the US, were a major issue debated by both academics and politicians.

As Chinese trade surpluses gradually shrank toward the end of the last decade, attention has shifted to Germany. At the 2011 G20 Summit in Cannes, France, Germany insisted that countries should agree on specific economic indicators to help "monitor" the causes of trade imbalances. Such indicators, however, should not be quantifiable. This meant that Germany was not going to accept a ceiling on its trade surplus. German representatives pointed out that capital flow volatility and cross border financing that allowed the increase of the trade surpluses must also be a concern.[8] This implied that Northern European banks that extended credit to finance the trade surpluses should have recognized the risk they were taking.

Figure 6.3 demonstrates how the German trade sector increasingly became more important for the entire German economy. Both the real GDP and the trade balance of Germany are presented as indices for the period 1950–2014 in this figure.[9] Starting in the early 1970s, the German trade balances began fluctuating above and below the GDP index. In 2001, nevertheless, Germany's trade

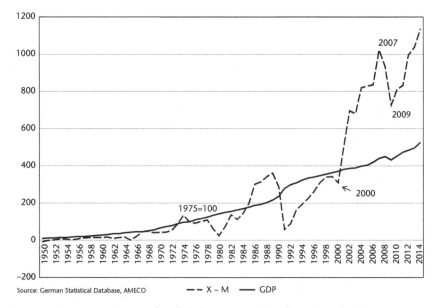

FIGURE 6.3 German GDP and trade balance (X – M) indices 1950–2014

surpluses began expanding almost exponentially. This turning point approximately coincided with the establishment of the Economic and Monetary Union (EMU). An exception to this upward trend, however, occurred during the subprime mortgage crisis (2007–9), when the US and other countries experienced stagnation and were forced to reduce their imports from Germany.

The German unemployment rate

Although the rate of growth of the West German economy declined after the end of the first postwar decade (1950–60), the economy was still in a very healthy condition as the unemployment rate stayed very low, below two percent for approximately ten years (see Figure 6.4). In the early 1970s, particularly during the first oil crisis (1973–4), the unemployment rate increased rapidly until it almost doubled in 1976. A more drastic increase in the German unemployment rate began in 1979–80 during the second oil crisis that lasted till 1985. After a decline in the years 1985–90, the German unemployment rate increased substantially by more than five percentage points between 1990 and 1997. This last increase is mainly attributed to the reunification of Germany and to the Maastricht Treaty; the latter induced a contractionary fiscal policy on all candidate EMU members that were required to meet the Maastricht convergence criteria. In 1997, the German unemployment rate reached a peak of 12.7 percent before it began declining for four years; thereafter it increased sharply to hit its all-time peak of 13 percent in 2005.

During the early 1990s, Germany's economy stagnated to the extent that its performance ranked last in comparison to the world's major economies.[10] It was

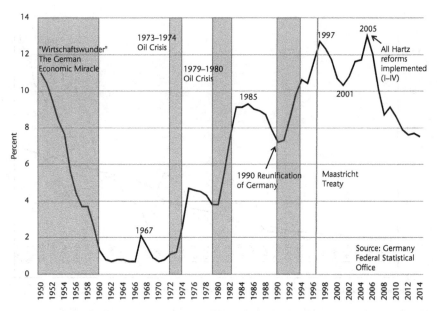

FIGURE 6.4 German unemployment rate 1950–2014

obvious then to many Germans, especially to business representatives, that the German social market economy model was no longer capable of withstanding international competition. Many business people were convinced that the economy was overregulated and the government was very protective of the workers. Since 2005, a drastic decline in the German unemployment rate began. This decline in the unemployment rate is almost exclusively attributed to labor and other reform policies introduced by the coalition government of the Social Democratic Party (SPD) and the Green Party, headed by Chancellor Gerhard Schröder. Such legal reforms became known as Hartz I–IV, named after the president of the committee, Peter Hartz, which was charged with investigating the necessary measures for the German economy to return to growth and reduce unemployment.

Coping with EU stagnation: the Lisbon Agenda

In the early 1970s, the miracle growth period had ended. This can be seen in Figure 6.4 through the increasing German unemployment rate that only stopped rising in 2005 after hitting its peak of 13 percent, exactly when the Hartz reforms were launched.

During this period, the vast majority of Western European countries experienced stagnation. The two oil crises in 1973–4 and 1979–80 negatively affected almost all Western European economies. Over-regulation of the European economies, rigidity of labor markets, and liberal unemployment and pension benefits rendered EU firms internationally uncompetitive. Germany was not an exception to this general trend. There was a clear understanding at that time that the EU was falling behind the US and Japan. Another problem that afflicted most European economies was the aging populations which threatened to render the pension systems unsustainable unless fiscal consolidation was introduced.

At the March 2000 EU Summit in Lisbon, EU leaders decided to launch a major EU program aiming to help transform the EU economy within ten years into the most competitive economy in the world. The new program was named the Lisbon Agenda, after the capital of Portugal where the treaty was drafted and signed. To achieve the Lisbon Agenda goals, all governments agreed to launch a set of new programs to improve business innovation and competitiveness. EU member governments became committed to pursuing macroeconomic stability and transforming their labor markets to become more flexible and efficient.

Labor reforms entailed reduction in pension payments through fiscal consolidation, reduction in wages, and other benefits to labor. In addition, businesses sought more freedom in hiring and firing workers. Such labor reforms were perceived by laborers in many EU countries as a direct shift of wealth from workers to businesses.[11] These reforms were carried out with the full support of many governments, which were convinced that they were both necessary and unavoidable. As a result, the countries were able to regain international competitiveness, return their economies to growth, and reduce chronic unemployment. Like other Western European countries, Germany also suffered from over-regulation and rigid labor markets that were encouraged by the social market economy environment.

For many years, Germany's social market economy evolved as a successful economic system. Under this system, it was possible for the country to achieve economic growth based on exports by concentrating mainly on high-quality and technologically advanced products in the manufacturing sector. Economic growth was the result of the close cooperation between workers and employers. In an amicable environment, employee training was of vital importance as it helped boost labor productivity. Consequently, Germany attained high and rapidly rising standards of living. In addition, the government's social policy promoted social inclusion through various policies that provided a liberal social safety net to prevent people from falling into poverty. It is, however, true that other Western European countries also attained high rates of growth and a rising standard of living.

For a long time, the core of Germany's economy was based on small and medium-sized enterprises (SMEs).[12] In German, these firms are known as *Mittelstand*, which are often family-owned companies. The owners of these firms always develop excellent relations with their employees who receive continuous training and remain with the company for a lifetime. To help companies withstand international competition during the crisis, employers often ask their employees to accept reduced wages and even to work longer hours for reduced pay.[13] The flexible arrangement within the *Mittelstand* firms allowed them to adjust both the work hours per week and the wages. In German, this program is called *Kurzarbeit* (short work). This has been a labor practice in Germany for over one hundred years. During the European sovereign debt crisis, unlike in other countries, *Kurzarbeit* helped Germany maintain low unemployment rates.

In the early 1990s, Germany's economy nevertheless revealed serious weaknesses. It had become an unattractive place for both domestic and foreign investors as a result of high tax rates and high labor costs. Large companies such as Siemens and Volkswagen preferred to invest in other countries.[14] High tax rates were necessary to support the liberal welfare benefits and the generous and long-lasting unemployment insurance programs. Beyond the common West European problems of over-regulation, excessive taxation, and labor rigidity, Germany experienced additional challenges as a result of the reunification of the country in 1990, following the collapse of the Berlin Wall.

The celebration of the reunification had just ended when the integration process was launched and problems began to surface. It soon became evident that economic convergence was not going to be a quick or a painless process, particularly for East Germany, the New Länder, since its economy was not catching up quickly with the more advanced economy of West Germany.[15] Although East Germany was the most industrialized country among the Eastern European countries, its technology was lagging far behind West Germany's. As a consequence of deindustrialization in the New Länder, the unemployment rate rapidly increased from 0 to 20 percent.[16] Many East European workers moved to West Germany in search of employment, exacerbating the unemployment situation in West Germany. However, East Germany's stagnation was unprecedented as West German exporting companies which were "destroying jobs in foreign countries now turned to East Germany."[17]

Chancellor Helmut Kohl's government plan to impose a parity, a one-to-one rate, between the currencies of the two Germanies indicated that integration in Germany was based on strong political commitment and determination that was pursued at any economic cost. It is interesting that a similar approach to the formation of the currency union between the two Germanies in the 1990s was also adopted in the launching of the euro and the establishment of the EMU in 1999. EU country leaders decided to create the EMU rapidly – they did not choose the gradual integration approach by maintaining fixed exchange rates for a certain period to allow market adjustments to facilitate a smoother convergence process. EU leaders decided then not to require real economic convergence among candidate countries, which would have allowed them to reach the same level of economic development prior to joining the EMU. Instead, nominal convergence was required of all candidate countries according to the five Maastricht convergence criteria.[18]

The trade unions requested quick adjustments in East German wages to West German wages, despite existing differences in labor productivity. Consequently, high wages made East Germany uncompetitive and unable to attract investment, and as a result it fell behind in terms of competitiveness in relation to the other East European countries.[19] Massive fiscal transfers from the former West Germany intended to assist in the catch-up process created additional issues among the people of the two Germanies. First, such large fiscal transfers made it difficult for

Germany to exercise fiscal discipline to meet the Maastricht fiscal convergence criteria prior to joining the EMU. Second, fiscal transfers to East Germany changed the perception of their compatriots in the West from considering the East Germans as innocent victims of Soviet totalitarianism for over forty years to "lazy recipients of their taxes."[20] The natural feeling as a result of such negative development according to Schmidt (2009) was "betrayal and estrangement" for the peoples of East Germany.[21] The perception of the Germans and other Northern Europeans about the bailout recipients of the periphery EA countries is almost identical to the views of West Germans about East Germans. There is, however, a major difference between the two cases. Germany and the other Northern EA countries made relatively small direct contributions from their treasuries to the bailout countries at the expense of their taxpayers. The vast majority of the funds for the bailouts were borrowed through the issuance of bonds that the EMU countries guaranteed to pay if the bailout countries declared bankruptcy.[22] Almost all funding for the European Financial Stability Facility (EFSF) and the European Stability Mechanism (ESM), the two bailout funds created by the EU amounting to €1 trillion, was borrowed by issuing bonds. Only €80 billion was paid by the treasuries of the EA member countries of which €27 billion, the largest amount, was paid by Germany. EU countries contributed a total of €110 billion to the first bailout of Greece in May 2011, of which Germany paid €22.4 billion. This bailout is one of the main reasons that the news media were able to turn public opinion against Greece. However, not the entire amount of €110 billion was paid to Greece as instalments were discontinued when the second bailout was approved.

The launching of Agenda 2010 in Germany

A few years prior to the end of the millennium, European policy circles and academia were involved in intense discussions regarding the need to liberalize the European economies. The EU responded to the challenge of the chronic high unemployment and stagnation by launching the Lisbon Agenda in 2000. In Germany, the coalition government of the SPD with the Green Party, headed by Chancellor Gerhard Schröder, introduced its own version of the Lisbon Agenda for Germany. After long discussions and extensive research involving several German research institutions, Chancellor Schröder asked all political parties and trade unions to engage in debates about adopting the necessary reforms that would render the German economy internationally competitive. Lastly, many agreed to support the reforms to reinvigorate the German economy, which had been faltering for several years.

Chancellor Schröder invited Peter Hartz, a former personnel director of Volkswagen AG, to head a committee charged with the preparation of the proposed reforms to be written into laws that would help transform Germany into a very competitive economy. The Hartz reforms were in line with the Lisbon Agenda that all EU governments agreed to introduce into law in their countries.

Many Germans who had voted for the Social Democrats and the Green Party that had formed the SPD-Greens coalition government became frustrated as soon as the 2000 election was over because the new government campaigned for the introduction and launching of a set of more neoliberal programs instead of social protections. The new programs were designed to assist businesses gain international competitiveness, which would boost economic growth and reduce chronic unemployment. The Agenda 2010 reforms were submitted by Chancellor Schröder to the German parliament (the *Bundestag*), which approved a great number of the proposals to become laws.

The Hartz reforms created incentives for workers to search for work and find employment, because it was no longer in the workers' interest to remain unemployed since the liberal long unemployment benefits were drastically cut. The German agenda restructured the Federal Employment Agency and modernized the welfare system.[23] Wages and other benefits, such as pensions and healthcare for workers, were substantially reduced as new types of employment were introduced. Wages under these new types of employment were set outside the contracts that customarily were agreed and signed through negotiations between trade unions and employers associations.

The new type of employment that the Hartz reforms encouraged is also known as precarious employment. Examples of this type of employment are fixed-term contracts, agency work, temporary work, mini-jobs, midi-jobs, and others.[24] Such new forms of work are contingent on the needs of the employer. Consequently, job dissatisfaction and insecurity both increased with the Hartz reforms, since workers are employed when needed and dispensed with easily without much cost to the employers. The situation regarding precarious employment is better in Germany than in other countries, but still constitutes a major social problem exacerbating income inequality.[25]

High unemployment in Germany after 1990 tilted the bargaining power away from the trade unions to companies, which imposed their conditions under the threat that they would invest abroad and close factories in Germany.[26] Laborers employed in precarious types of employment were those who lost the most from the neoliberal policies promoted by Agenda 2010. These workers not only received very low wages and benefits, but also lost the liberal welfare benefit transfers that existed in Germany prior to the launching of Agenda 2010 if they become unemployed.[27]

Many analysts in Germany attributed the quick recovery of the German economy from the financial crisis to the Hartz reforms that were adopted. Although Germany experienced a severe recession in 2009, its economy recovered remarkably well and generated positive rates of growth while its unemployment rate was kept exceptionally low since the introduction of the Hartz reforms in 2003–5. Several other analysts, however, are convinced that the resilience of the German economy that helped it to quickly recover from the recession and maintain a low unemployment rate is due to other factors that pre-dated the crisis and made it possible for the Hartz reform programs to be effective. Such characteristics of the German economy include the decentralization of labor union agreements, *Kurzabeit* (short work), and the weakening of trade unions.

Decentralization of collective bargaining

Chronic unemployment in Germany was caused by labor market rigidity and over-regulation of the economy. The high German unemployment rate was also partially explained by the organizations that negotiated labor agreements. Specifically, for many years prior to the launching of the Hartz reforms, labor agreements in Germany were decided at the national and regional levels through bargaining of the respective trade unions and the employers' association representatives. Negotiations and agreements regarding labor compensation at such high aggregation levels, however, could not take into consideration differences in labor productivity, and as a result such agreements were neither efficient nor equitable.

Nevertheless, long before the announcement of the German agenda in one important sector of the German economy, namely engineering, labor compensation agreements for many employees were negotiated and agreed at the company-specific level, i.e. by the employer and the respective plant union. Several engineering firms had left the employers' associations in order to avoid paying the high wages agreed between the national union, IG Metal, and the employers association, the Gesametmetall.[28] Six thousand companies sought and concluded company-specific collective agreements as far back as 2002, and the trend continued after the adoption of the Hartz reforms.

Short work **(Kurzabeit)** *and working time accounts*

Kurzabeit is an agreement between workers and employers on wages and the work week at the plant level.[29] These agreements take place during periods of low demand for a firm's products. In such a situation, a firm reduces the working hours and the wages of certain employees. The interested company must apply to the Employment Office to participate in the program for short-time work support. The Employment Office upon approval reimburses the company for the short hours that the employees did not work but got paid. This payment for unworked hours takes place at a reduced rate in the range of 60–67 percent of standard wages, as the government Employment Office indirectly pays these wages for hours not worked. *Kurzabeit* is a direct subsidization program of wages by the government and is paid by the unemployment insurance fund.

According to some analysts, the moderate increase of the unemployment rate during the 2008–9 recession is also attributed to a related program known as a "working time account." Under this program, the employee accumulates working hours above the standard hours without being paid regular or overtime wages; the employee saves these unpaid hours in the working time account.[30] During times of low demand for the company's products, these employees are paid as if they were working full time although they are working fewer hours than standard. There exists evidence that short work accounts began increasing prior to and after the launching of the Agenda 2010. Both short work and working time accounts helped Germany reduce unemployment by allowing firms to cut hours during the recession instead of laying off workers. The two programs made firms more efficient and internationally competitive as they reduced the cost of laying off skilled workers, thus avoiding the rehiring and retraining process.

Short work and working time accounts are negotiated by the Works Councils, i.e. the representatives of the workers in each plant. The question arises as to why short work and working time accounts were introduced in Germany? These two schemes are important in saving jobs by shedding working hours and not workers; therefore, they are in line with the goals of the social market economy model that for years provided social protection. *Kurzabeit* and working time accounts were successful programs for Germany because they maintained a high employment level, especially during the recession.

Weakening of trade unions

Labor compensation and other related issues for both private and public sector workers in Germany were customarily decided through negotiation between the regional or national trade unions and the employer association's representatives. This institutional practice, nonetheless, has drastically changed since the German reunification in 1990, as for a brief time there was a sharp increase in union membership. In 1991, trade union membership in the unified Germany was 11.9 million workers. This was a substantial increase from the trade union membership prior to 1990 – the trade union participation rate increased by approximately five percentage points. But by 2011, trade union membership dropped by 5.6 million whereas the trade union participation rate dropped by 17.96 percentage points. The drastic decline in trade union participation was mainly the consequence of the sharp increase in the unemployment rate after reunification. The reduction in the trade union participation rate weakened the bargaining power of the trade unions.[31]

By the mid-1970s and even more so after the reunification of Germany, businesses responded to globalization and international competition by cutting the costs of production. Many firms requested that agreements on labor remuneration be made on a plant-specific basis to take into consideration labor productivity differences. German businesses also sought new forms of employment agreements, of the precarious type, that were not negotiated with the trade unions. Such forms of employment are less costly to firms because precarious workers are paid lower wages than union workers and receive very low or no benefits for the same amount and type of work. Furthermore, these workers are not provided with job security. The German government leaders became convinced that labor cost reduction was the way to reduce unemployment and to gain international competitiveness. This was the German response to the globalization challenge. Several German leaders approved and encouraged the suppression of labor remuneration and, thus, a reduction in the standard of living of the lowest paid workers and the unemployed.

Agenda 2010 legalized labor practices that were already taking place without official government endorsement. Several economists, who adhered to the theory of functional integration, criticized the trade unions for demanding a quick

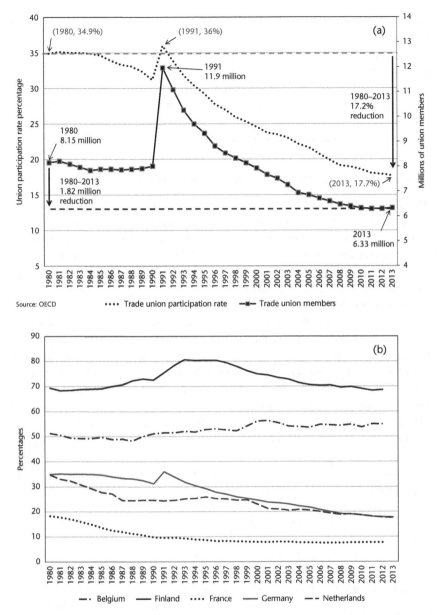

FIGURE 6.5 (a) Trade union membership rate in Germany 1980–2013; (b) Trade union membership rate in Northern EA countries

adjustment of the East German wages and benefits to the level of the West German workers' wages. The trade unions' demands totally ignored labor productivity differences and did not allow market forces to bring about a gradual adjustment. The same analysts were also critics of Chancellor Kohl's political decision to force an immediate currency union by imposing a one-to-one parity between the currencies of the two Germanies. East Germany, as a result of the currency union, became a less competitive economy because costs of production increased substantially.

Figure 6.5(b) shows that the German, Dutch, and French trade union participation rates dropped the most out of the five Northern EA countries. No other country's trade union participation rate, however, displays the 1990–1 abrupt change caused by the German reunification.

Did the Hartz reforms pose unfair competition?

The question arises as to whether the German Agenda 2010 posed unfair competition against Germany's trading partners. A country exercises unfair international competition if it subsidizes its exports or manipulates its currency to create a comparative advantage. As a member of the World Trade Organization (WTO), Germany cannot legally subsidize its industries via direct payments or through any other hidden subsidies. Germany was not, however, accused of such subsidization or any other form of protectionism.

It is, however, a well-known fact that the German government subsidized labor compensation. This was done through the *Kurzarbeit* (short work) program for many years but particularly during and after the Eurocrisis. The government subsidized wages of workers for additional hours that firms could not afford to pay for on their own. Therefore firms were able to keep their skilled workers instead of firing them and rehiring new workers. This means when market conditions improved, firms were able to save a lot of money. Such a program created an uneven level of competition against foreign importing firms competing against German exports.

German exporting firms remained competitive in relation to competing foreign import firms by using the time account program as well since they did not have to lay off their skilled workers. German firms were also able to reduce production costs through negotiating labor agreements at the plant-specific level. All of these schemes enabled German exporting firms to establish a comparative advantage.

The creation of precarious types of employment and the decrease in welfare benefits reduced personal disposable income for many Germans. As a result, consumption on domestic and foreign goods declined. In addition, such policies helped Germany become the leading exporting country in the world through the promotion of its own exports and indirectly discouraging imports, as it suppressed the income of many German workers.

Germany, however, could not manipulate the exchange rate to keep the euro undervalued and promote its exports. The value of the euro, the euro exchange rate in terms of foreign currencies, is determined in the market and can be affected by the ECB and the ECOFIN, the two institutions responsible for the euro exchange rate policy. Germany, nonetheless, succeeded in promoting its exports through a reduction in labor compensation. Can reduction in wages and benefits constitute unfair competition? Not necessarily, if other countries were also allowed to adopt similar policies by impoverishing their workers. This is something the Lisbon Agenda promoted for all EU countries.

Many exporting countries around the world have succeeded in achieving growth by adopting export-led policies, relying mainly on supply side pro-business policies and deregulation. In the EU, all countries had the opportunity to adopt neoliberal pro-business policies after the EU launched the Lisbon Agenda (2000). This is exactly what Germany did. The only difference is that Germany pushed such policies much harder than any other country did in the EU, thus suppressing the standard of living of a large number of its own workers. A major fallacy, however, exists in the campaign taken up by the German government advising other countries to follow its policies to attain economic growth. It is impossible within the EU for all member countries to generate trade surpluses, since this is simply the old mercantilistic advice of the self-defeating trade policy, that countries only trade as long as they generate surpluses. Furthermore, the German government kept giving the same advice about generating trade surpluses to all the trading partners of these countries.

The periphery EU countries began generating trade surpluses from 2013, thus German surpluses vis-à-vis the periphery EA members practically dissipated. However, this did not affect the magnitude of the German exports because Germany generated trade surpluses with other countries outside the EU and the EA. Consequently German trade surpluses with the EU were substantially reduced, whereas trade with EA countries had almost disappeared by the second quarter of 2013 (see Figure 6.6).

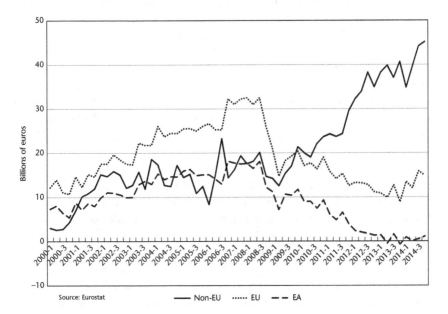

FIGURE 6.6 German trade balances by region 2000–14

Since Germany adopted the social market economy model, it provided more protection to its citizens than other countries with a possible exception of the Scandinavian countries. Germany was able to reduce income inequality for many years till the mid-1990s. The adoption and the launching of the Agenda 2010 reversed the trend on income inequality.

Because neoliberal policies and precarious employment were adopted by many countries, Germany alone cannot be criticized. It is incorrect to single out Germany when the OECD, the IMF, and the World Bank advised countries to adopt neoliberal policies that increase precarious employment.[32] Several analysts strongly believe that neoliberal policies promoting precarious employment, leading to income inequality and job insecurity, must not continue. Such policies ought to be reversed, as they contribute to the deterioration of the standard of living of the German people, especially in the lowest income classes, and furthermore destroy the competing import industries of trading partners.[33]

German leadership and its stance towards the EU

Almost all political German parties since the end of World War II were very supportive of Germany's position and membership of the EU. All of Germany's leaders followed a European course for Germany. As a result Germany has been at the forefront of deeper integration. This course lasted until the beginning of the Eurocrisis. The two biggest political parties in Germany are the Christian Democratic Union (CDU) and the Social Democratic Party (SPD). These two main political parties have been alternating in governing Germany, either in a coalition with one or two of the smaller parties or jointly. The close cooperation of the German political parties has created a stable political environment which turned out to be both a necessary and an important condition for the economic growth and prosperity that Germany achieved. Chancellor Helmut Kohl was the Chancellor of Germany from 1982 to 1990 and was the most pro-European Chancellor in Germany's history. He visualized the future of Germany only within the EU. He was also the first Chancellor of the unified Germany. After his term as Chancellor he was replaced by Angela Merkel as the leader of the CDU. Merkel has been elected for three consecutive terms as the Chancellor of Germany.

Angela Merkel's third term in the office of Chancellor was also when the Eurocrisis began. Chancellor Merkel's career in German Politics will be mostly remembered in reference to her handling of the European sovereign debt crisis. As the leader of the largest economy in the EU, the Chancellor of Germany was expected to play a decisive role along with the other EU leaders to find an exit from the crisis. The recession has been going on for many years, mostly in Southern European countries. The prolonging of the deep recession is explained by the failure of the EU leaders to convince the markets that EA and EU member countries were united and would not allow speculators to devastate certain EA economies as a result of panic and short selling of their government securities.

Chancellor Merkel's obsession with austerity is a primary reason for the inability of EA countries to recover from the prolonged recession which devastated the periphery countries and still threatens the rest of the EU and the world economy. Germany, under Chancellor Merkel's leadership, is often blamed by the news media and many analysts as the main reason the Eurocrisis has not yet been resolved. In Box 6.1, we employ four metaphors to explain Chancellor Merkel's approach to the Eurocrisis.

BOX 6.1 Summary of Chancellor Merkel's handling of the crisis

The Swabian housewife

In 2008, Chancellor Angela Merkel spoke at an event in Stuttgart, the capital of the South-Western State of Baden-Würtenberg, where she stated that failing American banks could have learned from the Swabian housewives of the region who have a reputation of knowing how to manage money.[a] Since then, Chancellor Merkel has frequently invoked the Swabian housewife metaphor in her speeches about the Eurocrisis as the Chancellor is convinced that the periphery EA countries have been living beyond their means and can learn from the housewife. Chancellor Merkel, however, is neither Swabian nor a housewife. She is the daughter of a pastor and grew up in former East Germany; she was a physical chemist prior to entering politics.[b] Chancellor Merkel's Finance Minister Wolfgang Schäuble, a lawyer and native of Baden-Würtenberg is a great supporter of austerity as being the only way out of the crisis. Although neither the Chancellor nor her Finance Minister are trained economists, they should have been advised that although saving and frugality are beneficial for an individual and a family, it may be detrimental for a whole country or the entire EU. The concept of the "Paradox of Thrift" may be useful to help explain why austerity has prolonged the crisis, since what is good for the part may not be good for the whole. The European obsession with austerity even by those countries which do not need it turned out to be detrimental.

Salami tactics

Chancellor Merkel's dealing with the crisis has often been described by a metaphor portraying the Chancellor cutting thinner and thinner slices of a sausage to give at any new request of aid to the financially distressed countries. In this way, the Chancellor remained popular at home and was re-elected to office. However, she did not help resolve the crisis, and as a result Chancellor Merkel will not be remembered as a great pro-European German leader. She was very far from matching the generosity of US President Dwight Eisenhower who extended massive aid through the Marshall Plan to help the reconstruction of

Europe. Chancellor Merkel's fiscal frugality is exactly the opposite to Chancellor Kohl's pro-European approach especially during the historical German reunification period that involved massive fiscal transfers from West to East Germany to serve a noble cause, to reunite the country.

The infected leg theory

This metaphor is based on a proposed solution for dealing with Greece which was perceived as a bottomless pit when receiving aid thus wasting rescue funding intended to save the country. Greece was the infected limb that had to be amputated to save the body or the rest of the EMU countries. High-level government officials in Chancellor Merkel's coalition were divided into two groups. The first was convinced that a Greek exit should be avoided as it would trigger a domino effect leading to the financial collapse of other countries. The other group was convinced that Greece must be kicked out of the EMU since it was the gangrenous leg that would destroy the entire European project. Wolfgang Schäuble is one of the biggest proponents of this latter theory. It is well understood that many German officials in the Chancellor's government were concerned about the survival of the EMU and the euro particularly since Germany benefitted greatly from membership of the EMU. What is not understood is the comparison of an entire country with an infected leg. It takes a certain type of human character to even think of such a medical metaphor. Many will agree that it is difficult to believe that such a group of people belong to a civilized country in the middle of Europe. Chancellor Merkel did not follow this group's advice on how to deal with Greece in 2012. However, when the Greek public debt crisis was reignited in the middle of 2015, the leaders of the infected leg theory of Chancellor Merkel's party seemed to have the upper hand in the dealings with Greece as they forced the Greek Prime Minister, Alexis Tsipras, to pull out of negotiations about solving the Greek debt problem.

Driving by sight

The last metaphor describes the cautious approach of Chancellor Merkel in dealing with the Eurocrisis: *auf Sicht fahren* (translated as "Driving by sight"). This means that drivers are responsible for being able to stop their vehicles at any time within the distance they can see. This is a customary expression for Germans who often have to drive in fog. Similarly, decisions regarding the handling of the crisis should be such as to protect the German economy. Such a metaphor is very much liked by Chancellor Merkel and her government officials, especially her Finance Minister who claims that Germans are safe under this government even during fog. However, such a cautious and hesitant approach can be credited for the endurance of the recession.

[a] "Hail, the Swabian Housewife," *The Economist*, Stuttgart, February 1, 2014.
[b] Marcus Walker (2013) "Inside Merkel's bet on the Euro's future," *Wall Street Journal*, April 23.

Many analysts argued that saving the euro and the periphery economies required a commitment of funds from the EA countries to create firewalls to protect EA countries' sovereign debt from speculative attacks.[34] Critics of Chancellor Merkel repeatedly stressed that Germany was not doing enough to reverse the crisis. This certainly was the opinion of Radoslaw Sikorski, Poland's Foreign Minister.[35] German inactivity was criticized by many people and political leaders, especially in the periphery countries as their economies were badly battered. Also, some EU officials and major world country leaders criticized Germany for not doing enough to avert the crisis. Some analysts pointed out that Germany gained more than any other country since it generated a sequence of extraordinarily large trade surpluses with the peripheral EA countries. Germany also gained during the crisis since it was able to borrow at exceptionally low interest rates since it became a recipient of massive financial capital flows because it was and still is considered a safe-haven country for investment purposes.

The crisis deepened and spread because both the bailout recipient countries and the Northern EA countries failed to act promptly and take preventive measures prior to the explosion of the crisis. Once the recession spread, it became clear that in order to reverse the crisis, a commitment of large amounts of funds were required. Chancellor Merkel's CDU party governed in coalition with other political parties, the Free Democrats, the Bavarian Christian Social Union (CSU) and even with the main opposition, the Social Democratic Party (SPD). The popularity of Chancellor Merkel among voters/taxpayers is attributed to a large extent to her handling of the crisis and, particularly, the bailouts to the financially distressed countries.

Chancellor Merkel faces multiple constraints in her job. She must satisfy domestic demands and keep bailout payments at a minimum, but in her role as the leader of the economically strongest EU country, she is under pressure to help financially devastated countries overcome the crisis and to save the euro.

For a variety of reasons, political decisions in Germany are very complicated, more so than in other EU countries. This turned out to be particularly true when decisions had to be made to approve the bailouts to periphery EA countries. The first priority of Chancellor Merkel was to keep the voters/taxpayers satisfied who despised the idea of bailing out financially distressed countries with their taxes. The strong opposition of the voters/taxpayers to support the periphery countries with their taxes is explained by the fact that a very large number of the voters are workers who, as a result of the Hartz reforms, have not witnessed increases in their wages and benefits for several years. Many workers have also experienced a reduction in wages as a condition of keeping their jobs as they are employed in precarious work such as part-time and temporary work.

A second constraint faced by Chancellor Merkel is the fact that some politicians in her own party or in the CDU coalition parties tried to gain popularity by strongly opposing the bailouts and by telling voters exactly what they wanted to hear. One such populist politician was Phillip Rösler, the head of the Free Democratic Party, a junior coalition partner in government with the CDU during the term 2009–14, a time of three-party coalition government with the CSU. Mr Rösler frequently made the news, and in almost every one of his public appearances he did not miss the opportunity to speak about his favorite topic: how Greece either complies with the austerity programs imposed by the Troika or has to leave the euro.

The German voters paradoxically punished the Free Democratic Party despite the frequent polemics of its leader against bailouts and, particularly, against Greece. The party lost representation both in the upper and lower levels of the parliament, the *Bundesrat* and the *Bundestag*, respectively. In addition, because of the lack of consensus among government officials on how to deal with the crisis, the German government never spoke with a single voice during the crisis. Consequently, it sent conflicting messages, irritating investors who almost always reacted by dumping their sovereign holdings of the periphery countries in large quantities. This caused sharp increases in long-term interest rates, thus punishing those countries which could no longer borrow in the market.[36]

Many German politicians support the view that fiscal austerity is the right medicine for the bailout countries in order to exit the crisis.[37] A few other politicians in Germany and Northern allied EA countries practice populist politics and tell the voters what they like to hear. Both of these groups of politicians tend to support any EU programs that impose fiscal discipline and think it protects the taxpayers. Although fiscal austerity seemed like a plausible solution to the sovereign debt crisis, it turned out to be the wrong policy to pursue as it deepened and prolonged the crisis. Austerity simply means the application of contractionary fiscal policy. Under normal circumstances, contractionary fiscal policy is recessionary. This is more so when austerity is imposed on several countries simultaneously while some of them are already in a recession. The rest is simple arithmetic: if the goal of a government is to reduce the public debt to GDP ratio, the way to attain this is not by imposing contractionary, recessionary policies. Reducing the GDP, i.e. the denominator of the debt to GDP ratio, simply increases the ratio. This is exactly what the periphery countries were forced to implement in order to qualify for the bailouts.

Several German politicians have invoked the existing treaties to prohibit the ECB, other EU institutions, or the governments of EU members from bailing out financially distressed countries. This approach was adopted mainly to protect the voters/taxpayers. A new treaty was also signed after strong persuasion by Germany in 2012 to reassure the Northern EA countries that their taxpayers will be protected from future bailouts. The treaty became known as the Fiscal Compact Treaty. To reassure fiscal stability in the EA, through this treaty, Germany imposed on all EU member countries discipline and respect for the EMU fiscal rules. EMU member countries, by signing the fiscal compact, delegated fiscal authority to the EU Commission to approve the national budgets and impose penalties on countries violating the fiscal rules. Furthermore, national governments, according to the treaty, are required to operate on a balanced budget. This implies that there can be no discretionary fiscal policy left for the EMU member countries.[38]

One can easily see that recovery from the recession under these new fiscal rules is becoming difficult, as countries have lost a major policy tool in fighting recessions.

Another condition that the German government imposed on the EA member countries was the Private Sector Involvement (PSI) program. Chancellor Merkel's government requested that all bailout recipient countries include a PSI program in their bailout agreement. A PSI program requires that the bond holders (creditors) of a country which receives a bailout to bear a share of the burden by accepting a haircut on the private bond holdings. So far, a haircut has been imposed only on Greece's private bond holders as part of the second Greek bailout program. Most analysts are convinced that the PSI sank Greece into a deeper recession and caused an economic contagion that spread to many other countries. As a result, this was a major reason the crisis has spread and is yet to be resolved.

The lack of European commitment among German politicians explains why the crisis is not resolved. In 2012, Chancellor Merkel's government, however, decided to support the continuation of Greek membership in the EMU. The few rescue programs launched by the EU were approved by the German government, but the approval always came after fierce negotiations to keep the bailout funding to a minimum. An additional constraint to finding a quick solution to the crisis is that most of the important decisions regarding the rescue programs had to be approved by the Constitutional Court of Germany. The rationale for such approval is that any transfer of funding from the German taxpayers to the periphery countries shifts power from the German Parliament (*Bundesrat*) to Brussels. Since this authority must be vested with the German parliament, such transfers of funding require the Constitutional Court of Germany to decide on the legality of such a program. The Constitutional Court almost always approved the government's decision to meet its commitments to the EU. The major issue of the Court, however, is that it always takes a long time to make its decision. This loss of time turned out to be detrimental to the periphery EA countries as markets operate around the clock and speculators do not miss any opportunities to profit at the expense of financially distressed countries.

Euroscepticism in Germany and elsewhere in the EA

Euroscepticism refers to the dissatisfaction of the people of a country or their government or of one or more political parties regarding their EU experience. Euroscepticism usually arises when additional powers are transferred to Brussels and away from member states. Historically, the UK is considered to be a Euroskeptic country, even prior to joining the EU. Euroscepticism in the UK was deeply rooted among many British people. Several EU members and political parties oppose the EU's further concentration of power while they also complain that the existing authority exercised by the EU institutions is excessive and should be repatriated to EU member states.

The main reason for the anti-EU attitudes is based on the strong belief that EU un-elected Brussels bureaucrats make decisions that affect the lives of EU citizens of member countries. Such claims may be valid for the most important EU positions including the President of the EU Commission and the President of the European Council. However, even for these appointments, one can make a point that they take place through a democratic process involving the heads of states which themselves are elected officials, and by the European Parliament (EP) which consists of representatives directly elected by the European voters.

EU citizens, nevertheless, when they had the opportunity to influence the EU through electing their representatives, did not come out to cast their votes in large numbers. Since 1979, when the European Parliament began to be directly elected by the European citizens, the turnout has been declining in such elections, indicating apathy among many EU citizens. The EU parliament together with the EU Commission and Council enact three different types of laws, directives, decisions, and regulations. Such laws are enacted based on the principle of subsidiarity, i.e. the EU will only be delegated authority to regulate certain activities if such activities cannot be handled more efficiently at a lower level of government, i.e. by national, regional, or local governments.

The most recent EP elections took place on May 22–25, 2014. The outcome of these elections carried a strong message for EU leaders as pro-EU parties suffered major losses to anti-European parties of the extreme right or left. More shocking were the large gains of the extreme right, consequently the election results were characterized as "a political earthquake."[39]

The amount of damage and the degree of embarrassment to the countries depended on the outcome of the elections. In general, the results reflected the economic performance of each country during the EP's previous tenure from 2009 to 2014. Germany, the largest economy in the EU, came quickly out of the crisis while performing much better than the other large economies. Consequently, the CDU and SPD, the two major political parties, were ranked first and second in the EU elections followed by a new party initially formed to pursue a single objective, to lead Germany out of the EMU.[40] The new party, Alternative for Germany (AfD), which received 7 percent of the vote is a strong Euroskeptic populist party but is not supporting Germany's exit from the EU. A great embarrassment for Germany was the election of a single neo-Nazi party EP member, Udo Voigt, the former leader of the extreme right-wing National Democratic Party (NPD). The German courts are still examining whether there is a case for banning this neo-Nazi party as the newly elected representative was convicted in 2009 for praising the infamous Waffen SS.[41]

Euroscepticism in other EU countries

In France, an embarrassment was directed towards the two main political parties, the Socialist Party which ranked next to the Union for a Popular Movement (UMP). The two parties jointly received only 35 percent of the votes. The leading party in France was the National Front, an extreme nationalistic right-wing party which is Euroskeptic and anti-immigrant. Ms Marine Le Pen inherited the party from her father Jean-Marie Le Pen, but boosted its popularity and now she has an eye on the French presidency. As for President Hollande, he commented that France is not the only country to face such embarrassment and is in the company of other countries battered by the crisis. President Hollande mentioned that countries needed growth. However, when he had the chance to help organize other countries to form a strong coalition to stop the imposed neoliberal and austerity programs when he was the newly elected President of France, he decided to visit the wrong capital city, Berlin, where it is suspected he was lectured on the importance of German commitment to austerity.

None of the Socialist Party's policies reversed the downward trend in the French economy. Personal scandals concerning President Hollande did not help either. The leaked financial scandals of the UMP kept this party in second place behind the National Front. In the meantime, President Hollande's popularity sank below 20 percent, the lowest of any French president. In the spring and summer of 2014, Hollande appointed Manuel Valls as Finance Minister and Emmanuel Macron as Economy Minister, respectively, both committed to launch neoliberal policies hoping to return the French economy to growth and appease the Germans.

The third largest EU country, the UK, elected as first party a more Euroskeptic anti-EU party than the Conservative governing party of the Prime Minister David Cameron, who is committed to citizens deciding in a referendum by 2017 whether they wish to remain a member of the EU. The UK Independence Party (UKIP) grabbed 27.9 percent of the vote leaving the Conservative and Labor parties each to pick up a quarter of the votes. Such results can only lead to a faster exit of the UK from the EU after more than 40 years of rather troublesome relations. If UK citizens decide to secede from the EU, it will lead to disintegration of the EU.

The first choice for Italian voters was the Democratic Party under the new leadership of the young and ambitious Prime Minister Mateo Renzi who promised to take the economy to a fast recovery. *The Economist* interpreted the election's strong outcome of 40 percent for Mr Renzi as possibly empowering him to go up against both Chancellor Merkel and the austerity programs. As for the next two parties, the Five Star Movement (M5S) led by comedian and blogger Pepe Grillo captured 20 percent of the vote while Sylvio Berlasconi's Forza Italia received 17 percent. Both of these parties are Euroskeptic. The M5S has already announced that it prefers to challenge the Euro membership of Italy in a referendum.[42] The election results in Spain, the Netherlands, and Finland did not favor anti-EU parties. There is much frustration and anger in Spain related to the bad shape of the economy, but this anger was not directed at the EU. However, the new political party Podemos, meaning "We Can", won five of Spain's 54 European Parliament seats. Podemos in 2015, is increasing in popularity along with another new party, Ciudadanos, that after the financial crisis threatened to permanently break the traditional two-party system in Spanish politics. Podemos ranks number one in the polls for the upcoming national election on December 20, 2015, but its popularity decreased after Syriza's confrontation with the Troika.[43]

Lastly the Greeks elected Syriza, a left-wing party that is very critical of the austerity programs and Angela Merkel. Syriza is a protest party that is branded by some in the news media as a populist party. Syriza is expected to play a major role in the national politics of Greece and possibly in the future of the EU as it is opposing all the EU neoliberal policies adopted and, particularly, the austerity programs that have sunk Greece and other periphery countries into deep recessions. Syriza was the leading party in the national elections on January 25, 2015, which quickly formed a government in coalition with a small nationalistic anti-austerity party. The party that ranked third in the EP elections in Greece is a neo-Nazi and anti-immigrant party, Golden Dawn, which received 10 percent of the vote. Most of its leaders are in prison being investigated for organized criminal activities. Golden Dawn has brought shame to Greece, the country that introduced democracy to the world. The success of Golden Dawn in Greece is related to the austerity programs imposed by the Troika. This rise of the neo-Nazi Party is reminiscent of the Versailles treaty that imposed sanctions on Germany and brought the fall of the Weimar Republic regime that was replaced by an elected tyrant, Adolf Hitler.

Figure 6.7 shows the composition of the European parliament for the two most recent elections in 2009 and 2014. Figure 6.7 clearly indicates that the pro-EU parties lost approximately 10 percent of the votes in 2014 in comparison to the 2009 election results. However, pro-EU parties still command a large majority of about 70 percent. That does not mean that the shocking results of May 2014 would be irrelevant to the future course of European integration. Many European people are very dissatisfied with the way the EU is functioning, particularly in reference to the health of the economy with a more than 10 percent unemployment rate and with a rather liberal EU immigration policy. These two issues constitute the clear message of the election outcome. If nothing changes in the EU, a bigger "tsunami" could possibly appear in the next national elections of member countries which could shock the present status quo of the EU. The election of Syriza is certainly one such shocking event, not only for Greece, but also for the future course of the EMU and the euro.

Neoliberal policies work slowly; thus austerity has had a negative impact by prolonging the recession in several countries. It is clear that Chancellor Merkel cannot change her mind to save Europe as she does not perceive other EU countries' problems as Germany's problems, and she is a firm believer in austerity. If a disaster occurs, however, it will not start in the EP because Euroskeptic parties will not form a common front to challenge the establishment of the EU. It is also highly unlikely that the extreme-right wing parties will form a common front as they disagree among themselves despite their similar political ideologies. Furthermore, it is almost impossible for the extreme right-wing parties to join forces with the extreme left-wing parties. As a result, in the next five years, the EU parliament is expected to continue functioning with a comfortable pro-EU majority, but not without serious criticism from the Euroskeptic parties

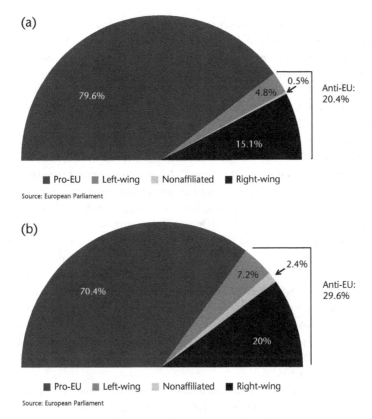

(a)

79.6%

4.8%

0.5%

Anti-EU:
20.4%

15.1%

■ Pro-EU   ■ Left-wing   ▨ Nonaffiliated   ■ Right-wing

Source: European Parliament

(b)

70.4%

7.2%

2.4%

Anti-EU:
29.6%

20%

■ Pro-EU   ■ Left-wing   ▨ Nonaffiliated   ■ Right-wing

Source: European Parliament

FIGURE 6.7   (a) Election results: 2009; (b) Election results: 2014

and possibly directly from the European voters themselves, who are frustrated with the recent developments in the EU.

The reluctant hegemon – lack of leadership

Germany's economy recovered very quickly from the financial crisis and evolved to be economically stronger than any other EU country. Consequently, Germany gained the admiration and respect of other EU countries' leaders and citizens. This admiration and respect was also directed towards Chancellor Merkel who became a popular and preeminent EU leader. During the first term in office, the CDU formed a coalition government with the SPD. The SPD helped Chancellor Merkel take a more balanced approach with regard to the crisis during that period. Angela Merkel's approach to the crisis was always very cautious, never revealing her final decisions without being absolutely certain it would not upset her voters. However, Chancellor Merkel was also criticized for lacking both a vision for the future of the EU as well as the "empathy and emotionalism" for the completion of the European project.[44]

As the crisis spread and deepened, Chancellor Merkel became more cautious in making commitments and decisions to fight the crisis which had already begun having destructive effects on the periphery countries. When the Chancellor intervened, it was either to block or postpone proposed programs that would have required the commitment of resources. Such commitments would have turned voters against the CDU and the two coalition parties in government during her second term in office. The Chancellor's indecision and over-cautious approach was frequently criticized during the crisis. The first misstep of the Chancellor was her decision to refuse support to Greece as soon as it was understood that Greece could not finance its public debt alone.[45] An announcement expressing support for Greece would have calmed the markets and put an end to investors' panic. Her SPD finance minister Peer Steinbrük, however, suggested that assistance could be expected for Greece from other EA member countries.[46] Chancellor Merkel instead stated that the solution to the problem was the adoption of strict austerity programs by Greece. Since that time, Chancellor Merkel according, to William E. Paterson, began taking Germany toward the center of the stage to become the reluctant hegemon of the EU.[47] Paterson claimed that Chancellor Merkel was lacking the commitment and dedication for the European project. Such an attitude was the exact opposite of the strong and friendly pro-European approach followed by her predecessor Chancellor Helmut Kohl. It became clear that a higher priority for the Chancellor to remain in office, and as a result voters/taxpayer came first.[48]

Chancellor Merkel knew that continuous support for her cannot be taken as given as voters would abandon the CDU and her if their built-up expectations were not met.[49] German voters had already revealed their disappointment over the handling of the crisis by expressing disapproval of the bailouts during the state elections in 2011 as both the CDU and the Free Democratic Party were badly battered. These elections took place after the approval of the creation of the European Financial Stability Facility (EFSF) by the EU and the IMF for a total of €750 billion of which Germany, as the largest EA economy, guaranteed the largest share of the EU's part of €500 billion.

When the crisis spread to Ireland and Portugal and economic conditions in Greece had deteriorated after the first bailout, it was clear that EU leaders had to intervene to prevent further spreading of the crisis. Particularly, the fear at that time was that the two large EA economies, Spain and Italy, would be next in line. At the twentieth summit of the EU since the European financial crisis began, EU leaders discussed the formation of a banking and monetary union and the issuance of medium-term Eurobonds. These crucial programs for the survival of the EMU were included in a seven-page report issued by the President of the European Council, Herman Van Rompuy.

Chancellor Merkel stated at the summit that mutualization of the public debt would not take place in the EA "as long as I live." She, therefore, killed the possibility of the issuance of Eurobonds to restore financial stability. The idea of Eurobonds, however, was heavily supported in the summit by France, Italy, and

Spain. The issuance of Eurobonds was also supported by Jean Claude Juncker, the Prime Minister and Treasury Minister of Luxembourg and President of ECOFIN.[50] Juncker, together with Guilio Trimonti, Minister of Economy and Finance in Italy, had publicized their views on Eurobonds in an article in the *Financial Times*.[51]

On December 14, 2010, Frank-Walter Steinmeier and Peer Steinbrük, the German Foreign and Finance Ministers in Chancellor Merkel's 2005–9 coalition government, also called for a limited introduction of European-wide bonds. In a joint article to the *Financial Times*, the two SPD ministers asked for an end to the cautious "wait and see approach" of Chancellor Merkel. The two former ministers were very critical of Chancellor Merkel, and advised her to end the painful austerity programs which led nowhere. An exit to the crisis could be achieved with more integration and the formation of a political union that is presently missing.[52] Jean-Claude Juncker, who in 2014 was chosen to be the new President of the EU Commission, his candidacy having been supported by Chancellor Merkel, characterized the rejection of Eurobonds as "Un-European."

Chancellor Merkel is the most popular politician in Germany, but she is not held in high esteem by the people of the financially distressed countries which are experiencing a painful recession. Chancellor Merkel is not popular among many Eurocrats either who support more European integration than she is willing to pursue. She is not popular with people that are convinced that she practices populist politics. It is understood that the Chancellor cannot risk her electability, thus she promotes her own rather narrow nationalistic interests rather than trying to keep the EU, the EA, and the euro afloat. Furthermore, Chancellor Merkel never explained the large benefits Germany received from the EU and the EMU. As a result, Germans were influenced by the policy elite which in general belong to an economic school of thought known as ordoliberalism ("ordo" means order). This school of thought supports a strong free market enhanced with two major principles: liability and credibility.[53] The bailouts, according to adherents of ordoliberalism, violate these principles. Ordoliberalism is similar to the Austrian school of economics as it relies heavily on the free market. Two of the best known proponents of this school are the President of the IFO Economics Research Institute in Munich, Hans-Werner Sinn, and the President of the Bundesbank, Jens Weidmann.

Mr Sinn is known as a most hawkish and conservative anti-bailout economist who has written a number of articles and given lectures presenting the case that Germany is the country which has lost the most from its EMU membership.[54] He recommended that the bailout recipients should exit the EMU to gain international competitiveness. It is, nonetheless, obvious that his true motive is to protect German taxpayers from having to extend transfers to periphery EA members. Mr Sinn is so extreme in his views that he has fallen out of favor even with the German government and, particularly, with another extremist, the Finance Minister Wolfgang Schäuble.

Mr Weidmann, the other proponent of ordoliberalism, became isolated in the ECB as he casted the only vote against the Outright Monetary Transactions (OMT) program that would allow the ECB to purchase bonds of financially distressed countries. This program has saved the euro simply by being announced on August 2, 2012, despite the fact that the ECB has yet to purchase a single bond. This was done by creating a positive climate in the markets encouraging investors to buy Italian and Spanish government bonds. As a result, interest rates in these and other EA countries drastically declined. Because OMT requires full sterilization, if employed it could not pose a threat of inflation.

A few analysts of the Eurocrisis tried to explain Chancellor Merkel's slow approach to addressing the problem during the Eurocrisis in the unique way that consensus politics works in Germany. The German political system relies heavily on consensus decision-making, but it also leaves the markets with a large role to play. On the other hand, the French political system gives far more weight to the central authority concentrated with the President of the Republic. Such a difference in the role of leadership among the two countries explains the uncertainty over the degree of commitment of the EU in rescuing Greece and resolving the crisis.[55]

When economic conditions worsened in Greece and officials in Merkel's coalition started talking about kicking Greece out of the euro, the Chancellor made her decision only after consulting the ECB executive board member, Jörg Asmussen, and the President of the Bundesbank, Jens Weidmann. Both of them told the Chancellor they were not certain what would be the effects on Germany and the rest of the EU of Greece exiting the euro. However, Weidmann responded that if Greece leaves then Cyprus will follow. He also stated that if Greece stays and does not keep up with the Troika-imposed reforms, then it would be risky. This was the time when the Chancellor spoke to the Greek Prime Minister, Antonis Samaras, of the coalition government who convinced Chancellor Merkel that Greece would follow all necessary reforms. Antonis Samaras visited Berlin and was received with all honors as a Head of State. Since Greece turned out to be a reliable partner, the Chancellor visited Athens to reconfirm her decision about Greece, as long as the austerity measures were implemented.

The EU, IMF, and particularly Germany imposed unprecedented conditions on Cyprus when it was revealed that its banking system was unstable. After strenuous negotiations, the Troika approved a €10 billion bailout to Cyprus. This, however, took place only after large bank depositors of amounts greater than €100,000 received a substantial 55.3 percent haircut. This decision, which was imposed almost exclusively by Germany, had a negative impact not only on Cyprus but elsewhere in the EU and beyond. As it turned out, this decision created uncertainty and risk for bank depositors not only in the EU, but everywhere in the world.

German press influences public opinion on Greece

When Greece was admitted into the EU in 1981 it was a small, less developed country. The EC accession negotiations were relatively easy and quick. The reason was that the small size of Greece did not pose a threat to the EC. After Prime

Minister George Papandreou, almost 30 years, later revealed to the EU Commission that the preceding government had misrepresented the public deficit statistics, the accusations leaked to the news media and spread quickly around the EU. In Germany the press began a long campaign that became known as Greek bashing. Starting in early 2010 many respectable newspapers and magazines began to publish a sequence of articles that created an impression that Greece was the sole cause of the crisis. Consequently many Germans were angry with Greece and were unwilling to show solidarity and provide support when it became clear that Greece would not be able to finance its public debt alone. Such perceptions of the German people and citizens of a few other countries played a major role in the crisis as CRAs began downgrading the public debt of financially distressed EA countries.

The German news media bashing began in February 2010, when the German magazine *Focus* published a highly derogatory and biased article "2000 years of decline from Europe's cradle to Europe's slum area: Greece's descent is unparalleled." On the front page of the issue, *Focus* presented the Greek goddess Aphrodite (Venus) in a digitally manipulated photo to give everyone the middle finger. The headline of the *Focus* issue was "Betrayers in the Euro-family." The article makes references to previous controversial publications to provide evidence for the decline of Greek culture which is the reason for Greece's detrimental role within the crisis. Although it is not necessary to defend Greece against such hideous attacks, it is very regrettable, nonetheless, that *Focus*, which is considered a serious magazine, should shamelessly publish such one-sided defamation stories against one country. More reputable publications followed *Focus* in publishing a sequence of articles shaping public opinion against Greece. The largest German newspaper, *Bild*, published many articles that portrayed the Greeks as lazy in comparison to the hard-working Germans that were asked to bail them out. The same line with *Bild* was followed by the reputable left-wing magazine *Spiegel*.[56]

The relentless attacks against Greece by the German news media lasted about two years until other countries, Ireland, Portugal, Italy, and Spain, also experienced financial turmoil. In 2012 the German Council of Economic Experts expressed the view that it is not possible for a single country to be solely responsible for the Eurocrisis as it was pointed out that the EMU was created with a structural problem and it had to be complemented with a banking and fiscal union to become resilient to economic instability.[57]

Amelie Kutter studied how the financial newspapers covered the crisis, claiming that the financial newspapers took a more objective approach. For example, the German financial newspaper *Handelsblatt* supported a "comprehensive restructuring" of the Greek debt. This newspaper has often disagreed with the rescue programs proposed by the German government and, instead, has proposed alternative programs based on economic theory either supported by the traditional ordoliberalism or the Keynesian approach.[58] Chancellor Merkel is so committed to and rigid in her views of austerity, she cannot even accept advice from Nobel laureate economists (see Box 6.2).

BOX 6.2 Challenging the Economics Nobel Laureates in Lindau Island (Germany)

On Sunday June 29, 2014 the 64th Lindau Nobel Laureate conference was launched with a speech by German Education Minister Johanna Wanka, who praised the successes of Germany. Lindau is a picturesque small island located in Lake Constance in southern Germany close to the Swiss-Austrian border. Besides the 600 brilliant young scientists selected to attend the conference, 37 Nobel Prize winners attended as well. The topic of economics dominated the debates as 400 young economists from 80 countries and 18 economics Nobel winners participated in the conference. The composition of the conference cannot be a surprise after taking into consideration the poor economic performance of the European economy and particularly the prolonged recession of the periphery EA countries.[a] There was much more dispute and controversy this year in comparison to other meetings. Chancellor Merkel also participated in the conference for the first time. The Chancellor had a question for the economists: she wanted to know why the discipline of economics had failed during the crisis of the last few years to "predict and describe the economic reality."

Chancellor Merkel wanted to know whether economists employed incorrect models or if she was being advised by the wrong economists. The Chancellor challenged the economists to develop new measures of good life – this is what is important for the citizens and not the statistics most often reported such as GDP and unemployment, the Chancellor stated. Joseph Stiglitz, a Nobel prize winner in economics and a past chief economist in the World Bank (1997–2000) was in the audience and seemed to be pleased with the Chancellor's request.[b] In an interview with the German broadcaster Deutsche Welle he claimed that markets are not always efficient. A second topic that was not important among economists was income inequality. His research shows that there is increasing income inequality among the poor and the rich, but more so in the US than in Europe. Chancellor Merkel's economists are neither concerned with market failures nor with income inequality which they have accepted as a way to reduce unemployment.[c] Both market failures and income inequality are definitely measures of good (bad) life, and are possibly the reason that Joseph Stiglitz was pleased to hear that Chancellor Merkel spoke of the good life which is getting out of reach for many hard-working unemployed and retired workers.

Professor Stiglitz was critical of EU/EA policies which he described as "disastrous failures" leading to depression that can last for many years, worse than "even Japan's Lost Decade." He suggested that EA leaders had grossly underestimated how contractionary austerity measures can be.[d]

Another Nobel laureate economist Peter Diamond also gave warning for many years of depression in the EMU; he strongly criticized EA country leaders' economic policies and found the European Central Bank's Monetary Policy to be "so stunningly destructive." Professor Diamond offered simple advice to get out of the recession – "better use of stimulus and spending on infrastructure" as this would trigger growth thus reducing the public debt to GDP ratio.[e]

A third Nobel laureate Christopher Sims observed that the EMU structural design flaws have not been corrected yet, forcing Southern EA countries into deeper recession by adopting incorrect "pro-cyclical policies." He feared that the probability of recovery of the Southern EA countries within the EMU is very small thus he offered advice for the Southern countries to design "contingency plans" outside the euro.[f] Chancellor Merkel's response to such strong criticism was that the financially distressed countries could have attained economic growth by reducing spending. Chancellor Merkel admitted, however, that is was very difficult to manage the currency of 19 countries, the euro, when the governments of these countries do not follow the rules of the EU governing institution. She also reported that there were signs of a slow recovery as EA countries reduced current account deficits.[g]

Lastly Claire Jones of the *Financial Times*, who wrote about the Lindau conference, reported that "analysts warn political intransigence and lack of leadership have undermined confidence." This seems a very accurate characterization of the Eurocrisis. Joseph Stiglitz, among so many others, is convinced that the EMU countries do not constitute an optimum currency area. This led him to conclude that the combination of "a flawed EMU structure with flawed economic policies" turned out to be devastating. Furthermore, Mr Diamond's view was a widely shared critique by almost all the economic Nobel prize winners in the conference who were convinced that the European strategy to fight the recession is "self-defeating."[h]

[a] Hannah Fuchs (2014) "Tomorrow's geniuses gather at Nobel meeting in Lindau," *Deutsche Welle*, June 30.
[b] Ibid.
[c] Manuela Kasper-Claridge (2014) "Chancellor Merkel challenges Nobel economists," Deutsche Welle, August 20.
[d] Ambrose Evans-Pritchard (2014) "Nobel economists say policy blunders pushing Europe into depression," *Telegraph* (UK), August 20.
[e] Ibid.
[f] Ibid.
[g] Claire Jones (2014) "Spectre of 'lost decade' haunting Europe," *Financial Times*, August 21.
[h] Ibid.

Concluding comments

Germany attained exceptionally high economic growth after the end of World War II. Although this growth declined over more recent years it remained relatively high for a long time. As a result Germany evolved to become the strongest and largest economy in the EU. Germany's economic growth is attributed to positive and increasing trade surpluses. Starting in the early 1970s the European economy stalled.

Germany was no exception to this trend and as a result the social market economy model was considered at least partially responsible for the high unemployment rate due to heavy protection of the workers and the over-regulation in the economy. In addition to the common European stagnation issues, the German reunification constituted a country-specific problem that only afflicted Germany.

Germany responded to the economic stagnation by launching the Hartz reforms that liberalized the economy and helped the country return to economic growth. The German reunification created a strenuous situation in Germany as fiscal transfers from West to East Germany generated a heavy demand on the budget and friction among the East and West German people. Between 2003 and 2005 the SPD-Green coalition government under the leadership of Chancellor Gerhard Schröder launched Agenda 2010. Agenda 2010 created a totally new economic reality in Germany both domestically and in terms of its relations to EU countries. At home, Agenda 2010 reduced over-regulation and suppressed wages and benefits to millions of workers. Agenda 2010 removed many labor rigidities including making easier hiring and firing of employees. The Hartz reforms allowed and encouraged the creation of new forms of employment known as precarious employment; such type of work is contingent on the needs of the employer. As a result millions of German workers experienced a reduction in their standard of living. The unprecedented reduction in labor costs gave a competitive edge to German industries that boosted exports as Germany's international competitiveness increased substantially.

Germany subsidized labor through short work and working time accounts, two programs that constituted unfair competition. Chancellor Merkel, although other countries could follow suit, turned out to be a very cautious leader during the Eurocrisis, such characterization being justified by the way she handled the creation of the two EU rescue funds, the EFSF and the ESM, along with the approval of the bailouts. Political decision-making in Germany was a deterrent factor, since several populist politicians exploited the Eurocrisis to gain political benefit by telling voters what they wanted to hear about the bailouts to financially distressed countries.

The Eurocrisis undoubtedly played an important role in the rise of Euroscepticism in almost every EU country. This is strongly supported by gains in the popularity of anti-EU parties. Germany's cautious approach in handling the Eurocrisis constitutes evidence that Germany became a reluctant hegemon of the EU and delayed the exit from the crisis by not acting promptly to calm the markets. Chancellor Merkel's firm determination to oppose the issuance of Eurobonds is a major blow to the long expected recovery. German news media bear a huge responsibility for the creation of a negative public opinion of Greece and a long campaign that became an endless criticism of Greece has for a long time poisoned relations between the people of these two countries.

Glossary

Agency worker – a temporary worker that a company hires through an agency that does not receive the wages or benefits a full-time employee does.

Agenda 2010 – a plan in Germany to reform the labor and welfare system of the country.

European Financial Stability Facility – the first of the two funds created by the Euro Area to act as a firewall to protect the financially distressed countries in the EA.

Euroscepticism – the conviction of certain citizens or political parties of EA countries that EU powers should be repatriated to the individual nations.

Fixed-term work – work that is only guaranteed for a short time, usually less than two years, and does not provide the employee with the job protection of a permanent contract.

Hartz reforms – a set of recommendations made by the Hartz committee from 2003 to 2005, including labor reforms, liberalizing markets, and adopting supply-side policies; its main goal was to reduce the unemployment in Germany.

Hegemon – a state that has political power over a majority of the other member states of a confederation.

Kurzarbeit **(short work)** – the strategy of the German government to keep workers employed by subsidizing the hours per week that they are not working.

Lisbon Agenda – a development plan adopted by the EU countries in 2000. This plan was designed to set up development goals for the EU from 2000 to 2010.

Mini-midi jobs – low-quality part-time jobs and established small grants for entrepreneurs to build a group of self-employed workers.

Mittelstand – medium and small-sized companies that comprise most of Germany's economy.

Ordoliberalism – school of thought that the state must be responsible for ensuring that the free market economy works to its full potential by adopting two principles: liability and credibility.

Social market economy – an economic system that supports a market-based economy supplemented with strong safety nets provided by the government for its population.

Wirtschaftswunder **(miracle growth)** – the period of rapid growth of the Germany economy during the decade after the end of World War II.

Notes

1 The name was in reference to the capital of West Germany, Bonn which is located by the Rhine River.
2 The US, nonetheless, assisted Germany, especially in the first years after World War II which had left Germany's infrastructure and economy totally devastated. With the important American Recovery Program widely known as Marshall Plan, the US assisted Germany and the other Western European countries to rebuild their economies through a massive aid package amounting to approximately $13 billion, and by imposing a requirement for the abolition of barriers to trade among all the Western European countries.
3 Martin Wolf (2013) "The German model is not for export," *Financial Times*, May 7. See also Zestos and Smith (2013).

4 This was the strong view of the first economics minister and second Chancellor of Germany, Ludwig Erhard.

5 Richard Reichel (2013) *Germany's Postwar Growth: Economic Miracle or Reconstruction Boom?* Cato Institute.

6 Each trade balance expansion period ends with a couple years of reduced trade balances that are followed by a new trade expansion surplus period.

7 The CA is a broader measure of a country's transactions with the rest of the world. Because the trade balance is often the largest component of the CA, the latter is frequently used instead of the trade balance (*The Economist*, June 2014).

8 "Germany seeks deal on global imbalances," *Financial Times*, February 16.

9 This is done in order to be able to compare the relative importance of the trade balance in relation to GDP.

10 Jacobi and Kluve (2006).

11 Ibid.

12 See Brian Blackstone and Marcus Walker (2011) "Germany's resiliency buoys Europe," *Wall Street Journal* [Online], September 1.

13 Ibid.

14 Martin F. Parnell (1999a) "Globalization, Eastern Germany and the 'Mittelstand,'" *European Business Review*, 99 (1): 32–41.

15 In 2015 the two economies have not converged as the GDP per capita is much lower in eastern than in western Germany.

16 Schmidt (2009).

17 Ibid.

18 Political determination was so strong that EU leaders violated the public debt to GDP ratio criterion and admitted three countries although they have failed to meet that fiscal criterion.

19 Martin F. Parnell (1999b) "Globalization, 'organized capitalism' and German labour II," *European Business Review*, 99 (5): 300–12.

20 Schmidt (2009).

21 Ibid.

22 It leaves one wondering why anyone would ever imagine that a country that received a bail-out was going to be left to bankruptcy, a guaranteed way for all creditors to lose their loans.

23 Holger Schmieding (2012) "Tough love: the true nature of the Eurozone crisis," *Business Economics*, 47 (3): 177–89.

24 See the glossary in this chapter for definitions of these terms.

25 John Evans and Euan Gibb (2009) *Moving from Precarious Employment to Decent Work*, Discussion Paper No. 13. Geneva: ILO.

26 Parnell (1999a).

27 Such benefits were entitlements to all Germans in the social market economy economic system that prevailed there since the end of World War II.

28 See Zestos (2006).

29 See Jacobi and Kluve (2006).

30 Gerhard Bosch (2009) *Working Time and Work Time Policy in Germany*. University of Duisburg-Essen.

31 See Schmieding (2012) "Tough love."

32 See Evans and Gibb (2009) *Moving from Precarious Employment to Decent Work*.

33 See Schmieding (2012) "Tough love."

34 This is something that the EU countries provided, but critics state that this was always too little and too late.

35 Radoslaw Sikorski (2011) "I fear Germany's power less than its inactivity," *Financial Times*, November 29, 2011.

36 G. K. Zestos and T. P. Rizova (2012) "US subprime mortgage crisis and the European sovereign debt: why the European sovereign debt crisis has not been resolved yet," *The State of the Union(s): The Eurozone Crisis, Comparative Regional Integration, and the EU Model*. Miami, FL: Thomson-Shore.

37 P. Allesandrini, M. Fratianni, A. Hughes Hallett, and A. F. Presbitero (2012) *External Imbalances and Financial Fragility in the Euro Area*, MoFiR Working Paper No. 66. Money & Finance Research Group.
38 The treaty was approved and signed by 25 of 28 countries. The UK and the Czech Republic opted out. Croatia was not a member at the time of the vote. The Czech Republic later signed this treaty.
39 "The Eurosceptic Union", *The Economist*, May 26, 2014.
40 After the EP elections it started gaining popularity as it broadened its position in additional conservative issues as it opposes gay marriage, relaxation of the public deficit, and immigration laws.
41 "Outrage as neo-Nazi joins European Parliament civil rights committee," *Haaretz*, July 8, 2014.
42 See "The Eurosceptic Union."
43 See William E. Paterson (2015) "Two-party system is the latest victim of financial crisis," *Financial Times*, June 25.
44 See W. E. Paterson (2015) "The reluctant hegemon? Germany moves centre stage in the EU," *Journal of Common Market Studies*, 49: 57–75.
45 See Paterson (2015) "Two-party system is the latest victim."
46 Ibid.
47 William E. Paterson was the Director of the Institute for German Studies and Professor of German and European Politics at Birmingham University from 1994 to 2008.
48 See Paterson (2015) "The reluctant hegemon?"
49 For this reason her government ignored the advice of many major world country leaders and top officials of international organizations to more actively intervene to stop the crisis.
50 Thorstein Severin and Catherine Bremer (2012) "Merkel buries Euro bonds as summit tensions rise," *Reuters*, June 26.
51 Jean Claude Juncker and Giulio Trimonte (2010) "E-bond would end the crisis," *Financial Times* [Online], December 6.
52 Frank-Walter Steinmeier and Peer Steinbrück (2010) "Much depends on German Chancellor: Germany must lead fightback," *Financial Times* [Online], December 14.
53 Hans Werner Sinn (2012) "Germany and the Eurocrisis: slow, but popular," *The Economist*, December 8.
54 Pedro Nicolaci Da Costa (2014) "Euro-Zone tensions flare at U.S economic gathering," an interview with George K. Zestos, *Wall Street Journal*, January 5.
55 F. Bohn and E. de Jong (2011) "The 2010 Euro crisis standoff between France and Germany: leadership style and culture," *International Economics and Economic Policy*, 8: 7–14.
56 Hans Bickes, Tina Otten, and Laura Chelsea Weymann (2014) "The *financial crisis* in the German and English press: metaphorical structures in the media coverage on Greece, Spain, and Italy," *Discourse and Society*, 25 (4): 424–45.
57 Ibid.
58 Amelie Kutter (2014) "A catalytic moment: the Greek crisis in the German financial press," *Discourse and Society*, 25 (4): 445–65.

References

Blackstone, B. and Walker, M. (2011) "Germany's resiliency buoys Europe," *Wall Street Journal* [Online], September 1.
Haaretz (2014) "Outrage as neo-Nazi joins European Parliament Civil Rights Committee," *Haaretz*, July 8.
Jacobi, L. and Kluve, J. (2006) *Before and After the Hartz Reforms: The Performance of Active Labour Market Policy in Germany*, 12A Discussion Paper, No. 2100. Bonn: Institute for the Study of Labor.

Juncker, J. C. and Trimonte, G. (2010) "E-bond would end the crisis," *Financial Times*, December 5.

Parnell, M. F. (1999a) "Globalization, Eastern Germany and the 'Mittelstand,'" *European Business Review*, 99 (1): 32–41.

Parnell, M. F. (1999b) "Globalization, 'organized capitalism' and German labour II," *European Business Review*, 99 (5): 300–12.

Paterson, W. E. (2011) "The reluctant hegemon? Germany moves centre stage in the EU," *Journal of Common Market Studies*, 49: 57–75.

Schmieding, H. (2012) "Tough love: the true nature of the Eurozone crisis," *Business Economics*, 47 (3): 177–89.

Schmidt, I. (2009) "German labour experiences since World War Two: a suggested interpretation," *Labour/Le Travail*, 63: 157–79.

Severin, T. and Bremer, C. (2012) "Merkel buries Euro bonds as summit tensions rise," *Reuters*, June 26.

Sinn, H. W. (2012) "Germany and the Eurocrisis: Slow, but popular," *The Economist*, December 8.

Steinmeier, F.-W. and Steinbrück, P. (2010) "Much depends on German Chancellor: Germany must lead fightback," *Financial Times* [Online], December 12.

Walker, M. (2013) "Inside Merkel's bet on the euro's future," *Wall Street Journal*, April 23.

Wolf, M. (2013) "The German model is not for export," *Financial Times*, May 7.

Zestos, G. K. (2006) *European Monetary Integration: The Euro*. Mason, OH: Thompson Learning South-Western.

Zestos, G. K. and Rizova, T. P. (2012) "US subprime mortgage crisis and the European sovereign debt: why the European sovereign debt crisis has not been resolved yet," *The State of the Union(s): The Eurozone Crisis, Comparative Regional Integration, and the EU Model*. Miami, FL: Thomson-Shore, pp. 69–83.

Zestos, G. and Smith, A. (2013) *Causal Links Between Northern-Southern Eurozone Trade Imbalances and Over-Indebtedness of Southern Eurozone Countries*. Paper presented at the World Finance Conference, Cyprus 2013.

7

GREECE

The epicenter of the Eurocrisis

Introduction

The history of modern Greece began with the formation of the Greek kingdom in 1830. Greece was one of the first countries to gain its independence from the Ottoman Empire after 400 years of brutal occupation. The Greek revolution brought freedom to Greece after a strong resistance and a long rebellion that began in 1821. Independence cost dearly – many rebels died in battles and the massacres of the non-combatant population were brought about by the frequent Ottoman reprisals.[1] The Greek revolution was one of several liberation movements that spread across the Ottoman Empire and against other autocratic regimes (monarchies) in Europe. Such rebellions were inspired by the French revolution (1789), which attempted to end feudalism, autocracy, and despotism by spreading the ideals of liberty, equality, and freedom to all people.

The Greek revolutionaries received much assistance from the combined naval fleets of the three big European powers at that time which accidentally destroyed the Sultan's fleet at a naval battle at Navarino (the ancient and modern city of Pylos).[2] This historical battle in 1828 facilitated and shortened the path to Greek independence that marked the end of the Ottoman Empire. The Greek revolutionaries also received assistance from many Philhellenes (friends of the Greeks) who offered their personal wealth and lives, volunteering to fight for the freedom of Hellas (Greece) alongside the Greek rebels. Since then, three powers, France, the UK, and Russia, have competed to have Greece under their influence. Germany should be added to the three big European powers that were seeking to influence Greece, as Germany gave Greece its first king, a young prince named by the Greeks Otto of Bavaria.

Accompanying the arrival in Athens of the young Bavarian prince, besides his wife Queen Amalia, was a group of government administrators and policemen to organize the modern Greek state as they assumed the Greeks lacked the ability to govern themselves. In addition, an army came from Bavaria along with three regents who ruled Greece until the king came of age and was enthroned. Since then, a long struggle for political and economic freedom and justice has ensued. The struggle, however, more than 185 years later, has at least partially failed to deliver its objectives of political and economic independence and equality among the Greeks. The failure to reach these goals can be attributed to several reasons, but a very important one is the fact that the country rarely stood united to confront its threats. The fact that modern Greeks are divided seems to follow from an ancient tradition, according to which the Hellenes (Greeks) were only united when an external enemy posed a major threat.

A few events of political advancement took place during the history of the Greek nation. Probably the most important one was the uprising against King Otto in 1843, forcing him to yield some of his powers and accept a constitution. The revolt took place because the Greeks, who fought for their freedom against the Turks, became angry from paying high taxes and living through a new tyranny imposed by the Bavarians. The Greek soldiers occupied the palace building and gave the king 30 days to send the Bavarians home and provide the country with a constitution. It is ironic that most of the demonstrations against the imposed austerity nowadays take place in front of King Otto's palace, which is presently the Greek parliament building. The square in front of the parliament was named Syntagma (Constitution) Square to commemorate the uprising. This was a sign of political progress, as Greece advanced from an absolute monarchy to a constitutional one.[3]

The present Eurocrisis is the latest national tragedy to bring human suffering, shame, humiliation, and economic devastation to the country. Other EU periphery economies and Cyprus were also severely affected by contagion as the crisis spread. Such economic disaster transformed Greece from a developed economy to a developing one.

Throughout the years after Greece gained its independence, foreign influences entered Greece through the royal family and also through the political parties which shamelessly identified themselves as pro-English, pro-French, or pro-Russian, but not as pro-Greek. The foreign influence was strengthened through economic dependence that emerged with the borrowing from abroad by the Greek government to an extent that the average Greek citizen of that time would be unable to comprehend well.[4] Greece throughout its modern history has also experienced the humiliation of several national bankruptcies in 1826, 1843, 1860, 1894, and 1932.

The Greek nation wrote a few glorious pages in its modern history during the enlargement of the country when most of the occupied Greek territories were liberated from the dissolving Ottoman Empire during the Balkan wars (1912–17). There were, however, national tragedies, sometimes self-imposed, but also a few originating from abroad. The most catastrophic of these were the Asia Minor catastrophe (1919–23) and the German occupation (1940–4), which was followed by a three-year Greek civil war that devastated the country. The most recent Greek national tragedy was the occupation of 38 percent of Cyprus in July 1974 by Turkey, during a period when Greece was ruled by a military Junta that gave Turkey an excuse to occupy part of the sovereign country, Cyprus.

The European course of Greece

In 1960 Greece became an associate member of the European Community (EC), aiming to eventually become a full member; under this transitional status, Greece agreed to prepare its economy for full EC membership which came about in 1981. As a result Greece became the tenth member of the EC, following the first enlargement that included the UK, Ireland, and Denmark in 1973.[5] Negotiations for full EC membership of Greece were relatively brief and rather easy since it was not expected then that Greece would ever become a systemic risk to the EC and its member states. This view was held because Greece was a small developing country, and its economy constituted only a very small share of the total EC. Throughout the years after World War II Greece experienced a steady economic growth that lasted till the onset of the Eurocrisis in 2009.[6] The major sectors of the Greek economy that contributed to economic growth were shipping, tourism, and agriculture; these are also the areas in which Greece enjoyed a comparative advantage in relation to its trading partners. The construction industry has also played a major role in the Greek economic development.

Greek public debt, the Achilles heel

In recent years, despite a long period of economic growth, Greece found itself in the exceptionally difficult position of public over-indebtedness. Greece's public debt to GDP ratio had been rising since the early 1980s. Furthermore, Greece became a member of the EMU with a public debt to GDP ratio of approximately 100 percent, far above the maximum 60 percent allowed by the Maastricht Treaty which established the EMU in 1999. Greece, nonetheless, was not the only EMU candidate country that suffered excessive government debt prior to joining the EMU.

Greece, nevertheless, has been at the center of the European sovereign debt crisis as it triggered the crisis. This started when the newly elected Prime Minister George Papandreou informed the EU Commission and the world that the predecessor government had fabricated the Greek fiscal data and reported only half of the expected public deficit to GDP ratio value for 2009. The Greek opposition immediately defended the 2009 public deficit statistics as the result of the accounting method employed to record a massive order of military expenditure that year. It was claimed that they employed the cash accounting method and thus recorded only the annual government expenditure for the military purchases delivered that particular year. If the accrual accounting method had been employed, this would have required them to record, as current government expenditures, all the military purchases agreed upon in 2009 but to be delivered in several future years. This would have increased the deficit substantially although Greece did not receive or pay for the military purchases it had ordered. In its defense, the Greek opposition also claimed that other EMU countries employed the same accounting method. The accusations involving the Greek public deficit were examined by the EU Commission, which decided that the former Greek government had incorrectly reported the deficit statistics and that the Greek fiscal statistics had to be revised.

There were disagreements in three previous years (1997, 2003, and 2004) between Eurostat, the official EU statistical agency, and Greek governments regarding the way the Greek fiscal data were reported.[7] The Greek fiscal violations were for years more or less common knowledge; for example, Greece was under the EU's excessive deficit procedure in 2004, which was abrogated in 2007 by the EU Council. The EU Commission wrote then in its report to the EU Council that there was a substantial improvement in the way Greece reported its fiscal statistics.[8] Then came the shocking revelation by the newly elected prime minister who spoke of the fiscal situation in Greece as a "horrendous political lie."[9] Such unexpected news shook the very foundations of the EMU and triggered a prolonged recession in Greece and several EA countries, and also threatened a severe crisis of potential global dimensions.

It is unknown why the Prime Minister of Greece took such an extreme and hostile approach when handling this issue which led his country into financial chaos, sending more than a quarter of the labor force to the army of unemployed. Furthermore, as a result of the crisis, many people experienced prolonged poverty, health deterioration, and permanent psychological trauma. Others left the country seeking employment elsewhere, emigrating abroad as many had done in the past, especially after World War II.[10] As a consequence of the crisis, Greece was severely affected and lost its sovereignty, starting with the first bailout in May 2010, the time at which the country came under the auspices of the Troika.

Some analysts believe that Prime Minister Papandreou was trying to get even with the opposition party (New Democracy) that had accused PASOK, his own party, a few years earlier when it was in government, that it had cooked the fiscal data in order for Greece to qualify for EMU membership. An alternative explanation as to why the Greek government would accuse its predecessor was to shift the blame elsewhere. This would have been necessary if the government were to defend itself when the EU Commission discovered the excessive Greek public deficit when it prepared the annual reports on the fiscal stability of the EA member countries.

It is also possible that Prime Minister Papandreou might have revealed the shocking information because he was certain that the fiscal data were fabricated, and he was reported to say that his country had been corrupted.[11] It is very likely that he believed that such revelations would be the beginning of a new era for Greece after a national cleansing, and through EU guidance Greece would return to normality like all the other EU members which respected EU laws. It is obvious that Prime Minister Papandreou never imagined that the market reaction to the news could lead Greece and other EMU countries to an unprecedented financial crisis.[12]

Although the resulting financial devastation was real and measureable, analysts cannot agree on the true motives of the financial managers of investment portfolios. One view is that unprincipled speculators did not hesitate to manipulate markets to trash foreign bonds and currencies to achieve profits. Such a position was taken by Mr Papandreou when he spoke in front of the US Congress in 2011. The opposite view is that financial managers' behavior is to protect their investors' interests and, according to this view, there is absolutely nothing wrong with such behavior that expedites market adjustments. Market speculators and credit rating agencies (CRAs) claim that without their positive role in the financial system, postponed adjustments would have actually taken place but they would have been much bigger, abrupt, and more painful. A third approach is that although speculators play a positive role in establishing the correct market prices, they should never be free to go to extremes by forcing a country to bankruptcy. Financial market regulations and prudent fiscal policies can prevent such extremes by suppressing destabilizing behavior such as excessive borrowing in both the private and public sectors. This is a more appropriate approach to prevent financial disasters, by suppressing destabilizing behavior when necessary.

Greek debt and GDP statistics

Greece, Belgium, and Italy were accepted into the EMU, even though they had accumulated excessive public debt to GDP ratios close to 100 percent, almost double the maximum allowed by the Maastricht Treaty. EU leaders who were committed to European integration had knowingly bent the rules of the treaty to expedite the economic and monetary integration of Europe, which was mainly a political decision for them. As was shown in Figure 3.5 in Chapter 3, the Greek public debt to GDP ratio reached very close to 100 percent in 1993. For the next decade it remained in the proximity of 100 percent. During the previous two decades, 1974–93, the Greek debt to GDP ratio had been drastically increasing regardless of which of the two major political parties was in government. During this period Greece was not a member of the EMU; however, Greek public debt increased fivefold from 20 to 100 percent. It is therefore evident that the Greek public debt to GDP ratio during 1974–93 increased substantially, but not because Greece could borrow at low interest rates as a result of its EMU membership. During the years 2006–9, the increase in the debt to GDP ratio could be attributed to low interest rates, but this period consists of only four years out of the total of 40 shown in Figure 3.5.

From 2005, Greek public debt began increasing almost exponentially, particularly after the revelation by Greek Prime Minister George Papandreou at the end of 2009. Starting in 2010, when Greece came under the guidance and auspices of the Troika, the public debt to GDP ratio kept increasing and reached an unprecedented, unsustainable level of 174 percent at the end of 2014. Such a high debt to GDP ratio prevailed despite the two bailouts from the EU/IMF and a voluntary haircut of the Greek public debt held by the private sector of approximately €100 billion.

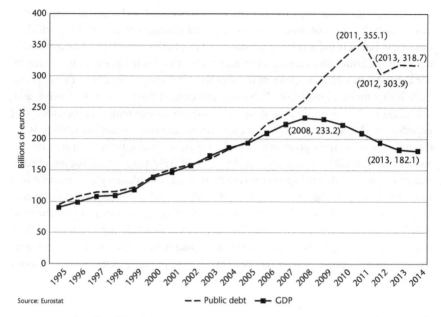

FIGURE 7.1   Greek public debt and GDP at current prices

Figure 7.1 shows that the Greek nominal GDP and public debt moved closely together during the years 1995–2005, just two years prior to the onset of the US subprime mortgage crisis. After 2005, the Greek public debt and the GDP growth paths diverged. The nominal GDP reached its peak in 2008 at €232.2 billion and since then it has been declining and is estimated to have lost more than 20 percent of its pre-crisis level. Such a sharp decline in the GDP made the Greek recession one of the worst in Europe after World War II, thus it can justifiably be called the Great Greek Depression. In 2014, Greece finally had a positive, but anemic, annual rate of growth of its nominal GDP of 0.6 percent.[13]

Nominal public debt kept rapidly increasing till 2011. This was only a year after Greece had received its first bailout and the EU Council had agreed to extend a second bailout if necessary. Indeed Greece did received a second bailout of €130 billion and agreed to restructure its public debt accompanied by a voluntary haircut of the Greek public debt held by the private sector.[14] This decision to impose a haircut – or the Private Sector Involvement (PSI) as it is also called – was adamantly demanded and imposed by Germany. The PSI is considered to be the primary cause of the spread of the crisis to other EA countries, as it ruined investor confidence in European government bonds.[15]

The second bailout was portrayed as a prudent monumental EU political decision that would not only reverse the Greek path from financial collapse, but would end the Eurocrisis. The truth, however, is that the only thing the second Greek bailout did was simply buy time for the markets to be able to better handle the Greek financial failure, which was inevitable with or without the negotiated PSI and bailout.[16]

Christian Rickens, in a commentary in the German magazine *Spiegel* in 2012, challenged the European leaders and the Eurocrats by openly expressing the view that Greece was bankrupt and required 100 percent debt forgiveness to recover. According to the *Spiegel* article, about a quarter of the €130 billion bailout would never arrive in Greece but would pass directly to Greece's international creditors, the bond holders. For example, €30 billion was to be received by the holders of the Greek bonds as "sweeteners" to induce them to swap the old bonds with new ones which have longer maturity and lower interest rates. The rest of the €100 billion would not go towards reconstructing the Greek economy but to reward the speculators who had gambled on high-risk financial investments. The return to fiscal stability for Greece by 2020 when its debt to GDP ratio was predicted to be 120 percent is highly unlikely to be feasible because this figure was estimated assuming the most favorable economic development for Greece and the European economies, which is very unlikely to occur. Similar criticism was also raised in July 2010 for the first bailout that also promised the quick reduction of the Greek public debt.

In an exceptionally "prophetic" article, Ronald Janssen questioned the terms and conditions of the first bailout package offered to Greece, suggesting it would have been possible to achieve the objective to reduce public debt to sustainable levels and save the country from speculators.[17] Very simple calculations convinced Janssen that the Greek bailout program which required fiscal cuts of €30 billion imposed on Greece for 2010–14, with hardly any funding for the Greek economy, would lead Greece into a prolonged recession that would increase the public debt to GDP ratio. Janssen then raised a rhetorical question: "Who exactly is being saved?" Indeed, the question was an appropriate one. Certainly it was not Greece that would be saved, Janssen answered.

The Troika's aim was to save the banks, insurance companies, and pension funds which were holding the sovereign Greek debt. According to estimates, about 80 percent of the Greek public debt was held by European banks. The Greek bailout transferred the Greek public debt from the balance sheets of banks and other institutions to the balance sheets of the European governments. Such a bailout of Greece therefore was not similar to other bailouts offered by the IMF that imposed fiscal consolidations to countries and austerity in return for fiscal sustainability. As a result Janssen predicted that on July 20, 2010, Greece would experience a deep recession and hardship for its people, but no benefits would be forthcoming as a reward for the austerity programs imposed. He nevertheless realized that the IMF and the EU must have done a similar calculation, but politics were such that EU leaders were not permitted to offer favorable terms with the first bailout. This is a main reason that the Greek crisis spread quickly and became a Eurocrisis.

Did reckless fiscal management trigger the crisis?

If reckless fiscal management could be indicated by the size of the public debt to GDP ratio, then Greece is the worst performer during the Eurocrisis. Greece is indeed responsible for triggering the crisis. Nonetheless, two other countries, namely Italy and Belgium, for many years had very high public debt to GDP ratios during the same period. Neither of the two countries has experienced speculative attacks on their sovereign debt nor were they forced to receive a bailout. It is therefore important to examine several factors that increased Greece's public indebtedness. Such factors may be related to direct fiscal mismanagement of the country or to long-acquired individual and social habits of the Greek citizens.

High public debt often is related to the share of the public sector in the total economy: the higher the government's share in the total economy, the higher the public debt to GDP ratio is likely to be. The reason this relation holds is because highly indebted countries finance large parts of their public expenditures by issuing public debt. Such governments as a result frequently generate excessive public deficits and debt. Furthermore, if a relatively large share of government expenditures is allocated to government consumption, such as expenditure for administration, the public debt will increase. The cost of government administration mainly consists of employee compensation and pensions. This was the case for Greece, therefore, these components of public expenditures are at the core of the public debt problem. In addition, public debt is divided into domestic debt owned by national citizens and to external debt held by foreigners. High foreign debt is the result of low national savings and chronic trade deficits.[18]

Figure 7.2 shows total Greek saving divided into private and public. Public saving was negative in every year, with minor exceptions in 1999 and 2014. This means that public saving was a drag on total Greek saving and indicates that the only saving in the Greek economy was generated by the private sector. Private saving in comparison to other EA countries was relatively low. Starting in 1995 private Greek saving was the lowest of all eleven EA countries, as was shown in Chapter 3.[19]

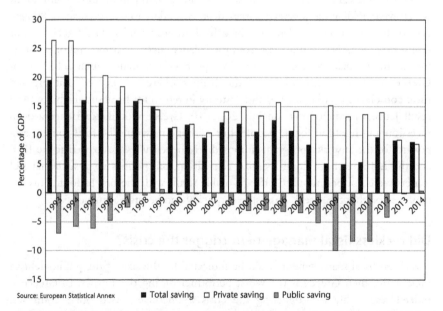

Source: European Statistical Annex   ■ Total saving   □ Private saving   ▨ Public saving

FIGURE 7.2 Greek private and gross national saving as a percentage of nominal GDP

Several factors, including a low savings rate, contributed to the explosion of the Greek public debt that became unsustainable, forcing the country to request a bailout from the EU and the IMF to avoid a disorderly default. Fiscal recklessness and mismanagement is another factor that is responsible for Greek over-indebtedness. This could have been avoided if government decision-makers were vigilant and fiscally prudent. Although several factors played important roles in rendering the Greek public debt unsustainable, some of these factors were more important than others.

Figure 7.3 shows the growth of the real GDP during the period 1961–2014. The entire period is divided into four distinct sub-periods, which are discussed below. Greece achieved a very high growth rate during the first sub-period 1961–73, averaging an annual rate of 7.86 percent. In the next sub-period 1974–93, which consists of two decades, Greece generated a mixed record with regard to its economic performance. It attained a negative rate of growth during five out of the twenty years and a feeble average rate of growth of only 1.29 percent. Indeed, this was a turbulent and slow growth period not only for Greece but also for the world economy. Several negative shocks occurred during this period, including the two oil crises, the breakup of the Bretton Woods International Foreign Exchange and Monetary System, and the 1992–3 exchange rate crisis of the European Monetary System (EMS). In the third sub-period 1994–2007, monetary integration took place in the EU; it began one year after the launch of the EMU with the Maastricht Treaty (1993). The 14-year annual growth rate of GDP was 3.26 percent, which is relatively high.

It is evident from both Figures 7.1 and 7.3 that the period 1994–2007 was a period of growth and expansion for Greece. It would therefore have been fiscally

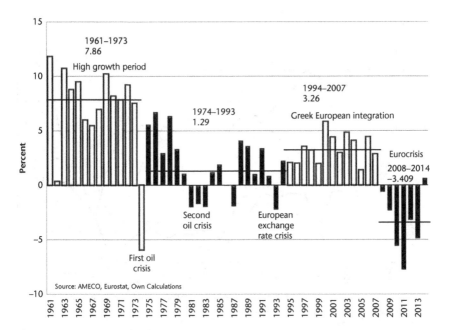

FIGURE 7.3 Real Greek GDP growth

prudent for the Greek government not to have applied pro-cyclical (expansionary) fiscal policy. This is obvious from Figure 7.4 where the government balance, i.e. government expenditures minus tax revenue (G – T), and the trade balance, exports minus imports (X – M), are shown. The government balance shows that during this sub-period the public deficit was kept above the maximum 3 percent allowed by the Stability and Growth Pact (SGP). The public deficit as a percentage to GDP has been declining since 2008.[20] Although the public deficit had been declining, it was still negative thus the public debt kept increasing. Greece was and still is required to make extraordinarily large interest payments to finance its mountainously high public debt. This continued even after the two bailouts and the PSI Greece received. The exception was 2013, when the deficit to GDP ratio increased.

The preventive arm of the SGP requires all EMU countries to meet a Medium-Term Objective (MTO) of "close-to-balance or surplus budget." Since 2005, the SGP also added a new requirement of cyclicality which must be taken into consideration to achieve fiscal stability. This means that EMU countries must use public surpluses generated during periods of economic growth to reduce deficits and debts generated during recession years. It is evident from Figures 7.1–7.4 that Greece did not comply with this prudent fiscal policy rule. Greece generated government deficits during a time of a relatively high average growth of 3.27 percent per annum during the pre-crisis 1994–2007 sub-period.

It is evident that pro-cyclical fiscal policy constitutes reckless fiscal management and this contributed to making the Greek public debt unsustainable. It is therefore crucial to investigate the reasons that deterred the Greek government

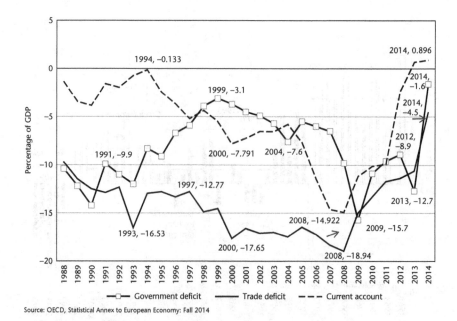

Source: OECD, Statistical Annex to European Economy: Fall 2014

FIGURE 7.4 Greek trade, current account and government deficit as a percentage of GDP

from stabilizing and even reducing the Greek public debt, especially during a period of solid economic growth. To analyze the source of the fiscal instability it is necessary to examine the data for both government expenditures and revenues. The last sub-period (2008–14) constitutes one of the worst recessions experienced by a developed economy after World War II. This is the period that Greece lost approximately 20 percent of its pre-crisis GDP. During this sub-period Greece, under the strong EU/IMF austerity and fiscal consolidation program, reduced its deficit so abruptly that it drove its economy to a severe and prolonged depression. Figure 7.4 also shows the trade account, the current account, and government balances to GDP ratios for the period 1988–2014.

Greece had made serious progress in reducing its public deficit by approximately 11 percentage points, from −14 percent in 1990 to −3.1 percent in 1999. This, nonetheless, marked the end of the contractionary fiscal policy period, which almost coincided with the end of the campaign to meet the Maastricht convergence criteria. After 1999, Greece applied a highly expansionary fiscal policy till 2009 when its public deficit reached −15.7 percent per annum. Since 2009, Greece, under pressure from the Troika, applied the most contractionary fiscal policy in the EA and EU. In 2014, Greece's fiscal deficit to GDP ratio was reduced to −1.6. For the first time ever, the deficit to GDP ratio was below the 3 percent of the Maastricht and SGP reference value. Such a massive fiscal contraction is at least partially responsible for the economic stagnation in Greece which began in 2008 when the ECB stopped accepting Greek sovereign bonds as collateral. This was the time when the markets were given untamed powers to demolish the EMU. Greece throughout the years failed to stabilize its public finances, and as a result its economy became vulnerable to business cycles; specifically after 2009, Greece was unable to finance its huge public debt.

Greece, as has been shown in the figures of this and other chapters, borrowed heavily prior to joining the EMU. Thus it became a member of the EMU having a more than 100 percent debt to GDP ratio which it maintained till 2004. From 2005 Greece continued to borrow from abroad and increased its debt to GDP ratio. Through borrowing Greece was able to boost domestic demand although domestic production was consistently short of domestic demand. Greece, as a result of low international competitiveness, generated massive trade deficits, which is consistent with low saving and increased borrowing from abroad. Figure 7.4 clearly shows that the Greek trade deficit (X − M) has been increasing from 1988 to 2008.

What is evident from this figure is that the trade deficit has been a chronic problem for Greece. This was the result of low international competitiveness caused by high labor unit costs, high profit margin rates, and since Greece joined the EMU, a shared and overvalued currency. Since 2008 the trade deficit decreased substantially to about 4.5 percent in 2014. Such a drastic decline is attributed to many factors; the most important of these is the reduction in the Greek national income, which played a major role in the reduction of Greek imports. Furthermore, the reduction in real employee earnings triggered a depreciation of the real exchange rate making Greek exports cheaper; this created an increase in the demand for Greek exports. Similarly there was an increase in demand for Greek services as well, particularly tourism.

In 2014 Greece had a very successful tourist season, which helped the country generate a positive real rate of growth for the year. Proponents of the internal devaluation approach to recovery would be quick to point out that the approach works well. These proponents must be reminded that it takes a very long time for the recovery to arrive and so far it has inflicted unnecessary pain on millions of people. A quick reduction in the trade balance deficit did very little to reduce the Greek foreign debt. Furthermore, it is exceptionally difficult for Greece to pay the huge public debt interest payments, not to mention reducing the principal amount of the bailouts.

Along with the public and the trade deficit, the Greek current account (CA) is also shown in Figure 7.4. It is clear from this figure that Greece, according to this broader measure of international balances which includes income inflows (out-flows), performed much better than it did in the trade balance. It can be seen in Figure 7.4 that the CA deficit was never as large (negative) as the trade balance. Also after the Eurocrisis the CA began improving more rapidly than the trade balance. As a result, in 2014, for the first time since 1988 Greece generated a small but positive CA balance.

Tax evasion

A major problem that contributed to the rise in the Greek public debt was tax evasion. Greece, prior to its EU/EMU membership, lacked an efficient tax system to finance its public expenditures. The country was relying on inflationary finance, raising public revenues through the creation of inflation, i.e. by taxing the money balances of businesses and households without legislating the introduction of new taxes. Greece also relied on some other taxes to raise government revenues such as excise, inheritance taxes, and tariffs on foreign imports. Public employees, how-ever, always paid payroll taxes, as it is impossible for these employees to hide earned incomes.

Greek fiscal policy in general remained outside the EU/EMU jurisdiction with the only exception that countries which joined the EMU are required to respect the Maastricht criteria and the SGP. The SGP was enacted upon the strong insistence of Germany to assure that member countries continue to respect the 3 and 60 per-cent deficits and public debt to GDP ratio limits respectively after the countries had adopted the euro. Such fiscal rules, nevertheless, have been repeatedly violated by many countries including Germany, the country which insisted on introducing them into EU law. As a result, the SGP has long ago lost its credibility.

After the crisis, the EU kept very busy introducing several new fiscal rules – perhaps too many according to a few experts. All these new fiscal rules aimed at promoting and establishing fiscal discipline. As a result, EA governments became legally liable to respect and maintain fiscal stability, balance their government budgets, and even have their budget approved by the EU Commission, starting in 2014.

To many Greeks, the necessity and importance of the social responsibility for paying taxes was never well understood. Perhaps the tradition of not paying taxes goes back to the Ottoman occupation when many Greeks preferred to leave their homes and properties in the valleys and climb into the mountains to join the rebels.[21] At that time this was a heroic action for the Greek peasants to pursue, joining the resistance movement against the oppressors instead of helping them grab the lion's share of their produce. Of course this tradition should have ended long ago after the liberation. However, economists and other experts on the EU must work closely to develop improved taxation systems that are both efficient and equitable and take into consideration, as much as possible, the country-specific indigenous conditions. This approach to taxation would suppress or even come close to eliminating tax evasion. For example, in Greece analysts pointed out that collecting Value Added Tax (VAT) was never very successful. Such an observation should be seriously examined and not taken lightly.[22]

After the crisis deepened, Greece negotiated and received two bailouts. As a condition of the bailouts, the Greek government agreed to reduce tax evasion, consequently they quickly introduced new taxes, practically taxing anything that theoretically could be taxed, to comply with its promises to the Troika and raise public revenue. However, the recession substantially reduced GDP; such a huge reduction in GDP also reduced the tax base and consequently the government was unable to keep its promise to raise tax revenues.

Some estimates found that the informal economy was as much as 25 percent of the total economy. Based on this information, Greek officials hoped to increase taxes from this sector.[23] However, even if the claim for the actual size of the informal sector is correct, its economic activity has shrunk substantially in the severe recession as it has in the formal sector, thus the overall ability of the country to pay taxes has been significantly reduced.

Greek resistance to structural reforms

Many analysts long before the onset of the Eurocrisis were convinced that the Greek economy needed a major overhaul and restructuring in order to become internationally competitive. The major criticism was that Greece had a very large public sector in relation to other developed economies. Many Greeks were working in professions protected by the government and others in heavily subsidized public or quasi-public enterprises. Also, the strong presence of cartels in several private sectors of economic activity contributed to maintaining very high prices. It therefore became evident that the Greek economy needed a major structural overhaul to become internationally competitive and to comply with EU competition law. This was particularly important as most EU countries were rapidly adopting market-oriented polices supported by neo-liberal governments and other political parties.

Greece on its own initiative began a few structural reforms prior to the bailouts; however, the vast majority of the reforms came after the bailouts, while several programs were still expected by the Troika to be implemented. Greece in 1995 sold 30 percent of the quasi-public telecommunication agency, the Hellenic Telecommunications Organization (OTE) to the German Deutsche Telecom. Proponents of such types of foreign investments in the Greek economy believed this sale would facilitate the inflow of new technologies and help reduce prices to consumers. Opponents claimed that such foreign investments increased dependency and amounted to selling off the country to foreigners.[24]

One public company that attracted the attention of the news media and the people in Greece for several years was the country's National Olympic Airlines, which was reported to cost the government €1 million every day. After it had accumulated €2.6 billion in losses, it was finally privatized in 2008. Privatization turned out to be the only way to lay off redundant employees who had been offered employment throughout the years as political favors. Several public enterprises for many years were accruing losses; such companies became known as "problematic" and were a major liability in the government's budget for years.

Pressing Greece to adopt reforms

To receive the first bailout, on May 2010 Greece agreed to launch a fiscal contraction of €30 billion during the next three years (2010–13). Greece also agreed to increase various tax rates, such as VAT by 2 percent, as well as the excise tax on fuel and alcohol by 10 percent. Furthermore, the government agreed to raise the retirement age to 60 years in some professions. This was a first priority to appease the Germans as it was publicized in Germany that Greeks retired at a younger age than Germans, yet Germany was asked to bail out Greece. In May 2010 Greece received its first bailout. It was agreed that Greece would receive the entire amount of €110 billion within a three-year period in 12 installments on condition that Greece adopted the promised reforms and the austerity measures. Greece made tremendous progress the first year in most conditions of the bailout, but towards the end of the first year due to external and internal factors the entire program was at risk of being sidetracked as the reforms slowed down. Because of the slowdown in the reforms, Greece was denied the fifth tranche (installment) of the bailout. The Troika demanded more rigorous reforms to be adopted to achieve the initial objectives of sustainable public debt and economic growth through increased production, not by a reduction of the demand which leads to recession.[25]

In order for Greece to receive the fifth tranche, upon pressure from the Troika, Greece agreed to adopt a Medium-Term Fiscal Strategy (MTFS), which would have reduced the Greek public deficit by the end of 2014 to 3 percent. The MTFS focused on fiscal consolidation for the period 2012–15 in the amount of €28 billion through an almost equal reduction in public expenditure and an increase in public revenues.[26]

The Troika requested that the Greek parliament approve the MTFS; thus it would become binding law not only for the present government, but also for any other governments that may emerge by future elections. The approval of the MTFS not only released the fifth tranche from the first bailout program, but also opened the negotiations for a second bailout to Greece since the first one admittedly had failed. Mr Bob Traa who was the IMF resident representative in Athens at that time praised Greece for its accomplishments in several areas. However, in a speech he gave just one day prior to the approval of the MTFS, he urged Greece to continue with the privatization plan and the economic structural reforms in the real economy that would help promote efficiency. These reforms included the improvement of labor laws, the liberalization of protected professions, and a reduction in tax evasion.

In the fall of 2011, as the situation in Spain and Italy worsened when interest rate spreads began rising, the ECB responded by purchasing the government bonds of these two countries. Together, Spain and Italy constituted a systemic risk as they could not be bailed out due to the large amount of total outstanding public debt, approximately €3 trillion. The protests against the bailout conditions of austerity and the required reforms in Greece have never ended. Participants in the demonstrations were from different backgrounds who peacefully protested against measures that affected them. It was a grassroots movement inspired by a similar movement in Spain, *Indignados*, which had begun a little earlier. Some demonstrations were organized by the political parties, mainly on the left wing such as Syriza, PASOK, and the Communist Party of Greece (KKE). Another group of demonstrators are the anarchists, who for many years prior to the crisis have been violently demonstrating "with or without cause" according to Anna Visvizi (2012). Although the anarchists had little to do with the crisis, they receive media attention since they are the most violent group. As the situation worsened some Greeks began moving their deposits to safe haven countries, motivated by the CRAs continuing to downgrade Greek government bonds to junk status. Such overall conditions in Greece increased the fear of a disorderly default that could trigger the exit of the country from the EMU and a return to the old currency, the drachma.

As time passed, because of the frequent demonstrations and protests, Greek reforms slowed down as a result of political fatigue. New EU/IMF programs therefore had to be initiated to keep the process going, not only to help Greece exit the crisis, but also to suppress the contagion and protect other countries. Thus, in July 2011, a Greek haircut was negotiated which was designed to provide a major public debt relief of the order of €100 billion.

How to reduce the government deficit

The Greek government was also criticized due to its reliance on raising taxes instead of cutting government expenditure to reduce the public deficit. Several studies have found that the most effective way to reduce public debt is to reduce government expenditure rather than raising taxes.[27] The Greek coalition government of the New Democracy Party (ND) with PASOK, in order to comply with the terms of the second bailout, was desperate to reduce its deficit; it therefore introduced new taxes which caused much distress to millions of its citizens and businesses that were unable to pay their overdue taxes. This forced the Greek government to introduce various new tax schemes to help citizens pay overdue taxes; for example, they could pay their taxes in installments and sometimes at a discount. After its victory in the Greek national election in January 2015, Syriza has been negotiating the new reforms required by the EU and the IMF in order for the last installment of the Greek bailout to be released. Without an agreement about the reforms Greece will not be able to pay its creditors and remain solvent.

Regardless of the original design in the bailout plan or the Greek government's priority for reducing government deficits, Figure 7.5 shows that the actual government expenditures and government revenues after 2009 have both declined. At first sight it does not seem plausible to observe government tax revenues declining when both tax rates and the number of taxes have increased. Nevertheless, economists have no problem explaining such statistics. The massive reduction in the Greek GDP during the crisis substantially decreased the tax base and as a consequence reduced the total tax revenue taken from that smaller tax base. The improvement in the Greek deficit as a result came only from the decreases in government expenditure. Thus the policy imposed on Greece to reduce public deficit through increasing taxes did not work, as can be seen in Figure 7.5.

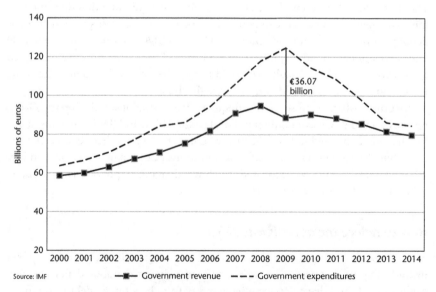

Source: IMF   ■— Government revenue   – – – Government expenditures

FIGURE 7.5   Greek government revenue vs. government expenditures

Slow privatization but bloated public sector

Another major reform that the Greek government failed to implement is privatization. Greece failed to raise government revenue through the sale of public property although it was initially expected to raise €50 billion. However, with all the negative publicity surrounding Greece, the downgrading of its public debt, and the haircut (PSI), it was difficult for Greece to attract investors. Nonetheless, Greece in 2014 generated a primary government surplus; it also generated a current account (CA) surplus and positive real GDP growth for first time since 2007.[28]

Another suspected factor that has contributed to the unsustainability of the Greek public debt is the bloated public sector, caused by a steady increase in public employment. According to a 2004 OECD study Greece had the highest expenditure on public administration as a percentage of GDP among OECD countries.[29] This problem is the result of a clientelistic culture in which politicians swapped votes for positions of employment in the government, even when such positions were redundant. Such overstaffing of public agencies and the government administration does not necessarily mean improved public services in terms of quality or quantity. As a matter of fact, many complain that red tape and slow services are such that the average citizen suffers on a daily basis.[30] Similarly, the government throughout the years prior to the crisis liberally increased pension payments to almost all applicants without carefully examining if the applicants were legally entitled to such benefits.[31] Numerous other government expenditures, especially military spending, contributed to a bloated public sector.[32] The vast majority of violations have now been corrected as the government carefully scrutinizes itself to correct all employee records.

The Greek state, regardless of which party was in government, has always applied interventionist and protectionist policies in the economy. This approach is based on the conviction that the government must provide for the citizens who should reciprocate and support their politicians. Politicians, for their part, eagerly trying to deliver on their pre-election promises, have overstaffed the government administration.

Not so fast

On October 13, 2014, the Greek government announced that it planned to exit the bailout, expressing its intention to borrow directly from the markets without any support credit line from the EU or the IMF. A support credit line could safeguard Greece: if interest rates were to rise Greece would be able to use such a credit line instead of having to borrow at very high interest rates from the market and falling victim to speculators. The markets reacted nervously to the announcement of the Greek Prime Minister's willingness to borrow up to €9 billion in 2015 and Greek ten-year government bond yields reached as high as 9 percent. Such a strong reaction forced the Greek premier Antonis Samaras to shelve the plan.[33] Greece, after all, could not follow Ireland and Portugal, the two countries that were both successfully able to get out of their memoranda (bailouts) clean without support credit lines. This asymmetric treatment of Greece in relation to the other two countries by the market reveals differences between Ireland and Portugal on one hand and Greece on the other.

The asymmetric market response to Greece on the one hand and to Ireland and Portugal on the other could be explained by the fact that Greece was the country that triggered the Eurocrisis. This happened with the revelation of the Greek Prime Minister who started a modern Peloponnesian war by exposing the predecessor government to the world for fabricating the reported Greek public deficit statistics.

Another factor in the differential treatment of Greece by the market is that leaders of major EU countries and some EU officials rarely spoke about Greece with one voice. This caused small Greek and EA crises every few weeks, with everyone wondering when Greece's exit from the EMU would occur.

However, Greek politicians did not speak with one voice either; as a matter of fact, many were terrified by the idea that the left-wing opposition party Syriza, which was ahead of the New Democracy governing party of Antonis Samaras in the polls by a few percentage points, might form the next government in Greece. Fresh in the memory was the Syriza leader Mr Tsipras who once said that he would tear apart the Memorandum when his party formed a government. Another possible source of the rough treatment of Greece by the markets is that the country had not adopted all the structural reforms and policies recommended by the Troika. According to an OECD report on Greece, it was stated that Greece had "made impressive headway in consolidating its finances." Indeed Greece was successful in boosting productivity by substantially lowering the real unit labor costs. OECD Secretary General Angel Gurria admitted, however, that the increase in the Greek public debt was the result of sluggish economic growth, which was much lower than was initially anticipated.[34]

On January 25, 2015, Syriza was the leading party in the Greek national elections. It formed a government coalition with a small, nationalistic and anti-austerity party, ANEL. For about five months, Syriza negotiated about the future of the Greek public debt with the Troika (renamed as the "Institutions") to reach an agreement without a Memorandum of Understanding, which Syriza had criticized prior to the elections. Prime Minister Tsipras, frustrated from the adamant position of the international lenders, pulled out of the negotiations and decided to ask the Greek people if they wished to accept their imposed terms in a referendum scheduled for July 5, 2015. In the meantime, Greece ran out of liquidity and was forced to introduce capital controls by closing its banks on June 29, 2015 to prevent capital outflows from the country. On June 30, 2015, Greece missed a payment of €1.6 billion due to the IMF, thus Greece became the first developed country to default on its debt to the IMF.

Greek politics fermented the crisis

The crisis in Greece was caused by both external and internal factors. Of the internal factors, politics in Greece played a major role in fermenting the crisis. However, the politicians did not act alone; they interacted with their constituency within a long-established and continuously evolving social, cultural, and financial environment. Since the early 1950s after the end of the German-Italian occupation and the civil war Greece was a politically divided country. However, its economy was growing at a relatively high and steady rate. Along with the real economy Greece's public debt was also growing in terms of both absolute levels and as a percentage of the country's GDP. The two major political parties each independently ruled Greece and both contributed to the increase in the public debt to GDP ratio to 100 percent by 1993.

From 1975, just one year after the restoration of democracy in Greece, until 2009, the outset of the crisis – a period of 35 years – the Pan-Hellenic Socialist Party (PASOK) governed Greece for 20 years; in the remaining 15 years, the conservative New Democracy party was in government. PASOK campaigned and elected on the promise that it would rule as an egalitarian welfare state. Many Greeks supported PASOK because its policies eliminated the discrimination and exclusion of many Greeks from many government benefits. From 1975, the two Greek political parties worked hard to attract and keep as many supporters as possible faithfully attached to their party. Since many public departments and public agencies were overstaffed with unqualified employees, it became customary to allow outside private companies to be assigned via contracts to complete large parts of the work that was supposed to be done by public employees. In this way the outside contractors performed two tasks. First, they performed a lot of public works by employing competent workers, and, secondly, they facilitated public employees, allowing them to keep their jobs but at the expense of increasing public deficits. This is how the Greek public sector became bloated by the overstaffing of every public entity. Politicians influenced employment in the private sector as again they exchanged favors for votes.

Both political parties are therefore responsible for the heavy indebtedness of the country. Political parties nevertheless did not act alone as everything they did was with the tolerance of the society and with the cooperation of a large share of the population. The problems of clientelism, corruption, tax evasion, and low employee productivity have all played a role in the formation of a bloated public sector within the country's politico-economic system. Consequently, both politicians and the voters who live, work, and interact within the democratic political system are jointly responsible for the explosion in the Greek public debt. Several critics of the large governmental sector in Greece also laid responsibility on the public unions which are powerful and are able to protect their members' jobs even if they were redundant. There exists evidence showing that Greece has one of the highest shares of government employment relative to its GDP than any other OECD country.[35]

Prominent Greek political families dominate

The blame for the fiscal deterioration that led to the country's financial collapse cannot be attributed to a single individual, even if this person held the highest political office in the country. However, voters should bear some responsibility because starting in the early 1950s, members of three prominent political Greek families were repeatedly appointed to cabinet posts and elected to the highest political office in government, i.e. the positions of the Prime Minister and President of the Republic. The political Greek system is anachronistic, resembling those older systems where leadership was inherited. For instance, Prime Minister George A. Papandreou has exactly the same name as his grandfather, a popular liberal politician who began a movement to end political discrimination of Greek citizens. Andreas Papandreou was the father of the younger George Papandreou and referred to as Andreas since he was identified as a simple person close to the common people despite his elitist educational background and the high-level political offices he held.

The revelation of the fabrication of Greek public deficits by George Papandreou triggered the crisis in Greece and the EA and now even threatens a global crisis. Millions of people have already suffered from this shocking revelation as a result, despite the intent of Papandreou's initiative, for which he bears significant responsibility. Millions of people have paid dearly as they were thrown into poverty, others forced to emigrate, and several have committed suicide as they could not tolerate the psychological trauma and humiliation.

The Prime Minister of Greece and leader of the New Democracy party Konstantinos Karamanlis is the nephew of a long serving right-wing politician with the same name as his nephew, who was in government in 2009 just before George Papandreou was elected. The elder Karamanlis served in many political posts including that of the Prime Minister and as President of the Hellenic Republic. This took place when the political system of Greece changed from that of a kingdom to a presidential democracy following a referendum. He became popular and respected because he tried to end the political divide of the country, especially the heavy persecution and discrimination against the communists. This, however, happened after his return from a long absence from Greece in Paris.

The younger Karamanlis is one of the few elected politicians who gave up his premiership and called a national election that he knew he was going to lose during his second four-year term in office. His government raised the public debt to unprecedented and unsustainable levels consequently with his resignation; he tried to minimize embarrassment by shifting the blame elsewhere. George Papandreou had won the election and inherited a bankrupt country, but he did campaign with the slogan: "The country has money." Neither of these two prime ministers would most likely have been elected had they not had the names of their famous ancestors. It is suggested here that the political system in Greece lacks the characteristics of a fair system that gives all qualified citizens an equal opportunity to serve in the highest political positions in the country.

With the same reasoning and for the sake of fairness, politicians, especially those in key positions who handled the fiscal management of the country such as the Ministers of Economics and Finance and other high-level political appointees in key positions, bear major responsibility merely because they had more information and authority to prevent the fiscal deterioration. A few of them are already being investigated by the Syriza-led government, and most likely others will follow as the efforts of the new government to eradicate corruption and raise public revenue increase.

The Greek press often publicized embezzlement cases that were leaked or discovered by journalists. Several of these cases involved reimbursements of public funding for non-existing or inflated public expenditures and tax evasion. Many of these cases end up in the courts and take a long time to be decided.[36] It seems plausible that all such recovered public funds, if any, should be directed to a general account fund created and earmarked exclusively for the reduction of public debt. Similarly, unpaid taxes on amounts transferred abroad out of fear that Greece would exit the EMU must be collected and directed to the same fund. Many wealthy Greeks indeed transferred large amounts of money abroad.

A group of such individuals who transferred money abroad was reported on the notorious Lagarde list. The list was handed by the former Finance Minister of France Christine Lagarde, and then the IMF Director, to Greek government officials in the form of a CD. The CD was kept in the drawer of a government official until a Greek journalist leaked the names on the list creating a big scandal. The journalist was sued for publishing the names on the list and luckily was found innocent. The Greek Minister of Finance during that time, George Papakonstantinou, also sued for not delivering the CD to the justice department. The suspicion was that he withheld the disk and deleted the names of his relatives which were on it. The court found the Finance Minister of Greece under the PASOK government guilty.

Among the names were well known figures and even a few politicians. After so much publicity, it is still not known if the government collected any taxes from those on the list. Unfortunately, justice often does not prevail, and many people are able to evade taxes. Some of these people are those who purchased apartments in London, Berlin, and other European cities. However, neither the Greek justice system nor those of other European countries did much to catch the big tax evaders. Therefore the poor and the middle class have to pay for some of the crimes they did not commit.

Grexit

"Grexit" is a term introduced by William Buiter, the chief economist of Citigroup, on February 6, 2012. Grexit refers to the possibility that Greece willingly or unwillingly leaves the EMU. Since the Greek Prime Minister Papandreou revealed to the EU Commission the public deficit statistics misreported by the previous government, Grexit became a possibility. Grexit increasingly became a major news topic; it remained an issue even after Greece received the second bailout and restructured its public debt by signing an agreement for a haircut of its public debt held by the private sector. Grexit became a cover-page story by the news media in several countries, particularly in Germany, where the news media began an insidious campaign against Greece demanding that it sell some of its islands or the Acropolis to finance its debt. The Grexit was still on the front page of newspapers and magazines in June and July 2015 after the Greek public debt crisis again burst into flames and especially after the default of Greece to the IMF at midnight of June 30, 2015.

Several German and other Northern European politicians at various levels communicated their strong views against a Greek bailout to protect their tax-payer/voters and themselves in order to gain popularity and get re-elected. Such an initial reception of the Greek request for support not only worsened the situation in Greece, precluding the country from borrowing in the market, but it also soon spread to other countries that were punished by the markets. Interest rates increased in several countries (Ireland, Portugal, Spain, and Cyprus) and as a result they eventually were also forced to seek financial support, making the rescue programs exceptionally large and hardly affordable for the EU. One of the most critical moments regarding the decision whether Greece would remain in the EMU took place in Cannes, France prior to the G20 Summit on November 2, 2011.[37]

The European sovereign debt crisis took an abrupt turn for the worse during the months of October and November 2011. This was indicated by a sharp increase in interest rates in the periphery EA countries. Several events during this period played an important role in determining the future of Greece in the EA and the EU. On October 27, 2011, after long negotiations, Greek bondholders agreed to accept a major restructuring (haircut) of the Greek debt that constituted the largest public debt default in the world. The program is also known euphemistically as PSI and concerns €200 billion of privately held Greek public debt. Greece was experiencing a social upheaval during this time as demonstrations and strikes became the normal situation because economic conditions in Greece were drastically deteriorating. Unemployment had reached depression levels and wages and pensions were reduced to extremely low levels.

The cancelled referendum

Upon his return from the EU Summit in Brussels where the PSI program was agreed, Prime Minister Papandreou, after consulting with a few members of his party, announced on October 31 a referendum by the Greek voters to approve or reject the second bailout. The Prime Minister, knowing the situation in Greece, chose to seek a mandate from the Greek people to be able to successfully implement the reforms that entailed great hardships for the majority of the society. He meant well because he was convinced that in the end, after the reforms were implemented, Greece would be better off than if there had been a disorderly default and an exit from the EMU and the EU.

The information about the referendum spread around EU policy circles and among EU country leaders. After some communication between the then president of France Nicolas Sarkozy and Chancellor Merkel, it was agreed that Prime Minister

Papandreou would be invited to a meeting to be held prior to the G20 Summit which was going to take place in Cannes, France. Mr Papandreou was invited on November 2, one day before the G20 Summit began. This was an important meeting regarding the future of Greece in the EMU and the EU. Beside Merkel, Sarkozy had also invited the Managing Director of the IMF, Ms Christine Lagarde. The President of the European Council Herman Van Rompuy and the President of the EU Commission José Manuel Barosso were also invited along with the President of the Eurogroup Jean-Claude Juncker.

The invited officials met one hour before George Papandreou and his Finance Minister, Evangelos Venizelos, arrived to decide how to handle Papandreou. Mr Sarkozy was behind this arrangement as he was very angry with Papandreou for not consulting the EU leadership, especially after the EU had already done so much for Greece. Sarkozy's initial position was that Prime Minister Papandreou would be given the offer to take the bailout or exit the EU/EA. Finally, he agreed with Merkel that Greece could have a referendum, but the question asked would be whether Greece would stay in the EA.[38] The decision at the meeting seemed predetermined to inform Papandreou to abandon the referendum. However, the meeting was very strenuous and even made a few of the EU officials uncomfortable. How could two large EU country leaders forcibly impose their views on an elected smaller country leader? This attitude of the two large countries' EU leaders may easily be the current major problem of the EU as it has lost the democratic connection with the EU citizens. This is something that was vividly shown in the May 2014 European Parliamentary elections when Euroscepticism was the new shocking development in EU politics. Similar problems resurfaced in the last week of June 2015, when another referendum for the same reason was scheduled for July 5, 2015. This was proposed by Prime Minister Tsipras after he broke off negotiations with the EA member countries and the IMF when he thought that the negotiating partners were not willing to accept any compromise.

Everyone in the room was against Papandreou's referendum on the bailout. After so much hardship from the first bailout, it was highly unlikely that Greeks, many of whom were still in the streets protesting almost daily, would have had approved another bailout. Such an approval would have been pure masochism. Perhaps all the participants in the meeting remembered the 2009 revelations by Mr Papandreou of the misreported deficits which triggered the Eurocrisis. Now the referendum could finish the European future of Greece and cause irreparable damage to the European Project.[39]

By blocking the referendum both European leaders and EU officials aimed to prevent the destruction of the EMU. Nonetheless, if they had taken earlier action neither the huge bailouts nor the referendum would have been necessary. During the entire Eurocrisis, the EU country leadership only intervened at the eleventh hour to save financially distressed countries and the euro. EU country leaders did not address other important problems such as trade imbalances, rising unemployment, or maintaining peace in their own backyard. The European leadership has failed to visualize what it would take to make Europe a better place to live. The principles of integration and harmonious development that are explicitly stated in the second article of the Treaty of Rome is what they grossly ignored, but embraced non-European policies such as fierce competition to promote efficiency for both firms and countries that compete in the product, labor, and credit markets.

Harmonious development, unity, solidarity, and clear communication of the rules and responsibilities would have been sufficient to make the EU/EA a better and more stable union of countries. This Europe could serve as an example for other continents and regional trading blocs to follow because it is clear that the world has almost lost a regional development model. Papandreou was not the only victim of the Cannes meeting. When interest rates in Italy exceeded 6 percent, this was a strong and clear message that something had to be done to help Italy. Nevertheless, Italy with a public debt of more than €2 trillion was "too big to save." The IMF chief came up with some small amount of €80 billion accompanied by the usual bitter pill of reforms and austerity. The meeting at Cannes turned out to be significant not only for the future of Greece in the EU/EA, but also of the type of government to be formed in Greece and Italy as well as who would be the next Greek and Italian prime ministers.

Replacement of elected EU country leaders by Eurocrats

Only five days after the return of the Greek delegation to Greece, Mr Papandreou resigned as prime minister. It is clear that he was pressured to step down. He also lost the leadership of PASOK in the party elections to his Finance Minister, Evangelos Venizelos, who was against the referendum and had accompanied him in Cannes. Another opponent of the Greek referendum was the opposition leader Mr Antonis Samaras. Before the meeting in Cannes the President of the EU Commission Mr José Barosso had called upon Mr Samaras and asked him if he would take part in a coalition government headed by a non-elected Eurocrat. Mr Barosso quickly found such a person in Mr Lucas Papademos, the former Vice President of the ECB whose term had expired about a year ago. Mr Samaras strongly opposed the referendum and agreed now to serve in a national unity government with PASOK, although initially he was aiming to move alone to the premiership with his New Democracy Party.

For the President of the Commission to undertake such an initiative before the meeting, it seems that he must have known the outcome. Although it is difficult to criticize the two European leaders and Mr Barosso for their unwillingness to take a chance and gamble with the future of the EU/EA, their approach has damaged to the long-run reputation of the EU as a democratic union of independent countries.

Italy, without accepting a bailout, agreed to allow the monitoring of its economy by the IMF. However, a second elected leader, Silvio Berlusconi, the Prime Minister of Italy, was replaced by another European technocrat, Mario Monti, the former EU Commissioner for Competition. The end result of the Cannes meeting was the dumping of two elected EU country leaders who were merely replaced with two EU Eurocrats. This is something new in the European political decision-making process that Europeans should revisit if this should be allowed to become a precedent for the governance of the EU.

Pressing the Chancellor

The European country leaders met again at 9:30 p.m. on the same day, November 2, 2011, without the Greek delegation. This time Sarkozy surprised his European colleagues because he invited President Barack Obama to chair the meeting. In this session Chancellor Merkel was cornered as Sarkozy tried to put pressure on her to increase the amount in the rescue fund, so the EA would be in a similar position as the US was during the 2007–9 crisis – this would protect the EMU and the financially distressed countries. The Fed had then purchased massive amounts of government and private securities and the US Treasury launched two massive fiscal programs to save the US economy. Chancellor Merkel fought back against the suggestion and informed the group that she could not decide for the Bundesbank. The Central Bank's independence, she said, guarantees the prevention of hyperinflation, similar to that experienced by Germany during the interwar period when the Bundesbank kept printing Deutschmarks to repay the World War I reparations imposed by the US, France, and the UK. She told the EU leaders and President Obama that the hyperinflation of that time was a partial cause of the fall of the Weimar Republic that was replaced by the tyranny of Adolf Hitler and his monstrous Nazi party.

Lastly, Obama and Sarkozy proposed a program under which the EA countries would transfer their Special Drawing Rights (SDRs) to a rescue fund to provide protection to the EMU member countries that were at risk.[40] Such news quickly spread, reaching the President of the Bundesbank Jens Weidmann who called the Chancellor and informed Merkel that he opposed the program. SDRs are part of a country's international reserves and are managed by the country's central bank. When President Obama insisted that Germany participate in the SDRs program, Ms Merkel broke down in tears, shocking everyone in the room. She tearfully explained, "That is not fair. I cannot decide in lieu of the Bundesbank. I cannot do that." The first interpretation of Ms Merkel's reaction was that she was very sad because she could not help all those people suffering from the rigidity of the German policy. Now, it appears that the Chancellor was upset rather than sad because everyone in the room continued to press Germany on issues that concerned mainly other countries. The Cannes meetings were a clear failure as the Italian ten-year bond yields increased sharply to unprecedented levels close to 7.5 percent and the Greek rates shot up to 33 percent making the Grexit even more likely to happen.

The Cannes meetings left no doubt that historical institutional constraints in Germany render monetary policy in the EMU impotent, thus limiting the beneficial effects of monetary policy throughout the entire EA. One wonders why the EA countries would ever agree to sign such a treaty that requires them to surrender the two most important macroeconomic policies. As President Obama observed, the preferred policy of the ECB during the Eurocrisis should be similar to that of the Fed during the 2007–9 US subprime mortgage crisis. However, he quickly noticed that this choice was not possible therefore the crisis could not be resolved. Consequently, either Germany had to change its policy to help countries cope with the contemporary problems in Europe of high unemployment and very low inflation or it had to allow other countries to resolve the problem on their own. This suggests a Germexit (German exit) was a possible solution as Germany with a few of its close allies could form their own Northern European monetary union, or Germany could returns to its old currency, its beloved Deutschmark.

Plan Z

After the Cannes meetings the economic and political situation in Greece continued to deteriorate. Riots, strikes, and demonstrations were a daily occurrence as economic conditions in Greece were going downhill. More than a quarter of the Greek labor force was unemployed. Both wages and pensions were drastically cut while existing taxes were increased and new taxes were introduced and implemented. The uncertainty about Greece's future in the EMU had been a common theme in news around the world. The neo-Nazi party Golden Dawn and the main opposition party Syriza were gaining popularity; both were a threat to the EU/IMF status quo regime of the bailouts and strict conditionality.

Many Greeks were withdrawing their deposits from their bank accounts for fear that the country would return to the old currency, the drachma, and that therefore they would lose most of their money. The possibility of a Grexit became common knowledge deterring the Greek recovery and wasting the bailout funds and sacrifices of the Greek people who had been trying to survive under the austerity conditions imposed upon them by the Troika. If the ECB at any time refused to lend to the Greek banks because it no longer accepted Greek government bonds as collateral, Greece would have to issue its own currency because it no longer would have access to the liquidity of the euro. It was not clear who was to make the decision "to pull the plug." A Grexit, however, seemed a highly likely event as Greek voters did not elect a majority party in the May 2012 election that would have supported the bailout program assuring that Greece would repay its loans to its international lenders.

As the return of Greece to its old currency seemed likely to occur to some, a group of two dozen people were preparing a plan to facilitate Greece to convert to its old currency. The people involved kept "Plan Z" a secret, since such secrecy was necessary to avoid market speculation that could have had devastating effects of the Greek economy.[41] The name, Plan Z, was used to indicate that it was only a plan of last resort. The group members of Plan Z came from the IMF, the EU

Commission, the ECB, and the Eurogroup. Their job was to build a new economic and financial system for Greece based on the old currency. In order to avoid any possible leaks the group excluded Greeks. The team was headed by Jörg Asmussen from the ECB, Marco Buti from the Commission, Thomas Wieser from Eurogroup, and Paul Thomsen from the IMF. During this period, the word Grexit was repeatedly used not only by the news media but also by the large EU country leaders such as Sarkozy and Merkel and as a result it seemed it was becoming a self-fulfilling prophecy. Considering the approach used, it should not be a surprise that the rescue of Greece became very expensive, and disastrous, for the Greek economy and its people.

The Greek election results of June 15, 2012 reduced the intensity of the crisis and the Grexit debates in most European policy circles. Antonis Samaras of the New Democracy party in these elections received the largest share of the vote. His party formed a coalition government with Evangelos Venizelos' PASOK which ranked third in the elections behind Syriza. Chancellor Merkel for several weeks was undecided regarding the Grexit. Her advisors were divided. One group strongly believed that Greece should be expelled from the EMU in order to teach the other members a lesson to respect the fiscal rules. This group of Merkel's advisors was known as the "infected leg camp." The most notorious and strongest proponent of this group was Merkel's Finance Minister Wolfgang Schäuble. He was still the strongest proponent of a Grexit in the newly rekindled Greek public debt crisis during June–July 2015. The opposite group supported the view that if one country is forced to leave the EMU this will trigger a bigger crisis with unknown effects on the rest of the EMU countries. This was the "domino effect" group that was concerned with contagion and thus was against a Grexit.

A temporary end of the Grexit

As the President of the EU Commission which is the guardian of the EU treaties, President Barosso took it upon himself to save the euro, thus he decided to pay a visit to Athens. Prior to visiting Athens, Mr Barosso had visited Berlin where he had a lengthy discussion with Ms Merkel advising her that there were many risks involved with a Grexit. In Athens he met the Prime Minister Antonis Samaras and convinced him to begin implementing the conditions of the bailout, and not to ask for any changes to the terms of the bailout for at least a year. Mr Samaras accepted the strong recommendation and immediately restarted the austerity programs and the reforms.

Then there was a major turn in Berlin. After consulting with many experts and her close advisors, Chancellor Merkel made up her mind. Because none of her close advisors were sure what effects the Grexit would have on the EMU she decided it would be more prudent to support Greece as this would be the safest way out from the crisis. Then she decided to work closely with the Greek Prime Minister, inviting him to Berlin where he was accepted by her with all the honors of a head of state. Mr Samaras promised her that his government would work hard to implement the conditions of the bailout. In October 2012 Chancellor Merkel made a symbolic visit to Athens to confirm her support.

Austerity brought misery and poverty

The austerity imposed on Greece starting with the first bailout in May 2010 caused an unprecedented rise in mental and physical diseases among many Greek people. These findings are based on several studies. One such study published in the *Social Science and Medicine* journal found that from the first year of the recession a substantial increase in suicides had taken place. Based specifically on the research conducted by the University of Portsmouth (UK) for every one percent reduction in government spending there was a 0.43 percent increase in male suicides.[42]

Many studies found a link between the recession and the general health of the population. The Eurostat reported 800,000 Greek people had no access to health services mainly because health insurance in Greece is related to employment. During the crisis Greece experienced the highest rate of unemployment. Stuckler and Basu reported in their book that the reduction in government expenditures had had a negative impact on the health of the people. As a result of the budget cuts in healthcare even diseases like malaria that had been eradicated as much as 45 years ago reappeared.[43]

A study of 22,093 patients in the city of Kalamata in the Peloponnese found a significant increase in heart attacks when comparing statistics from the pre-crisis period (2004–7) to the crisis period (2008–11). The overall increase in heart attacks was 29 percent, with 39.2 percent among women. The study pointed out factors that could have increased heart attacks in women more so than in men. Women experience higher unemployment rates and for a longer duration than men, which increases women's financial difficulties. Financially distressed people often do not seek medical treatment to avoid the medical expenses. Women holding outside jobs usually work more than men as their work continues at home taking care of their household and children.[44]

As the crisis deepened, public health expenditures drastically decreased. Lack of medical equipment, supplies, and drugs are a common phenomenon. Doctors, nurses, and other hospital employees have seen pay freezes and reductions in wages, and often are kept unpaid for several months. Such a situation affects both the morale of employees and their productivity. The government delays payments to almost all medical suppliers. The German pharmaceutical group Merck, for example, discontinued supplies of Erbitux, a cancer drug, to all Greek public hospitals.[45]

On February 21, 2014, *The Independent* presented a gloomy picture of the medical conditions in Greece. According to experts from Oxford, Cambridge, and London School of Hygiene and Tropical Medicine, the budget for public Greek hospitals was reduced 25 percent between 2009 and 2011, but pharmaceutical spending was slashed by more than 50 percent. These drastic reductions had a severe impact on the health of many ordinary Greek people. The joint report of the three universities mentioned above criticized the Greek government and the Troika for imposing such drastic cuts and refusing to recognize the magnitude of the hardship inflicted on ordinary people who depend on government health services. Several diseases have been increasing according to the Greek National School of Public Health while there has been, for example, an increase of 21 percent in stillbirths and a 43 percent increase in infant mortality in the period 2008–11.[46]

Since the health system in Greece is incapable of providing adequate health services, especially for the very poor, a small number of international humanitarian organizations, such as Doctors Without Borders and Doctors of the World, along with a few Greek humanitarian groups have provided free medical services to those in need and unable to pay by going to the private sector. As a condition of receiving the bailout Greece agreed to cut its medical spending to a limit of no more than 6 percent of its GDP. Such cuts in medical expenditure affected almost all medical services. Since Greece is traditionally heavily dependent on public health services such large cuts had an immense negative impact on both the quality and quantity of health services. The large cut in the budget for public hospitals caused a tremendous deterioration in medical services.[47] For example, because public hospitals in Greece are understaffed there is always a queue for patients receiving medical services for major treatments. The black market worked in a diabolical way in this regard; some patients and physicians discovered and practiced a method that expedites health services for candidate patients who are willing and able to bribe physicians, an arrangement that comes in the form of an envelope of cash. Thus the Hippocratic Oath had been repeatedly violated along with Greek law for many years. This arrangement only worked in the past for those who had the money, but it was not an option for the poor.

International healthcare to the very poor was provided by international healthcare non-governmental organizations (NGOs). However, since the crisis began Greek volunteer physicians and medical personnel provided health services usually in clinics in municipal buildings known as social medical centers. Many people who visited Greek hospitals were highly frustrated and shocked by the poor quality of the services they received. Wishing "not to become sick in Greece" was an expression often heard. The grave deterioration of healthcare in Greece is supported by numerous statistics as the major share of the medical costs have been shifted from the state to individuals who often cannot afford to pay because they are unemployed. Health insurance is provided to employed workers but is only available for one year after they lose their jobs.

For several years prior to the crisis many critics had stressed the inefficiencies, corruption, and waste that existed in the Greek health sector. A few health specialists believed the structural changes imposed by the Troika were a welcome opportunity to overhaul the entire healthcare system. The new health system, however, had to become more efficient, save costs, and thus better serve the people. A few government representatives claimed that the reforms imposed by the Troika were necessary and did not affect the quality and quantity of health services. Such claims, nevertheless, are grossly incorrect because studies conducted by many Greek and foreign scientists support the findings that healthcare in Greece has gravely deteriorated.

Hungry and homeless

The crisis did not spare anyone, even children, some of whom go to school hungry, often asking their classmates for leftovers and are sometimes forced to look in the trash cans for food. Prior to the crisis, teachers can't remember children revealing to them that their unemployed parents are desperate and they do not know what to do. Teachers often witness children bending over with pain in their stomachs while others faint. The government initially refused to recognize the existence of the problem but then admitted it after several international humanitarian and Greek organizations – including the Greek Orthodox Church – began providing food for the Greek children and others in need. Nevertheless, the government's priority was to repay the bailouts from the international lenders.[48]

Starting in 2008 a local humanitarian organization Prolepsis began a pilot program in 34 schools reaching 6,400 families providing the children with a sandwich, fruit, or milk. The program was financed by the Stavros Niarchos International Philanthropic Organization, and in 2013 covered 120 schools feeding 20,000 students. The Greek government also received EU financing to provide meals to schools.[49]

The bailouts did not bring a quick recovery nor a reduction in public debt; Greece fell deeper and deeper into recession. The longer the duration of unemployment, the more people became financially distressed and unable to provide basic needs for their families. Large numbers of people seek food in soup kitchens in Athens and in a few other large Greek cities. The number of people who are in need of free food continues to rise as both hunger and homelessness are on the increase. Food surpluses donated by food-related businesses, such as restaurants, grocery chains, and bakeries, are distributed to more than 700 soup kitchens all over Greece.[50]

Those who seek assistance do not necessarily come from the lower-income classes or the poorer neighborhoods any longer. A very large number of middle-class unemployed workers and business people who were forced to shut down their stores now seek free meals. Humanitarian organizations quickly realized a niche for their role and acted accordingly. The Greek Orthodox Church provides food daily for 55,000 people whereas the local governments and municipalities offer 7,000 meals in Athens and the periphery.[51] The new unemployed and homeless who lost their incomes long ago contributed to the reduction in consumption of all goods and services in Greece. Young people who received an apprenticeship or higher education cannot find a job.

According to journalist Julianne Mendelsohn, the stereotype of the "lazy Greek" publicized by the German *Bild* is nonsensical as there are simply no jobs to be had. Mendelsohn, who met many people and has seen the homeless and hungry, was struck by the pain and sadness in the eyes of these people "at moments when they thought nobody was watching them." It is almost certain that the Prime Minister and the Vice President of the Greek government never offered to give the Troika representatives a tour of Athens to meet these people.[52] Although the bailouts saved the banks and the government, they also destroyed the private sector since the Troika imposed the wrong policies. As a consequence of the brutal austerity and the sharp reduction in the unemployment compensation and welfare benefits to large families, the number of homeless reached 40,000 in 2014.[53]

In addition to the homeless there are many others who still live in their homes or apartments. Being unemployed or having had their pensions cut so drastically that they are unable to pay their bills and the rent, they are without electricity and water and are close to eviction. Since 2010, Greece has been transformed into a different country; once a relatively affluent economy, in 2015 it depicts all the characteristics of a country with a multitude of social and economic problems.

Poverty, malnutrition, homelessness, and a lack of basic health and decent education are now prevalent everywhere. It is widely accepted that Greece is in a failed state status, far from being a modern European welfare state. Draconian austerity and cuts in wages, pensions, and social services have created a vacuum for the introduction of new institutional forces and networks to assist both Greeks and foreigners who arrive in Greece for a better future in Europe. A serious effort to fill in the gap of the missing Greek state was made by formal NGOs and informal groups. The NGOs existed prior to the crisis and were financed by the Greek government, but as the recession deepened, the government reduced their funding and in 2012 cut it off completely. As a result, during the crisis, these NGOs sought and found new sources of funding from non-profit institutions such as the Stavros Niarchos, Ioannis Latsis, George Soros, and other similar foundations. The informal groups act independently of the government and big businesses that consider them and the Troika primarily responsible for the crisis.

Informal groups were innovative in creating a variety of new opportunities to improve the dysfunctional social and economic systems in both the production and distribution of goods and services. Such innovations include the Local Exchange Trading System which created bartering networks, where people exchange goods or services for online credit. Another initiative of social solidarity that has received much publicity was the informal distribution networks under which farmers began distributing their produce directly to the consumer to avoid the middlemen who were known to jack up the prices to earn an extraordinarily large profit margin.[54]

The unpaid, forced, World War II loan to Greece

The austerity programs imposed on the periphery countries by the Troika and supported mostly by Germany and its northern allies triggered strong protests in the bailout recipient countries. Austerity protests started in 2010 and continued throughout the crisis, particularly in Spain and Greece, two countries in which about a quarter of the labor force became unemployed. One of the fiercest anti-austerity protesters in Greece is Manolis Glezos, a left-wing politician who is widely known and much admired by many Greeks. Glezos gained the respect and admiration of the Greek people on May 20, 1941 during the Nazi occupation of Greece, when at the age of 18 he climbed the Acropolis with his friend, Apostolos Santas, of the same age, and brought down the swastika to replace it with a blue and white Greek flag. Such a heroic act brought great joy and encouragement to his compatriots and all other peoples oppressed by the Nazis, but produced shock and anger among the Nazi occupiers. Mr Glezos lived in Greece during the occupation and has strong memories of and statistics that reveal the horrendous atrocities committed by the Nazis. Today, he still fights for democracy and against the unfair treatment of Greece.[55] Mr Glezos is a left-wing politician that served as a member of the European Parliament representing Syriza. He received over 500,000 votes in the May 2014 elections to the European Parliament, surpassing any other Greek candidate for the Parliament.

Glezos is angry that the German news media portrays the Greeks as lazy when in reality this is a false accusation according to many statistics. He opposes the bailouts as their purpose is to save the banks rather than support the people who are suffering during the crisis. He strongly believes that Germany must help Greece, not only as a gesture of European solidarity, but as partial repayment for the famine, the plundering of factories and homes, and the looting of the entire country during the occupation of Greece by Nazi Germany. Greece suffered many losses during the occupation, both in terms of physical assets, such as vehicles, buildings, and food stuffs, and in terms of human life. Greece lost a substantial percentage of its population, mostly in mass executions as reprisals for guerilla attacks against the occupying Nazi forces.[56]

The Greek newspaper, *To Vima*, in its Sunday issue of April 8, 2013, reported that the extensive work of an appointed commission by the government charged to estimate the amount that Greece must demand from Germany came to a conclusion. The work was compiled by a group of experts that worked in the Greek Finance Ministry for several months before the 80-page report was released. After examining numerous documents and some 761 volumes of archives the commission came to the conclusion that Greece has not received war reparations from Germany.[57]

The report estimated the amount of the unpaid reparation at €162 billion, which consisted of €108 billion for the destroyed Greek infrastructure and another €54 billion for the two forced loans that the occupying Nazi regime received from the Bank of Greece to finance its military operations in the country.[58]

Following the report, the New Democracy/PASOK Greek government did not take any action because it is highly likely that any such move would increase the tension in Greek-German relations at a critical time when rescue programs were being negotiated. Deputy Finance Minister Christos Staikouras said the report has been in the hands of the Greek government and "will act when it considers appropriate."

Chancellor Merkel accused over-indebted countries of being reckless prior to and during the crisis, therefore they should be responsible for paying their debts and saving their banks. The British newspaper, *The Guardian*, was critical of Chancellor Merkel's view that Greece must repay Germany the full bailout amounts and with interest. Germany never paid back the forced World War II loan from Greece nor has it paid any other war reparations.[59] Germany's economy was devastated at the end of World War II and, thus, was unable to pay. However, the US paid instead because the Americans did not wish to witness the return of Nazism and Fascism in any of the axis countries. Nevertheless, Germany's current policies lack the US's prudence, sensitivity, and foresight, as Euroscepticism, Nazism, and fascism become popular in Europe.

The Guardian is also critical of Greece stating that if it demands war reparations from Germany, then it should also demand them from Italy, which was equally guilty of war damages and crimes against Greece. Most of the Marshall Plan aid to Greece came in the form of weapons and military equipment to help the government suppress the Communist revolution after the end of World War II. As a result, the civil war in Greece after the liberation of the country from the Nazis and Fascists devastated Greece for a second time within ten years.

In a historical visit to Greece by the President of Germany Joachim Gauch, the issue of German war reparations to Greece resurfaced. In a joint appearance with the Greek President Karolos Papoulias, Mr Gauch stated that Germany dismissed Greek demands for World War II reparations. President Gauch stated that after Germany paid $115 million Deutschmarks in 1960 the issue is considered closed.[60] His Greek counterpart, however, Karolos Papoulias, a member of the Greek anti-Nazi resistance at a very young age, instead said the two countries must begin discussing the war reparations as soon as possible. German President Gauch recognized that Germany was bearing a "moral debt" for dozens of massacres by the occupying Nazi army. He indicated Germany would set up a "future fund" of a large amount of money as a reminder to the new German generations of the Nazi war crimes in Greece.[61]

The suggestion of the German President for the formation of a "future fund" are well intentioned, but his estimation of dozens of massacres committed by Nazis is certainly deflated. Although there are only a few widely known official monuments such as Distomo, a village in central Greece near Delphi and Kalavryta in the Peloponnese where the barbaric atrocities of the Waffen SS troops' reprisals have surpassed the imagination of the human mind, there are numerous mass executions that took place during the occupation. Every few kilometers in most parts of Greece, there are places that usually the local populations (the elderly) know very well where massacres by Nazis took place. Many villages were burned to ashes and the people killed or shipped to Germany to work and be humiliated in concentration camps. Greek property was confiscated as persistent looting was the norm during the occupation. Many Greeks are now convinced that it is in the nature of a large percentage of Germans always to want to be dominant, whether via military force or economically.

Many Greeks are now very angry with such a German attitude because, since 2010, Germany has dictated the austerity programs that so far have deepened the recession and punished Greece. According to several experts, Greece has a valid claim against Germany, but any settlement will be arrived at through a political rather than a legal decision.[62] A settlement is more likely to be negotiated and possibly agreed for the two forced loans as Germany paid little to other countries for all its other crimes involving massacres and destruction of infrastructure.

The recent friction between Greece and Germany regarding the most recent version of Grexit after Syriza was elected attracted a lot of attention from many people, politicians, and journalists in Europe and beyond. Both the Germans and Greeks were vocal in support of their views. The questions about the World War II reparations resurfaced again. This time, Berlin's position that the case was closed regarding Greek World War II requests was rebuked from inside Germany. The challenge came from three German politicians, two from Merkel's coalition SPD party Gesine Schwan and Ralph Stegner, while the third is Anton Hofreiter, the parliamentary chief of the opposition Green Party.[63]

Gesine Schawn disagrees with the German government's response to the Greek war-reparation claims; she stated that "Germany does not want to face up to its responsibilities." Several other people are offering a sympathetic ear to the Greek claims although they see why Greece presently raised the request, as it is pressed by the EU to meet its financial obligation to the creditors of the bailout. Everyone, however, wants to keep the two issues separate. Gesine Schwan suggested to the *Financial Times* that Germany could find a solution with Greece just as a solution was found between Germany and Poland.

A German historian Eberhard Rondholz, who investigated the case of the German World War II reparations to Greece, concluded that the case is not like the German government claims it to be. Mr Rondholz studied the agreements that the German government referred to when it reached its decision that the case is closed. He concluded that the agreements "cast doubt" on the German government's interpretation to consider the case of the German war reparations to Greece closed.[64] (See Box 7.1 for another approach to the German war reparations to Greece.)

A neo-Nazi party on the rise

One of the worst and most unwelcome side effects caused by the crisis in Greece is the rise to popularity of an extreme right-wing neo-Nazi party named Golden Dawn. Golden Dawn is very different and more extreme than any other right-wing European party. Golden Dawn forcefully intervenes in many areas to fill in the vacuum created by the disabled Greek state. To fill in the gaps, Golden Dawn intervenes in many areas in addition to providing political representation of its constituency in the parliament. The party is organized almost as a state within the state, providing food for people who are in need and protection of businesses

BOX 7.1 A moral lesson to the world by a German couple

Lessons in morality and kindness can come from the least expected people. After several years of Greek bashing by German news media, one is surprised to find modern heroes who are not swayed to think that most Greeks are lazy tax-evaders. Some people have the courage to teach lessons of morality to the entire world. Ludwig Zacaro and Nina Lahge went on vacation in Greece and visited the picturesque town of Nafplio in East Peloponnese in March 2015. While in Nafplio, they paid a visit to the mayor of the town and offered him a check of €875. They explained to the mayor that they were not wealthy, but the couple wanted to repay their share of the war reparations to Greece that Germany owes.

Both were aware of the forced loans that the occupying Nazi regime extracted from the central bank of Greece in 1942. The loans were worth €11 billion, and with interest amounted to about €70 billion. The rest was simple arithmetic the couple divided this amount by the population of Germany of about 80 million and found that every German owes an amount of €875, thus they took the symbolic action to hand the check to the mayor, which was deposited in a local charity. Nina Lahge was interviewed at a press conference where she stated, "We are guests in this beautiful country and we wanted to give something back. Not charity, but something that belongs to you." Such words I know are very touching to many people, and bring tears to many eyes. Furthermore, the couple noted that they love and support Greece and that they are embarrassed for the way the news media and the German politicians treat Greece. They are also convinced that the Greek people are not responsible for the old debt that the previous governments created for the benefit of oligarchs.

and people. The Golden Dawn members took it upon themselves to clear the city squares of foreign immigrants.

Many of its members are organized as paramilitary units and intervene to impose the law according to their strong convictions, sometimes in the presence of police who often are simple spectators tolerating illegal acts. Golden Dawn is an extremely nationalistic party and strongly anti-immigrant and anti-Semitic; its objective is to expel all illegal immigrants from Greece. The party is strongly against the bailouts and the international lenders which consider them to be exploiters. Golden Dawn is also involved in humanitarian work; however, even this noble activity is carried out in the most distasteful and discriminatory way: Food for Greeks, Blood for Greeks, and more recently Jobs for Greeks.

Golden Dawn first attracted attention in the 1990s as waves of immigrants were arriving in Greece from Eastern European countries, Asia, Africa, but mostly from Albania.[65] At that time it began a fierce campaign against immigration. Golden Dawn became popular by strongly opposing the harsh treatment of Greece by the

Troika and the subsequent deterioration of the standard of living in Greece. Crime, which was almost unheard of in Greece before the 1970s, became a common theme with the arrival of the first waves of immigrants. Many people, especially the elderly, became the targets of robberies. The Greek police, according to many people, was unable to provide protection for the people as it was understaffed and underpaid. As a result, many in the police force did not seem to be bothered if Golden Dawn members turned into vigilantes.

A large percentage in the Greek police, for historical reasons, were supporters of Golden Dawn and closed their eyes to crimes against foreigners, leftists, and homosexuals. After receiving 0.29 of 1 percent in the 2009 national elections, Golden Dawn surprised everyone when it received 6 percent of the popular vote in the June 2012 election, sending 18 members to the national parliament. This was an astonishing election outcome for an extremist party with a criminal record. Political analysts interpreted this startling victory to be the result of a protest vote to punish the two major political parties that had shamelessly led the country to bankruptcy, and had allowed an extraordinary number of foreigners to arrive in Greece thus changing the demographics of the country. Many of the foreigners were publicized by the news media to be involved in criminal activities that raised a negative perception of them among the general public.

There is no doubt in anyone's mind that Golden Dawn is a neo-Nazi party as the members salute by extending the right hand and have blind obedience to their leader Nikolaos Michaloliakos who likes to be addressed as "Führer." It is frustrating that the political system has not stopped a series of crimes committed against foreign immigrants, especially when international human rights organizations have often given many warnings. In a country like Greece, which has suffered so much from Nazi crimes, it is difficult to believe that a neo-Nazi party can flourish and be allowed to go against immigrant workers when half of the Greek population are immigrants themselves in other countries.

A change in the wind against Golden Dawn began in September 2013 when a group of 30 Golden Dawn members attacked and killed an anti-fascist, left-wing musician named Pavlos Fyssas. This crime was publicly investigated and the assassin admitted that he was a member of Golden Dawn. This crime may be the beginning of the demise of the party, its downfall would be attributed to the Greek judiciary system. The great irony is that three women were destined to play a major role in the punishment of the violent male-dominated political party. A "gutsy" female prosecutor appointed two judges, Ioanna Klapa and Maria Dimitropoulou, to investigate Golden Dawn.[66] Helena Smith of *The Guardian* wrote that the two judges "will . . . dissect Golden Dawn with the precision of a surgeon."

The two female judges and friends have been working for about three decades on some of the most difficult criminal cases. For the Golden Dawn case they have accumulated an immense amount of information to examine and use for the prosecution, which includes speeches, confiscated computer drives, videos and other documents, all summing up to a dossier of some 15,000 pages compiled by the court officials. The two judges have a great reputation as fearless, non-partisan, diligent and meticulous.[67] The two judges are provided with police protection and were given 18 months to place members of the parliament belonging to Golden Dawn on trial. After spending a month in prison with five other members of the party, the Golden Dawn leader appeared in parliament where a vote to lift his immunity was going to take place. Michaloliakos was accused of murder, assault, and illegal possession of weapons. Michaloliakos gave the Nazi salute in the parliament and told the speaker of parliament to "shut up."

In Syntagma Square outside of the parliament Golden Dawn supporters dressed in their usual black shirts "gave a hearty rendition of the Nazi Horst Wessel song" with lyrics in Greek. All this happened after they insisted that they are not a Nazi party. Golden Dawn had fresh memory of its victories in the European elections on May 25, 2014. The Golden Dawn members were aggressive in that election practicing the politics of hate. A respected Greek journalist Pavlos Tzimas commented on the recent behavior of the Golden Dawn members and leaders, saying that Golden Dawn is a much different neo-Nazi party to any other party in Europe, because it aims to destroy democracy.

Why is Golden Dawn such an extreme party that not even Jean-Marie Le Pen would agree to cooperate with it? The answer to this question is based on the unique history of Greece in comparison to all other Western European countries. After liberation from the Nazis, Greece never experienced the immediate and smooth democratization that other European countries did. Greece lived through another catastrophic period of civil war from 1946 to 1949. The civil conflict not only split the country for three years, but left many wounds in the Greek population for many years to come. In addition, since the right-wing forces won the civil war, the Greek state has almost always been dominated by such forces, especially in the military and the police. This is the reason Golden Dawn had many sympathizers within the state ranks.[68]

Golden Dawn to stand trial

On October 16, 2014, in a 697-page report Isidororos Dogiakos, the Greek public prosecutor, accused 69 members of Golden Dawn and made them stand trial for a variety of criminal offenses. Among the 69 accused, the 16 members of the Greek parliament were included. The crimes are: murder, theft, arson, blackmail, and violent hate crimes.[69] The trial would determine the fate of the Golden Dawn party. Helena Smith of *The Guardian* once commented on the source of the strength of Golden Dawn. Such strength, she claims, lies in the "grueling austerity" that allowed Greece to make the largest fiscal consolidation in the history of the world. The same fiscal consolidation and austerity gave Golden Dawn its deep roots.[70] It seems that the new development involving the Greek judiciary may be able to almost eradicate neo-Nazism in the country that gave democracy to the world. Prosecutor Dogiakos is certain that the party which "employs violence" to achieve its objectives cannot be legal and he has started the process to prove it in the courts.[71]

Concluding comments

Undoubtedly, Greece has always been at the epicenter of the European sovereign debt crisis. The Eurocrisis was triggered by the shocking leak by the Greek Prime Minister Papandreou. Such onerous revelations opened a Pandora's Box at the end of 2009 and released untamed market forces that demonstrated how vulnerable the EMU was. Free financial markets proved to be more powerful than the joint IMF/EU efforts to stabilize Greece. Unregulated and unchecked markets provided the framework that allowed speculators to profit by forcing Greece into a depression. The crisis devastated the middle class and poor people of Greece, making them jobless, homeless, and ill. This is the ugly face of the markets.

Greek governments, regardless of which political party was in power, are responsible for the fiscal macroeconomic mismanagement of the country. A long-established clientelistic system encouraged corruption and created a bloated public sector.

The crisis was both avoidable and unnecessary. When Papandreou's revelations were made, many Germans realized that what they had always feared would happen had already occurred. The fiscal rules of the EMU were violated, and they were prepared to give the violators a good lesson. The fact that Germany was one of the first violators of the SGP was not seen as important. The Old Testament was dictating their behavior. It took Chancellor Merkel a long time to convince her voters and her party to support the bailouts as they would be better off without them.

Although Greece received a bailout that appeared massive in 2010, it was soon realized that it was insufficient because it was offered under very unfavorable terms. A second bailout – to replace the first, not in addition to it as many misconstrue it – had the same effects as the first. The reason is that very little of these bailout funds went into the Greek economy. As it is now known, the bailouts to Greece were intended to suppress the contagion and to bail out the European banks, and the banks were indeed bailed out. In addition, the bailout to Greece came with many strings. Greece had to adopt austerity measures and reforms supervised by the Institutions. As a result, Greece lost its sovereignty on May 10, 2010 when it received the first bailout. It turned out that, that instead of helping Greece out of the crisis, the fiscal consolidation imposed by the Troika on Greece drove its economy in an increasingly deeper depression.

The Greek New Democracy/PASOK government, in its effort to bring down the deficits, reduced government expenditures and increased taxes, policies which had contractionary effects on the Greek economy. In conclusion, the policies adopted by the Greek government and imposed by the Troika sank Greece into a long and unprecedented recession. As a result, neither the government nor the Troika was popular in Greece. On January 25, 2015 the Greek people elected Syriza, an anti-austerity party, which promised to expel the Troika and renegotiate the Greek bailout with the EU and the IMF. Finding a solution to this question is a big challenge for Greece, the EA, and the IMF as much is at stake, including the exit of Greece from the EA and the survival of the euro and the EU.

After five months of negotiations between the new Greek government and the Institutions, the two reached a deadlock. Things became worse when Syriza pulled out of the negotiations and announced a referendum to let the Greek people decide whether the government should accept the terms of the agreement with the Institutions that Syriza considered very harsh.

Notes

1 Such atrocities are well portrayed up to this date by the French painter Delacroix at the Louvre Museum, in Paris.
2 The combined naval fleets of the three big powers came to Southern Greece in the Peloponnese to enforce the London Treaty (1827) to maintain the balance of powers in the region. However, when a small boat with an English crew was accidently shot by the Turks and their Egyptian allies, the naval battle began and almost the entire Ottoman fleet was destroyed.
3 Since the uprising took place in Athens, the street where the demonstration took place was renamed September 3rd to commemorate the date of the historical event.
4 This is depicted with the common saying often used up to this date that the English loans can never be repaid, implying the perception of the common people was that the country will always be indebted to England.
5 The associate EC membership of Greece was frozen during the period 1967–74 when Greece was ruled by a military dictatorship as the EC accepts only democratic countries as members.
6 The exceptions were the two oil crises and the 1992–3 European exchange rate crisis.
7 Visvizi (2012).
8 However, in the past several candidate EMU governments were suspected of using "creative accounting" to calculate public deficit and debt statistics in order to show that they met the Maastricht convergence criteria to qualify for EMU membership.
9 Visvizi (2012).
10 It is estimated that presently as many Greeks live abroad as in Greece. However, emigration has ceased and Greece has been experiencing an inflow of foreign immigrants and repatriated Greeks.
11 It was reported he claimed this when he made his revelations about the deficits being deflated by the previous Greek government, although Papandreou later said that he had been misinterpreted.
12 Several EU leaders during the crisis have also failed to understand the way markets react to news and how sometimes news can have very favorable effects but other times be destructive of an economy. Such underestimation of the markets by Papandreou is considered a huge political mistake that has marked his political career, since the damage to the country was immense.
13 Based on estimated data.
14 Greece did not receive the entire first bailout but only 5 of the first 12 installments.
15 Zestos and Williamson (2012).
16 Rickens (2012).
17 Janssen (2010).
18 Statistics on these two important macroeconomic variables are presented in this section of the chapter.
19 See Figure 3.6.
20 In Figure 7.4 this is shown as an increase, i.e. approaching zero.
21 A similar tradition continued during the German-Italian occupation.
22 Only tax evasion can explain a merchant's usual question "with or without receipt" to potential buyers when negotiating a price. This practice was customary in the Greek countryside and the small towns where people knew each other well and the risk of being caught was slim since the buyer and seller were usually friends or relatives.

Furthermore, they had never had to pay such taxes in the past. In addition many people do not trust the government, thus not paying taxes may not be considered such a bad thing.

23 Congressional Research Service.

24 This belief is held by an increasing number of people and is especially influenced by the extreme and non-cooperative position taken by German politicians and news media.

25 Traa (2011).

26 Visvizi (2012).

27 Cafiso and Cellini (2012).

28 Greek National Reforms Program, April 2014, Primary surplus (deficit) refers to government revenues minus expenditures excluding interest payments to service the public debt.

29 Zoan NG (2014).

30 Greek public employees do not have an incentive to be very productive or eager to help the citizen as they get paid regardless.

31 Rumors have it that even some people who have not worked in Greece sometimes received pensions.

32 Military spending has always been a major component of public spending as the country has the largest military budget as a percentage of GDP in the EU. This is mainly due to the adversarial relations and distrust that Greece has with regard to Turkey. Even the most peaceful and dove-like people in the country have never criticized military purchases.

33 "Greece's bailout: not so fast" (2014) *The Economist*, October 25.

34 Gurria (2015).

35 "Social Expenditure Update," OECD (2014).

36 By prolonging a case, either in the parliament or in the courts, people become fed up with hearing so much about it and all the accused are found innocent in the end. This is how politicians of opposing parties end up resolving issues by going soft on each other's supporters. This is a commonly held view by Greek people, most of whom are frustrated with the way the justice system works.

37 This section on the November 2, 2011 pre-Summit Cannes meeting draws very much on the *Financial Times* article by Peter Spiegel, "How the Euro was saved," Part 1, May 11, 2014, of the services they provide.

38 This referendum would have had a agreeable answer – the Greeks were not angry with the EMU, but only with the Draconian austerity measures.

39 These may have been some of the thoughts of the participants in this important pre-Summit meeting.

40 Special Drawing Rights are a weighted average accounting currency created and held by the IMF in which countries hold reserves. The currencies included in the SDR are the US dollar, the euro, the yen, and the UK pound.

41 *On the Year that Changed Europe*, May 16, 2014. The material in this section draws heavily on the "Inside Europe's Plan Z" by Peter Spiegel of the *Financial Times* in the second installment of a three-part series.

42 Allen (2014).

43 Stuckler and Basu (2013).

44 The study was conducted by Dr Emannouil Makaris and presented at the American College of Cardiology Annual Meeting, "From heart attacks to maternal care: the human cost of austerity in Greece," *New Statesman*, April 13, 2013.

45 *On the Year that Changed Europe*, May 16, 2014.

46 Cooper (2014).

47 Kentikelenis *et al.* (2014).

48 Alderman (2013).

49 Cooper (2014).

50 The last time that Greece was inflicted by such a massive famine was in 1941 when it was estimated that 100,000 people died from starvation. When pictures of starving people falling and dying in the streets of Athens were publicized by the international news media, this influenced the Allies to lift the blockade of the German occupied city of Athens and thus some food slipped in.

51 Smith (2013).
52 Mendelsohn (2013).
53 Zikakou (2014).
54 Sotiropoulos and Bourikos (2014).
55 Manolis Glezos worked for the statistics office of the International Red Cross and was one of the people responsible for recording daily human losses from starvation and Nazi executions (Smith, 2011).
56 Sotiropoulos and Bourikos (2014).
57 Christisis (2013).
58 These figures were calculated by Greek organizations.
59 Inman (2013).
60 The payment to Greece was one of 12 war compensation agreements the Germans had signed with western nations (Papachristou, 2014).
61 Inman (2013).
62 Psaropoulos (2014).
63 Gesine is the former SPD Presidential candidate that later became SPD Vice Chairman (Wagstyl, 2015).
64 Ibid.
65 *Guardian Newspaper*, "Fear and loathing in Athens: the rise of Golden Dawn and the far right." See: http://www.theguardian.com/world/2012/oct/26/greece-golden-dawn.
66 *Guardian Newspaper*: "Golden Dawn: the courage of two women stems the rise of Greece's neo-nazis." See: http://www.theguardian.com/world/2014/mar/23/golden-dawn-women.
67 Ibid.
68 *Guardian Newspaper*: "SS songs and antisemitism: the week Golden Dawn turned openly nazi." See: http://www.theguardian.com/world/2014/jun/27/greece-golden-dawn.
69 *Guardian Newspaper*: "Greek prosecutor orders all Golden Dawn MPs to face criminal trial." See: http://www.theguardian.com/world/2014/oct/16/greece-golden-dawn.
70 Ibid.
71 Greek independent press (2014) *EnetEnglish.gr*, October 17.

References

Alderman, L. (2013) "More children in Greece start to go hungry," *New York Times*, April 17.
Allen, K. (2014) "Austerity in Greece caused more than 500 male suicides, say researchers," *The Guardian*, April 21.
Cafiso, G. and Cellini, R. (2012) *Evidence on Fiscal Consolidations and the Evolution of Public Debt in Europe*. Munich: CESifo Group.
Christisis, G. (2013) "Berlin owes Greece billions in WWII reparations," *Spiegel Online*, April 8.
Cooper, C. (2014) "Tough austerity measures in Greece leave nearly a million people with no access to healthcare, leading to soaring infant mortality, HIV infection and suicide," *The Independent*, February 21.
"Greece's bailout: not so fast" (2014) *The Economist*, October 25.
Gurria, A. (2015) *OECD's 2015 Going for Growth: Breaking the Vicious Cycle*. OECD, Speech, Istanbul.
Inman, P. (2013) "Greece is right to expose German loans hypocrisy," *The Guardian*, April 26.
Janssen, R. (2010) *Who Exactly Is Being Saved*. Center of Economic Policy Research, July.
Kentikelenis, A. *et al.* (2014) "Greece's health crisis: from austerity to denialism," *The Lancet*, 383 (9918): 748–53.
Mendelsohn, J. (2013) "Hardship in Greece," *The European*, September 19.
Papachristou, H. (2014) "Germany offers fund to defuse Greek war reparations claims," *Reuters*, March 6.

Psaropoulos, J. (2014) "Greece pressure Germany on WW II reparations," *Al Jazeera*, April 26.

Rickens, C. (2012) "Stop the second bailout package! EU should admit Greece is bankrupt," *Spiegel Online*, February 20.

Smith, H. (2011) "Greek protestors who resisted Nazi rule turn fire on EU," *The Guardian*, August 2.

Smith, H. (2013) "Greece's food crisis: families face going hungry during summer shutdown," *The Guardian*, August 6.

Smith, H. (2014) "Greek prosecutor orders all Golden Dawn MPs to face criminal trial," *The Guardian*, October 16.

Sotiropoulos, D. and Bourikos, D. (2014) "Economic crisis, social solidarity and the voluntary sector in Greece," *Journal of Power, Politics and Governance*, 2 (2): 33–53.

Stuckler, D. and Basu, S. (2013) *The Body Economic: Why Austerity Kills*. London: Allen Lane.

Traa, B. (2011) *Achieving Sustainable Economic Reforms in Greece in 2011 and Beyond*. Lecture, International Monetary Fund, Washington, DC.

Visvizi, A. (2012) "The crisis in Greece and the EU-IMF rescue package: determinants and pitfalls," *Acta Oeconomica*, 15–39.

Wagstyl, S. (2015) "Greeks find support for German reparations claims – in Germany," *Financial Times*, Berlin, March 17.

Zikakou, I (2014) "One night in Athens homeless shelter," *Greek Reporter*, August 20.

Zoan NG (2014) *Finance – Professional Essays and Assignments*. Zoan NG.

Zestos, G. and Williamson, M. (2012) "German rigidity: an obstacle to the resolution of the European crisis," *Journal of Regional and Socio-Economic Issues*, 2 (3): 6–20.

8

FINANCIAL STRUGGLES IN
THE EU AND EA

Housing bubbles in Europe

Many economists are convinced that the US subprime mortgage crisis spread to Europe and the rest of the world via contagion. Financial integration made it possible for US investment banks to transfer mortgage-backed securities (MBSs) and other toxic financial derivatives onto the balance sheets of European banks. This began when the US applied expansionary monetary policy to cope with the dot-com crisis in 2001, driving US interest rates to unprecedentedly low levels. The combination of low interest rates with a global savings glut and financial deregulation generated a housing bubble in the US. The financing of homes through the issuing of securities facilitated contagion of the crisis as investment banks spread the risk abroad through the sale of mortgage-related securities.[1]

In addition to the US, several European countries experienced prolonged increases in home and commercial real estate prices. Figure 8.1 shows the housing price indices of nine European countries. Eight of these countries formed housing price bubbles during the period 2005–9. The housing price indices of most of these countries turned upwards after the burst of the bubble at different times, depending on the idiosyncratic economic and financial conditions in each country. In four countries the housing price indices declined only for a very short period after the burst and thereafter began increasing. The house price indices of the UK, Finland, Belgium, and Sweden have been increasing since the initial downturn. The housing price index of Sweden increased so rapidly that a second housing bubble is almost imminent for this country. Another group of four countries experienced prolonged declines in their housing price index. Ireland experienced both the steepest increase and decrease in its housing price index among the four countries. Similarly, Spain and the Netherlands followed Ireland's housing price indices, thus they also formed housing bubbles and experienced prolonged declines after they hit

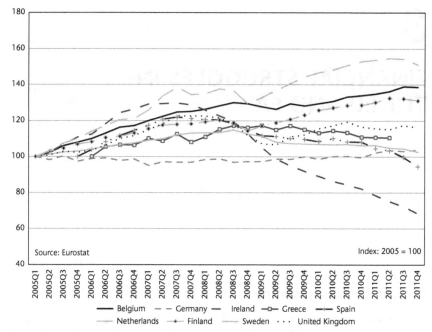

FIGURE 8.1 European housing price indices

their peaks. On the other hand, the home price index of Greece indicated such a mild increase that it can hardly be characterized as a bubble. The financial problems of Greece are mainly related to its public debt explosion.

It may be difficult to explain the absence of a housing bubble in Greece which experienced the worst economic crisis in Europe. However, it is now generally accepted knowledge that the cause of the crisis in Greece was its foreign debt that skyrocketed mostly since 2004 when New Democracy was the governing party. This Greek public debt accumulation continued increasing even more rapidly during the years Greece was under the supervision and monitoring of the Troika. During this time, the country was obligated to conform with the conditionality imposed by its creditors and face large interest payments to the international lenders.

Unlike other European countries, Germany was also an exception; its housing price index remained relatively constant during the period 2005–11. Since 2011 Germany's housing price index has increased by approximately 10 percent. Mortgage markets in Germany and in neighboring Austria are not as well developed as in the Anglo-Saxon countries. In both countries, housing markets have evolved in their own unique ways following strict national rules and regulations of their housing industry. For example, Germany has the lowest loan value to house price ratio requirement in Europe; borrowers are required to have a down payment of 30–35 percent. Furthermore, German public policy favors renting to owning a home. As a result, home ownership in Germany is only 42 percent, but 67 percent in the US and 79 percent in Spain.

The common perception that the global financial crisis was triggered by the US subprime mortgage crisis was challenged by the Freddie Mac chief economist Frank E. Nothaft.[2] Mr Nothaft claimed that the "boom-bust housing" cycles were not only generated in the US, but also in European countries. He provided evidence that home prices in some European countries increased and declined by more than they did in the US. Nothaft concluded that the roots of the housing crisis in some European countries were as "endemic in their own countries" as the crisis was in the US. Ireland, the UK, Spain, and the Baltic countries generated their own bubbles.

According to Nothaft, during the period 1996 to the peak of the housing market, Ireland observed the highest increase in its real housing price index amounting to 182 percent, followed by the UK which increased by 152 percent. The US experienced a 47 percent increase in its real housing price index far behind the housing price increases in France and Spain.[3] Figure 8.2 shows the housing price indices of seven EA countries and the house price index of the US for the period 2011–2014. According to this figure, although the US house price index started above the index of six of these European countries, it ended up to be below four European country housing price indices after the bubble burst. This means that some of the EA countries experienced more volatility as they formed larger bubbles than the US. In the next section, we look at the role of the Credit Rating Agencies (CRAs) during the subprime mortgage and European sovereign debt crises.

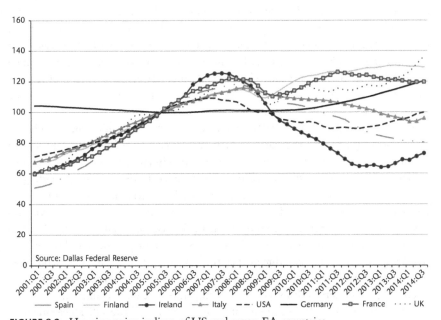

FIGURE 8.2 Housing price indices of US and seven EA countries

The overzealous credit rating agencies

CRAs are sued in the US

In August 2011, the US Department of Justice began an investigation of Standard & Poor's (S&P), the largest US CRA, to determine if it had correctly rated many mortgage-related securities. This investigation started before S&P stripped the US sovereign debt of its AAA rating.[4] On February 5, 2013, the US Department of Justice filed a lawsuit against S&P accusing the CRA of highly overrating residential mortgage-backed securities (RMBS) and collateralized debt obligations (CDO), therefore defrauding investors. The highly rated securities convinced many investors and several federally insured financial institutions to unknowingly buy low-quality securities as they were not aware of their low quality. As a result they lost billions of dollars.

Several US federal and state legal representatives in addition to the US Attorney General, Eric Holder, joined as plaintiffs in the legal trial. This lawsuit was part of a larger campaign to fight financial crime that began in 2009 with the establishment of the Presidential Financial Fraud Enforcement Task Force by President Obama. As a result, 20 federal agencies along with 94 US attorneys launched a campaign to punish financial crime and bring justice to the victims. The Justice Department continues to prosecute a large number of accused persons involved in over 10,000 financial fraud suits prosecuting about 15,000 individuals of which 2,900 were involved in mortgage fraud cases.[5]

A lawsuit was filed against the three major CRAs: S&P, Moody's, and Fitch by the liquidator of the two Bear Stearns hedge funds. The three CRAs were sued for one billion dollars for misleading investors by providing inflated ratings in order to fraudulently increase their own business.[6] It is interesting to note that the two Bear Stearns hedge funds were the early harbinger of the financial crisis in 2007, which triggered numerous downgrades of MBSs and other housing-related complex securities that were rated as very safe and high quality, although a few days later the same securities were rated as junk.

On January 21, 2015, S&P agreed to pay the Securities and Exchange Commission (SEC) and the states of New York and Massachusetts an amount of $77 million. S&P was accused by the SEC of "fraudulent misconduct" in its effort to boost its own businesses. In addition, S&P agreed to discontinue providing its services for a year for certain synthetic, structured, financial derivatives although it did not agree or disagree with the accusations.[7] The fine of $77 million, nevertheless, is a very small penalty in comparison to the damages caused to the US and global economy by the financial crisis. The US Justice Department and several US regulatory agencies are convinced that the CRAs not only failed to send early warnings to prevent the crisis but also contributed to the creation of the crisis, by overrating the creditworthiness of many companies that went bankrupt.

On February 3, 2015, a settlement between S&P and the US Department of Justice and 19 states was announced. In this settlement, S&P, without admitting any guilt, agreed to pay $1.38 billion, which was divided almost equally between the Department of Justice and the 19 states.[8] The accusation this time was that S&P failed to warn investors of the low quality of the toxic, mortgage-related securities they were buying and holding as safe investments. According to US Attorney General Eric Holder, S&P purposefully ignored analysts' warnings concerning the low-quality financial products it was endorsing. S&P admitted in this settlement that it ignored the company executives' advice when it did not downgrade low-quality securities for fear of losing business.

The Australian lawsuit against S&P

In another part of the world, on November 5, 2012, Australian Federal Court Justice Jayne Jagot ruled against S&P and ABN Amro Bank NV. This case was brought at a Federal Court in Sydney by twelve Australian municipality councils, which invested in securities given AAA ratings by S&P.[9] This was the first such ruling against a CRA, and it was expected to have an influence in other similar cases in Australia, the US, Europe, and possibly other parts of the world. In addition, a second class-action lawsuit against S&P was brought by IMF Australia Ltd, a company that funds large class-action lawsuits. IMF Australia Ltd represented 90 councils, churches, and charities that claimed to have lost $207 million. IMF Australia Ltd accused S&P of giving AAA and AA ratings to CDOs purchased from Lehman Brothers, which was the first US investment bank to collapse at the outset of the US subprime mortgage crisis.[10]

Many analysts were critical of the US government for not bailing out the Lehman Brothers as this triggered the US subprime mortgage crisis. The treatment of Lehman Brothers by the US government is often compared to the treatment of Greece by the EU during the Eurocrisis, which kept Greece in "intensive care" for many years contributing to the spread and intensity of the crisis.

S&P and ABN Amro Bank NV unsuccessfully appealed the decision of the Federal Australian Court; both S&P and the Amsterdam-based ABN Amro NV were found to have misled the 12 municipality councils in New South Wales. The councils were awarded 30 million Australian dollars for the losses.[11]

The CRAs proved to be unable to send early warnings by announcing the upcoming financial crisis in the US by downgrading banks, financial institutions, and other firms that were holding in their balance sheets almost worthless mortgage-related securities. Many such financial institutions were assigned a perfect credit rating by the three CRAs a few days prior to the crisis. The subprime mortgage crisis is the result of the explosion of complicated securities that markets could not correctly price, but it was sensed by investors that they were worthless.

The CRA experience in the EU

A large number of analysts and politicians accused the CRAs of overreacting by downgrading the government bonds of European countries that were financially distressed, exacerbating financial instability in the EA. A few countries (Greece, Ireland, Portugal, Spain, and Cyprus) experienced a large increase in interest rates; therefore, it became prohibitively expensive for them to borrow in the market and they were forced to seek bailouts which were jointly offered to these countries by the EU and the IMF. Several EU officials and country leaders became angry with the CRAs for not refraining from downgrading the countries' government bonds (sovereigns) even when bailout negotiations about these countries were still taking place. From that point the EU began a long process of evaluating the role of the CRAs in the European economy, and a campaign to change the importance of the CRAs in rating countries in order to reduce financial fragility in the EU/EA economic and financial system. This was going to be achieved through stricter regulation of the CRAs and by increasing the competition and transparency of the credit evaluation process of government bonds.

Since the G20 Summit in Washington DC on November 16, 2008, the leaders of the 20 richest and larger emerging economies agreed to jointly introduce new financial regulations to safeguard the international financial system. Among the top priorities at the G20 Washington DC Summit was a joint policy of reforms, a promise to avoid protectionism, and the enactment of financial rules and regulations that would govern complex financial derivatives and CRAs.[12] All such provisions were aimed at preventing the US financial crisis from spreading.

EU officials and country leaders quickly became aware that there were several deficiencies in the EU/EA financial system and that there was a need to introduce financial regulations to safeguard member countries from the financial crisis, which rapidly spread in Europe in 2008 and 2009. The EU Commission drafted a proposal curbing the CRAs' freedom by laying out stricter operating rules and regulations. The EU Commission expressed its view of the CRAs by stating that ratings are not "simple opinions" but are extremely powerful pieces of information that can bankrupt corporations and countries. The Commission, according to this proposal, seems to be well aware of the CRAs' role in both the US subprime mortgage crisis and the Eurocrisis.

Because the CRAs provided incorrect ratings for sovereigns that led to a drastic rise of interest rates in Greece, Ireland, Portugal, Spain, Italy, and other countries, CRAs are partially responsible for the crisis. The EU Internal Market Commissioner, Michel Barnier, is convinced that CRAs are sometimes disruptive and increase market volatility that turns out to be detrimental to some EA countries. According to the EU Commissioner, when there exists evidence of "infringement or gross negligence," the CRA should be prosecuted. The EU Commission proposal stated that there should be less reliance on CRAs. Furthermore, to avoid the conflict of interest, the introduction of other methods than the "issuer pays model" of how CRAs should be paid must be sought.

EU Internal Market Commissioner, Mr Barnier, proposed that investors must also undertake their own evaluation of the bonds they are purchasing. Lastly, the proposal calls for more transparency in the rating process and more accountability by the CRAs as their mistakes are suspected of having partly triggered the crisis.

The EU Commission is not alone in its effort to curb the power of the three CRAs: S&P, Moody's, and Fitch. The G20 Financial Stability Board (FSB) has examined how to reduce the CRAs' power to influence investors.[13] Meanwhile, German Foreign Minister Guido Westerwelle had long ago recognized the issue of the lack of competition, and back in 2008 had recommended the establishment of a new European Credit Rating Agency.[14]

The concern of the EU officials and country leaders that CRAs can trigger an increase in volatility turned out to be well justified because on January 20, 2012, S&P announced the downgrade of nine EA countries. The first two, France and Austria, were stripped of their AAA status to AA, one notch down. The public debt of another group of countries – Malta, Slovakia, and Slovenia – was downgraded by one notch as well. Lastly, the public debts of Italy, Spain, Portugal, and Cyprus were downgraded by two notches. S&P explained its decision to downgrade the nine countries was the result of the slow response by the EA leaders to convince the markets that they were determined to resolve the crisis.[15]

During this time, Greece and the EA were negotiating with the private investors of Greece to reach an agreement to restructure the Greek debt through a PSI program (haircut), which would reduce the public debt and render it sustainable. The PSI agreement was reached on February 22, 2012, creating a temporary euphoria among EU leaders and EU officials. However, unlike the initial expectation, the PSI did not resolve the Greek public debt problem despite the drastic reduction of the privately held public debt by 53.5 percent, and a massive second bailout of €130 billion that followed the PSI program. Indeed, this was not only a disaster for Greece but for other countries as well, as they were infected via contagion as interest rates increased substantially. If the severity and duration of the European sovereign debt crisis could have been predicted knowing the record of the three CRAs in Australia, Europe, and the US, a case could have been made for at least a temporary shutting down of the three CRAs while legal investigations were pending. It is highly likely that the crisis would not have evolved into such a disastrous recession without the uninterrupted fuel provided by the CRAs.

The second largest CRA, Moody's, followed S&P and downgraded six EA countries: Italy, Malta, Portugal, Slovakia, Slovenia, and Spain. The reason for the downgrades, according to Moody's, was the lack of commitment by the countries to implement fiscal and economic reforms. In addition, Moody's criticized the EA country leaders for not committing sufficient resources to cope with the crisis. These were problems that markets already sensed, so Moody's comments enhanced the fragility in the financial system.

Italy has been the focus of attention by CRAs and the financial markets for its high debt to GDP ratio, only second to that of Greece, for some time. S&P put Italy on a negative watch list in May 2011 and downgraded Italy's rating by one notch. In January 2013, S&P downgraded Italy by two notches. Fitch also followed S&P when it downgraded Italy from A+ to an A− rating.

Unlike previous suits, the plaintiff that filed charges against the CRAs, the Italian prosecutor Michele Ruggiero, sued a former S&P president and five of its employees. He argued that the CRAs destabilized Italy because the information leaked to traders was biased and distorted.[16] S&P responded to the prosecutor's accusations, saying that their decisions were based on independent opinions according to the standard and transparent methodologies that are always used with every country. The court in Trani, Italy, decided that ECB President, Mario Draghi, Economy Minister, Carlo Padoan, and former Prime Minister, Mario Monti, will all be called to testify in the trial. Interestingly, Mario Monti, as Italy's Prime Minister for a little over a year, is credited to have calmed the markets in his country until Silvio Berlusconi withdrew support from his government. Mario Monti was the Internal Market and Financial Services Commissioner for two terms, 1994–2004. During this period, he blocked several mergers and went against vast interests promoting competition in the EU and thus earned the title "Super Mario."

The EU, in line with the G20 November 14–15, 2008 Washington DC Summit spirit to regulate all financial institutions, products, and markets, introduced into EA law Regulation 1060/2009, The EU Credit Rating Agencies. Furthermore, because the EU had created the European Securities and Markets Authority (ESMA), a supervisory authority over all CRAs, it was compelled to revise its CRA regulation in 2011. Lastly, the EU introduced new laws in 2013 to enforce stricter regulatory rules of CRAs – these included Regulation 462/2013 and Directive 2013/14/EU.[17]

The new laws became effective on June 20, 2013. Since June 20, 2013 CRAs have become more accountable and transparent when rating countries' securities. The new regulations require investors to undertake their own evaluations and to rely less on the CRAs' mechanistic approach to rating government bonds. The new regulations aim to reduce conflicts of interest, although the "issuer pays" model has not changed. The new 2013 regulations require companies' issuers to rotate CRAs when they securitize complex structured financial derivatives. Such an arrangement is helpful, because it breaks up a long and mutually beneficial relation between the issuer and CRAs in order to protect investors.

Similarly, it is prohibited for CRAs to rate companies if shareholders of the CRAs which hold at least 10 percent of the CRA capital also hold 10 percent, or more, of capital of the company being rated. The new regulations provide that starting in June 2015 all ratings will be published on a new European rating platform; such innovation will improve transparency and assist investors. Although it was an initial idea, the new 2013 regulations did not include the creation of a new European CRA, public or private.[18]

A CRA and an investment bank, S&P and the Royal Bank of Scotland, were sued in Amsterdam in the Netherlands by a group of institutional investors for up to €250 million. The European institutional investors had purchased constant proportion cost obligations (CPDOs) during 2005–6 just before the global crisis. These are the same type of complex securities that were purchased by the 12 municipal councils in Australia that had won their case against S&P. The European institutional investors were very hopeful, considering the favorable decision of the Federal Australian Court for the 12 councils, especially because the CPDOs they purchased were also rated AAA by S&P.[19]

Besides downgrading EU countries, S&P decided to also downgrade the EU, thus on December 20, 2013, S&P reduced the EU AAA rating by a notch.[20] The explanation provided was a concern by S&P for the financing of the EU budget. This downgrade was surprising because the EU has hardly any debt of its own, and its budget is about one percent of the EU GDP, which can be characterized as exceptionally stable. Mr Ohlin Wren, the Economics and Finance Commissioner, then responded that the EU never experienced problems with its budget. Even during the crisis member countries always promptly paid their share.

The credit rating performance of the periphery EA countries' government bonds

The credit ratings of all the periphery countries are presented and discussed in this section, beginning with Greece and proceeding onto other countries that experienced financial distress and were rescued by the EU and the IMF. The ratings by all three CRAs are shown for each country. S&P and Fitch use identical letter grades, although their ratings do not always match. The three CRAs were exceptionally active in changing the ratings of the periphery countries' public debt during the Eurocrisis. This meant mostly downgrades by one or sometimes two notches at a time. Prior to the downgrades countries were usually placed under a negative outlook for a certain period. Equivalent letter ratings of the three CRAs have a numerical scale ranging from 1 (corresponding to default) to 21 (corresponding to highest quality). Any letter rating of BBB–, Baa3, and above 11.5 is considered investment status. Any letter rating of BB+, Ba1, or below 11.5 numerical score is considered as speculative junk. (See Table A8.1 in the appendix to this chapter for the credit rating scale of the three CRAs.) What follows in this chapter is the presentation of the historical credit ratings of the ten-year government bonds for each of the five bailout recipient countries. The public deficit and debt to GDP ratios, which are closely related to credit ratings, along with the real rate of GDP growth are also presented for each country.

Greece

The credit ratings of countries' government bonds depend on the economic performance of the country. Economic performance is always indicated by the real GDP growth and the unemployment rate. During the European sovereign debt and banking crisis, the public deficit and debt to GDP ratios played a very important role in the rating of the countries' public debt.

What is crucial for the ratings assigned by the CRA is that Greece, from 2008 to 2013, experienced a severe recession causing the country to lose approximately a quarter of its pre-crisis GDP. The rate of growth of real GDP for Greece is shown in Figure 7.3 in Chapter 7. Figure 8.3 shows Greece's public debt and deficit to GDP ratio on the left-hand and right-hand sides respectively. Although Greece had a very low public debt to GDP ratio in the early 1980s, it has steadily increased to become one of the highest debt to GDP ratios of all developed countries.

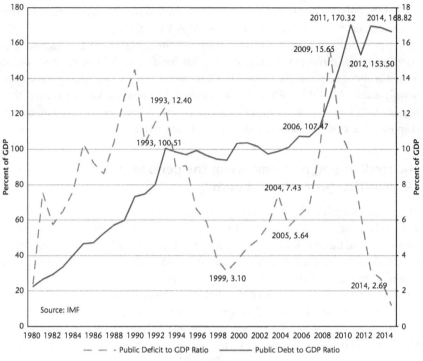

FIGURE 8.3 Greece: public deficit and debt to GDP ratios

The public deficit to GDP ratio is directly related to the public debt. During the first decade, 1980–89, Greece experienced a rapid rise in its public debt to GDP ratio till 1993 due to the high increase in public deficits. The public debt to GDP ratio leveled off at around 100 percent in the early 1990s up to 2004. From 1989, the public deficit to GDP ratio declined for about a decade until the euro was launched in 1999. After this event, the deficit to GDP ratio increased drastically when it reached 15.65 percent in 2009. Thereafter, we observed an almost unparalleled reduction of the Greek public deficit as a result of the fiscal consolidation imposed on Greece by the Troika. The Greek public deficit to GDP ratio reached 2.69 percent in 2013. Since 2004, the Greek public debt to GDP ratio almost exploded to reach the extraordinarily large number of 174.25 percent and is forecasted by the European Commission to reach 180.2 percent by the end of 2015. Note the deficits are measured in all EA country graphs as positive, whereas surpluses are denoted as negative. This is done for the purpose of presenting government surplus/deficits in the same figures as the public debt to GDP ratios.

Figure 8.4 presents the credit ratings of Greece by the three CRAs. What is observed in Figure 8.4 is the financial devastation of a country brought about by the changes in the ratings of its public debt-worthiness by the three CRAs. The first downgrade of Greece was announced by S&P on January 14, 2009. Since then, a drastic deterioration in the quality of Greek public debt as evaluated by the three

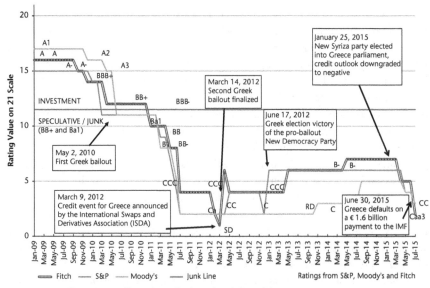

FIGURE 8.4 Greece: credit ratings during the debt crisis

CRAs followed, until March 9, 2012 when a credit event (default) was announced by the International Swaps and Derivatives Association. This was a necessary announcement after the agreement between the private creditors and Greece for the PSI (haircut). This is denoted by SD using Fitch notation. During this period a few hedge funds were able to collect insurance, that is they received cash for the credit default swaps (CDS) they had purchased. However, the amount they collected was relatively small, equal to €3.2 billion, in relation to the amount of loss (haircut) that the private creditors (bondholders) received.

Moody's much earlier had downgraded Greece to Ca and then to C. All three ratings reported by S&P, Fitch, and Moody's after the announced credit event of Greece, the ratings of its government bonds were reported as near default with the possibility of recovery. After March 12, 2013, Greece's credit ratings were upgraded by S&P and by Fitch, but not by Moody's. However, all three CRA ratings of the Greek ten-year government bonds remained at speculative/junk, thus precluding Greece from the market as interest rates remained high through June 2015.

Such low credit ratings for Greece were justified since the Greek public debt was unsustainable, and a sequence of mini crises left the CRAs unconvinced that the Greek public debt ought to be upgraded in the near future. Political uncertainty is another negative factor, particularly the pre-election promise of Syriza to seek another major haircut. Such a negative climate still prevailed despite the fact that Greece generated a primary surplus in the government account, a current account surplus, and positive economic growth for 2014.

The prolonged Greek public debt crisis flared up again at the end of June 2015. After negotiating for about five months with the EU and IMF, the Greek government decided abruptly to pull out from the negotiation table on June 27, 2015.

This happened after the Greek representatives were convinced that the international lenders were not willing to reach a fair compromise solution. The Greek government announced a referendum on July 5, 2015 to ask the Greek voters whether they approved the proposed EU/IMF proposal for the settlement of the Greek debt issue. The Greek government strongly believed that the EU/IMF proposal was too harsh and, if adopted, would have violated the coalition government's pre-election promises to the Greek people to end austerity. Economic conditions in Greece further deteriorated as Greece defaulted on a €1.6 billion payment to the IMF at midnight on June 30, 2015. To prevent capital outflows, the Greek government closed its banks and imposed capital controls by only allowing Greek residents limited access to their bank accounts through ATMs. In the early part of July 2015, all three CRAs downgraded Greece, as depicted in Figure 8.4 with notations Caa3 and CCC– (numerical value of 3) by Moody's and S&P, respectively. Such low ratings denote very high credit risk. Fitch, which was more aggressive, reduced its rating to an even lower status of CC (numerical value of 2) that corresponds to near default with possibility of recovery. The outcome of the referendum was a strong no as more than 61 percent voted against the EU/IMF proposal to resolve the Greek public debt problem. The Greek government, thereafter, returned to the negotiation table with its partners after also receiving endorsements by all the Greek political parties except the Communist Party and the Fascists, Golden Dawn.

Interest rate increases follow downgrades

Credit ratings are negatively related to interest rates. If corporate government bonds are downgraded, investors rush to sell their securities. This type of investor behavior would drive the price of the securities down and increase the interest rates. Investors require a higher interest rate to buy a downgraded security because they want to be compensated for the increased default risk they take by holding such securities. As a result, under these circumstances, it will become very expensive for the company or the country to raise funding in the market.

Figure 8.5 shows the relationship of the ten-year Greek government bond interest rate (right axis) and the average numerical rating (left axis) of the three CRAs. It is clear that the line plots of two time series variables are almost mirroring each other, moving in exactly opposite directions. Such results are plausible. The credit rating announcement of course leads to a change in the Greek interest rates. The response of the interest rates to credit rating announcements is almost instantaneous as financial markets are very efficient and very quick in responding to all available information. It is very clear therefore that the CRAs' announcement was instrumental in raising interest rates to extraordinarily high levels. Furthermore, the exceptionally low ratings of Greece by all three CRAs contributed to keeping the Greek bonds at speculative/junk status triggering extraordinary increases in interest rates that precluded Greece from borrowing from the market.

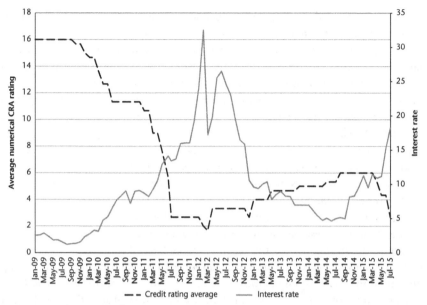

FIGURE 8.5 Greece: credit rating vs. interest rate

Ireland: the Celtic Tiger downgraded

The second country after Greece to sign a Memorandum of Understanding to receive a bailout and accept supervision and monitoring by the Troika was Ireland. After initially insisting that it did not need a bailout, Ireland finally agreed to receive an EU/IMF rescue package for its banking sector and to finance its large deficits.[21] Ireland's financial problems are related to its booming real-estate sector and the excessive lending by its banks to real-estate developers, which led to the banking collapse. On September 30, 2008, the Irish government announced a blanket to guarantee all the banks' liabilities. Indeed this decision increased the Irish public deficit in 2010 to an unprecedented level of 32 percent, higher than in any other EU country.

The amount of the bailout was €85 billion of which €17.5 billion was to be paid by Ireland, primarily the National Pension Reserve Fund; the rest was paid by the EU/IMF. The amount paid by the EU was equally divided between the European Stability Mechanism (ESM) and the European Financial Stability Facility (EFSF), as each contributed €22.5 billion.[22] The IMF also contributed €22.5 billion to the bailout fund. Ireland was given the freedom to decide its spending and tax plans and allowed ten years to repay the loan, which was not going to start until four years after the drawdown of the bailout.[23]

After the November 28, 2010 bailout, Irish people lived under austerity as the government imposed tax increases and cut government expenditures. The governing Fianna Fáil party that offered a blanket guarantee to Irish banks on February 25, 2011 was voted out of government. The coalition, consisting of the Fine Gael and

Labor parties headed by Prime Minister Enda Kenny, took over and was able to negotiate an interest rate reduction with the EU Council on the EU portion of the bailout. The Prime Minister also resisted pressure from Germany and France to raise the 12.5 percent corporate tax rate. Ireland considers the low tax rate central to its economic and industrial policy that all political parties, along with some labor unions, support. This is consistent with the government's decision to oppose a financial transaction tax (Tobin's Tax) in the EA.[24] Irish a tax policy along with a very flexible labor market and many supply-side policies have created a business-friendly environment that was expected to boost exports and lead the country to recovery. Indeed this was a strategy that had worked well for Ireland in the past. Ireland, prior to the crisis, had one of the highest real GDP per capita in the EU, next only to Luxembourg.

Ireland has been criticized for adopting a very low corporate tax rate to induce foreign firms to invest and move their operations to Ireland. After three years of recession, the Irish export sector began reviving. Several firms, mostly American, such as Microsoft, Google, EBay, Facebook, Eli Lily, and Twitter, have set up operations in Ireland.[25] These firms were recently attracted to Ireland, in addition to many other foreign firms that had also invested in Ireland after the launching of the EMU. Ireland as a result is the most open economy among the bailout recipient countries. This is indicated in Table 8.1 by the exports to GDP ratio. Ireland, since 1999, the year of the launching of the euro, has increasingly become a more open economy. As a result, it outperformed the other four bailout recipient countries in terms of trade openness (measured by exports to GDP ratio), as shown in Table 8.1.

Figure 8.6 shows Ireland's real GDP growth for 1980–2014. The entire period was divided into three sub-periods. In the first sub-period (1980–92), Ireland grew at a relatively low rate of growth of 2.84 percent. In the second sub-period (1993–2007), after the EU countries signed the Maastricht Treaty and launched the EMU in 1999, Ireland grew at the phenomenal rate of 6.74 percent, earning the title of the Celtic Tiger. The next sub-period 2008–14 was a period of stagnation since the recession prevailed in most of these years, and Ireland stalled at an annual rate of −0.43 percent.

As the Eurocrisis is associated with sovereign debts and public deficits, we now turn to examine the fiscal situation in Ireland during the past 35 years. Figure 8.7

TABLE 8.1 Exports to GDP ratio of five bailout recipient countries for selected years

	1999	2005	2010	2013	2014
Ireland	86.7%	78.3%	95.7%	105.3%	112.1%
Cyprus	67.3%	56.2%	47.7%	50.8%	55.4%
Greece	19.2%	21.3%	22.1%	30.2%	33.0%
Spain	26.4%	24.7%	25.5%	31.6%	32.0%
Portugal	26.5%	26.7%	29.9%	39.3%	39.7%

Source: Eurostat.

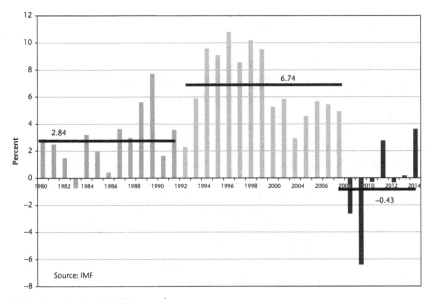

FIGURE 8.6   Ireland: GDP growth

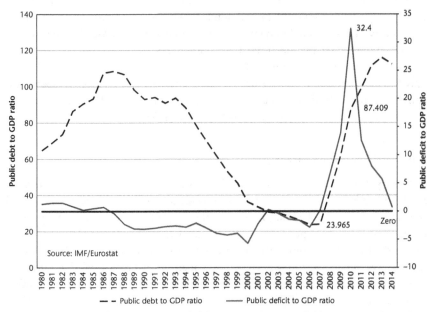

FIGURE 8.7   Ireland: public deficit and debt as a percentage of GDP

shows the Irish public deficit to GDP ratio on the right-hand side axis and the public debt to GDP ratio on the left-hand side axis. Ireland's public debt to GDP ratio had been increasing in the 1980s until it reached a peak in 1987 at a value above 100 percent (108.5 percent). From 1987, the public debt to GDP ratio began to decline for the next 20 years and reached an amazingly low minimum rate of approximately 24 percent in 2007 at the outset of the crisis. The government surplus to GDP ratio was increasing from 1980 to 2000, and in 2007, at the outset of the crisis, Ireland had a small government surplus. This was quite an accomplishment of fiscal tightening for Ireland. When the crisis began spreading in the years 2006 and 2007, both the public deficit and debt to GDP ratios rose exponentially to reach unprecedented levels.

First, the public deficit to GDP ratio reached its maximum of 32.4 percent, an exceptionally high record in comparison to all EU countries and an unprecedented violation of the Maastricht Convergence Criterion by about 30 percent. The Irish public debt to GDP ratio reached its maximum value in 2013 at 116 percent, which is one of the highest in the EU and almost double the maximum allowed by the Maastricht Treaty. However, both fiscal measures are declining, particularly the public deficit to GDP ratio, which was close to zero in 2014. (Note that the public deficits are measured with positive numbers and public surpluses with negative numbers. This is done with the purpose of allowing both public deficit and public debt to GDP ratios to be shown in the same figure.)

Figure 8.8 shows Ireland's credit rating during the Eurocrisis. It is clear that the downgrading of Ireland's public debt began immediately after the announcement on September 30, 2008 when the Irish government offered a blanket guarantee to the country's bank liabilities. This announcement caused a sharp downgrading in the country's government bond ratings by the three major CRAs. The rollercoaster of the downgrading by the three CRAs was based on concerns regarding the increased deficit and the inability of Ireland to remain solvent. Of the three CRAs, only Moody's degraded Ireland's debt to junk/speculative status since Moody's was convinced that Ireland needed a second bailout.[26] The other CRAs kept their ratings very low, but above junk status as Baa1 and BBB+.

The first to exit the bailout

In January 2013, Ireland took over the six-month rotating EU Council presidency. At that time Prime Minister Enda Kenny made an announcement that he hoped Ireland would exit the bailout program by the end of 2013. After remaining almost three years under the supervision of the Troika, Ireland decided in December 2013 to exit the bailout program without a precautionary credit line. Such a decision by Ireland was the correct one, claimed the managing director of the European Stability Fund (ESM), Klaus Regling, because the country did not require another restructuring.[27]

The Troika's monitoring and supervision of Ireland caused much hardship for many Irish people as they suffered from financial distress. However, the Irish people were not angry with the Troika, but only with their own leaders and banks that had lent to Irish businesses which often had made huge fortunes on property investments. It was publicized that the ECB encouraged the Irish government not to shift some of the burden of the financial crisis to the bank creditors through a haircut.

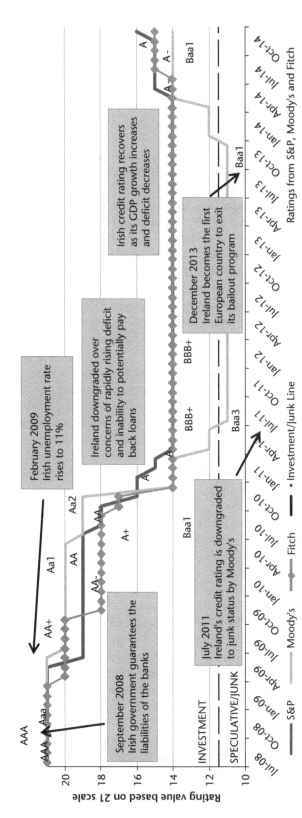

FIGURE 8.8 Ireland: credit ratings during the debt crisis

As a result, the ECB was criticized by several analysts that an unelected European institution exercised too much power by refusing a sovereign state the freedom to impose a haircut on its bank creditors. Following the exit from the bailout program, Ireland's credit ratings improved substantially. This was achieved because of Ireland's drastic reduction of its public deficit and the high economic growth that it achieved in 2014.

Ireland's GDP increased in 2014 as was expected by the Troika, which had imposed fiscal consolidation, austerity, and reforms; the Troika, along with Germany, claimed Ireland as a success story.[28] *The Economist* agrees that Ireland was indeed a success story, but is convinced it has little to do with the austerity and reforms imposed by the EU and the IMF. The Irish success was based on the economic growth of the US and the UK, because these countries increased imports from Ireland. The export-led growth model succeeded thanks to the foreign firms, mostly American, that were attracted by Ireland for several reasons related to the domestic strength of the Irish economy, the business-friendly environment, the well-trained English-speaking labor force, and an ideal location for the island nation in Europe. The Irish success has very little to do with the austerity measures and the structural reforms imposed by the Troika as Ireland had introduced many such reforms prior to 2010.[29]

However, positive economic growth does not mean that most Irish people are doing well. Many construction workers are still unemployed, and many well-trained young people have already left the country seeking employment abroad. The dissatisfaction of Irish citizens is indicated by a poll in February 2015 which found that both political parties, Fine Gael and Fianna Fáil, that have dominated Irish politics since the early 1930s were behind Sinn Fein, the anti-austerity party and the political arm of the Irish Republican Army (IRA).[30] However, high economic growth in Ireland may reduce the popularity of Sinn Fein. Although national elections will not be held until 2016, everything is possible considering the developments in Greece, where Syriza was elected to government, and in Spain, where Podemos was leading in the polls. Irish people became very angry with the EU when information leaked out that the ECB had threatened to cut liquidity to the Irish banks unless the government accepted the negotiated bailout.

The decision of the government to offer full guarantees to creditors of its banks was criticized as it made the rescue program very expensive. The intervention of the Irish government to shift some of the burden of the bailout to senior bondholders was rebuffed by the EU and the ECB. During the third quarter of 2008, only about a couple months prior to the bailout, German banks had invested about €208.3 billion in Ireland.[31] When the Irish government expressed interest in a haircut on its senior bondholders to reduce the cost to its taxpayers, the ECB intervened and stopped such a solution for fear of contagion or pressure from financial interest groups, i.e. German banks.[32]

In Greece, unlike Ireland, nobody from the Troika was against the PSI agreement that was imposed on creditors. Many analysts agree that the PSI sank Greece into a prolonged recession which spread to other EU countries. In Ireland, Prime Minister

Enda Kenny followed the advice of the Irish Attorney General and called for a referendum for the approval of the EU Fiscal Compact Treaty. Country leaders did not try to stop Ireland out of fear of possible rejection of the treaty. Thus Ireland was the first country to democratically decide whether to approve the fiscal rules imposed by Germany on EA countries.

Unlike Ireland, Greece, at the Cannes Summit, was prevented from having a similar referendum regarding the approval of the second bailout by the Greek people. The suppressed referendum resurfaced later in the form of an election that gave the Greek people an opportunity to elect an anti-bailout, anti-austerity party Syriza. With about two years' delay from the first cancelled referendum, the new government announced another for July 5, 2015.

There is a strong conviction among many Irish people that their country's taxpayers took on a very large burden to prevent a repeat of the Lehman Brothers collapse in Europe. This would have caused a much larger financial disaster for the entire European banking and financial system.[33]

The failure of the policy-makers to impose a haircut on the unsecured creditors of Irish banks resurfaced again when the IMF criticized the decision. According to the IMF report, the spillover effects from imposing losses on the bank creditors, as was claimed by the ECB, was not so "obvious." Even if there was spillover as a result of contagion, the report claimed that appropriate policy measures could have been taken to suppress the "ringfencing" of the spillover.

Portugal

The third country forced to seek a bailout from the EU and the IMF was Portugal. After first resisting the bailout, on June 4, 2011, caretaker Prime Minister and leader of the socialist party, José Sócrates, agreed for his country to receive a Memorandum of Understanding (bailout). This announcement followed the prime minister's resignation on March 23, 2011 after his party lost its majority in the Portuguese parliament.

The Portuguese economy, claims Ricardo Reis, a Professor of Economics at Columbia University, never experienced the growth seen in Ireland, Greece, or Spain after the adoption of the euro. Nevertheless, Portugal's economy grew in the period prior to the launch. Portugal's economy during the 2002–12 period, according to Professor Reis, grew by less than the US during the Great Depression and Japan during the "lost decade" (1990–2000).

Figure 8.9 shows Portugal's real rate of economic growth for the period 1980–2014. As shown in the figure, Portugal attained a respectable rate of growth for the first 20 years, 1980–2000, of 3.52 percent. The second period, 2001–14, is a time identified with the launching of the euro, and during this period Portugal experienced stagnation as it attained an average rate of growth of only 0.03 of one percent. It is, nevertheless, well-documented that the crisis in Portugal which began in 2009 had devastating effects that lasted until 2013. In 2014, the Portuguese real rate of growth was low, but positive.

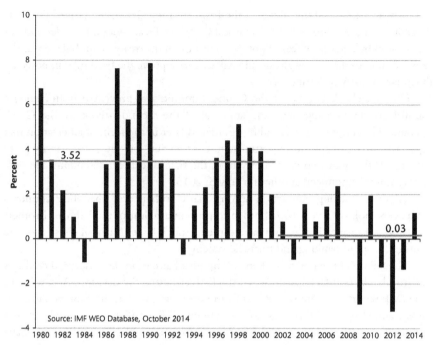

FIGURE 8.9 Portugal: GDP growth

As shown in Figure 8.10, from 1990 to 2000, Portugal's public debt to GDP ratio was low and remained below the Maastricht Treaty limit of 60 percent. Then Portugal's public debt to GDP ratio began increasing in 2000 at about the onset of the launching of the euro. At the beginning of the Eurocrisis, the public debt to GDP ratio, which is shown on the left-hand side axis, began increasing to reach 131.26 percent of GDP in 2014. Portugal's public deficit to GDP ratio is shown on the right-hand side axis; it declined for about a decade up until 2000, but drastically increased in the period 2007–9 as the result of the adopted countercyclical expansionary fiscal policy to cope with the crisis. After 2009, the public deficit to GDP ratio began declining as Portugal adopted a contractionary fiscal policy.

Many explanations were offered regarding the cause of the Portuguese crisis, such as rigid labor markets, competition from countries such as China, and other rigidities in the Portuguese economic system. However, Professor Reis claims that capital inflows to Portugal after the introduction of the euro were wasted on inefficient investment in the non-tradable sector.[34]

The official bailout agreement took place on May 3, 2011: Portugal received €78 billion and had to comply with the IMF conditionality, which included austerity, reforms, fiscal consolidation, and a serious privatization program.[35] The austerity program caused suffering and distress to many Portuguese people as welfare benefits were reduced and unemployment rose to 18 percent. During this period, CRAs were very active, downgrading the Portuguese government bonds as seen in Figure 8.11. Moody's was the first to downgrade Portugal's government bonds.

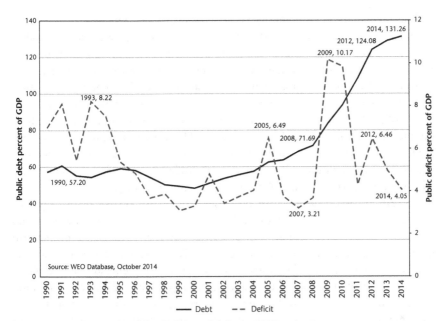

FIGURE 8.10 Portugal: public deficit and debt to GDP ratio

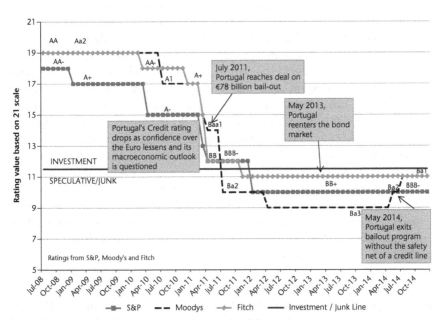

FIGURE 8.11 Portugal: credit ratings during the debt crisis

The austerity measures in Portugal took their toll, causing a prolonged recession as government expenditures were reduced and taxes increased according to the Troika's directives aiming to decrease public deficits. However, the Portuguese government chose to rely more on tax increases rather than reductions in government expenditures.[36]

Labor strikes and demonstrations became an increasingly common occurrence after the bailout as a growing number of people were affected by the crisis. On April 5, 2013, Portugal's Constitutional Court found four out of the nine bail-out measures in the 2013 budget to be illegal. The impact of the four measures on the budget was very small, approximately 1.2 to 1.3 percent, so the court's decision did not cause a political crisis, although the ruling per se was very important. The question remains: what factors caused the crisis in Portugal?

Several Portuguese analysts are very critical of the EU/IMF bailout. Professor Ricardo Cabral considers the EU/IMF plan for recovery to be one with "no adherence to reality" because the program required Portugal to outperform Germany in its foreign trade account, particularly during a time when several EA country trading partners of Portugal were also advised to generate trade surpluses just like Portugal. The bailout program for Portugal called for the recapitalization of banks and guarantees for the bank creditors. These are the same policies that were imposed on Ireland.[37] The total support of the Portuguese banking system amounted to 27.2 percent of its GDP.

Several Portuguese journalists, commentators, and many economists were long ago convinced that the EMU was launched as an incomplete structure. Since the crisis began, the policies adopted played a major role in the deterioration of the standard of living, especially of the weaker groups in the periphery countries. Another deficiency that surfaced during the crisis is that EU politics undermined the demo-cratic processes in Greece, Italy, and Ireland. One frustrated commentator stated that EU leadership left "everything to the vulgarities of the bond markets and CRAs."[38]

Ricardo Cabral, an economist at the University of Madeira, is very critical of the architects of the EMU, the EU, and the country leaders who adopted policies that deepened the recession. He claims that "widespread hardship, despair, hunger, and suicide are not unavoidable random events, but predictable outcomes" caused by wrong policies.[39] It is difficult to argue against the claim of Cabral that misguided EU policies have caused many problems for the Portuguese people. Easily avoida-ble hardship and social problems were experienced in other European countries that also received bailouts. Lastly, Ricardo Reis criticized the EU/IMF response to the crisis in the EA countries as they imposed the same structural reforms and aus-terity regardless of the economic conditions and the causes of the crisis in each country. For example, Portugal did not suffer from a housing boom as did Ireland and Spain, nor did Portugal experience the Greek public debt explosion problem or the continuous political instability of Italy.[40]

On May 17, 2014, Portugal exited the bailout program cleanly without a credit line, exactly like Ireland and Spain. Portugal's economy has undergone many struc-tural changes, and these positive effects have started to materialize. In 2013, Portugal generated its first trade surplus in goods and services since 1943. In 2014, Portugal generated a positive rate of growth and as a result enjoyed a substantial reduction in its ten-year government bond yield. These achievements required a great sacrifice by the people of Portugal who faced many severe hardships. Many people suffered as many workers, for example, were burdened with unemployment and many other social and economic problems.

Spain

The second Iberian country to receive a bailout was Spain. After insisting for a long time that his country would not need a rescue package from the EU/IMF, Prime Minister Mariano Rajoy succumbed and requested a bailout. The Spanish request for a Memorandum of Understanding, however, was different to those received by Greece, Ireland, and Portugal. Spain originally requested to receive up to €100 billion without the usual IMF conditionality that accompanied similar rescue packages. Furthermore, the entire amount that the Spanish government was going to borrow from the €100 billion would be used for the financial sector, i.e. its banks, and not for the real economy.[41]

The Eurocrisis devastated the Spanish economy as the country experienced a prolonged and severe recession that had detrimental effects on the most vulnerable groups in its population. Figure 8.12 shows the real GDP growth of Spain for the period 1980–2014. According to this figure, from 1980 to 2007, the Spanish economy experienced steady growth for almost three decades – only two of the 28 years recorded negative growth rates. Figure 8.12 indicates how Spain was transformed

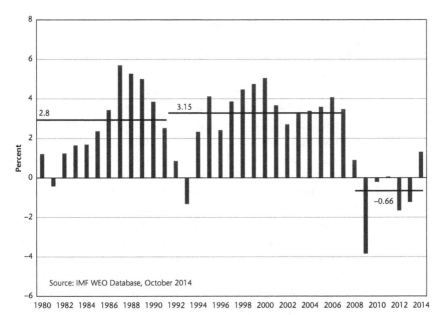

FIGURE 8.12 Spain: real GDP growth

from a developing economy to an advanced one. Such an achievement took place after the oppressive regime (1936–76) of the brutal dictator Francisco Franco was replaced. Spain has since peacefully transitioned to a democracy.[42]

The entire period (1980–2014) can be divided into three sub-periods, the first of which can be labeled the pre-EU sub-period, 1980–91 when Spain attained an average annual rate of growth of 2.8 percent. The second sub-period (1992–2007) covered the time after the Maastricht Treaty, a period during which EU countries prepared their economies for the adoption of the euro in 1999. This sub-period ended in 2007, the year before the crisis. The Spanish economy grew at a respectable average rate of 3.15 percent during this time. The last sub-period covers the period of the Eurocrisis. During these years a reversal took place in Spain and the country fell into stagnation, attaining a negative annual rate of growth of –0.66. The source of the crisis in Spain was its banking sector; in this respect, it is similar to Ireland. The government, in its efforts to support the private sector, rapidly inherited the problem from the banking sector and its fiscal standing, which was one of the best in the EU, deteriorated.

Spain's major problem was a booming real-estate and construction sector financed by Spanish banks that had borrowed heavily from abroad. Spain experienced an extraordinarily strong housing boom from 1997 to 2007. Such a boom increased home ownership in Spain, which rose to be one of the highest in Europe.[43] The housing boom led to a phenomenal growth in the construction and real-estate sectors, accounting for up to 43 percent of the Spanish GDP. The booming housing sector as a result required large amounts of financial capital beyond that provided by domestic savings. Consequently, Spanish banks sought external financing through borrowing abroad.[44]

Several banks, therefore, had over-borrowed from abroad in order to lend to developers and families for home purchases. By April 2012, credit conditions deteriorated in the EU, as interbank liquidity became extremely tight. Interest rates reached unprecedentedly high levels for Spain after a two-notch downgrade of its public debt by S&P. The Spanish interest rate increased 4.2 percentage points above Germany's. During this period, Spanish unemployment rose from 8 percent in 2008 to 25 percent in the third quarter of 2012.[45] Several banks that lent heavily and became over-indebted throughout the booming real-estate and construction years were rescued by the government. The government spent about €34 billion on the banking system. Spain nationalized its fourth largest bank, Bankia, which had requested €19 billion from the Spanish government. Bankia had been created in July of 2010 when several regional *cajas* (savings banks) joined to form Bankia because they were considered to be too vulnerable to survive the crisis alone.

Cajas specialize in real-estate lending, and performed well for more than 200 years. During the present crisis, however, they were affected more heavily than the banks.[46] Unlike the *cajas*, some banks turned out to be safe as they were well managed. Examples of such banks, according to the IMF, are Santander and BBVA.[47] On December 11, 2012, Spain requested and received a €41 billion bailout, an amount that was only part of the maximum €100 billion that was agreed on June 2,

2012. The funding was to be used for recapitalizing the nationalized banks that are known as Group 1 banks, constituting one-fifth of the entire national banking system.[48] Besides Bankia, Catalunya Bank, Banco de Valencia, and Novag Banco were nationalized as well.

The Spanish government took many measures to prevent the spread of the crisis, including austerity, reductions in pension, and capping its public debt which was explicitly written in the country's constitution.[49] A €65 billion austerity package was launched during the third week of July 2012. Such measures were a response to increased uncertainty indicated by the rise of the ten-year government bond yield to 7.5 percent.[50]

In Figure 8.13 the public deficit and debt to GDP ratios are shown on the right- and left-hand side axes respectively. Figure 8.13 clearly shows the crisis was not a public debt crisis. The fiscal problems were caused by the over-indebtedness of the private sector, which had financed the real-estate and construction sectors. The public debt to GDP ratio in Spain was one of the lowest in Europe, 36.3 percent in 2007. The country's deficit declined from 1995 to 2006, a year that Spain generated a surplus of 2.4 percent. The prolonged reduction of public deficit and debt is explained by the large amounts of revenue raised by the government from the booming real-estate and construction sectors.

During the crisis both public deficit and debt to GDP ratios increased exponentially, reaching 11 and 98 percent respectively. Although the public deficit to GDP ratio had been declining, from 2012 the public debt to GDP ratio continued to increase. Meanwhile, fiscal conditions in Spain have still been deteriorating.

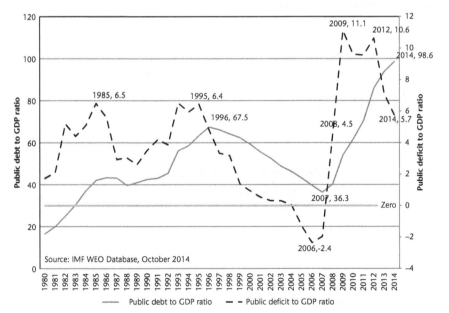

FIGURE 8.13 Spain: public deficit and debt to GDP ratio

When the blue-chip stock market index hit a record low and the insurance on government bonds (CDSs) increased substantially, the government tried to calm the markets and introduced a temporary ban of short selling. Between the last quarter of 2011 and the fourth quarter of 2012, CRAs were exceptionally busy downgrading the Spanish public debt. CRAs, nonetheless, stopped short of driving the quality of the sovereign debt of Spain, the fourth largest economy of the EA, to speculative/junk status. It is plausible that such a move would have definitely triggered contagion to neighboring EA countries, such as Italy and Belgium, and possibly to the entire EU and the rest of the world.

Such a scenario of course would have had an impact on the financial health and viability of the CRAs themselves. This possibility may have deterred the CRAs from downgrading Spanish public debt to junk. A more plausible explanation why the CRAs did not reduce Spanish public debt to junk was the announcements of the ECB President Mario Draghi to "do everything it takes" to save the euro. The decision of Spain's government to agree to receive a bailout could be another reason that may have kept its credit rating above the speculative/junk status. Figure 8.14 shows Spain's credit ratings by the three CRAs.

On January 23, 2014 Spain officially exited the bailout. It was the second country after Ireland. All three CRAs raised Spain's credit rating by one notch (see Figure 8.14). Although it implied that the economy was on a path to recovery, as the Spanish Prime Minister Mariano Rajoy announced, exit from the bailout did not mean the crisis is over. Spain was stuck at the time with a two-digit unemployment rate of 26 percent. According to the Spanish Memorandum of Understanding for the financial sector, Spain was required to impose haircuts on both bank shareholders and bank creditors (bondholders) for banks to receive bailouts.

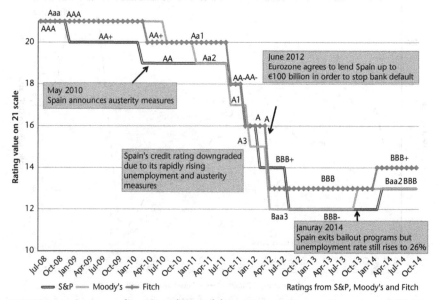

FIGURE 8.14 Spain: credit ratings during debt crisis

Such haircuts were to be imposed before banks were to receive any funding from the bailout. In order to understand where most of the private funding for the Spanish banks was coming from and how it had dried out during the crisis, the following information may offer an explanation. In the first quarter of 2008, German and French banks had claims on Spanish banks equal to €315 and €209 billion respectively. In the fourth quarter of 2012 during the peak of the crisis, the German and French bank claims were drastically reduced to €120 and €100 billion, as such funds were looking for safe-haven investments elsewhere, most likely repatriation to the respective countries.[51] It is interesting that the same pattern regarding inter-European bank lending that took place in Ireland reoccurred in Spain as the German and French banks pulled out their investments from Spain, another financially distressed country.

Such massive private inflows and outflows of financial capital in a country obviously contributed to both booms and busts. It is therefore to the benefit of a country to monitor such flows for the purpose of financial and macroeconomic stability. As foreign banks' financial investments were pulled out from Spain, the ECB was able to make up the difference, thus Spain borrowed through the Target 2 (T2) program of the European System of Central Banks (ESCB). Thus the T2 account of the central bank of Spain increased from a zero balance prior to the crisis in 2007 to €400 billion in 2012.[52]

Two-digit, prolonged unemployment, evictions and foreclosures – all had an unprecedented negative impact on the welfare of the most vulnerable groups in Spanish society.[53] The government had done much to prevent the negative impact of the housing crisis on these groups, but the inability of the two major Spanish political parties to do enough gave rise to a new political party Podemos (translated as "We Can").

Podemos was born from the "dissolution of the Indignados" ("the outraged"), or 15-M Movement, established on May 15, 2011 that protested against the crisis and austerity. When Podemos was 100 days old, it took 5 out of the 54 seats in the European Parliament in May 2014.[54] The question arises, how did Podemos become so successful? The answer is rather easy. The major reason is that the two major Spanish political parties failed to address very important issues concerning basic human rights, issues such as the right to work, and access to health services, food, and shelter. Podemos is committed to resurrecting the Athenian democracy where all issues are openly debated and decided by all the people.

To achieve such an ideal form of democracy, Podemos relies on online communication and party elections. Citizens have an input on all issues whether at the local, regional, or national level – even party contributions are done online by individuals and not banks and big businesses so the party will not be corrupted. As of January 30, 2015, Podemos is the most popular party in Spain. Its main stand is against the austerity measures, the rising public debt, and privatization, i.e. against all the policies employed in most European countries. The good news for the Spanish economy, however, as of June 2015, regarding the forecasted 2015 rate of GDP growth of 3.3 percent may be a setback for Podemos.

Cyprus

The fifth country to sign a Memorandum of Understanding with the EU and the IMF was Cyprus. This small Mediterranean island country got into financial trouble because its two major banks, Laiki and the Bank of Cyprus, invested in toxic Greek government bonds. The Cypriot misfortune began late in the night of October 11, 2011, when the EU and IMF representatives "planted a time bomb" in the financial and banking system of Cyprus.[55] At this meeting the EU and the IMF decided to resolve the Greek public debt problem through the negotiation of a haircut of the Greek public debt that was held by private holders of government bonds. Between the two Cypriot banks, it was estimated that they had purchased approximately €4.5 to €5 billion in Greek bonds. This was a very large amount for the government of Cyprus to provide, if it was to rescue its two banks. As a result, the vicious cycle from failing banks to failing governments was resurrected and effective in bankrupting another EA country, despite the many promises by the EU leaders and officials to break that cycle.

As it turned out, Cyprus found itself with two insolvent major banks and its government, although fiscally sound, unable to rescue them since the banks were too large. As a result, the government of Cyprus was unable to protect its financial system and avoid an economic downfall. Cyprus had a very strong country leading up to the onset of the Eurocrisis, therefore factors which caused the collapse should be examined.

Cyprus joined the EU in 2004, together with nine other countries. At that time Cyprus was the richest of all the new countries in terms of GDP per capita. Immediately after it became an EU member, it started preparing to join the EMU and after only four years it joined the EMU in 2008, together with the other small Mediterranean country Malta. EMU membership implied that Cyprus and Malta had met the Maastricht criteria. As a result, like all the other countries, Cyprus experienced a decrease in interest rates. Cyprus experienced high interest rates prior to joining the EU due to the presence of occupying Turkish troops on the northern part of the island and because of the breakdown of the inter-communal negotiations that led the Greek Cypriots to apply for EU membership without the Turkish Cypriots.[56]

Long before joining the EU, Cypriot governments had promoted Cyprus to be an "offshore international business service center." In 2003, it adopted a very low corporate offshore tax rate of 10 percent.[57] Furthermore, in 2008, Cyprus signed a double taxation treaty with Russia. This allowed Russians and Cypriots to pay taxes in only one country. As a result, the Russians were able to pay the low Cyprus capital gains and dividends tax of 10 percent instead of the high Russian rate of 20 percent.[58] Furthermore, Cyprus allowed foreign firms to register as Cypriot firms. This move gave foreign firms the advantage of access to the EU market, but it also became a source of future problems for Cyprus. Russia became an important factor for the Cypriot economy. Since 2008, Russia's most important platform for its "trans-shipped and round-tripped foreign direct investment" (FDI) was Cyprus.[59]

"Trans-shipped" refers to Russian FDI that goes through Cyprus to third countries whereas "round-tripped" indicates FDI originating in other countries destined for Russia. The statistics for the two Russian FDIs for 2011 were $129 and $122 billion respectively. This meant that Cyprus was a very important conduit for Russia. These statistics are even more important for Cyprus considering the country's GDP for 2011 of €18 billion was several times smaller than Russia's bank deposits to finance its FDI.

Prior to joining the EU, there were suspicions of money laundering and corruption, most of it related to Russian oligarchs. However, in preparation to join the EU, Cyprus worked hard to clean the record and comply with EU law. The presence of these firms in Cyprus became detrimental to the country just at the moment that Cyprus needed support. EU countries demonstrated a great degree of apathy and anti-solidarity. Let us now look at some statistics of the economy of Cyprus and analyze this data to explain how the country found itself in a situation that led to its default.

Figure 8.15 shows Cyprus' real GDP growth for the period 1980 to 2014. It can be seen in this figure that Cyprus from 1980 until the onset of the crisis generated a phenomenal rate of growth. During the last sub-period (2008–14), Cyprus, however, experienced a recession, which unlike in other bailout countries extended to 2014. Cyprus grew at a rate of 5.56 percent from 1980 to 1993 and a rate of 4.29 percent during the period 1994–2007. These were exceptionally high rates of growth. During the third sub-period, 2008–14, the Cypriot economy shrank as it generated a negative rate of growth of −1.08 percent during this period.

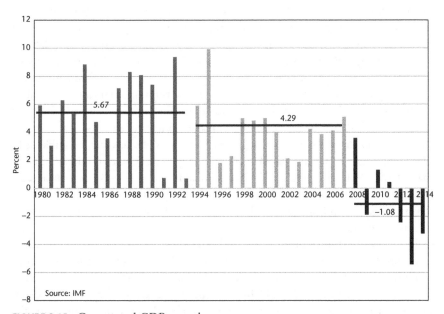

FIGURE 8.15 Cyprus: real GDP growth

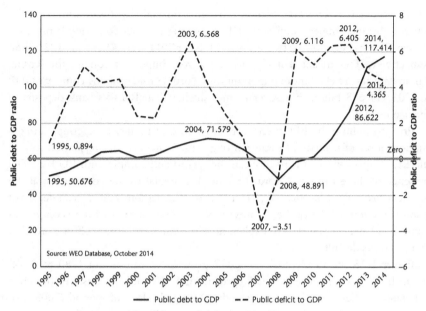

FIGURE 8.16 Cyprus: public deficit and debt to GDP ratio

Figure 8.16 shows the debt to GDP ratio on the left-hand side and the public deficit to GDP ratio on the right-hand side. According to this graph, the public debt from 1995 to 2008 was fluctuating near the 60 percent Maastricht limit. On the right-hand axis, the public deficit to GDP ratio is shown. The year before the recession began, Cyprus's public debt to GDP ratio was only 49 percent. Since 2008, however, the public debt to GDP ratio kept increasing, to reach 117 percent by 2014. As the Cypriot government resumed responsibility for the private debt, its public debt began drastically increasing. It seems that the story of Ireland was repeating itself in another country, with the end result the same; a transformation of the excessive private debt to public debt, rendering the latter unsustainable. The public balance prior to the onset of the crisis was in surplus both in 2007 and 2008. In 2012, Cyprus's deficit began declining, to reach 4.3 percent in 2014.

Figure 8.17 shows the credit ratings for Cyprus. It is obvious that the public debt of Cyprus began to be downgraded at almost the same time as the leaks surfaced that a Greek PSI was going to take place. In addition both banks demonstrated a lack of prudence as they expanded operations in several countries including Greece, Russia, Ukraine, and Serbia. The banks were too large in relation to the size of Cyprus's economy.

In its first effort to protect its two banks the government of Cyprus requested a loan from Russia. Indeed, Cyprus received a €2.5 billion loan from Russia which, although very large for Cyprus, proved to be inadequate to save the two banks. Then Cyprus turned to the EU but European country leaders were adamant; they decided to give a second hit to Cyprus after the first one came with the announcement of the Greek PSI. The EU/IMF offered a €10 billion bailout to

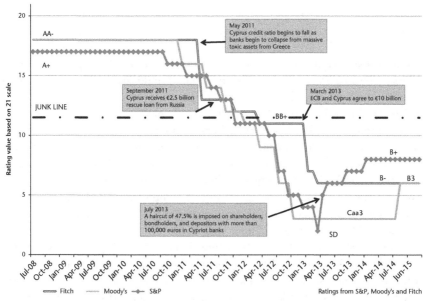

FIGURE 8.17 Cyprus: credit ratings during the crisis

Cyprus provided it dismantled the Laiki bank and imposed a haircut of up to 40 percent for its depositors of over €100,000. Deposit accounts of less than €100,000 were not taxed. This was a major setback for the Cypriot economy and its effects will last for a long time.

No matter how insistently the Cypriot leader Nikos Anastasladis disagreed and argued against a deal that could not be worse, it was to no avail. EU leaders and particularly Angela Merkel wanted to change the Cypriot economic model. The banking sector of Cyprus was too large in relation to its economy. Besides, she wanted to show the German voters and the opposition parties that she could stand strong against the Russian oligarchs. This stand was also going to help her in the upcoming national elections a few months later in September 2013 in which she wanted to be re-elected.

Repealing the Dodd-Frank Act

The Dodd-Frank Act was introduced into US law in July 2010 to save the US economy from panics similar to that which followed the collapse of the Lehman Brothers in the fall of 2008. The Fed was able to rescue the US economy by acting as a lender of last resort to banks and other US institutions. However, the Dodd-Frank Act weakened the Fed by pulling back its power to act as lender of last resort to non-bank institutions.

The Dodd-Frank Act also imposed restrictions on the Federal Deposit Insurance Corporation (FDIC) providing additional guarantees to demand deposits. The Act also imposed restrictions on the US Treasury guaranteeing money market funds.

The powers that were taken away from the Fed, the FDIC, and the Treasury are vested now with the legislative branch of the US government, i.e. Congress. Legislators were also kept very busy once the Dodd-Frank Act had been passed to free the banks from the restrictions imposed by the Act not allowing them to invest in risky assets. In other words legislators aimed to undo the most important aspect of the financial reform bill to protect the taxpayers.

The House of Representatives voted on October 29, 2013 to repeal the provisions of the Dodd-Frank Act allowing banks to keep and not push out the trading of risky derivatives. These are the same derivatives that caused the crisis in September 2008. In this vote the House of Representatives shifted the burden of risk-taking from the banks back to the taxpayers, implying that the country had not learned anything from the subprime mortgage crisis. It is important to note that in a review of relevant emails the *New York Times* reported that 70 out of 85 lines of the bill were drafted by lobbyists working for Citigroup.[60]

On December 11, 2004, just about three hours before the government ran out of money, the US House of Representatives passed a 1.1 trillion dollar budget. A few hours later the US Senate passed the same budget bill of 1.1 trillion dollars. The budget bill also included provisions that allow banks with US FDIC-insured deposits and other subsidies from the government to gamble by investing in financial derivatives. Alas the House and Senate bills received support from the Democrats and even from President Obama, since it was believed that a new bill in 2015 produced by the Republican-dominated Congress would be worse, giving more power to the banks at the expense of financial stability.[61]

The George Washington University law professor, Arthur Wilmarth, was exceptionally critical of Congress when he said, "Shame on Congress if indeed it allows megabanks to continue to pursue the same business strategy that brought us the financial crisis." Such harsh statements may be justified if one takes into consideration that, in the current election cycle, Wall Street spent $1.2 billion corresponding to $2.3 million on each of the 535 US legislators in both houses.[62]

A second setback against the Dodd-Frank Act was engineered by Wall Street, the second in the month of December 2014. This happened when the Fed decided to partially repeal the Volcker Rule and allow banks to keep risky assets on their balance sheets for two more years, the same type of asset that caused the meltdown in the fall 2008.[63]

Concluding comments

The US subprime mortgage crisis spread to Europe via financial integration as US investment banks sold MBSs based on toxic assets to European banks and other financial institutions. The chief economist of Freddie Mac, Frank E. Nothaft, believes that a few countries in Europe have generated their own housing bubbles, just as the US did. This implies that the UK, Ireland, Spain, and the Baltic countries are partially responsible for their own crises. CRAs were accused in the US of assigning AAA ratings to firms which a few days later declared bankruptcy. In Europe, the CRAs were blamed for overreacting in downgrading countries and not giving the EU a chance to complete bailout programs designed to save these countries.

Investors who purchased high-rated securities and lost money have sued the three agencies. Several suits were filed in the US, Australia, and Europe. Courts have found the CRAs guilty of negligence because they did not inform investors of the low quality of the securities they were purchasing. CRAs were also sued by governments including the US and Italy. CRAs have often pleaded not guilty but have tried to settle the cases outside the courtroom. The EU introduced new regulations to protect countries from aggressive downgrading. Thus the EU's new rules require more transparency and competition, allowing investors more options in rating the securities they are purchasing. However, the "issuer pays" model has not changed and the three CRAs still serve almost the entire international market.

As the crisis spread in Europe and CRAs began downgrading the EA countries' government bonds, the interest rates on these securities began increasing rapidly. There is a symmetric relationship between the numerical rating of a country's government securities and its interest rates for such securities. Five EA countries were affected by the Eurocrisis. Ireland and Spain's crises are similar because they were the result of the formation of bubbles in the housing and real-estate markets that created boom and bust cycles. Cyprus was a unique case. The crisis in Cyprus was mainly a bank crisis. Its two large banks made bad property loans and purchased Greek government securities at a discount after the Greek PSI was announced. EA assistance was relatively small and came with severe conditions aiming to punish the presence of Russian oligarchs in Cyprus. Portugal's economic conditions deteriorated for different reasons, including competition from abroad and inefficiencies in the non-tradable sector, where much funding from abroad was directed. Lastly, the case of Greece is purely that of a public debt crisis. All five countries experienced high interest rates as the default risk for their securities increased substantially and the countries were precluded from the bond markets. Thus Greece, Ireland, Portugal, Spain, and Cyprus received bailouts from the EU and IMF.

The bailouts were provided by the IMF and the EA under the condition that the countries adopt austerity, reforms, and privatization programs. It is believed by many economists that austerity prolonged the recession in these countries. However, in 2014, all countries except Cyprus generated positive growth. Furthermore, Ireland, Portugal, and Spain exited the bailouts cleanly, without a precautionary credit line. The crisis, however, is not over as several of these countries suffer from high unemployment and other social and economic problems, which the Greeks call a humanitarian crisis. For the first time since World War II, peoples of Western Europe have experienced hunger, homelessness, and widespread physical and mental disease. Although the crises in Ireland, Portugal, and Cyprus have weakened and in some cases have been resolved, in the middle of 2015 Greece is stuck in a bitter and prolonged dispute with the EU and IMF regarding an agreement on the Greek public debt issue. The new government of Greece pulled out of negotiations and announced a referendum on July 5, 2015, in which the Greek voters supported the Greek government's position not to accept the EU/IMF proposal to settle the Greek public debt issue.

In June and July of 2015, the Greek public debt saga reignited as Greece defaulted on a €1.6 billion loan to the IMF. The country ran out of liquidity, closed its banks, and imposed capital controls. Such developments caused more misery and suffering among the Greek people whose lives have been pawns on the negotiation table for the duration of the crisis. Greece returned to the negotiation table with the EU/IMF aiming to reach a final settlement by mid-July 2015.

Lastly, we report indicators of economic activity before and after the Eurocrisis for all five EA bailout recipient countries. In Figure 8.18, the real per capita GDP is portrayed. It is clear that all five EA countries suffered from the crisis starting in 2008. However, all countries made a comeback to growth in 2014 except Cyprus, which was the last country to receive a bailout. Nonetheless, Cyprus is also recovering since the country has quickly taken all necessary policies and measures to return to growth.

Figure 8.19 shows the unemployment rates of the five countries for the period 1982–2015. According to this figure, two countries, Spain and Ireland, were burdened by much higher unemployment than the others. This, however, changed in the 1990s. Prior to the Eurocrisis, all EA countries recorded unemployment rates of less than 10 percent. However, in 2007 and 2008, all unemployment rates shot up. Greece and Spain were affected the most as both countries had a quarter of their labor forces unemployed. In both countries, the unemployment rates began declining in 2014, but are still approximately 10 percent above the other countries. It is interesting to note that in both countries, there was a major political repercussion and response, since many attributed the high unemployment to the austerity measures imposed by the Troika. Consequently, two anti-austerity parties rose to power. Syriza in Greece is already in government and Podemos in Spain is a contender in the next elections.

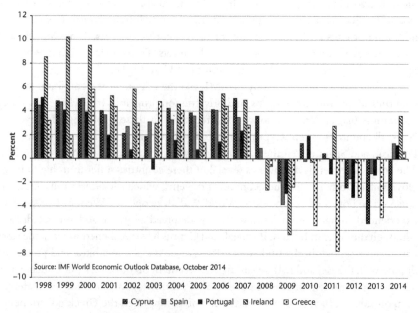

FIGURE 8.18   Real GDP growth of bailout countries

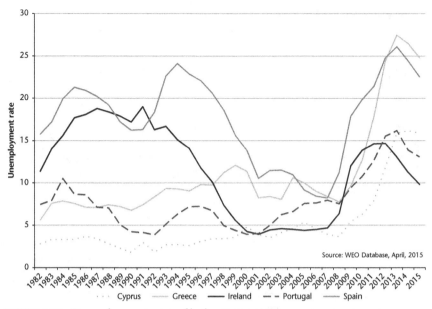

FIGURE 8.19 Unemployment rates of bailout countries

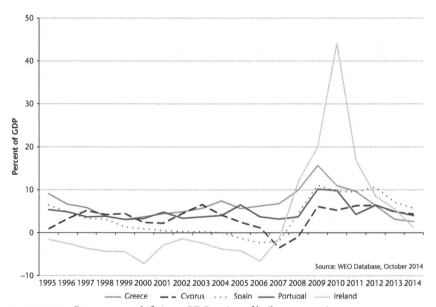

FIGURE 8.20 Government deficit to GDP ratios of bailout countries

Figure 8.20 shows the public deficit to GDP ratios from 1995 to 2014. It is interesting to note that all countries responded to the crisis by increasing the public deficit. However, all countries in 2010–11 started reducing the public deficits as the recession began weakening.

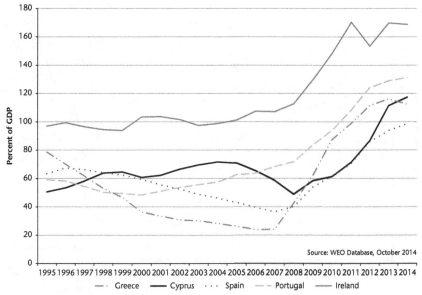

FIGURE 8.21 Public debt to GDP ratios of bailout countries

Lastly, Figure 8.21 shows the public debt to GDP ratio of the five bailout recipient countries, which is the economic variable that the crisis was correctly associated with and named after, European sovereign debt. It is evident that the crisis had a tremendous effect on the countries' public debt to GDP ratios, which increased substantially. In addition, although the crisis has in many ways been subdued, all five countries have experienced a significant increase in their public debt that for many years will remain high and impose a major constraint on their future fiscal policies.

Appendix

Table A8.1 explains the notation employed by the three CRAs. They use an alphanumeric scaling method. Two of them (S&P and Fitch) use the same letter notation while Moody's uses its own.[64]

TABLE A8.1 Credit rating scales of the three CRAs

S&P	Moodys	Fitch	Scale	Quality	Investment/ speculative
AAA	Aaa	AAA	21	Highest quality	Investment
AA+	Aa1	AA+	20	High quality	Investment
AA	Aa2	AA	19	High quality	Investment
AA−	Aa3	AA−	18	High quality	Investment

(Continued)

TABLE A8.1 Credit rating scales of the three CRAs (Continued)

S&P	Moodys	Fitch	Scale	Quality	Investment/ speculative
A+	A1	A+	17	Strong payment capacity	Investment
A	A2	A	16	Strong payment capacity	Investment
A–	A3	A–	15	Strong payment capacity	Investment
BBB+	Baa1	BBB+	14	Adequate payment capacity	Investment
BBB	Baa2	BBB	13	Adequate payment capacity	Investment
BBB–	Baa3	BBB–	12	Adequate payment capacity	Investment
BB+	Ba1	BB+	11	Likely to fulfill obligations, ongoing uncertainty	Speculative/junk
BB	Ba2	BB	10	Likely to fulfill obligations, ongoing uncertainty	Speculative/junk
BB-	Ba3	BB–	9	Likely to fulfill obligations, ongoing uncertainty	Speculative/junk
B+	B1	B+	8	High credit risk	Speculative/junk
B	B2	B	7	High credit risk	Speculative/junk
B-	B3	B–	6	High credit risk	Speculative/junk
CCC+	Caa1	CCC+	5	Very high credit risk	Speculative/junk
CCC	Caa2	CCC	4	Very high credit risk	Speculative/junk
CCC–	Caa3	CCC–	3	Very high credit risk	Speculative/junk
CC	Ca	CC	2	Near default with possibility of recovery	Speculative/junk
SD	C	SD	2	Near default with possibility of recovery	Speculative/junk
C		DDD	1	Default	Speculative/Junk
		DD	1	Default	Speculative/junk
		D	1	Default	Speculative/junk

Notes

1 Ewland Walterskirchen (2010) "The burst of the real estate bubble – more than a trigger for the financial crisis," *Austrian Economic Quarterly*, 1: 86–93.
2 Frank E. Nothaft (2011) "The boom, the bubble, and the bust abroad," February 14. http://www.loansafe.org/chief-economist-frank-nothaft-on-the-boom-the-bubble-and-the-bust-abroad
3 S. Kapner (2011) "Study finds endemic European housing bubble," *Financial Times*, February 14.
4 W. Brandimarte and D. Bases (2011) "United States loses prized AAA credit rating from S&P," *Reuters*, August 7.
5 Department of Justice Press Release (2015) *Justice Department and State Partners Secure $1.375 Billion Settlement with S&P for Defrauding Investors in the Lead Up to the Financial Crisis*, February 3.
6 Karen Freifeld (2013) "Moody's, S&P, and Fitch sued over failed Bear Sterns funds," *Reuters*, November 11.
7 Sarah N. Lynch and Karen Freifeld (2015) "S&P to pay $77 million to settle U.S. civil charges over ratings," *Reuters*, January 21.
8 "S&P to pay $1.4 bn to regulators in sub-prime debt case," *BBC*, February 3, 2015.

9 David Fickling and Matthew Robinson (2012) "McGraw-Hill plummets after Australian court ruling," *Bloomberg*, November 5.

10 "Australian investors launch second class-action lawsuit against S&P," *Reuters*, April 17, 2013.

11 Swati Pandey (2014) "Australian court rejects S&P, ABN Amro appeals on derivatives ruling," June 5. http://www.reuters.com/article/2014/06/06/australia-sp-courts-idUsL3N0ON0EM20140606

12 "Not a bad weekend's work," *The Economist*, November 16, 2008.

13 "EU targets credit rating agencies," BBC, November 15, 2011.

14 Many people found it odd that three mainly US CRAs serving the entire world market managed to contribute to the creation of the global financial crisis.

15 Nobody can argue against such an opinion because, since the crisis began, it was repeatedly demonstrated that EU country leaders were not committed or able to do what it took to resolve the crisis.

16 Louise Armistead (2012) "S&P and Fitch accused of market manipulation in Italy," *The Telegraph*, November 12.

17 European Commission Press Release (2013) *Stricter Rules for Credit Rating Agencies to Enter into Force.* Brussels, June 18.

18 However, by December 2016, the EU Commission will submit a report to the EU Council and the EU Parliament to recommend whether the establishment of an EU CRA is appropriate to reduce the power of the three large CRAs.

19 The case, however, was somehow complicated because S&P was never in the Netherlands thus it filed for the trial to be held in London.

20 Luke Baker (2013) "S&P cuts EU's AAA rating, European officials dismiss move," *Reuters*, December 20.

21 "Ireland says it doesn't need a bailout despite EU pressure," *Reuters*, November 15, 2010.

22 Karl Whelan (2013) "Ireland economic crisis: the good, the bad, and the ugly," UCD Centre for Economic Research, June 18.

23 Shawn Pogatchnik and Gabrielle Steinhouser (2010) "Ireland bailout, EU agrees to €89.4 billion loan," *Huffington Post*, November 28.

24 Such a tax is supported by many economists who are interested in creating a large fund to rescue ailing financial institutions and reduce fragility in the financial system.

25 David Gardner (2011) "Warily on the way back," *Financial Times*, December 6.

26 Daniel Kruger and Dave Liedtka (2011) "Ireland cut to junk by Moody's as EU seeks to contain crisis," *Bloomberg*, July 13.

27 "Ireland 'right' in clean bailout exit – ESM chief," *RTE News*, December 4, 2013.

28 "The emerald shines again," *The Economist*, November 8, 2014.

29 Niamh Hardiman and Aidan Regan (2013) "The politics of austerity in Ireland," *Intereconomics*, 48 (1): 4–32.

30 Mandy Johnson (2015) "Negative campaigning continues to bring positive poll results for Sinn Féin," *Irish Independent*, February 24.

31 Such information was provided by the Bank of International Settlements.

32 "IMF criticizes Irish failure to impose 'bail in,'" *Financial Times*, January 30, 2015.

33 "'We took one for the team' said Ireland's Prime Minister." See A. Greely (2013) "Ireland's finance minister renegotiates euro bailout via diplomacy," *Bloomberg Business*, September 12.

34 Ricardo Reis (2013) *The Portuguese Slump and Crash and the Euro Crisis*, Brookings Papers on Economic Activity, August.

35 "Portugal's €78 bn euros bailout is formally approved," *BBC*, May 17, 2011.

36 The average income tax rate, for example, increased from 9.8 to 11.8 percent.

37 The difference is that, unlike Ireland, a substantial part of the bailout was designated for the real economy.

38 Robert Fisherman (2011) "Portugal's unnecessary bailout," *New York Times*, April 12.

39 Ricardo Cabral (2013) "The Euro crisis and Portugal's dilemma," *Intereconomics Review of European Economic Policy*, January.

40 Ricardo Reis (2013) *The Portuguese Slump and Crash and the Euro Crisis*, Brookings Papers on Economic Activity, August.

41 This provision of the rescue package is identical to the one offered to Ireland. It is highly likely that this is not coincidental since both countries were victims of a housing bubble.

42 Many political analysts recognize the positive role of the Spanish King Don Juan Carlos for contributing to the peaceful transition to democracy.

43 "Spain: rights at risk in housing crisis," *Human Rights Watch*, May 28, 2014.

44 J. Jimeno and T. Santos (2014) "The crisis in the Spanish economy," *SERIEs*, 5: 125–41.

45 N. Davies (2012) "Spain unemployment hits record high at 25 percent," *Reuters*, October 26.

46 "Thinking outside the box," *The Economist*, July 29, 2010.

47 C. Towe and R. Moghadam (2012) *Spain: Financial Stability Assessment*, International Monetary Fund Country Report No. 12/137. Washington, DC: IMF.

48 "Spain receives European bailout funds," *Reuters*, December 11, 2012.

49 "The Euro crisis, how to save Spain," *The Economist*, June 2, 2012.

50 This rate was above the 7 percent benchmark that triggered the crisis in the other EA countries. Jesus Aquado and Julien Toyer (2012) "Spain slump deepens as bailout fears grow," *Business Finance News*, July 23.

51 "Spain forced to impose haircut on savers, private investors as part of bailout deal," *Forbes*, July 10, 2012.

52 Such funds of course are temporary transfers to finance trade deficits and as deficit countries like Spain fall into a recession and the trade deficits shrink the T2 balances also shrink. This implies that the ECB does not transfer funds to EMU countries.

53 "Spain: rights at risk in housing crisis," *Human Rights Watch*, May 28, 2014.

54 Nigel Davies (2012) "Spanish economy in 'huge crisis' after credit downgrade," *Reuters*, April 27.

55 Andrew Higgins and Liz Alderman (2013) "Europeans planted seeds of crisis in Cyprus," *New York Times*, March 26.

56 Alexander Apostol (2013) "Beware of German gifts near their elections: how Cyprus got here and why it is currently more out than in the Eurozone," *Capital Markets Law Journal*, June 24.

57 Even lower than Ireland's which is 12.5 percent. In 2003 Cyprus reduced the local corporate tax rate to 10 percent.

58 This is the moment when Russian money stated flowing into Cyprus. Lynnett Lopez, *Business Insider*, March 21, 2013.

59 Kalman Kalotay (2013) "The 2013 Cyprus bailout and Russian foreign direct investment platform," May 24. *Baltic Rim Economies – Bimonthly Economic Review, No3/2013*, pp. *58–59*.

60 E. Lipton and B. Protess (2013) "House, set to vote on 2 bills, is seen as an ally of Wall St," *New York Times*, October 28.

61 S. Denning (2014) "With Dodd-Frank rollback, the big bad banks are back," *Forbes*, December 12.

62 Ibid.

63 "Federal Reserve delays parts of Volcker rule until 2017," *BBC*, December 18, 2014.

64 Any rating about BB+ (Ba1) or above an 11.5 on a 21-point scale is considered worthy of investment. Any rank below this is considered to be speculative/junk.

9

CONCLUDING COMMENTS

It is now close to a decade since the financial crisis began in the US, but its effects are still being felt as the crisis is well rooted in Southern Europe, particularly in Greece, Spain, and Cyprus, and to a lesser extent in Portugal and Ireland. Unemployment rates remain very high in several EA countries. Furthermore, severe social problems such as hunger and homelessness have created a humanitarian crisis.

The international financial crisis that began in the US, according to the vast majority of analysts, was caused by a combination of factors. Some of these factors go back to the 1930s when the US government established a new financial regime to safeguard the economic financial and banking system from possible future financial crises. The US government, in order to promote home ownership for the poor and minorities, intervened decisively in the housing market.

The US government created several public and quasi-public agencies to assist in the purchases of homes by the less privileged Americans. The government subsidized purchases of homes, home insurance, and increased liquidity for the housing sector. The two governmentally regulated housing entities, now both publicly owned, Freddie Mac and Fannie Mae, securitized half of all mortgages in the US. By buying mortgages from banks, they provided liquidity to the US banking sector as they sold the securitized mortgages in global financial markets. The US government encouraged banks to issue home loans (mortgages) to families that did not qualify without government assistance to purchase a home. In such a financial system, banks could sell their home loans to the GSEs, so they did not carry any risk. Therefore, banks issued as many loans as possible and earned their income from loan fees without having to service the loans. It is no surprise that many of the mortgages were of low quality, such as subprime and Alt-A. Many of these low-quality mortgages were securitized by the investment banks and two GSEs and then sold in the US and many other countries.

Investment banks were very innovative in creating financial structured products known as financial derivatives. These novel financial derivatives were very complex as there was no limit to the imagination of the financial engineers. They combined MBSs with other financial assets that they sliced and recombined to create new types of securities and again rebundled and diced them to produce higher-order structured financial products. Because these novel and exotic financial products were so complex, the markets failed to price them correctly. However, investors sensed that such products were mainly based on subprime mortgages and were practically worthless; this is when the subprime mortgage crisis began. Several financial institutions in the US and around the world found themselves holding US property-related securities that were worthless. Since many people had placed their savings and retirement funds in these types of securities, we witnessed an ugly phenomenon: US investment banks were practically stealing the savings of people from poorer countries.

Most analysts agree that the subprime mortgage crisis was the result of both public and private failures. The main difference is that the motive of the government was to help home ownership for the poor and minorities, but the motive for the private sector investment banks was greed and profit. The greediness of a few bank executives disappointed and outraged the US public, especially after it became known that a number of these institutions had been bailed out by the government.

The US subprime mortgage crisis caused many families to lose their homes and millions of workers to lose their jobs. Most of the borrowers were punished without being guilty or careless. There was asymmetric information between the banks and mortgage applicants – the banks always knew more than the home loan applicants about the mortgage contracts. Similarly, there was asymmetric information between the bank executives and the shareholders. Investment banks knew more than investors, who purchased their MBSs and other toxic securities. Moral hazard in the presence of asymmetries explains the crisis.

The US monetary and fiscal authorities, unlike the European counterparts, were decisive in effectively addressing the crisis. The Fed, the US President, and Congress launched extraordinarily expansionary monetary and fiscal policies that ended the Great Recession. Three monetary stimulus programs were adopted by the Fed and three fiscal stimulus programs were launched by two US presidents and Congress. The fiscal and monetary stimuli were gradually absorbed by the Fed and US Treasury. Thus the US public deficit and debt began decreasing, as did the monetary stimulus, as the Fed exited the quantitative easing policy and planned to raise interest rates after September 2015.

The European sovereign debt crisis has lasted a very long period. Each of the EA bailout recipient countries has been devastated by economic and social problems such as prolonged unemployment, financial distress, poverty, and homelessness. The decision of the EU to adopt austerity and fiscal consolidation through increased taxation led to a prolonged recession for the EA periphery countries. The decision of Germany and its Northern allies to bring the IMF to enforce austerity was detrimental. Strong austerity caused recession, and as a result the public debt to GDP ratios for almost all countries, instead of declining, increased. It is now obvious that the invitation of the IMF by the EU, and mostly by Germany, to participate in the bailout programs to impose austerity was a major policy mistake that Germany and its allies, the Netherlands and Finland, still do not admit. It is possible their position is such because these countries were hardly affected by the crisis. The relative success of the US which pulled out of the recession via extraordinarily expansive monetary and fiscal policies did not convince them.

The Eurocrisis was accidentally triggered by the revelations of the incorrectly reported fiscal statistics by the Prime Minister of Greece, George Papandreou. Thus Greece triggered the crisis but did not cause it. Prompt response by the EU and EU leaders could easily have prevented the Eurocrisis. Unregulated financial markets and unregulated CRAs allowed speculative attacks on the weaker countries' government bonds. Such countries either were not internationally competitive or they had accumulated a high public debt to GDP ratio, or both.

Once the crisis began spreading, the EU/EA countries were unable to contain and reverse the crisis. The main reason for this is the fact that the construction of the EMU was incomplete. The EMU took away monetary and exchange rate policies and a major part of fiscal policy; this left member countries vulnerable to asymmetric shocks that affect only a few individual countries.

The monetary policy exercised by the ECB, especially after the outset of the crisis, was in general contractionary and slow in responding to deteriorating economic conditions. Monetary policy in the EMU is exercised by the ECB, which is not an independent central bank as other central banks of major world economies, such as the US, UK, and Japan. The ECB operates in the shadow of the member countries' national central banks, especially the German Bundesbank, which tries to impose its views through voting in the ECB Governing Council, through threats by publicizing its views in the press, or even taking the ECB to the Constitutional Court of Germany. Of course, the ECB is not like the central banks of other major world economies. The ECB capital, for example, is owned by the EA national central banks. As a result, the ECB cannot be a lender of last resort as the Fed is, and thus is not capable of assisting countries when a threat appears on the horizon. Consequently, the ECB cannot apply discretionary monetary policy to help countries when necessary. Two fears of the Bundesbank – inflation and the monetization of public debt of countries at risk – deter the exercise of an independent ECB monetary policy to promote price stability and growth in the EMU.

The monetization of public debt entails the ECB buying countries' government bonds in order to keep interest rates low, so countries can borrow in the market. To comply with the low inflation target, the ECB kept relatively high interest rates. In general, the ECB rates were higher than the corresponding US rates. As a result, the euro was kept expensive in relation to the US dollar and other currencies, making European goods, services, and assets "expensive." Thus, the EMU could not employ its exchange rate policy to make European goods cheap and help its recovery.

The EMU does not have a complementary fiscal policy. The EU has a small budget, totaling approximately 1 percent of its GDP. The EU budget has to be balanced annually; this means that the EMU does not have a discretionary fiscal policy. In addition, the Maastricht Treaty, the SGP, the fiscal compact, and other EU agreements impose straitjacket policies, such as low deficit and public debt limits, below 3 and 60 percent of their GDP. In addition, EA countries must have a balanced budget approved by the EU Commission and public debt ceilings inscribed in the countries' constitutions. Every one of these fiscal treaties and rules was a result of strong insistence by Germany that eventually became EU laws.

These imposed fiscal rules are part of a bigger program by Germany to transform Europe. The idea is to make Europe comply with the German economic and political paradigm, in other words to create a Germanic Europe. These are the views of a few political analysts and citizens of the impoverished periphery EA countries. After losing World Wars I and II, Germany is now trying to impose its views on Europe economically instead of militarily as it had in the past.

After World War II, Germany adopted the social market economy model. This model was based on a market economy with strong government participation that was very protective of German workers and with a major role played by the trade unions. As the US, UK, and other countries in the 1980s adopted strong pro-market models and supply-side neoliberal policies, Germany joined the EU countries and adopted the Agenda 2010 policies, suppressing the social part of the social market economy model. Germany launched its own version of the Lisbon Agenda known as the Hartz IV reforms. The Hartz reforms helped Germany become an internationally competitive economy. This happened for two reasons: first, Germany developed a very efficient manufacturing sector and a highly skilled labor force; second, Germany reduced many labor benefits including wages, unemployment compensation, and pensions. Thus Germany generated large trade surpluses with most of its trading partners and the country grew rapidly.

Germany, during the last few years, generated one of the largest current account surpluses in the world, often exceeding even that of China. The German neomercantilistic policies, although working well for Germany, were destructive to its trading partners in Europe. Once the trade balances with the periphery countries dissipated due to the recession caused by the Eurocrisis, Germany began generating trade surpluses with countries outside the EU, including the US and Asian countries.

There were two problems with the export-led growth model. The first is that German growth implies the destruction of foreign industries, and second, this growth is achieved by suppressing real wages in Germany through numerous policies that German workers accepted as many of them were promised permanent jobs. Many German workers have not seen a raise in years; some workers have even accepted pay reductions and millions have moved to precarious employment, under which workers have very limied rights. There is no doubt that German society is divided into economic classes. One class is that of the privileged company and government managers plus the highly skilled workers; the other class consists of those who are employed in temporary work, under contract work, agency work, and so forth, receiving hardly any benefits, and most became convinced they should be thankful to have a job.

There is no doubt that Germany was one of the least affected EA countries during the Eurocrisis. One can easily make the case that the crisis worked well in Germany's favor as capital flows from periphery countries were invested in Germany, which is considered a safe haven in Europe. As a result, Germany enjoyed exceptionally low interest rates to finance projects in both the public and private sectors during a period in which EA partner countries were starving for liquidity, particularly in countries like Greece where interest rates went through the roof. The largest bond company in the world, PIMCO, based in California and owned by German Allianz Insurance and Asset Management Company, pulled out all of their investments from the periphery EA countries as soon as the crisis entered Europe. At the same time, the three CRAs were left free to rate the securities of the financially distressed countries as junk status as interest rates rose as a result of capital outflows. The CRAs have now been found guilty in the courts that they were negligent when they downgraded companies and countries.

Is this the Europe we want?

Many German politicians, especially in the CDU, and a substantial part of the German population have convinced themselves that they know better than other European people. Such a perception of superiority can be revealed by observing the decision-making process within the EU. When any European leader speaks proposing something, at the end of the speech everyone looks to Chancellor Merkel to see if she approves of the proposal. German politicians in the CDU and its partners in government never get tired of reminding all political leaders that any requests for approval by Germany must go through the Eurogroup; however, nothing seems to get approved unless Germany agrees to it. The logic of this is absurd and it is very demeaning that EU members must follow Germany because they are economically weaker.[1]

The German government's philosophy is that since they have the strongest economy in the EA, they are the de facto leaders regardless of whether other countries disagree. A few years ago, the Polish Prime Minister Donald Tusk told the Chancellor that he and others had fundamental doubts over the German austerity model as a solution to the crisis; he then asked Merkel, "Why do you have to ferment division?" He did not get an answer during the summit. After nine months, however, the EU approved the fiscal compact treaty along with several other "German-made" austerity policies. In this respect, German dominance is obvious. Chancellor Merkel took an extreme position in Europe and is "successfully" dominating EU decision-making. She has almost restricted cooperation among equal member European states. Merkel and her government team are not able to see that their attitude is poisoning relations between member countries in the EU, although this is not all her fault because several former Eastern European country leaders behave as if they were leaders of satellite states, that is they have replaced Soviet Union with Germany.

Inviting the IMF to Europe was a gigantic mistake but it allowed Chancellor Merkel to impose austerity measures, thus creating an army of unemployed in the periphery EA countries. If such high unemployment rates were to emerge in Germany as a result of her austerity measures it is certain she would dropped her failing austerity policies. However, the misery has occurred in other countries, so the German government has held fast to its decisions regardless of who disagrees with the austerity programs. Even the advice and input of Nobel Prize-winning economists is not heeded because she believes she knows better.

Once Chancellor Merkel said that she was alone in Europe. However, she does not mind because "she knows that she is right."[2] She mentioned also that Germany is to Europe as the US is to the rest of the world. The only thing she forgot to say is that when the US was dictating policy to the Europeans, none of them cooperated, including herself. The US and EU built a better climate for relations with President Obama who likes to discuss matters with European and other countries' leaders instead of dictating policies, even though the US is both economically and militarily much stronger than any of the countries in the EU.

German dominance will never be accepted in Europe. The present model, which gave Germany a few brief years of dominance, can never be the ultimate European economic and political system. Merkel's leadership has often been characterized as a Fourth Reich but Merkel's empire will end at some point and be remembered as a very sad episode of European economic disintegration. Economic dominance is simply another type of dominance, and one which can be as bad as that imposed through the barrel of a gun. Economic dominance has also killed people and destroyed many countries' economies, just in a different way. The first country to strongly oppose this dominance was Greece, the country which has been bailed out twice and whose people were considered ungrateful to their creditors and other EA leaders.

It is true that Greece committed serious mistakes, particularly in failing to collect sufficient taxes; in addition, for years Greek governments supported the elite oligarchic class at the expense of the common people. But the crisis constitutes an opportunity to cleanse the country of bad habits such as clientelism and corruption. The present government, with the support of the EU, has promised to do so and has a good chance of being successful, otherwise, the future of Greece seems grim. The new Prime Minister has asked European governments to help the Greek government uncover cases of bribery and tax evasion. It is already known that Mr Tsipras has requested that the German government help with bribery investigations against Siemens and other companies. The Greek government is also working with the Swiss government to uncover tax evasion that took place during the crisis as billions of euros left Greece. If such funds are recovered it could certainly help to reduce the Greek public debt.

However, EU country leaders are responsible for keeping Greece in "economic intensive care" since May 2010. However, they do not see it like this, thus they perceive themselves as benefactors of Greece. There are two major problems with the way Greece was treated: the first pertains to the invitation of the IMF to impose conditionality in Europe. Greece should have received aid quickly from the EU and particularly from the ECB as this would have put an end to the crisis.

However, German obsession with controlling the ECB did not allow this, thus the crisis spread. If the ECB had been allowed to purchase Greek government bonds, interest rates would have been kept low and Greece would have been able borrow from the market, rendering the bailouts unnecessary. The second problem was the decision of the EU/IMF to approve the PSI program that was also strongly supported by Chancellor Merkel. The decision to impose PSI spread the crisis to the rest of Europe as it caused financial capital to flee from financially distressed countries. If European leaders knew the negative knock-on effects of the PSI program, they would never have adopted such an experimental program. No investors would bring their money to a country that previously had imposed a haircut. This is the reason other countries such as Ireland, Portugal, and Spain have better weathered the crisis. Cyprus is the other country that has not recovered. Cyprus is also a victim of the PSI as its two banks purchased about five billion euros of Greek government bonds that received a haircut. When Mario Draghi expressed his views about the failure of the PSI program to help the Greek economy in the Eurogroup meeting on July 11, 2015, Wolfgang Schäuble fiercely reacted against his comment. The atmosphere became so intense that the President of the Eurogroup, Jeroen Dijsselbloem, was forced to interrupt the meeting for ten minutes.

At the informal meeting on Greece just before the European Council Summit of March 19, 2015, Donald Tusk, the President of the European Council, said it was very obvious to him that Grexit or Grexident is in nobody's interest. Mr Tusk went on to characterize this possibility of Greece leaving the EA as "the most dramatic chapter in the EU." He explained that there was so much at stake, as the issue involves not only money and geopolitics, but dignity and emotions. This latter concern of the thoughtful and sincere President of the EU Council had never been mentioned before in the numerous meetings of the EU institutions – in particular money was of the utmost concern for Germany, Finland, the Netherlands, and a few other Baltic and Eastern European countries.

Mr Tusk insisted that a Grexit, whether accidental or not, was an "idiotic scenario" that must be prevented.[3] He also reminded people that World War I was started by an accident. If the President of the European Council is so determined and certain that Grexit does not make sense, then why all the rigmarole about throwing Greece out of the euro? Can anyone imagine the total costs for all those involved in resolving this issue and covering the potential Grexit? Imagine the airfares and other transport expenses, the television and radio time for the endless debates, and the cost of newspapers and other news media used to communicate with and to convince taxpayers and voters. It is highly likely that all these large expenditures are greater than the Greek public debt itself. The most important cost of the discussions on Greece's future in the EA – and most likely in the EU as a country leaving the EMU might leave the EU – is the opportunity cost of the time of the country leaders and EU officials. One can make a case that EU leaders did not spend their time efficiently and effectively. We can be convinced about this by assessing the geopolitical conditions in the EU proximity and around the world. EU country leaders ought to play a much more important role in promoting peace and prosperity around the world. It should be unacceptable that the Mediterranean Sea has been transformed into a cemetery for so many people who are trying to reach Europe. It is also unacceptable for ISIS to be allowed to commit heinous crimes against the people of Syria and Iraq and be allowed to destroy historical monuments and art that are thousands of years old. If these leaders had been taking their responsibilities seriously, the bloodshed in the Middle East would have ended long ago and the ISIS leaders would have been in The Hague at the International Court of Justice to defend themselves for the crimes they had committed against humanity. Instead, EU country leaders have had a lot of time to discuss the expulsion of Greece from Europe, never mind that Greece is an indispensable part of Europe, not to mention the origin and foundation of European and Western civilization.

The EU is obligated to more vigorously promote human rights, democracy, and economic development outside EU. The EU did not help those countries that begged for help to give democracy and peace a chance to flourish. The EU approach to influence peace and prosperity has not been vigorous enough to make a difference, thus conditions have deteriorated very rapidly. The Arab Spring that began a few months before the first Greek bailout is a good example of a wasted opportunity for the EU to improve the political and economic condition in a large part of the world.

Close attention to the countries neighboring the EU could have prevented the situation in Russia and Ukraine. Both countries could have been offered transitional associate memberships to the EU, provided that they both agreed to meet the Copenhagen Criteria establishing democratic regimes, to respect human rights and minorities, and to meet all the other requirements to qualify for EU membership. The EU instead went half way and invited only Ukraine. Similarly in Africa, the situation has gotten out of control. What is the EU contribution to establishing peace in these afflicted areas of the world? How much time did the EU decision-making bodies devote to discussing possible peaceful proposals for these and other troublesome areas of the world? Many short-sighted people may say that this is not a European problem, but in reality it is everyone's problem because it will eventually affect all countries.

The EU jointly with non-EU countries that are seriously interested in world peace and prosperity should embark on major peace and prosperity projects to save the world. Such an objective cannot be accomplished with the miniscule 1 percent budget of the EU GDP. Such a major initiative will require vast resources to which many countries could contribute. Humanitarian organizations and volunteers from every country should participate in the programs. Similarly the private sector must participate, but will have to be kept under control and carry out meaningful and massive investments to promote economic development and peace. As a matter of fact, several mini-Marshall types of plans will be necessary to help regions in different parts of the world. This cannot happen if nationalistic and ethnocentric parties rule Europe.

Similarly the US cannot contribute if its politicians are busy repealing important legislation such as the Dodd-Frank Act and the Volcker Rule. This has already begun at the end of 2014 and continues to allow investment banks to earn large profits at the expense of rendering the financial system more fragile again. As a result, another financial crisis will soon be highly likely to occur; this would devastate the entire world economy. The EU will be able to help itself and the world if a new generation of leaders and intellectuals emerge similar to those altruistic European statesmen and visionaries that created the EU. The challenge is therefore ahead of us.

For the first time, Greece has a new government that opposes the way it has been treated since 2010 when the crisis began. Greece has been suffering from a humanitarian crisis that has to be immediately resolved; the country has sufficient resources and a relatively small population that it should easily be able to attain reasonable standards of living. It is a good thing that Greece is the first country to resist a system that allowed the oppression and humiliation of human beings in modern Europe. If it was not Syriza, it would have been another political party with another name, but it would have been a party that was ready to stand against the status quo. In other countries, political parties are resisting austerity, such as Podemos in Spain and Sinn Fein in Ireland.

Europe must change if its people are to come first. Markets should not be allowed to promote human suffering. Therefore the European peoples and political parties need to intervene and reject the model which, for the sake of efficiency, allows the wealthy few to exploit and destroy the weaker groups and the middle class in each society. The civilization of a country is measured by the way the country treats its weakest groups in its society. This should apply to EU countries as well. Europe has a good reputation in this aspect. The European project of Richard Coudenhove Kalergi, Robert Schuman, and Jean Monnet was never intended to suppress any group of people in any country. It is time for European people, EU country leaders, and EU officials to recognize that and work hard for the harmonization of development, increased stability and convergence of their standard of living. This was the objective of the Treaty of Rome that established the European Community. Europe must emerge from the crisis more united, stronger, and more prepared to defend itself from another crisis. EU countries, along with the rest of the world, must also join forces to pursue peace and prosperity for all countries and people in the world.

We must remember that both crises were man-made as well as unnecessary and easily avoidable.

A third bailout for Greece

On July 12, 2015, at the Brussels Summit of the EU Council, it was decided by the 28 EU leaders that Greece would remain in the EMU and receive a third bailout of €86 billion. All money would come from the European Stability Mechanism (ESM). This decision was made only after a heated and exhaustive debate that lasted 17 hours, the longest on record in the EU Council's history. Indeed it was a very strenuous summit with the EU country leaders divided. On one side was Germany and its allies which demanded the surrender of the economic sovereignty of Greece. The leader of this group was Chancellor Merkel who was mainly guided by the Finance Minister of Germany, Wolfgang Schäuble. The idea was simple: to punish Greece for defying the EU proposal when Greek Prime Minister, Alexis Tsipras, pulled out from negotiations and asked the Greek voters to decide on a referendum whether they support the EU proposal for the settlement of the Greek public debt issue. The Greek voters responded with an astoundingly strong response of "no" of more than 61 percent as they were fed up with austerity. On the previous day, at the Eurogroup meeting on July 11, Mr Schäuble managed not only to make sure there was no agreement among members, but convinced his colleagues that the proposal for a Grexit should be included in the report to the summit. A timeout for Greece, as he said, from the euro for about four or five years was the only viable solution.

The next day at the Summit, the Greek Prime Minister was grilled by Germany and its Northern allies for several hours. Finally, a new proposal for a Memorandum of Understanding, admittedly much worse than the former one, was made. The proposal was described by many analysts as a national humiliation. The proposed program by the EU partners damaged the EU and Greece. The reason is simple because it revealed the true face of the present EU.

In the Summit, the negotiating parties went on for many hours with no indication that the gap between their differences was closing. Greece received strong support from France and Italy. French President, François Hollande, was very supportive of Greece and convinced his colleagues that a Grexit was not an option. Chancellor Merkel also said a Grexit was not a solution unless Greece wanted to leave the euro, but she knew well that the vast majority of Greeks want to remain in the EA. However, after 14 long hours of negotiations, it was evident that an agreement was not possible and both Tsipras and Merkel approached the way out of the room.

As they tried to leave, the President of the European Council, Mr Donald Tusk, saved the day and the Eurozone from a certain break-up. He told the two leaders "Sorry, but there is no way you are leaving this room."[4] President Hollande played a major role in the breakthrough as he arranged a short meeting between Tsipras, Merkel, himself, and Tusk in Mr Tusk's office.

The agreement was very harsh as it demanded strict austerity. Some of the demands were plausible and necessary, but some could easily be considered vindictive and insulting to Greece. One can make out that the rough treatment of Mr Tsipras was coming from Mr Schäuble and his supporters who are convinced that Greece cannot be trusted.

The main points of the agreement were summarized as follows in five main areas:

- The first was for Greece to broaden the general tax base in order to increase total tax revenue. The agreement includes a detailed list of tax rates for various groups of commodities and activities.
- Second, Greece must reform its pension system to render it sustainable. The retirement age, in general, should be increased.
- Third, the Greek government must safeguard the full independence of the Greek national statistical agency.
- Fourth, was the creation of a fiscal council, in accordance with the Fiscal Compact Treaty that Greece has not yet enacted. The fiscal council, which is independent from the government, would have the power to cut government expenditures if the government's primary surplus is short of its target.

- Lastly and the most controversial of all was the requirement for the creation of €50 billion worth of Greek public assets that were to be privatized, and which the EU leaders, mainly Schäuble, wanted to place in an account in Luxembourg to be supervised by the Institutions.[5]

Mr Tsipras considered this last requirement as the most intrusive as the amount constituted about one-third of Greek GDP and neither the government nor the parliament would approve. When this point was discussed, Mr Tsipras took off his jacket and told his European colleagues "you might as well take this too," showing his jacket. Then he said: "If this deal is a part of the agreement, I better get a ticket for another destination and not for Greece."

Finally, a compromise was reached and it was agreed that the fund would remain in Greece and be managed by the Greek authorities, but would be supervised by the "relevant European Institutions."

The *Financial Times* reported the sources of the bailout and where the approximately €82–86 billion will be spent over the next three years. It was reported by the *Financial Times* that €65.5 billion will be paid by the European Stability Mechanism and €16.4 billion by the IMF. The entire amount will be paid towards debt repayment, interest payments, arrears, bank recapitalization, and the cash liquidity for the banking system. Greece will also receive more than €35 billion from the European Commission up through 2020 to support growth, jobs and investments; this is not part of the third agreed bailout.[6]

Table 9.1 reveals that the bailout will be spent in repayment of Greek public debt to the ECB, the national central banks, the IMF, and to privately held debt and amount in arrears. The second item is interest payments, which are equal to €17.2 billion. The third item is for bank recapitalization and for the creation of a cash buffer for liquidity in the banking system. Zero funds from the third bailout are to be invested in the real Greek economy. Therefore, those who were pointing a finger at Mr Tsipras or to the Greek Finance Minister, Mr Tsakolotos, are either not knowledgeable of the real nature of the Greek bailout or like to misrepresent the facts. It is no surprise that most commentators criticized the program as a bad

TABLE 9.1 Greek debt repayment

ECB and national central banks	€14.3 billion
IMF	€9.9 billion
Privately held debt	€5.5 billion
Arrears (owned to contractors)	€7.0 billion
Sub-total	€36.7 billion
Interest payment	€17.2 billion
Sub-total	€53.9 billion
Banks	
Bank recapitalization	€25.0 billion
Cash buffers for liquidity banking	€7.7 billion
Total	€86.6 billion

deal for Greece and rightly identified it to be recessionary. Greece however, could have been offered a much better deal to overcome the crisis at an earlier date.[7]

There was also no surprise that 39 members of Syriza (the left wing of the party), did not vote for approval of the program. They argued that the Greek voters did not approve such a program in the referendum of July 5, 2015. However, the agreement passed because it received support from the other parties, which support the country remaining in the EA. After the elections in the Greek Parliament on July 16, 2015, 229 members of parliament approved the agreement for a third bailout. It is estimated that 80 percent of the Greek people support Greece remaining in the Euro Area, or in the hard core of Europe as they often say. However, the EU and the EMU must change. No country should ever be punished as Greece has been. French President Hollande stated that France will propose legislation for the Euro Area to adopt a "common budget" and form an "economic government."

President Hollande stated he had always supported deeper economic convergence and social policies to counterbalance the strict fiscal discipline imposed by Germany. The agreement of the Greek bailouts, according to many commentators, was a personal success for President Hollande, and France, together with Italy, should push in the direction of persuading Germany to change. If Germany does not choose to yield on this issue, the inevitable will happen and a new reality will emerge with no euro or a split of the EA into two, one in the Northern states and one in the Southern, with each region using its own currency.

In the meantime, the IMF released a report as soon as Ms Lagarde arrived in Washington, DC, from the Brussels Summit. According to the report, the IMF would not participate in the Greek bailout unless the EU countries offered debt relief to Greece. This was required because the situation in Greece has worsened so much after the closing of the banks. However, the EU governments cannot offer another haircut, thus the third bailout program faces another barrier.[8]

As long as Germany pursues nationalistic interests and imposes programs such as austerity and fiscal discipline, economic and monetary integration will stall. Despite the fact that the German economy is thriving, such growth and prosperity cannot be sustained in the long run. This implies that even the most popular politicians like Wolfgang Schäuble have to be pushed aside as this is for the long-term benefit of Germany as well as for the long-term benefit of the EU and EMU members.

The Bundesbank's rigid monetary policy destroyed the European Monetary System as a result of the Exchange Rate Mechanism crisis in the early 1990s. The German people should rein in their country from destroying the second sincere attempt of economic and monetary integration during the last 25 years. This objective ought to be achieved even if they have to ask their finance minister to retire early. He has done enough damage. Many other populist politicians in Greece, Germany, the UK and elsewhere, have also inflicted damage to the European project. For European integration to be given a chance to remain an option in Europe, both Greece and Germany have to undergo major transformations. Greece has to quickly modernize its economy and place its people to work to attain a decent standard of living above the level attained prior to the crisis. Germany must willingly begin relaxing the rigid rules it imposed on the EU/EA members and embrace growth policies for the EU. Only growth policies will raise the standard of living and reduce the debt to GDP ratios of indebted EU/EA countries. If Germany fails to compromise the European project will become a small interval of failing uncoordinated national policies in the European history. EU leades must confront the real economic and political issues to allow the EU to escape its perpetual sovereign debt and banking crisis.

Only a few hours after the European Stability Mechanism (ESM) approved a partial disbursement of €13 billion for Greece on August 20, 2015, Prime Minister Alexis Tsipras announced his resignation. He then asked the President of Greece, Prokopis Pavlopoulos, to set a date for a national election as soon as possible. It seems that the Greek political and economic saga has no end as the Greek people were asked three times to vote in two national elections and one referendum during 2015.Tsipras called for this latest election because his party lost its parliamentary majority after members voted against the EU agreement on July12, 2015. As a result of this new election, Tsipras hopes to gain renewed support from the Greek voters. His popularity has increased because he stood up to the EU leaders, particularly against Germany.[9] It is ironic, nonetheless, that the EU agreement his government signed reversed the astounding "No" outcome of the EU/IMF bailout referendum on July 5, 2015. The EU/IMF bailout agreement of July 12, 2015 undermined the anti-austerity position that the Syriza party fervently campaigned about before the January 25, 2015 national election. Syriza has previously attacked other political parties for signing bailout agreements with the Troika.

In the national election that is set for September 20, 2015, Tsipras will try to gain support that will offset the loss of his extreme left-wing party members who split from Syriza and formed the Popular Unity party, consisting of 25 parliament members under the leadership of Panayotis Lafazanis. Lafazanis accused Tsipras of betraying the Syriza supporters who expressed their strong opposition to a new bailout. Tsipras admits that his government made mistakes; however, Syriza never campaigned for an exit from the EMU. In the new elections, he expects his party will gain support because he believes that Greece should remain in the EA, a position held by the vast majority of the Greek people, which is estimated around 80 percent. I personally believe that Greece, or any country, can more easily influence the EA/EU as an insider (member), rather than an outsider. If a country were to be expelled from the EA/EU, it would definitely carry a stigma and severely diminish its economic and political influence.

Notes

1 Bernhard Riedmann (2015) "The Fourth Reich: what some Europeans see when they look at Germany," *Der Spiegel*, March 21.
2 Ibid.
3 "European Council Chief D. Tusk–Greek PM A. Tsipras: 'Open and frank' talks," *Protothema News*, February 5, 2015.
4 A. Chassani, A. Barker, and D. Robins (2015) "Greece Talks: 'Sorry, but there is no way you are leaving this room,'" *Financial Times*, July 13.

5 "Text of Euro Summit Statement on Greece," *New York Times*, July 12, 2015.

6 A. Barker, L. Noonan, and C. Jones (2015) "Recapitalisation of up to €25bn called for to inject life into finance sector," *Financial Times*, July 14.

7 Zestos, George, K. (2015). "A compromise that will give Greece both freedom and responsibility," *Financial Times*, London, June 10.

8 P. Spiegel and S. Donnan (2015) "IMF raises doubts over its bailout role," *Financial Times*, July 15.

9 Kerin Hope (2015) "Somersaulting Tsipras prepares next trick" *Financial Times* 22 August/23 August.

INDEX

Added to a page number 'n' denotes notes.
Page numbers in *italic* refer to figures and tables.